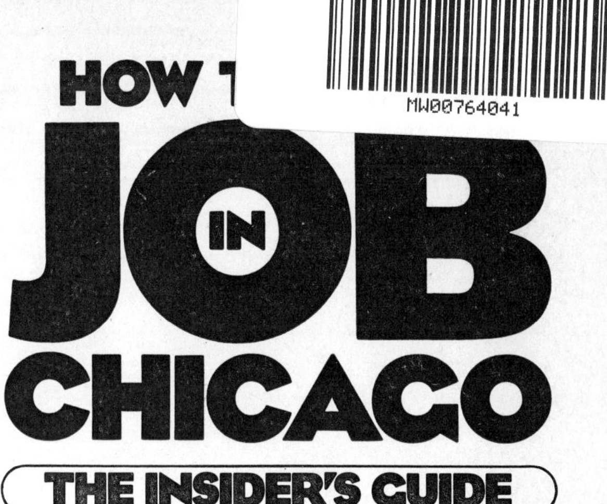

THOMAS M. CAMDEN
SUSAN SCHWARTZ

SURREY BOOKS
230 East Ohio Street
Suite 120
Chicago, Illinois 60611

HOW TO GET A JOB IN CHICAGO—The Insider's Guide.
Published by Surrey Books, Inc., 230 E. Ohio St., Suite 120. Chicago, IL 60611. Telephone: (312) 751-7330.

This book is manufactured in the United States of America.

4th Edition. 1 2 3 4 5

Library of Congress Cataloging-in-Publication data:

Camden, Thomas M., 1938-
How to get a job in Chicago: the insider's guide / Thomas M. Camden, Susan Schwartz—4th ed.
490p. cm.
Includes bibliographical references and index.
ISBN 0-940625-27-X: $15.95
1. Job hunting—Illinois—Chicago—Directories. 2. Job vacancies—Illinois—Chicago—Directories. 3. Vocational guidance—Informational services—Chicago—Directories. I. Schwartz, Susan H., 1946- . II. Title.
HF5382.75.U62C43 1991 90-24554
650.14'09773'11—dc20 CIP

AVAILABLE TITLES IN THIS SERIES — all $15.95

How To Get a Job in Atlanta by Thomas M. Camden, Diane C. Thomas, and Bill Osher, Ph.D.
How To Get a Job in Chicago by Thomas M. Camden and Susan Schwartz.
How To Get a Job in Dallas/Fort Worth by Thomas M. Camden and Nancy Bishop.
How To Get a Job in Europe by Robert Sanborn, Ed.D.
How To Get a Job in Houston by Thomas M. Camden and Robert Sanborn.
How To Get a Job in Southern California by Thomas M. Camden and Jonathan Palmer.
How To Get a Job in New York by Thomas M. Camden and Susan Fleming-Holland.
How To Get a Job in San Francisco by Thomas M. Camden and Evelyn Jean Pine.
How To Get a Job in Seattle/Portland by Thomas M. Camden and Sara Steinberg.
How To Get a Job in Washington, DC, by Thomas M. Camden and Karen Tracy Polk.

Single copies may be ordered directly from the publisher. Send check or money order plus $2.00 per book for postage and handling to Surrey Books at the above address. For quantity discounts, please contact the publisher.

Editorial production by Bookcrafters, Inc., Chicago
Cover design by Hughes Design, Chicago.
Typesetting by On Track, Chicago.

Acknowledgments

The authors would like to thank Dana Metes, who was responsible for revising this edition. Thanks also go to editorial consultant Valjean McLenighan, production editor Gene DeRoin, art director Sally Hughes, editorial contributors Drs. Bill Osher and Robert Sanborn, David Rouse and his staff at the Chicago Public Library's Business Information Center, and Kathleen Prendergast, who checked the bibliographical references.

Note to Our Readers

We, the authors and editors, have made every effort to supply you with the most useful, up-to-date information available to help you find the job you want. Each name, address, and phone number has been verified by our staff of fact checkers. But offices move and people change jobs, so we urge you to call before you write, and write before you visit. And if you think we should include information on companies, organizations, or people that we've missed, please let us know.

CONTENTS

unique list of selected networking groups in the Chicago area: professional organizations, trade groups, clubs, and societies, with addresses, phone numbers, areas of activities, and contact persons (where possible).

6 Using Professional Employment Services *Page 104*

Employment agencies—what they can and can not do for you, how they charge, how to get the most from them. Listing of selected employment agencies and their specialties. Career consultants; some words to the wise and questions to ask before retaining one; selected list. Executive search firms—how they operate, pros and cons; selected list. Social service and government employment agencies.

7 How To Succeed In an Interview *Page 122*

The interview objective and how to prepare. Mastering the five-minute resume. The interview as a sales presentation. Steps to a successful interview. What interviewers look for. Handling the interview, anticipating tough questions, and making sure you get your own questions answered. What to do following the interview. Books on interviewing. How to use your references.

8 What To Do If Money Gets Tight *Page 133*

Reviewing your assets and liabilites. Pros and cons of part-time and temporary work. List of selected sources for part-time work. Books on part-time and flexible employment. Government and private assistance programs.

9 Where To Turn If Your Confidence Wilts *Page 144*

Tips for dealing with rejection. What to do if you get fired. Dealing with emotional stress. Guidelines for seeking professional counseling or therapy. Selected crisis and mental health centers. Career transition issues.

10 Selecting the Right Job for You *Page 151*

You don't have to jump at the first offer. What you should find out before accepting any job offer. Finding the right employment "culture." Tips on negotiating salary. How to compare job offers—sample checklist. What to do after you finally accept a job.

11 Where Chicago Works *Page 157*

Names, addresses, and phone numbers of the Chicago area's top 1,500 employers, arranged by industry, with descriptions and contacts, where possible. Useful professional organizations, professional publications, and directories. Candid interviews and helpful hints.

Employers Index *Page 453*

General Index *Page 473*

How To Get the Most from This Book

So you want to get a job in the Chicago area? Well, you've picked up the right book. Whether you're a recent graduate, new in town, or an old hand at the Great Chicago Job Search; whether or not you're currently employed; even if you're not fully convinced that you *are* employable—this book is crammed with helpful information.

It contains the combined wisdom of two top professionals: Tom Camden, a seasoned personnel consultant who is Vice President of EnterChange, a national consulting firm, specializing in career transition management; and Susan Schwartz, a publishing professional known for her extensive, city-wide network of contacts.

Tom contributes expert advice on both basic and advanced job search techniques, from how to write a resume to suggestions for racking up extra points in an employment interview.

Susan combines extensive knowledge of the Chicago working world with an impressive contact network developed over the past 20 years. Her extensive listings are designed to save you hours of research time.

Dozens of other Chicago insiders have contributed tips, warnings, jokes, and observations in candid, behind-the-scenes interviews. All of which is to say that we have done our level best to pack more useful information between these covers than you'll find anywhere else in town.

We would love to guarantee that this book is all you need to find the job of your dreams, but we are not miracle workers. This is a handbook, not a Bible. There's just no getting around the fact that finding work *takes* work. *You* are the only person who can land the job you want.

What we *can* do—and, we certainly hope, have done—is to make the work of job hunting in Chicago easier and more enjoyable for you. We have racked our brains, and those of many others, to provide you with the most extensive collection of local resources in print.

To get the most from this book, first browse through the Table of Contents. Acquaint yourself with each chapter's major features, see what appeals to you, and turn to the sections that interest you the most.

It may not be necessary or useful for you to read this book from cover to cover. If you're currently employed, for example, you can probably safely skip Chapter 8—What To Do If Money Gets Tight. If you have no interest in using a professional employment service, you may only need to browse through Chapter 6.

There are certain parts of this book, however, that no one should overlook. One of them is Chapter 4—Researching the Chicago Job Market. Unless you're a professional librarian, we'd bet money that you won't be able to read this chapter without discovering at least a few resources that you never knew existed. We've tried to make it as easy as possible for you to get the inside information that can put you over the top in an employment interview.

Chapter 5 is another Don't Miss—especially our unique listing of organizations that you should know about to develop your network of professional contacts. We strongly suggest that you read Chapter 7, even if you think you already know all about how to handle an interview. And then, of course, there's Chapter 11—listings of the Chicago area's top 1,500 employers of white-collar workers.

There's another thing you should know to get the most from this book. Every chapter, even the ones you don't think you need to read, contains at least one helpful hint or insider interview that is set off from the main text. Take some time to browse through them. They contain valuable nuggets of information and many tips that you'll find nowhere else.

Keep in mind that no one book can do it all for you. While we've touched on the basic tasks of any job search—self-analysis, developing a resume, researching the job market, figuring out a strategy, generating leads, interviewing, and selecting the right job—we don't have space to go into great detail on each and every one of them. What we *have* done is to supply suggestions for further reading. Smart users of this book will follow those suggestions when they need to know more about a particular subject.

New in town?

Have you just moved to Chicago? In addition to this book, you could probably use some personalized assistance. The Travelers Aid Society (327 S. LaSalle St., Suite 1500, (312) 435-4500) offers counseling and referral services for newcomers. In addition to its other services, the Chicago Association of Commerce and Industry (200 N. LaSalle St., (312) 580-6900) publishes numerous studies and guides describing the business climate in Chicago.■

Chicago in the '90s

What's the job outlook for the Chicago area through the rest of the century? Surprisingly optimistic! A mid-1990 forecast by the Illinois Department of Employment Security predicts about 4 million jobs by the year 2000; that's an addition of 400,00 new jobs in the 1990s. Most of the gain from the base year of 1986 will be in white-collar employment: finance, insurance, and real estate jobs are projected to increase by 22 percent (60,000 jobs); retail will jump 25 percent (138,000 jobs); construction will increase 27 percent (34,000 jobs); and a very healthy service sector will forge ahead 27.4 percent (286,000 jobs). In general, service, administrative support, sales, and marketing are expected to account for half of the new jobs to the year 2000.

Speaking of the overall employment picture, Jim Sullivan, Senior Vice President at LaSalle National Bank, says, "I think everyone would say that the service sector is still expanding. Chicago is taking on more importance in world trade, and futures and options exchanges continue to build. Service-oriented businesses, including law firms, stock brokerages, banks, engineering, architectural, and accounting firms, and food service companies have grown. Most people are confident that this will continue."

Paul Pieper, Assistant Professor of Economics, University of Illinois at Chicago, agrees. "One reason growth in the service sector will continue," he says, "is that as incomes rise, people spend a higher proportion of their income on services. Another is that the service sector, unlike the manufacturing sector, does not face import competition."

The outlook for manufacturing and heavy industry in the Chicago area is not nearly so optimistic, although construction, chemicals, and plastics have held their own. Manufacturing jobs will probably continue to decline or remain flat, and import competition will be tough for both the short and long term.

Experts see the high-technology industries as a growth area for Chicago and vicinity. In fact, many people seem to be unaware of Chicago's high-tech industries, such as software firms, already located here.

The Chicago area also is an important center for high-tech research. "We have Argonne National Laboratory, an outstanding research facility," says Pieper. "We also have several of the nation's top universities where significant high-tech research is being carried out. Tremendous potential exists for commercial ventures that will utilize the knowledge gained through such research." Economists and other observers also feel that the climate for small business—both new and existing—is better than it has been in some time.

With plans for a third major airport under consideration, the area will probably continue to rank number one in air transportation. Chicago is second only to New York as a financial market and center for corporate headquarters, and it is an important employer in the health care industry. Other strengths include the area's diversified economy, as well as its generally high quality of life.

On that optimistic note, we hope to provide you with the resources you need to find the job you want. Good luck from both of us, and happy hunting!

Getting around

Need help finding your way around Chicago and suburbs?

These phone numbers should come in handy:

CTA/RTA (Chicago/Regional Transportation Authority) offers 24-hours-a-day city and suburban travel directions and information about public transportation at (312) 836-7000. Handicapped people can call (312) 664-7100. Suburbanites can call toll free, (800) 972-7000.

The major Chicago cab companies are American United, (312) 248-7600; Checker, (312) 421-1300; Flash, (312) 561-1444; and Yellow, (312) 829-4222. If it's not raining or snowing, you should have little trouble finding a cab on any downtown street.

Major car rental companies are listed in the Yellow Pages under "Automobile Renting and Leasing." If you're short of cash and don't particularly care what kind of car you're driving, try Rent-a-Fender-Bender, (312) 280-8554, or Rent-a-Wreck, (800) 339-7368.■

Chambers of Commerce

Many area chambers of commerce assist in the orientation process by providing information and mailing free material about schools, utilities, businesses, and entertainment. Call to find out what is available. The largest chambers of commerce are:

Chicago Association of Commerce and Industry (312) 580-6900

Greater North Michigan Ave. Association (312) 642-3570

State Street Council (312) 782-9160

Oak Brook Association of Commerce and Industry (708) 572-0616

Chamber of Commerce of Southern Suburbs (312) 957-6950

Lake County Economic Development Corp. (312) 360-6350

2

Establishing an Objective: How To Discover What You Want To Do

One of the most common mistakes job seekers make is not establishing an *objective* before beginning the job search. Practically everyone wants a job that provides personal satisfaction, growth, good salary and benefits, prestige, and a desirable location. But unless you have a more specific idea of the kind of work you want to do and are qualified to do, the chances are high that your job search will be less than satisfactory.

Many of our readers already have a clear objective in mind. You may want a job as a systems analyst, paralegal, production assistant, sales manager, or any one of the thousands of other occupations at which Chicagoans work. That's all well and good—in fact, *establishing an objective is a necessary first step in any successful job search.*

But anyone who's looking for work, or thinking about changing jobs or careers, can benefit from a thorough self-appraisal. What follows is a list of highly personal questions designed to provide you with insights you may never have considered, and to help you answer the Big Question, "What do I want to do?"

To get the most from this exercise, write out your answers. This will take some time, but it will help to ensure that you give each question careful thought. The more effort you put into this exercise, the better prepared you'll be to answer the tough questions that are bound to come up in any job interview. The exercise also will serve as the foundation for constructing a decent resume—a subject we'll discuss in more detail in the next chapter.

When you've completed the exercise, consider sharing your answers with a trusted friend or relative. Self-analysis is a difficult task. Although we think we know ourselves, we seldom have the objectivity to see ourselves clearly, to outline our personal and professional strengths and weaknesses, to evaluate our needs, and to set realistic objectives. Someone who knows you well can help.

Questions About Me

1. Taking as much time as necessary—and understanding the purpose of this appraisal—honestly describe the kind of person you are. Here are some questions to get you started. Are you outgoing or are you more of a loner? How well disciplined are you? Are you quick-tempered? Easy-going? Are you a leader or a follower? Do you tend to take a conventional, practical approach to problems? Or are you more imaginative and experimental? How sensitive are you to others?
2. Describe the kind of person others think you are.
3. What do you want to accomplish with your life?
4. What role does your job play in that goal?
5. What impact do you have on other people?
6. What are your accomplishments to date? Are you satisfied with them?
7. What role does money play in your standard of values?
8. Is your career the center of your life or just a part of it? Which should it be?
9. What are your main interests?
10. What do you enjoy most?
11. What displeases you most?

Questions About My Job

1. Beginning with your most recent employment and then working back toward school graduation, describe *in detail* each job you had. Include your title, company, responsi-

bilities, salary, achievements and successes, failures, and reason for leaving.
2. How would you change anything in your job history if you could?
3. In your career thus far, what responsibilities have you enjoyed most? Why?
4. What kind of job do you think would be a perfect match for your talents and interests?
5. What responsibilities do you want to avoid?
6. How hard are you really prepared to work?
7. If you want the top job in your field, are you prepared to pay the price?
8. What have your subordinates thought about you as a boss? As a person?
9. What have your superiors thought about you as an employee? As a person?
10. Can your work make you happier? Should it?
11. If you have been fired from any job, what was the reason?
12. How long do you want to work before retirement?

Your answers to these highly personal questions should help you to see more clearly who you are, what you want, what your gifts are, and what you realistically have to offer. They should also reveal what you *don't* want and what you *can't* do. It's important to evaluate any objective you're considering in light of your answers to these questions.

People who are entering the job market for the first time, those who have been working for one company for many years, and those who are considering a career change need more help in determining their objectives. Vocational analysis, also known as career planning and life planning, is much too broad a subject to try to cover here. But we can refer you to some excellent books.

CAREER STRATEGY BOOKS

Allen, Jeffrey. *How to Turn an Interview into a Job Offer.* New York: Simon & Schuster, 1988.

Applegath, John. *Working Free: Practical Alternatives to the 9 to 5 Job.* New York: AMACOM, 1984.

Azrin, Nathan H. *Finding a Job.* Berkeley, CA: Ten Speed Press, 1982.

Bolles, Richard N. *What Color Is Your Parachute?* Berkeley, CA: Ten Speed Press, 1990. The Bible for job hunters and career changers, this book is revised every year and is widely regarded as the most useful and creative manual available. Try it! We think you'll like it.

Breidenbach, Monica E. *Career Development: Taking Charge of Your Career.* Englewood Cliffs, NJ: Prentice-Hall, 1988.

Camden, Thomas M. *The Job Hunter's Final Exam.* Chicago: Surrey Books, 1990.

Clawson, James G., et al. *Self Assessment and Career Development.* Englewood Cliffs, NJ: Prentice-Hall, 1985.

Figler, Howard. *The Complete Job-Search Handbook.* New York: H. Holt & Co., 1988.

Fink, Edward J. *Building a Career in the Business World.* New York: Vantage Press, 1984.
Haldane, Bernard. *Career Satisfaction and Success: A Guide to Job Freedom.* New York: AMACOM, 1982.
Kennedy, Joyce Lain. *Joyce Lain Kennedy's Career Book.* Lincolnwood, IL: VGM Career Horizons, 1988.
Lee, Patricia. *The Complete Guide to Job Sharing.* New York: Walker, 1983.
Mazzei, George. *Moving Up: Digging In, Taking Charge, Playing the Power Game and Learning to Like It.* New York: Poseidon Press, 1984.
Scheele, Adele. *Making College Pay Off.* New York: Ballantine, 1983.
Shapiro, Michele. *Your Personal Career Consultant: A Step-by-Step Guide.* Englewood Cliffs, NJ: Prentice-Hall, 1988.

For those of you involved in a **mid-life career change,** here are some books that might prove helpful:

Allen, Jeffrey G. *Finding the Right Job at Midlife.* New York: Simon & Schuster, 1985.
Bardwick, Judith M. *The Plateauing Trap.* New York: AMACOM, 1986.
Falvey, Jack. *What's Next? Career Strategies After 35.* Charlotteville, VT: Williamson Publishing Co., 1987.
Gerberg, Robert J. *Robert Gerberg's Job Changing System.* Kansas City: Andrews-McMeel, 1986.
Hecklinger, Fred J., and Bernadette M. Curtin. *Training for Life: A Practical Guide to Career and Life Planning.* Dubuque, IA: Kendall-Hunt, 1984.
Morgan, John S. *Getting a Job After 50.* Blue Ridge Summit, PA: TAB Books, 1990.

And for people with **disabilities,** these titles could prove helpful:

Bolles, Richard. *What Color is Your Parachute?* Berkeley, CA: Ten Speed Press, 1990.
Lewis, Adele, and Edith Marks. *Job Hunting for the Disabled.* Woodbury, NY: Barron's, 1983.

For **women** in the work force, these titles will be of interest:

Gutek, Barbara, and Laurie Larwood, eds. *Women's Career Development.* Newbury Park, CA: Sage, 1986.
Morrow, Jodie B., and Myrna Lebov. *Not Just a Secretary: Using the Job to Get Ahead.* New York: Wiley Press, 1984.
Nivens, Beatryce. *The Black Woman's Career Guide.* New York: Anchor Books, 1987.

Professional Vocational Analysis

It would be great if there were some psychological test that would confirm without a doubt who you are and precisely what job, career, or field best suits you. Unfortunately, there isn't. Professionals in vocational planning have literally dozens of tests at their disposal designed to assess personality and aptitude for particular careers.

The test most commonly used is probably the Strong-Campbell Interest Inventory (SCII). This multiple-choice test takes about an hour to administer and is scored by machine. The SCII has been around since 1933. The most recent revision, in 1981, made a serious and generally successful attempt to eliminate sex bias.

The SCII offers information about an individual's interests on three different levels. First, the test provides a general statement about the test-taker's interest patterns. These patterns suggest not only promising occupations but also characteristics of the most compatible work environments and personality traits affecting work.

Second, the test reports how interested a person is in a specific work activity compared with other men and women. Finally, the occupational scales compare the test-taker with satisfied workers in some 90 different occupations. If you think you'd enjoy being a librarian, for example, you can compare yourself with other librarians and see how similar your likes and dislikes are. The occupational scales indicate the degree of probability, confirmed by extensive research, that you'll be satisfied with the choice of a particular occupation.

Personality/vocational tests come in a variety of formats. Many are multiple choice; some require you to finish incomplete sentences; others are autobiographical questionnaires. No single test should ever be used as an absolute. Personality tests are more important for generating discussion and for providing data that can be used in making judgments.

In Chicago, vocational guidance and testing are available from a variety of career consultants. A list of selected sources follows. One word of caution: career consultants are generally in business to direct an entire employment campaign. Vocational testing is only one of the services they provide. Because career consulting firms are private, for-profit businesses with high overhead costs, they usually charge more for testing than local community colleges or social service agencies (which are listed afterward). A fuller discussion of services offered by career consultants is provided in Chapter 6. Also in Chapter 6 is a list of social service agencies. Some of which offer vocational testing and guidance free of charge.

What To Expect from a Career Counselor

What kind of help can you expect from a career counselor that you can't find on your own?

For one thing, counselors offer an objective viewpoint, says one licensed professional career counselor we know. "You may not be able to discuss everything with family, friends, and especially coworkers if you happen still to be working. A trained professional can serve as a sounding board and offer strategies and information that you can't get elsewhere. We can essentially help a person become more resourceful."

This particular career counselor usually spends four sessions with individuals who want to establish a sense of direction for their careers. Here's what sessions cover:

- Exploring problems that have blocked progress and considering solutions.
- Establishing career objectives and determining strengths and areas to work on.
- Writing a career plan that outlines a strategy to achieve goals.
- Preparing an ongoing, self-directed plan to explore career goals.

"A counselor should help people develop methods and a framework from which to base continual exploration about what they want from a career, even after they are employed," our counselor friend says.

All too often people look for "quick fixes" in order to get back to work, she says. "In haste, they may not take time to reflect on where their career is going, to make sure they look for a job that will be challenging and satisfying."

Who's good? Who's not?

A listing in this book does not constitute an endorsement of any consulting firm or vocational testing service. Before embarking on a lengthy or expensive series of tests, try to get the opinion of one or more people who have already used the service you're considering. Reputable firms will provide references. You can also contact:

The Better Business Bureau
Inquiries: (312) 444-1188
Complaints: (312) 346-3313

The City of Chicago Consumer Services Office
(312) 744-4091

The City of Chicago Office of Consumer Complaints
(312) 744-4092

The Governor's Office of Consumer Services
(312) 814-4794■

CAREER COUNSELORS AND CONSULTANTS

American Personnel Consultants, Inc.
300 W. Washington Blvd., Suite 601
Chicago, IL 60606
(312) 263-6463
Supplies comprehensive testing in 12 to 15-hour period. Ph.D. supplies a written report. Vocational analysis. Fee: about $400.

Applied Potential
509 Halligan Circle
Lake Forest, IL 60045
(708) 234-2130
Testing program. Fees vary.

Aptitude Consultants
180 W. Washington Blvd., Suite 1200
Chicago, IL 60602
(312) 332-7449
Two-day program; Ph.D. business psychologists administer battery of standardized tests; counseling. Fee: counseling and testing package, $350; counseling alone, $80/ hr.

Ball Foundation/ Career Vision
800 Roosevelt Road, Suite 120
Glen Ellyn, IL 60137
(708) 469-6270
Interview with counselor; personality, interest, and aptitude assessment; standardized tests, career recommendations, follow-up sessions for one year. Fee: $395.

Career Directions
5005 Newport Drive, Suite 404
Rolling Meadows, IL 60008
(708) 870-1290
Vocational testing, workshops, seminars, individual counseling. Fee: $60/hr.

Educational Counseling Service
28 E. Jackson, Room 808
Chicago, IL 60604
(312) 427-2777
Vocational testing; counseling; each case handled individually. Fee: $75-$150 for complete package of tests and counseling.

Family Counseling Clinic, Inc.
19300 W. Highway 120
Grayslake, IL 60030
(708) 223-8107
Vocational testing. Fee: $58/session.

Friedland & Marcus
Civic Opera Building
20 N. Wacker Drive, Suite 3220
Chicago, IL 60606
(312) 567-3560
One-and-one-half day program tailor-made for each candidate; about 15 tests and homework; fee includes test materials,

counseling, computer analysis of scores. Fee: package, $495; extensive written report available for additional $80.

Gerald Greene, Ph.D.
500 N. Michigan Ave., Suite 542
Chicago, IL 60611
(312) 266-1456
Vocational testing. Fee varies.

Bernard Haldane and Associates
307 N. Michigan Ave., Suite 2001
Chicago, IL 60601
(312) 332-4516
President: Jack Chapman

Human Research & Data, Inc.
800 E. Northwest Highway
Palatine, IL 60067
(708) 358-8222
Preliminary interview, vocational testing, follow-up report by registered psychologists; also specific counseling with no testing. Fee: package, $250; counseling alone, $50/hr.

Human Resource Developers
126 W. Delaware Place
Chicago, IL 60610
(312) 644-1920
Vocational testing, counseling. Fee: first visit free; fees vary thereafter.

Johnson O'Connor Research Foundation
161 E. Erie St., Room 204
Chicago, IL 60611
(312) 787-9141
One-and-one-half day session: aptitude tests, counseling, career direction, and follow-up session. Fees vary.

Psychological Consultation Services
1103 Westgate St., Suite 205
Oak Park, IL 60302
(708) 386-1761
Ph.D.s administer vocational tests, supply counseling. Fee: $45-$75/hr.

University of Illinois Circle Campus
Office of Applied Psychological Services
1007 W. Harrison St.
Chicago, IL 60607
(312) 996-2540
Vocational testing and counseling. Fee: $300 for complete battery of tests taken over 12-hr. period; $50/hr. for counseling, with a sliding fee based on income.

Diane G. Wilson, M.A.
Career Development
55 E. Washington St., Suite 1221
Chicago, IL 60602
(312) 524-8113
Individual and corporate testing. Hourly fee varies.

Going back to work?

Displaced homemakers and women entering the job market for the first time can develop job skills, confidence, and support for adjustments they need to make at home and at work through the TARGET program of the West Suburban YWCA Employment Center. Privately funded and low cost, the program prepares women to make a smooth transition into the job world.

"The biggest thing many of these women feel is fear of getting back out there, or being employed for the first time. They don't realize that 30 years of being a homemaker is a solid skill that they can sell to an employer," says the Project Coordinator.

Classroom training introduces or improves skills and prepares women to handle common job situations effectively, such as asking for a raise. They are coached in time and money management, assertiveness, and in new ways to adjust family and working lives.

Job counseling is provided on an individual basis, and job placement is also offered, primarily in clerical fields. Following placement, women return to the center to attend a post-employment support group.

TARGET Program
West Suburban YWCA
739 Roosevelt Rd.
Building 8, Suite 210
Glen Ellyn, IL 60136
(708) 790-6600■

COLLEGES OFFERING TESTING AND VOCATIONAL GUIDANCE

College of DuPage
425 22nd St.
Glen Ellyn, IL 60137
(708) 858-2800
Career counseling and testing for residents of DuPage County.
Fee: free.

College of Lake County
19351 W. Washington St.
Grayslake, IL 60030

(708) 223-7200
Interest and aptitude testing for residents of Lake County; help with job search. Fee: free.

Elgin Community College
1700 Spartan Drive
Elgin, IL 60120
(708) 697-1000
Career counseling, vocational testing. Fee: counseling free; testing, $1.

Harper College
Algonquin & Roselle Roads
Palatine, IL 60067
(708) 397-3000
Vocational and psychological testing and counseling at three locations. Fee: counseling, $25/hr.; testing, $10/test.

Moraine Valley Community College
10900 S. 88th Ave.
Palos Hills, IL 60465
(708) 974-5721
Vocational testing, career counseling, seminars. Fee: package, $28.

Morton College
3801 S. Central Ave.
Cicero, IL 60650
(708) 656-8000
Vocational testing, career counseling. Fee: one credit hour in-district tuition, $24.

Oakton Community College
1600 E. Golf Road
Des Plaines, IL 60016
(708) 635-1600
Career counseling, vocational testing, and assessment. Fee: varies.

Prairie State College
202 S. Halsted St.
Chicago Heights, IL 60411
(708) 756-3110
Vocational testing, career counseling. Fee: free.

South Suburban College
15800 S. State St.
South Holland, IL 60473
(708) 596-2000
Vocational testing, career counseling. Fee: $4-$15.

Triton College
Office of Career Planning and Placement, S-122
2000 Fifth Ave.
River Grove, IL 60171
(708) 456-0300, ext. 671
Vocational testing; career counseling. Computerized job notification service available. Fee: comprehensive package, $115-150, options available.

Waubonsee Community College
Rt. 47 at Harter Road.
Sugar Grove, IL 60554
(708) 466-4811
Vocational testing, career counseling; job listings. Fee: counseling, free; testing, $5.

SOCIAL SERVICE AGENCIES OFFERING VOCATIONAL TESTING AND GUIDANCE

Jewish Vocational Service
1 S. Franklin St.
Chicago, IL 60606
(312) 346-6700
Nonsectarian agency provides vocational testing, counseling, skills training, and free job placement assistance. Fees based on ability to pay.

YWCA Employment Services
180 N. Wabash Ave.
Chicago, IL 60601
(312) 372-6600
Vocational testing, workshops, resume writing, individual follow-up. Fee: varies with service.

A banker's story

Susan Davis is a Vice President at Harris Trust and Savings Bank. We asked her for her job-hunting philosophy.

"Use the occasion of a job change to do some real self-searching about your beliefs and goals," she suggests. "I went to a 'career shrink'—a person trained in the techniques that Richard Bolles outlines in *What Color Is Your Parachute?* That's a book, by the way, that I can't recommend highly enough.
Anyway, my career shrink assigned me to write an autobiography. It took me a month to finish, and it was 80 pages long. But it made me take a good, hard look at myself.

"I would advise every job hunter to do the same thing. Read over what you've written, figure out what you said and what the implications are. Based on that thoughtful process, be willing to take a risk. That's what I did, and it certainly was a good investment. Women tend to take fewer risks than they ought to for their own self-interest."■

Thinking of Starting Your Own Small Business?

Free information available at **U.S. Small Business Administration** offices will answer many of your basic questions about starting a small business. Information packets deal with income tax preparation, loan programs for small businesses, assistance in obtaining government contracts, and solving management and technical problems.

To find out more, attend one of the SBA workshops. Or for individual assistance, call or drop by one of the SBA offices. Questions are answered by staff members and volunteers in the SCORE (Service Corps of Retired Executives) program. These retired executives draw upon years of experience in helping people start their own business or better manage the one they have. They in turn receive a great deal of support and advice from members of ACE (Active Corps of Executives), a group of professionals who volunteer their services.

You can find useful information on the ins and outs of becoming an independent contractor, too. Management training programs co-sponsored by the SBA are held all over the area, often at local community colleges.

You'll find the SBA offices at: **(312) 353-4520**

3

Writing a Resume That Works

Volumes have been written about how to write a resume. That's because, in our opinion, generations of job seekers have attached great importance to the creation and perfection of their resumes. Keep in mind that *no one ever secured a job offer on the basis of a resume alone*. The way to land a good position is to succeed in the employment interview. *You have to convince a potential employer that you're the best person for the job. No piece of paper will do that for you.*

The resume also goes by the name of *curriculum vita* (the course of one's life), or *vita* (life) for short. These terms are a little misleading, however. A resume cannot possibly tell the story of your life, especially since, as a rule, it shouldn't be more than two pages long. The French word *résumé* means "a summing up." In the American job market, a resume is a concise, written summary of your work experience, education, accomplishments, and personal background—the essentials an employer needs to evaluate your qualifications.

A resume is nothing more or less than a simple marketing tool, a print ad for yourself. It is sometimes useful in generating interviews. But it is most effective when kept in reserve until *after* you've met an employer in person. Sending a follow-up letter after the interview, along with your resume, reminds the interviewer of that wonderful person he or she met last Thursday.

The Basics of a Good Resume

The resume is nothing for you to agonize over. But since almost every employer will ask you for one at some point in the hiring process, make sure that yours is a good one.

What do we mean by a good resume? First, *be sure it's up to date and comprehensive.* At a minimum it should include your name, address, and phone number; a complete summary of your work experience; and an education profile. (College grads need not include their high school backgrounds.)

In general, your work experience should include the name, location, and dates of employment of every job you've held since leaving school, plus a summary of your responsibilities and, most important, your accomplishments on each job. If you're a recent graduate, or have held several jobs, you can present your experience *chronologically.* Begin with your present position and work backward to your first job. If you haven't had that many jobs, organize your resume along *functional* lines to emphasize the skills you've acquired through experience.

A second rule of resume writing is to *keep the resume concise.* Most employers don't want to read more than two pages, and one page is preferable. In most cases your resume will be scanned, not read in detail. Describe your experience in short, pithy phrases. Avoid large blocks of copy. Your resume should read more like a chart than a short story.

There are no hard and fast rules on what to include in your resume besides work experience and education. A statement of your objective and a personal section containing date of birth, marital status, and so on, are optional. An employer wants to know these things about you, but it's up to you whether to include them in your resume or bring them up during the interview. If you have served in the military, you ought to mention that in your resume.

Your salary history and references, however, should not be included in your resume; these should be discussed in person during the interview.

Keep in mind that a resume is a sales tool. Make sure that it illustrates your unique strengths in a style and format *you* can be comfortable with. Indicate any unusual responsibilities you've been given or examples of how you've saved the company money or helped it grow. Include any special recognition of your ability. For example, if your salary increased substantially within a year or two, you might state the increase in terms of a percentage.

Third, *keep your resume honest.* Never lie, exaggerate, embellish, or deceive. Tell the truth about your education, accomplishments, and work history. You needn't account for every single work day that elapsed between jobs, however. If you left one position on November 15 and began the next on February 1, you can minimize gaps by simply listing years worked instead of months.

Fourth, *your resume should have a professional look.* If you type it yourself or have it typed professionally, use a high-quality office typewriter with a plastic ribbon (sometimes called a "carbon" ribbon). Do *not* use a household or office typewriter with a cloth ribbon.

If your budget permits, consider having your resume typeset professionally or typed on a good quality word processor. In either case you have a choice of type faces, such as boldface, italics, and small caps. You can also request that the margins be justified (lined up evenly on the right and left sides, like the margins of a book).

No matter what method you use to prepare your resume, be sure to *proofread* it before sending it to the printer. A misspelled word or typing error reflects badly on you, even if it's not your fault. Read every word out loud, letter for letter and comma for comma.

Get a friend to help you.

Do *not* make copies of your resume on a photocopy machine. Have it printed professionally. The resume you leave behind after an interview or send ahead to obtain an interview may be photocopied several times, and copies of copies can be very hard to read. You should also avoid such gimmicks as using colored paper (unless it's very light cream or light gray) or using a paper size other than 8 1/2 x 11".

Our purpose here is not to tell you how to write the ideal resume (there *is* no such thing) but rather to provide some general guidelines. The following books are full of all the how-to information you'll need to prepare an effective resume and are available from bookstores or your local library.

BOOKS ON RESUME WRITING

Bostwick, Burdette. *Resume Writing.* New York: John Wiley and Sons, 1985.

Corwen, Leonard. *Your Resume: Key to a Better Job.* New York: Arco, 1988.

Foxman, Loretta D., and Walter L. Polsky. *Resumes That Work: How to Sell Yourself On Paper.* New York: John Wiley and Sons, 1984.

Jackson, Tom. *The Perfect Resume.* New York: Anchor/Doubleday, 1990.

Krannich, Ronald L., and William J. Banis. *High Impact Resumes & Letters.* Career Management Concepts, Inc., 1987.

Lewis, Adele. *How to Write a Better Resume.* Woodbury, NY: Barron's Educational Series, 1989.

Parker, Yana. *Damn Good Resume Guidelines.* Berkeley: Ten Speed Press, 1985.

Smith, Michael Holley. *The Resume Writer's Handbook,* 2nd ed. New York: Harper & Row, 1987.

Wilson, Robert F., and Adele Lewis. *Better Resumes for Executives and Professionals.* New York: Barrons, 1983.

Should You Hire Someone Else to Write Your Resume?

In general, if you have reasonable writing skills, it's better to prepare your own resume than to ask someone else to do it. If you write your own job history, you'll be better prepared to talk about it in the interview. "Boiler plate" resumes also tend to look and sound alike.

On the other hand, a professional resume writer can be objective about your background and serve as a sounding board on what you should and shouldn't include. You might also consider a professional if you have trouble writing in the condensed style that a good resume calls for.

Here is a list of area firms that will assist you in preparing your resume. Remember that a listing in this book does not constitute an endorsement. Before engaging a professional writer, ask for a recommendation from someone whose judgment you trust—a personnel director, college placement officer, or a knowledgeable friend. Check with the Better Business Bureau and other consumer advocates listed in Chapter 2 to see if there have been any complaints made about the resume service you are considering.

How to choose a professional

Before engaging a professional to help you write your resume, run through the following checklist of questions.

What will it cost? Some firms charge a set fee. Others charge by the hour. Though many firms will not quote an exact price until they know the details of your situation, you should obtain minimum and maximum costs before you go ahead.

What does the price include? Does the fee cover only writing? Or does it include typesetting? Most firms will charge extra for printing.

What happens if you're not satisfied? Will the writer make changes you request? Will changes or corrections cost extra?

How do this writer's fees and experience stack up against others? It's wise to shop around before you buy writing services, just as you would when purchasing any other service.■

PROFESSIONAL RESUME PREPARERS

A Frank Young Enterprise
P. O. Box 1205
Elmhurst, IL 60126
(708) 530-8818
Fee: $60-$100
Contact: Frank Young

Allen & Associates
1375 E. Woodfield Road
Schaumburg, IL 60173
(708) 517-7792
Fee: not available

American Resume Service
185 N. Wabash Ave.
Chicago, IL 60601
(312) 781-9590
Fee: varies

Banner Personnel
122 S. Michigan Ave., Suite 1510
Chicago, IL 60603
(312) 704-6100
Fee: varies
Contact: Ann Johnson

Bondar Executive Secretaries
5005 Newport Drive, Suite 800
Rolling Meadows, IL 60008
(708) 394-5055
Fee: $25/hr. for consulting; $25/page, $1 each additional page for typing

Cursor Characters
1021 W. Diversey Parkway
Chicago, IL 60614
(312) 975-6668
Fee: varies

Joan Masters & Sons
875 N. Michigan Ave., Suite 3614
Chicago, IL 60611
(312) 787-3009
Fee: $40/hr.
Contact: Joan Masters

Timesavers Secretarial Services
P.O. Box 1087
Morton Grove, IL 60053
(708) 470-0231
Fee: $95-$120
Contact: Barbara Friedman

What NOT To Do with Your Resume Once You Have It Printed

Do not change your resume except to correct an obvious error. Everyone to whom you show the resume will have some suggestion for improving it: "Why didn't you tell 'em that you had a scholarship?" or "Wouldn't this look better in italics?" The time to consider those kinds of questions is *before* you go to the typesetter. Afterward, the only thing to keep in mind is that there is no such thing as a perfect resume, except typographically.

A second point to remember: do NOT send out a mass mailing. If you send letters to 700 company presidents, you can expect a response of from 1 to 2 percent—and 95 percent of the responses will be negative. The shotgun approach is expensive; it takes time and costs money for postage and printing. You'll get much better results if you are selective about where you send your resume. We'll discuss this at greater length in Chapter 5. The important thing is to concentrate on known hiring authorities in whom you are interested.

The power of verbs

Jeff B. has been a sales manager in Chicago for 20 years. During those years he has changed jobs seven times, enhancing his career with each move. Jeff realized early that using powerful active verbs to describe his accomplishments made his resume stand out. Here are some sample verbs that job seekers in various career areas might use to help build a more effective resume.

Management
Controlled
Headed
Implemented

Methods and Controls
Restructured
Cataloged
Verified
Systematized

Public Relations/ Human Relations
Monitored
Handled
Sponsored
Integrated

Creative
Devised
Effected
Originated
Conceived

Advertising/ Promotion
Generated
Recruited
Tailored
Sparked

Communications
Facilitated
Edited
Consulted
Disseminated

Resourcefulness
Rectified
Pioneered
Achieved

Negotiations
Engineered
Mediated
Proposed
Negotiated■

Always Include a Cover Letter

This brings us to a third important "don't": do NOT send your resume without a cover letter. Whether you are answering a want ad or following up an inquiry call or interview, you should always include a letter with your resume. If at all possible, the letter should be addressed to a specific person—the one who's doing the hiring—and not "To Whom It May Concern."

A good cover letter, like a good resume, is brief—usually not more than three or four paragraphs. No paragraph should be longer than three or four sentences. If you've already spoken to the contact person by phone, remind him or her of your conversation in the first paragraph. If you and the person to whom you are writing know someone in common, the first paragraph is the place to mention it. You should also include a hard-hitting sentence about why you're well qualified for the job in question.

In the next paragraph or two, specify what you could contribute to the company in terms that indicate you've done your homework on the firm and the industry.

Finally, either request an interview or tell the reader that you will follow up with a phone call within a week to arrange a mutually convenient meeting.

Choosing a Resume Format

There are a number of different methods for composing a quality resume. Every career counselor and resume compiler has his or her own favorite method and style. As the person being represented by the resume, *you* must choose the style and format that best suits and sells you. Many resume books will use different terms for the various styles. We will highlight the three most popular types.

1. *The chronological resume* is the traditional style, most often used in the workplace and job search; that does not mean it is the most effective. Positive aspects of the chronological resume include the traditionalist approach that employers may

expect. It also can highlight past positions that you may wish your potential employer to notice. This resume is also very adaptable, with only the reverse chronological order of items as the essential ingredient.

2. *The functional resume* is most common among career changers, people reentering the job market after a lengthy absence, and those wishing to highlight aspects of their experience not related directly to employment. This resume ideally focuses on the many skills one has used at his or her employment and the accomplishments one has achieved. It shows a potential employer that you can do and have done a good job. What it doesn't highlight is where you have done it.

3. *The combination resume* combines the best features of a functional resume and a chronological resume. This allows job seekers to highlight skills and accomplishments while still maintaining the somewhat traditional format of reverse chronological order of positions held and organizations worked for.

Here are some sample resumes and cover letters to help you with your own. The books listed earlier in this chapter will supply many more examples than we have room for here.

SAMPLE CHRONOLOGICAL RESUME

GEORGE P. BURDELL
555 Maple Avenue
Wilmette, IL 60091
(708) 555-2436

OBJECTIVE

Position in technical management.

WORK EXPERIENCE

SAMPO CORPORATION 1978-1990

Manager, Marketing & Planning-(Taiwan) 1988-1990

- **Supervised** operations & staff of **new products development.**
- Instrumental in **making decisions** regarding **OEM new products** with clients such as: IBM, NCR, TI, Xerox, Quadram, etc.
- **Developed 4 new products:** Low-cost display monitor, oscilloscope, and two DEC-compatible terminals.
- Accomplishment: IPD **sales volume** in 1989: **$45,000,000; 50% increase** from 1987.

Manager, Midwest Division 1986-1988

- Generated **$3,000,000 in sales** of OEM display monitors to IBM(NC), NCR(SC), Quadram, Digital Control, & other local accounts.

Sales Engineer—(Chicago, IL) 1985-1986

- Successfully collaborated with OEM engineers to **develop** monitors for computer & laser games such as Jungle King & Dragon's Lair.

Production Engineer—(Chicago, IL) 1983-1985

- Member of team credited with building **new TV manufacturing plant.**
- **Involvement in this $7,000,000** project ranged from conceptualization to production of 600, 19" color sets daily.

Circuit Design Engineer-(St. Louis, MO) 1978-1983

- **Designed** PIF, deflection & remote control circuit for color TV.

EDUCATION

University of Chicago, Chicago, IL: **MBA in marketing,** 1986

Northwestern University, Evanston, IL: **B.A.,** 1977

REFERENCES

Furnished upon request

SAMPLE FUNCTIONAL RESUME

KATHY JONES
256 Lake Shore Drive
Chicago, IL 60611
(312) 555-5902

OBJECTIVE: Seek position as an **administrative assistant,** utilizing my adminstrative, organizational, and computer skills.

SKILLS

Administrative

- Independently straightened out a major client's account for an advertising agency.
- Kept books and managed funds in excess of $80,000 for a non-profit corporation.
- Managed two rental properties.

Organizational

- Set up procedure for assigned experiments and procured equipment for a research laboratory.
- Planned course syllabi, assessed weaknesses of individual students to facilitate learning.

Computer

- Managed data input and generated monthly reports.
- Completed courses in FORTRAN and BASIC.

EMPLOYMENT

Computer Operator, NSW Industries, Chicago, IL (1988-Present)

Trouble-shooter in accounting, Cargill, Wilson, and Acree, Oak Brook, IL (1986)

Instructor, Math Dept., Northern Illinois University (1982-85)

EDUCATION

M.S., Mathematics, Northern Illinois University (1981)

B.A., Mathematics, Cornell College, Iowa (1979)

REFERENCES

Furnished upon request.

SAMPLE COMBINATION RESUME

SUSAN SKINNER
122 Pine St.
Palos Park, IL 60464
(708) 555-0011

OBJECTIVE: Software development position utilizing software and computer skills.

EDUCATION:

UNIVERSITY OF ILLINOIS GPA 3.7/4.0
M.S., Information and Computer Science 12/86

ROOSEVELT UNIVERSITY (CHICAGO) GPA 3.5/4.0
A.B., Mathematics 5/81

QUALIFICATIONS:

Career-related projects:

- Designed and implemented multi-tasking operating system for the IBM-PC.
- Implemented compiler for Pascal-like language.

- Designed electronic mail system using PSL/PSA specification language.

Languages and operating systems:

- Proficient in **Ada, Modula-2, Pascal, COBOL.**
- Working knowledge of IBM-PC hardware and 8088 assembly language.
- Experienced in **UNIX, MS-DOS, XENIX,** CP/M operating systems.

Hardware:

- IBM-PC (MS-DOS, Xenix), Pyramid 90x (UNIX), Cyber 990 (NOS), Data General MV/10000 (UNIX, AOS/VS).

WORK EXPERIENCE:

Neil Araki Programming Services—
Chicago, IL 10/86-Present

- **UNIX Programmer**—Responsible for porting MS-DOS database applications to IBM-PC/AT running Xenix System V. System administration.

Strathmore Systems—
Des Moines, IA 11/83-9/86

- **Computer Programmer**— Performed daily disk backup on Burroughs B-1955 machine. Executed database update programs and checks. User assistance.
- From 8/81 to 11/83, held full-time positions as **Computer operator** for organizations in Chicago metropolitan area.

REFERENCES

Furnished upon request.

SAMPLE COVER LETTER

3420 Salmon Court
Evanston, IL 60071
June 26, 1990
(708) 555-6886

Ms. Jacqueline Doe
Wide World Publishing Company
1400 W. Superior St.
Chicago, IL 60602

Dear Ms. Doe:

As an honors graduate of Northwestern University with two years of copy editing and feature writing experience with the *Evanston Outlook,* I am confident that I would make a successful editorial assistant with Wide World.

Besides my strong editorial background, I offer considerable business experience. I have held summer jobs in an insurance company, a law firm, and a data processing company. My familiarity with word processing should prove particularly useful to Wide World now that you're about to become fully automated.

I would like to interview with you as soon as possible and would be happy to check in with your office about an appointment. If you prefer, your office can contact me between the hours of 11 a.m. and 3 p.m. at (708) 555-6886.

Sincerely,

Valerie Jones

SAMPLE/COVER LETTER

2239 Forest Park Blvd.
Chicago, IL 60646
May 31, 1990

Chicago Tribune
Box 1826
Chicago, IL 60611

Dear Employer:

Your advertisement in the May 29 issue of *The Tribune* for an entry-level bookkeeper seems perfect for someone with my background. I am about to graduate from Lacey Business School in a business preparatory course that includes two semesters of accounting.

As you can see from my resume, my work experience consists mainly of miscellaneous summer employment and part-time jobs while in school. But I hope to offset my lack of experience with hard work, enthusiasm, and a desire to succeed.

My activities with Junior Achievement should give you an idea of my aptitude for business. I would appreciate the opportunity of an interview at your convenience.

Sincerely,

Jim Clark
(312) 555-4414

SAMPLE COVER LETTER

228 Meadow Road
Northbrook, IL 60062
December 1, 1990

Dear Mike:

Just when everything seemed to be going so well at my job, the company gave us a Christmas present that nobody wanted—management announced that half the department will be laid off before the end of the year. Nobody knows yet just which heads are going to roll. But whether or not my name is on the list, I am definitely back in the job market.

I have already lined up a couple of interviews. But knowing how uncertain job hunting can be, I can use all the contacts I can get.

You know my record—both from when we worked together at 3-Q and since then. But in case you've forgotten the details, I've enclosed my resume.

I know that you often hear of job openings as you wend your way about Chicago and the suburbs. I'd certainly appreciate your passing along any leads you think might be worthwhile.

My best to you and Fran for the Holidays.

Cordially,

Emily Noir
(708) 555-9876

Seven ways to ruin a cover letter

1. Spell the name of the firm incorrectly.
2. Don't bother to find out the name of the hiring authority. Just send the letter to the president or chairman of the board.
3. If the firm is headed by a woman, be sure to begin your letter, "Dear Sir." Otherwise, just address it, "To Whom It May Concern."
4. Make sure the letter includes a couple of typos and sloppy erasures. Better yet, spill coffee on it first, then mail it.
5. Be sure to provide a phone number that has been disconnected, or one at which nobody is ever home.
6. Tell the firm you'll call to set up an appointment in a few days; then don't bother.
7. Call the firm at least three times the day after you mail the letter. Get very angry when they say they haven't heard of you.■

4

Researching the Chicago Job Market

To a large extent, the success of your job search will depend on how well you do your homework. Once you've figured out what kind of job you want, you need to find out as much as you can about which specific companies might employ you. Your network of personal contacts can be an invaluable source of information about what jobs are available where. But networking can't do it all; at some point, you'll have to do some reading. This chapter fills you in on the directories, newspapers, and magazines you'll need in your search and notes the libraries where you can find them.

Directories

When you're beginning your homework, whether you're researching an entire industry or a specific company, there are five major sources of information with which you should be familiar. All five of these "gospels" are available at the **Chicago Public Library's Business Information Center** (400 N. Franklin St., 4th Floor). Check your local branch library as well.

Standard and Poor's Register of Corporations, Directors, and Executives (Standard and Poor's Publishing Co., 25 Broadway, New York, NY 10004) is billed as the "foremost guide to the business community and the executives who run it." This three-volume directory lists more than 55,000 corporations and 70,000 officers, directors, trustees, and other bigwigs.

Each business is assigned a four-digit number called a Standard Industrial Classification (S.I.C.) number, which tells you what product or service the company provides. Listings are indexed by geographic area and also by S.I.C. number, so that it's easy to find out all the companies in Chicago that produce, say, industrial inorganic chemicals.

You can also look up a *particular* company to verify its correct address and phone number, its chief officers (that is, the people you might want to contact for an interview), its products, and, in many cases, its annual sales and number of employees.

If you have an appointment with the president of XYZ Corporation, you can consult *Standard and Poor's* to find out where he or she was born and went to college—information that's sure to come in handy in an employment interview. Supplements are published in April, July, and October.

The **Thomas Register of American Manufacturers** (Thomas Publishing Co., One Penn Plaza, New York, NY 10001) is published annually. This 23-volume publication is another gold mine of information. You can look up a certain product or service and find out every company that provides it. (Since this is a national publication, you'll have to weed out companies that are not in the Chicago area, but that's easy.) You can also look up a particular company to find out about branch offices, capital ratings, company officials, names, addresses, phone numbers, and more. The *Thomas Register* even contains seven volumes of company catalogs. Before your appointment with XYZ Corporation, you can bone up on its product line with the *Thomas Register.*

The **First Chicago Guide** (Scholl Communications, Inc., P.O. Box 560, Deerfield, IL 60015) is available for $24.95 and provides information on more than 250 publicly held northern Illinois companies in and around the Chicago area. It's not as detailed as the *Thomas Register,* but it does have the advantage of concentrating exclusively on Chicago. For each company, the guide provides an overview of the firm's business; names and titles of directors and officers; and financial and investment information. An index in the back lets you look up a product or service and find out what companies provide it;

another index ranks the companies by sales or revenues and by assets.

Moody's Complete Corporate Index (Moody's Investor Service, 99 Church St., New York, NY 10007) gives you the equivalent of an encyclopedia entry on more than 20,000 corporations. This is the resource to use when you want really detailed information on a certain company. *Moody's* can tell you about a company's history—when it was founded, what name changes it has undergone, and so on. It provides a fairly lengthy description of a company's business and properties, what subsidiaries it owns, and lots of detailed financial information. Like the directories above, *Moody's* lists officers and directors of companies. It can also tell you the date of the annual meeting and the number of stockholders and employees.

The **Million Dollar Directory** (Dun & Bradstreet, Inc., 3 Sylvan Way, Parsippany, NJ 07054) is a five-volume listing of approximately 160,000 U.S. businesses with a net worth of more than half a million dollars. Listings appear alphabetically, geographically, and by product classification and include key personnel. Professional and consulting organizations such as hospitals and engineering services, credit agencies, and financial institutions other than banks and trust companies are not generally included.

So much for the Big Five directories. The following list contains more than four dozen additional directories and guides that may come in handy. Most are available at the Chicago Public Library's Business Information Center (400 N. Franklin, 4th Floor).

USEFUL DIRECTORIES

Chicago Apparel Center
(Directory Publications, 470 Merchandise Mart, Chicago, IL 60654.)
Lists apparel retailers and wholesalers and Chicago area fashion events; published yearly.

Bacon's Publicity Checker
(Bacon's Publishing Co., 332 S. Michigan Ave., Chicago, IL 60604.)
Covers over 4,800 trade and consumer magazines, 1,700 daily newspapers, and 8,000 weekly newspapers in the U.S. and Canada. Organized geographically.

Blackbook Business and Reference Guide
(National Publications and Sales Agency, Inc., 1610 E. 79th St., Chicago, IL 60649, $4.90.)
Covers about 15,000 black-owned, consumer-oriented businesses and professionals in Chicago.

Business and Management Jobs
(Peterson's Guides, P.O. Box 2123, Princeton, NJ 08540.)
Lists employer information, job hunt hints, and directories for majors in business management, social sciences, and humanities.

The Career Guide—Dun's Employment Opportunities Directory
(Dun's Marketing Services, 3 Sylvan Way, Parsippany, NJ 07054, $295.)
Designed for those beginning a career; describes job prospects at hundreds of companies.

Chicago and Cook County Marketing Directory
(Manufacturer's News, Inc., 4 E. Huron St. Chicago, IL 60611.)
Thumbnail profile of manufacturers and service businesses in Chicago and Cook County.

Chicago Banks Directory
(Law Bulletin Publishing Co., 415 N. State St., Chicago, IL 60610.)
Lists banking institutions in Chicago and Cook County, including names of officers.

Chicago Creative Directory
(333 N. Michigan Ave., Chicago, IL 60601, $40.)
People and firms in the fields of photography, illustration, film, printing services, audio/visual, and music production; talent agencies, media reps, and firms that service the media industry.

Chicago Mercantile Exchange Membership List
(Chicago Mercantile Exchange, 30 S. Wacker Drive, Chicago, IL 60606, $6.)
National listing of traders who conduct business on the Mercantile Exchange; their firms and addresses.

Chicago Purchaser Roster Issue
(Purchasing Management Association of Chicago, 201 N. Wells St., Suite 618, Chicago, IL 60606.)
Annual listing of personal members and their firms.

Chicago Talent Handbook
(Swift Publishing Co., 445 W. Fullerton Ave., Chicago, IL 60614.)
Guide to modeling, acting, voice, trade show, and runway work in Chicago.

Chicago Talent Sourcebook
(Alexander Communications, Inc., 212 W. Superior St., Chicago, IL 60610, $50.)
Names and numbers of Chicago firms in advertising, photography, illustration; audio/visual, film, and tape production; music and printing services.

Chicago Unlimited Directory
(Chicago Unlimited, 203 N. Wabash Ave., Chicago, IL 60601, $7.)
Guide to Chicago audio/visual firms, facilities, and services.

College Placement Council
(College Placement Council, 62 Highland Ave., Bethlehem, PA, 18017, $30, set of 3.)
Directory of the occupational needs of over 1,200 corporations and government employers. Names and titles of recruitment representatives.

Consultants and Consulting Organizations Directory
(Gale Research Co., Book Tower, Detroit, MI 48226, $85.)
Contains descriptions of 6,000 firms and individuals involved in consulting; indexed geographically.

Contractors Trade Directory
(Contractors Trade Directory, Inc., 2538 W. Peterson Ave., Chicago, IL 60659, $50.)
Describes vendors of goods and services to the construction industry in a five-state area.

Corporate Finance Bluebook
(National Register Publishing Co., 3004 Glenview Rd., Wilmette, IL 60091.)
Annual directory of over 4,500 U.S. companies. Includes financial decision-making personnel and outside financial service firms.

Corporate Technology Directory
(Corporate Technology Information Services, Inc., 1 Market St., P.O. Box 81281, Wellesley Hills, MA 02181.)
Provides profiles of earnings and executives of over 30,000 high-technology manufacturers.

Data Sources: Hardware-Data Communications Directory and **Data Sources: Software Directory**
(Ziff-Davis Publishing Co., One Park Ave., New York, NY.)
Two-volume guide to most products, companies, services, and personnel in the computer industry.

Directories in Print
(Gale Research Inc., 835 Penobscot Bldg., Detroit, MI 48226.)
10,000 annotated descriptions of U.S. businesses and industrial directories that are nationwide or regional in scope or interest.

Directory of Agencies
(National Association of Social Workers, Publications Sales, 1425 H St., NW, Washington, DC 20005.)
Provides information on over 300 U.S. and international voluntary intergovernmental agencies involved in social work.

Directory of Chicago Fashion and Apparel Manufacturers
(Apparel Industry Board, Apparel Center, Suite 1346, 350 N. Orleans St., Chicago, IL 60654.)
Classified list of apparel manufacturers. Description includes label names produced by the manufacturer.

Directory of Community Organizing in Chicago
(Institute of Urban Life, 1 E. Superior St., Chicago, IL 60611, $2.50.)
Lists community organizations in Chicago having an office and one or more staff members.

The Directory of Directories
(Gale Research Co., Book Tower, Detroit, MI 48226, $195.)
Contains detailed descriptions of all published directories: what they list, who uses them, and who publishes them.

Directory of Human Resources in Health, Physical Education and Recreation
(ERIC Clearing House on Teacher Education, 1 DuPont Circle, Suite 616, Washington, DC 20036.)
Covers information centers in the U.S. and Canada concerned with health, physical education, and recreation. Geographic index.

Directory of Top Computer Executives/West Edition
(Applied Computer Research, Inc., P.O. Box 9280, Phoenix, AZ 85068.)
Lists top computer executives and systems in use at each company; includes geographic listings.

Dun's Consultants Directory
(Dun and Bradstreet Corp., 3 Sylvan Way, Parsippany, NJ 07054.)
Top 25,000 consulting firms in U.S. are briefly described here, with a separate index to Illinois firms.

Education Directory: A Woman's Guide to Education in the Chicago Area
(Applied Potential, Box 19, Highland Park, IL 60035, $4.)
Describes colleges and universities, trade schools, and specialized programs in the Chicago area.

Electronic News Financial Fact Books and Directory
(Fairchild Publications, 7 E. 12th St. New York, NY, $125.)
Background and financial information about leading companies in the electronics industry.

Encyclopedia of Associations
(Gale Research, Book Tower, Detroit, MI 48226.)
Lists 30,000 local and national associations, professional clubs, and civic organizations by categories; key personnel; indexed geographically.

Encyclopedia of Associations Regional, State, and Local Organizations: Vol 1, Great Lakes States
(Gale Research Co., Book Tower, Detroit, MI 48226.)
Five-state listing of 50,000 membership organizations; all Illinois organizations are in one section subdivided by city.

Encyclopedia of Business Information Sources
(Gale Research Co., Book Tower, Detroit, MI 48226, $220.)
Lists each industry's encyclopedias, handbooks, indexes, almanacs, yearbooks, trade associations, periodicals, directories, computer data bases, research centers, and statistical sources.

Everybody's Business
(Harper & Row, 10 E. 53rd St., NY, NY 10022, available at bookstores for $16.95.)
Candid profiles of 300 American manufacturers of well-known brand-name products.

Greater Chicago Minority Business Directory
(Chicago Regional Purchasing Council, 365 S. Wabash Ave., Chicago, IL 60603.)
Over 800 Chicago-area firms are profiled.

Guide to Illinois State Services
(Dept. of Commerce and Community Affairs, 222 S. College St., Springfield, IL 62706, $3.50.)
Describes state assistance programs; lists personnel.

Harris Illinois Industrial Directory
(Registry Publications, 425 Huehl, Unit 6B, Northbrook, IL 60062, $99.)
Lists over 28,000 manufacturers, wholesalers, and distributors in Illinois; parent firms, executives' names; indexed by company name and zip code.

Human Care Services Directory of Metropolitan Chicago
(United Way/Crusade of Mercy/Community Renewal Society, 560 W. Lake St., Chicago, IL 60606.)
Profiles the agencies of Chicago that help people in all areas; useful client descriptions.

Illinois Blue Book
(Illinois Secretary of State, State House, Rm. 213, Springfield, IL 62756, free.)
Descriptions of state departments and agencies; Chicago city government; key personnel.

Illinois Foundation Directory
(Foundation Data Center, 401 Kenmar Circle, Minnetonka, MN 55343, $625.)
Describes 2,000 active and inactive foundations; major contributors; financial data; indexed geographically.

Illinois Manufacturers Directory
(Manufacturers News, Inc., 4 E. Huron St., Chicago, IL 60611, $125.)
Describes all manufacturing companies located in Illinois; key personnel; cross-referenced and indexed geographically.

Illinois Media
(Midwest Newsclip, Inc., 213 W. Institute Place, Chicago, IL 60610.)
Lists daily and weekly newspapers, radio and TV stations in Illinois, and key personnel.

Illinois Services Directory
(Manufacturers News, Inc., 4 E. Huron St., Chicago, IL 60611, $135.)
Describes all wholesalers, jobbers, contractors, retailers, services located in Illinois; key personnel; cross-referenced and indexed geographically.

Illinois Solar Energy Directory
(Illinois Department of Energy and Natural Resources, 325 W. Adams, Springfield, IL 62706, free.)
Lists distributors and manufacturers of solar equipment; consultants; associations.

Internships
(Writer's Digest Books, F&W Publications, Inc., 1507 Dana Ave., Cincinnati, OH 45207.)
Lists 38,000 opportunities in 23 career fields.

Leadsource
(Leadsource, 1420 Kensington Road, Suite 115, Oakbrook, IL 60521, $560.)
Chicago business reference directory, listing company name, key personnel, location, and size.

Macmillan Directory of Leading Private Companies
(National Register Publishing Company, 30004 Glenview Road, Wilmette, IL 60091.)
10,000 companies and wholly owned subsidiaries are briefly profiled; especially useful for computer system/hardware data.

Madison Avenue Handbook
(Peter Glenn Publications, 17 E. 48th St., New York, NY, 10017, $40.)
Lists advertising agencies and related services such as TV producers, models, artists, actors, photographers, etc., for major cities, including Chicago.

Major Employers in Metropolitan Chicago
(Chicago Association of Commerce and Industry, 200 N. LaSalle St., Chicago, IL 60601, $45.)
Descriptions of 1,200 firms, employing at least 250 people in Chicago-area plants and offices; lists key personnel.

Merchandise Mart Resource Guide
(Merchandise Mart, 470 Merchandise Mart, Chicago, IL 60654.)
Classified A to Z listing of firms with offices in the Mart.

National Trade and Professional Associations
(Columbia Books, Inc., 1350 New York Ave., NW, Suite 207, Washington, DC 20005, $50.)
Lists all associations and labor unions in the U.S. and Canada; indexed geographically and by key words.

Occupational Outlook Handbook
(U.S. Department of Labor, Washington, DC 20212.)
Describes in clear language what people do in their jobs, the training and education they need, earnings, working conditions, and employment outlook.

O'Dwyer's Directory of Public Relations Firms
(J. R. O'Dwyer & Co., 271 Madison Ave., New York, NY 10016, $90.)
Describes 900 public relations firms in the U.S., their key personnel, local offices, and accounts; indexed geographically.

Peterson's Annual Guide to Engineering, Science and Computer Jobs
(Peterson's Guides, Inc., P.O. Box 2123, Princeton, NJ 08543, $19.95.)
Describes 800 government agencies, technical firms, and manufacturers that hire engineers and computer scientists.

Publicity Club of Chicago Membership Guide
(Publicity Club of Chicago, 1441 Shermer Road., Suite 110, Northbrook, IL 60662.)
Lists individuals and firms in media and public relations.

Reference Book of Corporate Management
(Dun & Bradstreet, Inc., 49 Old Bloomfield Ave., Mountain Lakes, NJ 07046, $625.)
National directory of 2,400 companies with at least $20 million in sales listed by name; biographies of key personnel and directors, including schools attended and past jobs.

Service Directory for Hispanic Americans
(Catholic Charities, 721 N. LaSalle St., Chicago, IL 60610, free.)
Lists services with bilingual staffs in Chicago.

Standard Directory of Advertisers
(National Register Publishing Company, 3002 Glenview Road, Wilmette, IL 60091.)
Geographic edition lists major Chicago companies.

Standard Directory of Advertising Agencies
(National Register Publishing Co., 3002 Glenview Road, Wilmette, IL 60091.)
The Red Book of 4,000 advertising agencies and their 60,000 accounts.

Training and Development Organizations Directory
(Gale Research Inc., Book Tower, Detroit, MI 48226.)
2,300 organizations and their products, courses, and training programs are described.

Try Us: National Minority Business Directory
(National Minority Business Directories, 2105 Central Ave., N.E., Minneapolis, MN 55418.)
Over 5,000 firms whose business is over 51% minority-owned and geared toward regional or national sales volumes.

Newspapers

Answering want ads is one of several tasks to be done in any job search, and generally among the least productive. According to *Forbes* magazine, only about 10 percent of professional and technical people find their jobs through want ads. Like any other long shot, however, answering want ads sometimes pays off. Be sure to check not only the classified listings but also the larger display ads that appear in the Sunday business sections of the major papers. These ads are usually for upper-level jobs.

Help-wanted listings generally come in two varieties: open advertisements and blind ads. An open ad is one in which the company identifies itself and lists an address. Your best bet is *not* to send a resume to a company that prints an open ad. Instead, try to identify the hiring authority (see Chapter 5), and pull every string you can think of to arrange an interview directly.

The personnel department is in business to screen out applicants. Of the several hundred resumes that an open ad in a major newspaper is likely to attract, the personnel department will probably forward only a handful to the people who are actually doing the hiring. It's better for you to go to those people directly than to try to reach them by sending a piece of paper (your resume) to the personnel department.

Blind ads are run by companies that do not identify themselves because they do not want to acknowledge receipt of resumes. Since you don't know who the companies are, your only option in response to a blind ad is to send a resume. This is among the longest of long shots and usually pays off only if your qualifications are exactly suited to the position that's being advertised. Just remember that if you depend solely on ad responses, you're essentially conducting a passive search, waiting for the mail to arrive or the phone to ring. Passive searchers usually are unemployed a long time.

Newspaper business sections are useful not only for their want ads but also as sources of local business news and news about personnel changes. Learn to read between the lines. If an article announces that Big Bucks, Inc., has just acquired a new vice president, chances are that he or she will be looking for staffers. If the new veep came to Big Bucks from another local company, obviously that company may have at least one vacancy, and possibly several.

MAJOR NEWSPAPER RESOURCES

The Chicago Sun Times
401 N. Wabash Ave.
Chicago, IL 60611
(312) 321-3000
The Sunday classifieds, though not as extensive as the *Tribune's*, are still a source for jobs; columnists cover local business, financial, and marketing news.

The Chicago Tribune
435 N. Michigan Ave.
Chicago, IL 60611
(312) 222-3232
At 6 p.m. on a Saturday, you will see people crowding newsstands to buy the *Sunday Trib*, which carries the most extensive classified advertising in Chicago. In addition to the classifieds, the daily and Sunday business sections carry display ads for jobs, notes about personnel changes, and a weekly calendar of events, conventions, and trade shows.

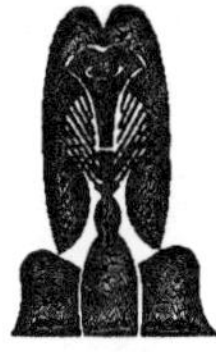

Using the Chicago Public Library's Computer-Assisted Reference Center

Let's say you have an interview next Thursday with the sales director of XYZ Corporation, a company for which you're *really* interested in working. You've done your homework by searching through the directories listed at the beginning of this chapter, you've familiarized yourself with the appropriate trade magazines, you have an "XYZ" information file bursting with the corporation's annual report, product brochures, and whatnot. You know where the sales director went to college and maybe what sorority she joined. But when you walk into that interview, you want to be absolutely up to date on what's going on with XYZ. So you call up the Computer-Assisted Reference Center at (312) 269-2915—one of the most valuable services offered by the Chicago Public Library (at the Business Information Center, 400 N. Franklin, 4th Floor—an address you should have memorized by now). For very little money you can find out if there are recent articles about the company. Tell the searcher/librarian you want to know the latest news on XYZ Corp., and especially any information on its sales department and director. The computer can search out anything that's recently appeared in print. You can generally find out what you want to know for under $30.■

Crain's Chicago Business
740 N. Rush St.
Chicago, IL 60611
(312) 649-5200
This weekly paper, available on newsstands or by subscription, prides itself on scooping other local papers with inside stories on Chicago businesses and people. Along with display and classified want ads, the magazine carries weekly listings of conventions and trade shows in town, personnel changes, and a calendar of meetings and seminars.

The National Ad Search
2328 W. Daphne Road
Milwaukee, WI 53209
(414) 351-1398
Weekly paper that lists job openings culled from 74 U.S. newspapers, including the *Chicago Tribune.* Ads are listed by career category.

National Business Employment Weekly
1 S. Wacker Drive
Chicago, IL 60606
(312) 750-4000
This weekly, published by *The Wall Street Journal,* appears every Sunday and reprints job openings nationwide that have been listed in the *Journal* during the week.

The Wall Street Journal
1 S. Wacker Drive
Chicago, IL 60606
(312) 750-4000
When you buy the nation's leading business daily from a Chicago vendor, you are getting the *Journal's* Midwest edition. Besides national business news, it carries items about local companies, personnel changes, and display and classified want ads for jobs in the Midwest.

NEWS AND CONSUMER MAGAZINES AND NEWS BUREAUS

Associated Press
230 N. Michigan Ave., 14th Floor
Chicago, IL 60601
(312)781-0500

Business Week
645 N. Michigan Ave.
Chicago, IL 60611
(312)616-3362

City News Bureau
35 E. Wacker Drive., Suite 792
Chicago, IL 60601
(312)782-8100

Ebony
820 S. Michigan Ave.
Chicago, IL 60605
(312)322-9200

House and Gardens
875 N. Michigan Ave., Suite 3648
Chicago, IL 60611
(312)649-3520

Inside Sports
Century Publishing Co.
990 Grove Ave.
Evanston, IL 60201
(312)491-6440

National Geographic
401 N. Michigan Ave., Suite 3000
Chicago, IL 60611
(312)467-1590

Newsweek
200 E. Randolph St.
Chicago, IL 60601
(312)565-3500

New Yorker
111 E. Wacker Drive
Chicago, IL 60601
(312)644-7666

People
303 E. Ohio St.
Chicago, IL 60611
(312)329-7815

Playboy
680 N. Lakeshore Drive
Chicago, IL 60611
(312) 751-8000

Redbook
1 S. Wacker Drive
Chicago, IL 60606
(312) 984-5180

Scientific American
333 N. Michigan Ave., Suite 912
Chicago, IL 60601
(312)236-1090

Self
875 N. Michigan Ave., Suite 3550
Chicago, IL 60611
(312)649-3519

Ski
625 N. Michigan Ave., Suite 1000
Chicago, IL 60611
(312)337-7208

Time
303 E. Ohio St.
Chicago, IL 60611
(312)321-7800

United Press International
360 N. Michigan Ave., 15th Floor
Chicago, IL 60601
(312)781-1600

U.S. News and World Report
435 N. Michigan Ave., Suite 1633
Chicago, IL 60611
(312)329-0890

Suburban and Community Papers

There are many outstanding community newspapers in the Chicago area. All carry want ads and stories and items about local businesses and business people that will give you more input for your job search. For a complete list of all the community newspapers published in Chicago and suburbs, see *Illinois Media,* available at the Chicago Public Library's Business Information Center, 400 N. Franklin, 4th Floor.

Chicago Tribune
DuPage Bureau
908 N. Elm St.
Hinsdale, IL 60521
(708) 850-2960
Publishes local section inserted into the *Chicago Tribune.*

Daily Herald
Paddock Publications
Box 280
Arlington Heights, IL 60006

(708) 870-3450
Daily paper, covering national news and northwest suburban news.

Daily Southtown Economist
5959 S. Harlem Ave.
Chicago, IL 60638
(312) 586-8800
Daily paper, covering national news and south suburban news.

Pulitzer-Lerner Newspapers
8135 River Drive
Morton Grove, IL 60053
(708) 966-5555
Large chain of weekly papers, covering city neighborhoods and suburbs.

Pioneer Press
1232 Central Ave.
Wilmette, IL 60091
(708) 251-4300
Large chain of weekly papers, covering suburban neighborhoods.

Star Publications
1526 Otto Blvd.
Chicago Heights, IL 60411
(708) 755-6161
Chain of weekly papers, covering south suburban neighborhoods.

Waukegan News Sun
100 W. Madison Ave.
Waukegan, IL 60085
(708) 336-7000
The voice of far northern Illinois; published daily.

Trade Magazines

Every industry or service business has its trade press—that is, editors, reporters, and photographers whose job it is to cover an industry or trade. You should become familiar with the magazines of the industries or professions that interest you, especially if you're in the interviewing stage of your job search. Your prospective employers are reading the industry trade magazines; you should be, too.

Trade magazines are published for a specific business or professional audience; they are usually expensive and available by subscription only. Many of the magazines we've listed here are available at the Chicago Public Library's Business Information Center, 400 N. Franklin, 4th Floor. For those that are not to be found at the library, call up the magazine's editorial or sales office and ask if you can come over to look at the latest issue.

The following magazines have editorial offices in metropolitan Chicago, reporting Chicago area news about the people and businesses in their industry. They all carry local want ads and personnel changes. For a complete listing of the trade press, consult the *Gale Directory of Publications and Broadcast Media* at the Library's Business Information Center.

ABA Banking Journal
175 W. Jackson Blvd.
Chicago, IL 60604
(312) 427-2729

Advertising Age
740 N. Rush St.
Chicago, IL 60611
(312) 649-5200

Adweek/Midwest
435 N. Michigan Ave., Suite 819
Chicago, IL 60611
(312) 467-6500

American Metal Market
Fairchild Publications
190 N. State St.
Chicago, IL 60603
(312) 609-0900

Assembly
Hitchcock Publications
191 S. Gary Ave.
Carol Stream, IL 60188
(708) 462-2339

Automotive News
740 N. Rush St.
Chicago, IL 60611
(312) 649-5200

Automotive Products Report
Irving Cloud Publishing Co.
7300 N. Cicero Ave.
Lincolnwood, IL 60646
(708) 674-7300

Back Stage
205 W. Randolph Ave.
Chicago, IL 60606
(312) 236-9102

Building Design & Construction
Cahners Publishing Co.
1350 E. Touhy Ave.
Des Plaines, IL 60018
(708) 635-8800

Building Supply Home Centers
Cahners Publishing Co.
1350 E. Touhy Ave.
Des Plaines, IL 60018
(708) 635-8800

Business Insurance
740 N. Rush St.
Chicago, IL 60611
(312)649-5275

Business Marketing
740 N. Rush St.
Chicago, IL 60611
(312)649-5260

Chicago Business Review
1407-B N. Wells
Chicago, IL 60610
(312) 944-1900

Chicago Film and Video News
2600 W. Peterson Ave.
Chicago, IL 60659
(312)465-7246

Chicago Lawyer
2015 N. State St.
Chicago, IL 60610
(312) 644-7800

Chicago Medicine
515 N. Dearborn St.
Chicago, IL 60610
(312) 670-2550

Chicago Metropolitan Real Estate Guide
415 N. State St.
Chicago, IL 60610
(312) 644-7800

Chicago Purchaser
201 N. Wells St., Suite 618
Chicago, IL 60606
(312)782-1940

Communications News
233 N. Michigan Ave., 24th floor
Chicago, IL 60601
(312) 938-2300

Construction Equipment
Cahners Publishing Co.
1350 E. Touhy Ave.
Des Plaines, IL 60018
(708) 635-8800

Consulting Specifying Engineer
Cahners Publishing Co.
1350 E. Touhy Ave.
Des Plaines, IL 60018
(708) 635-8800

Control Engineering
Cahners Publishing Co.
1350 E. Touhy Ave.
Des Plaines, IL 60018
(708) 635-8800

Daily News Record
Fairchild Publications
190 N. State St.
Chicago, IL 60603
(312) 609-0900

Datamation Magazine
Cahners Publishing Co.
1350 E. Touhy Ave.
Des Plaines, IL 60018
(708) 635-8800

Dental Lab Products
Irving Cloud Publishing Co.
7300 N. Cicero Ave.
Lincolnwood, IL 60646
(708) 674-7300

Dental Products Report
Irving Cloud Publishing Co.
7300 N. Cicero Ave.
Lincolnwood, IL 60646
(708) 674-7300

Editor & Publisher
8 South Michigan Ave., Suite 501
Chicago, IL 60611
(312) 641-0041

Electric Light & Power
Penwell Publishing Co.
1250 S. Grove Ave., Suite 302
Barrington, IL 60010
(708) 382-2450

Electronic Media
Crain Communications
740 N. Rush St.
Chicago, IL 60611
(312) 649-5200

Equipment Management
Irving Cloud Publishing Co.
7300 N. Cicero Ave.
Lincolnwood, IL 60646
(708) 674-7300

Food Service Equipment Specialist
Cahners Publishing Co.
1350 E. Touhy Ave.
Des Plaines, IL 60018
(708) 635-8800

Footwear News
Fairchild Publications
190 N. State St.
Chicago, IL 60603
(312) 609-0900

Hardware Merchandiser
Irving Cloud Publishing Co.
7300 N. Cicero Ave.
Lincolnwood, IL 60646
(708) 674-7300

Home Center Magazine
Vance Publishing Co.
400 Knightsbridge Parkway
Lincolnshire, IL 60069
(708) 634-2600

Hotels
Cahner's Publishing Co.
1350 E. Touhy Ave.
Des Plaines, IL 60018
(708) 635-8800

The Illinois Banker
111 N. Canal St.
Chicago, IL 60606
(312) 876-9900

Where to do your research

The Business Information Center of the Chicago Public Library (400 N. Franklin, 4th Floor, (312) 269-2814) is an invaluable source of career information. It systematically collects, files, and displays current career reference materials for easy access, including books, government documents, pamphlets, and directories. Most of the titles mentioned in this book can be found in the Business Information Center. Reference librarians are helpful and well informed, if somewhat overworked. The Business Information Center is open Monday through Thursday from 9 a.m. to 7 p.m.; Friday 9 a.m. to 6 p.m.; Saturday 9 a.m. to 5 p.m. ■

Industry Week
2 Illinois Center
233 N. Michigan Ave., Suite 1300
Chicago, IL 60601
(312) 861-0880

Inside Data Processing Management Association
505 Busse Highway

Park Ridge, IL 60068
(708) 693-5070

Jobber & Warehouse Executive
Hunter Publishing Co.
950 Lee St.
Des Plaines, IL 60016
(708) 296-0770

Jobber Topics
Irving Cloud Publishing Co.
7300 N. Cicero Ave.
Lincolnwood, IL 60646
(708) 588-7300

Lodging Hospitality
2 Illinois Center
233 N. Michigan Ave., Suite 1300
Chicago, IL 60601
(312) 861-0880

Modern Healthcare
Crain Communications
740 N. Rush St.
Chicago, IL 60611
(312) 649-5200

Modern Salon
Vance Publishing Co.
400 Knightsbridge Parkway
Lincolnshire, IL 60069
(708) 634-2600

Motor Age
Chilton Company
100 S. Wacker Drive, Suite 1850
Chicago, IL 60606
(312) 782-1400

National Underwriter
175 W. Jackson Blvd., Room A2110
Chicago, IL 60604
(312) 922-2704

Office Products Dealer
Hitchcock Publications
191 S. Gary Ave.
Carol Stream, IL 60188
(708) 462-2339

Packaging Magazine
Cahners Publishing Co.
1350 E. Touhy Ave.
Des Plaines, IL 60018
(708) 635-8800

Power Engineering
Penwell Publishing Co.

1250 S. Grove St., Suite 302
Barrington, IL 60010
(708) 382-2450

Professional Builder
Cahners Publishing Co.
1350 E. Touhy Ave.
Des Plaines, IL 60018
(708) 635-8800

Quality
Hitchcock Publications
191 S. Gary Ave.
Carol Stream, IL 60188
(708) 462-2339

Real Estate News
2600 W. Peterson, Suite 100
Chicago, IL 60659
(312) 465-5151

Realty & Building
311 W. Superior St., Suite 316
Chicago, IL 60610
(312) 944-1204

Research & Development
Cahners Publishing Co.
1350 E. Touhy Ave.
Des Plaines, IL 60018
(708) 635-8800

Restaurant Hospitality
2 Illinois Center
233 N. Michigan Ave., Suite 1300
Chicago, IL 60601
(312) 861-0880

Restaurants and Institutions
Cahners Publishing Co.
1350 E. Touhy Ave.
Des Plaines, IL 60018
(708) 635-8800

Screen Magazine
720 N. Wabash
Chicago, IL 60611
(312) 664-5236

Security
Cahners Publishing Co.
1350 E. Touhy Ave.
Des Plaines, IL 60018
(708) 635-8800

Security Distributing & Marketing
Cahners Publishing Co.
1350 E. Touhy Ave.

Des Plaines, IL 60018
(708) 635-8800

Semiconductor International
Cahners Publishing Co.
1350 E. Touhy Ave.
Des Plaines, IL 60018
(708) 635-8800

Sporting Goods Business
6160 N. Cicero, Suite 122
Chicago, IL 60646
(312) 545-0700

Telephone Engineering & Management
233 N. Michigan Avenue, 24th Floor
Chicago, IL 60601
(312) 938-2378

Variety
625 N. Michigan Ave.
Chicago, IL 60611
(312) 337-4984
Send Resume To:
P.O. Box 6519
Evanston, IL 60202

Women's Wear Daily
Fairchild Publications
190 N. State St.
Chicago, IL 60603
(312) 609-0900

Wood & Wood Products
Vance Publishing Co.
400 Knightsbridge Parkway
Lincolnshire, IL 60069
(312) 634-2600

Local Feature Magazines and Newspapers

The following periodicals do not necessarily cover business news but can be valuable sources of information about Chicago itself, information you need to be a well-informed Chicagoan.

Avenue M Magazine
60 E. Chestnut St., Suite 373
Chicago, IL 60610
(312) 943-9395
Covers "people" news of the Gold Coast—the area from Wacker Drive to North Avenue, bounded on the west by Wells Street and extending east to Lake Michigan.

Chicago Magazine
414 N. Orleans, Suite 800
Chicago, IL 60610

(312) 222-8999
Goings-on about town, restaurants, lectures and seminars, theater, sports, movies, intriguing articles about the city's neighborhoods and people, occasional business exposes, and a quarterly listing of social and service organizations, arts, community, career, political, and other special-interest groups.

Chicago Scene
414 N. Orleans, Suite 800
Chicago, IL 60610
(312) 222-8999
A spin-off of Chicago Magazine, this guide provides upscale hotel visitors with articles and information about Chicago's cultural life, entertainment and special events, shopping, and dining establishments.

Chicago Times
180 N. Michigan Ave., Suite 1440
Chicago, IL 60601
(312)372-6612
Bimonthly magazine with timely, well-researched local stories and fiction.

Chicago Welcome
32 W. Randolph St.
Chicago, IL 60601
(312) 338-5789
Free weekly, distributed through hotels and basically the same format as *Where Magazine.*

Inside Chicago
2501 W. Peterson Ave.
Chicago, IL 60659
(312)784-0800
Covers business, trends, local news, fashion, and lifestyle.

Key—This Week In Chicago
904 W. Blackhawk Ave.
Chicago, IL 60622
(312) 943-0838
Another free weekly, listing local happenings; also distributed through hotels.

North Shore Magazine
874 Green Bay Road
Winnetka, IL 60093
(708) 441-7892
Monthly guide to business, events, and activities of interest to those living in the North Shore suburbs (and to those who aspire to live there).

The Reader
11 E. Illinois St.
Chicago, IL 60611
(312) 828-0350
This formerly "underground" urban newspaper can be spotted even in the hands of middle-aged suburbanites these days. For the city's most complete entertainment listings, apartments to rent, interesting classifieds, and frequently innovative reporting, pick up this free

tabloid on Thursday afternoon at record stores and selected downtown and neighborhood locations. To locate your nearest distributor, call the *Reader* office.

Today's Chicago Woman
233 E. Ontario St.
Chicago, IL 60611
(312) 951-7600
Monthly magazine of features and events for Chicago women.

Where Magazine
1165 N. Clark St., Suite 301
Chicago, IL 60610
(312) 642-1896
Distributed through hotel lobbies, this weekly provides theater, restaurant, entertainment, and trade show listings of value not only to conventioneers but to the savvy job hunter as well.

General Business Magazines

The smart job seeker will want to keep abreast of changing trends in the economy. These magazines will help you keep up with the national business scene. They are available from libraries and may be purchased at most magazine stands.

Business Week

Forbes

Fortune

Money

Newsweek

Time

Venture

Working Woman

5

Developing a Strategy: The ABCs of Networking

The successful job search doesn't happen by accident. It's the result of careful planning. Before you rush out to set up your first interview, it's important to establish a strategy, that is, to develop a plan for researching the job market and contacting potential employers.

This chapter and Chapter 7 will cover specific techniques and tools that you'll find useful in your search. But before we get to them, a few words are in order about your overall approach.

It's Going to Take Some Time

Looking for a new job is no easy task. It's as difficult and time-consuming for a bright young woman with a brand-new MBA as it is for a fifty-year-old executive with years of front-line experience. Every once in a while someone lucks out. One of Tom's clients established a record by finding a new position in four days. But most people should plan on two to six months of full-time job hunting before they find a position they'll really be happy with.

According to *Forbes* magazine, the older you are and the more you earn, the longer it will take to find what you're looking for—in fact, up to six months for people over 40 earning more than $40,000. People under 40 in the $20,000-$40,000 bracket average two to four months.

Your line of work will also affect the length of your search. Usually, the easier it is to demonstrate tangible bottom-line results, the faster you can line up a job. Lawyers, public relations people, and advertising executives are harder to place than accountants and sales people, according to one top personnel specialist.

Be Good to Yourself

Whether or not you're currently employed, it's important to nurture your ego when you're looking for a new job. Rejection rears its ugly head more often in a job search than at most other times, and self-doubt can be deadly.

Make sure you get regular exercise during your job search to relieve stress. You'll sleep better, feel better, and perhaps even lose a few pounds.

Take care of your diet and watch what you drink. Many people who start to feel sorry for themselves tend to overindulge in food or alcohol. Valium and other such drugs are not as helpful as sharing your progress with your family or a couple of close friends.

Beef up your wardrobe so that you look and feel good during your employment interviews. There's no need to buy an expensive new suit, especially if you're on an austerity budget, but a new shirt, blouse, tie, pair of shoes, or hairstyle may be in order.

Maintain a positive outlook. Unemployment is not the end of the world; few people complete a career without losing a job at least once. Keep a sense of humor, too. Every job search has its funny moments. It's OK to joke about your situation and share your sense of humor with your friends and family.

Life goes on despite your job search. Your spouse and kids still need your attention. Try not to take out your anxieties, frustrations, and fears on those close to you. At the very time you need support and affirmation, your friends may prefer to stay at arm's length. You can relieve their embarrassment by being straightforward about your situation and by telling them how they can help you.

Put Yourself on a Schedule

Looking for work is a job in itself. Establish a schedule for your job search and stick to it. If you're unemployed, work at getting a new job full time—from 8:30 a.m. to 5:30 p.m. five days a week, and from 9 a.m. to 12 noon on Saturdays. During a job search, there is a temptation to use "extra" time for recreation or to catch up on household tasks. Arranging two or three exploratory interviews will prove a lot more useful to you than washing the car or cleaning out the garage. You can do such tasks at night or on Sundays, just as you would if you were working.

Don't take a vacation during your search. Do it after you accept an offer and before you begin a new job. You might be tempted to "sort things out on the beach." But taking a vacation when you're unemployed isn't as restful as it sounds. You'll spend most of your time worrying about what will happen when the trip is over.

Even if you're currently employed, it's important to establish regular hours for your job search. If you're scheduling interviews, try to arrange several for one day so that you don't have to take too much time away from your job. You might also arrange interviews for your lunch hour. You can make phone calls during lunch or on your break time. You'd also be surprised at how many people you can reach before and after regular working hours.

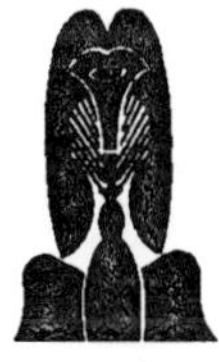

Tax deductible job-hunting expenses

A certified public accountant offers the following tips on deducting job-hunting expenses on the income tax form. To qualify for certain deductions, you must hunt for a job in the same field you just left, or in the field that currently employs you. For example, someone who has worked as a public school teacher could not be compensated for the cost of getting a real estate license and seeking a brokers job.

If you are unemployed or want to switch jobs, expenses can be deducted on the Income Tax Statement of Employee Business Expenses or itemized on Schedule A of Form 1040. Expenses you probably can deduct include preparing, printing, and mailing resumes; vocational guidance counseling and testing; and the standard government reimbursement for miles driven to and from job interviews. Telephone, postage, and newspaper expenses might also be deductible. While seeking work out of town, additional deductions are allowed for transportation, food, and lodging.■

Watch Your Expenses

Spend what you have to spend for basic needs such as food, transportation, and housing. But watch major expenditures that could be delayed or not made at all. The kids will still need new shoes, but a $200 dinner party at a fancy place could just as well be changed to sandwiches and beer at home.

Keep track of all expenses that you incur in your job search, such as telephone and printing bills, postage, newspapers, parking, transportation, tolls, and meals purchased during the course of interviewing. These may all be tax deductible.

Networking Is the Key to a Successful Job Search

The basic tasks of a job search are fairly simple. Once you've figured out what kind of work you want to do, you need to know which companies might have such jobs and then make contact with the hiring authority. These tasks are also known as researching the job market and generating leads and interviews.

Networking, or developing your personal contacts, is a great technique for finding out about market and industrial trends and is unsurpassed as a way to generate leads and interviews. Networking is nothing more than asking the people you already know to help you find out about the job market and meet the people who are actually doing the hiring.

Each adult you know has access to at least 300 people you do not know. Of course, a lot of them will not be able to do much in the way of helping you find a job. But if you start with, say, 20 or 30 people, and each of them tells you about 3 other people who may be able to help you, you've built a network of 60 to 90 contacts.

Mark S. Granovetter, a Harvard sociologist, reported to *Forbes* magazine that "informal contacts" account for almost 75 percent of all successful job searches. Agencies find about 9 percent of new jobs for professional and technical people, and ads yield another 10 percent or so.

Here's an example of a networking letter

Box 7457
Northwestern University
Evanston IL 60201
April 11, 1990

Dr. Norman Hartman
President
Combined Opinion Research
307 N. Michigan Ave.
Chicago, IL 60601

Dear Dr. Hartman:

Dr. Obrigon Partito, with whom I have studied these past two years, suggested that you might be able to advise me of opportunities in the field of social and political research in the Chicago area.

I am about to graduate from Northwestern University, with a B.A. in American History, and am a member of Phi Beta Kappa. For two of the last three summers I have worked in the public sector as an intern with the Better Government Association in Chicago and with Senator Claghorn in Washington. Last summer I worked as a desk assistant at *Newsweek's* Chicago office.

I am eager to begin to work and would appreciate a few minutes of your time to discuss employment possibilities in the field of social and political research. I will be finished with exams on May 24, and I would like to arrange a meeting with you shortly thereafter.

I look forward to hearing from you and in any case will be in touch with your office next week.

Sincerely,

Steven Sharp
(708) 555-2413■

How to Start

To begin the networking process, draw up a list of all the possible contacts who can help you gain access to someone who can hire you for the job you want. Naturally, the first sources, the ones at the top of your list, will be people you know personally: friends, colleagues, former clients, relatives, acquaintances, customers, and club and church members. Just about everyone you know, whether or not he or she is employed, can generate contacts for you.

Don't forget to talk with your banker, lawyer, insurance agent, dentist, and other people who provide you with services. It is the nature of their business to know a lot of people who might help you in your search. Leave no stone unturned in your search for contacts. Go through your Christmas card list, alumni club list, and any other list you can think of.

On the average, it may take 10 to 15 contacts to generate 1 formal interview. It may take 5 or 10 of these formal interviews to generate 1 solid offer. And it may take 5 offers before you uncover the exact job situation you've been seeking. You may have to talk to 250 people before you get the job you want. The maximum may be several hundred more.

Don't balk at talking to friends, acquaintances, and neighbors about your job search. In reality, you're asking for advice, not charity. Most of the people you'll contact will be willing to help you, if only you tell them *how*.

Turning volunteer work into a job

After spending many years working as a volunteer for various organizations, Marion Simon's daughters advised her to "stop giving it away." She decided to look for paid employment. But because she had never held a paid job, Marion was not sure how to begin her job search.

"As a woman in my middle years, I wondered where in the world I would go," says Marion. "I had a good education and a great deal of volunteer experience. I had planned and orchestrated large benefits and had done an inordinate amount of fund-raising over the years. I also had done community work in the inner city.

"I talked to some career counselors at a local college and they helped me put together a resume. Then I began to talk to people I knew. I was offered various jobs, none of which thrilled me.

"Then I happened to mention my job search to the president of a hospital where I had done a great deal of volunteer work," says Marion. "He asked me not to take a job until I had talked to him. Later, he hired me as his special assistant, with the charge to 'humanize the hospital.' Over a period of time, I developed a patient representative department.

"When I began the job 11 years ago, I was a one-person operation. As time went on, I added staff. I currently supervise a staff of 9, plus about 25 volunteers. The job of patient representative is now a full-fledged profession. Many women in the field began as volunteers. They knew a lot about the hospital where they were volunteering and thus made the transition into a paid position more easily."

We asked Marion what advice she has for volunteers who want to move into the paid work force. "Go to the career counseling departments of some of the small colleges. If they suggest that you need additional training, get it. But before you go back to school, investigate the kinds of jobs available in your chosen field. Think about how you can use your volunteer experience in a paid position. Take what you've done and build from it."■

The Exploratory Interview

If I introduce you to my friend George at a major Chicago bank, he will get together with you as a favor to me. When you have your meeting with him, you will make a presentation about what you've done in your work, what you want to do, and you will ask for his advice, ideas, and opinions. That is an exploratory interview. As is true of any employment interview, you must make a successful sales presentation to get what you want. You must convince George that you are a winner and that you deserve his help in your search.

The help the interviewer provides is usually in the form of suggestions to meet new people or contact certain companies. I introduced you to George. Following your successful meeting, he introduces you to Tom, Dick, and Mary. Each of them provides additional leads. In this way, you spend most of your time interviewing, not staying at home waiting for the phone to ring or the mail to arrive.

A job doesn't have to be vacant in order for you to have a successful meeting with a hiring authority. If you convince an employer that you would make a good addition to his or her staff, the employer might create a job for you where none existed before. In this way, networking taps the "hidden job market."

To make the most of the networking technique, continually brush up on your interviewing skills (we've provided a refresher course in Chapter 7). Remember, even when you're talking with an old friend, you are still conducting an exploratory interview. Don't treat it as casual conversation.

Developing Professional Contacts

Friends and acquaintances are the obvious first choice when you're drawing up a list of contacts. But don't forget professional and trade organizations, clubs, and societies—they are valuable sources of contacts, leads, and information. In certain cases, it isn't necessary for you to belong in order to attend a meeting or an annual or monthly lunch, dinner, or cocktail party.

Many such groups also publish newsletters, another valuable source of information on the job market and industry trends. Some professional associations offer placement services to members, in which case it may be worth your while to join officially. At the end of this chapter, we've provided a list of selected organizations that might prove useful for networking purposes.

If you're utterly new to the area and don't as yet know a soul, your job will naturally be tougher. But it's not impossible. It just means you have to hustle that much more. Here are some first steps you should take. Start attending the meetings of any professional society or civic organization of which you've been a member in the past. Find a church, temple, or religious organization that you're comfortable with and start attending. Join a special interest group. It could be anything from The Sierra Club to Parents Without Partners.

If you're just out of college (even if you flunked out), work through your alumni association to find out who else in the Chicago area attended your alma mater. If you were in a fraternity or sorority, use those connections. If you're not a member of any of the groups mentioned above, now's the time to join—or to investigate some of the networking groups that follow.

Once you've taken the trouble to show up at a meeting, be friendly. Introduce yourself. Tell people you talk to what your situation is, but don't be pushy. You've come because you're interested in this organization and what it stands for. Volunteer to serve on a committee. You'll get to know a smaller number of people much better, and they'll see you as a responsible, generous person, a person they'll want to help. Do a bang-up job on your committee and they'll want to help all the more.

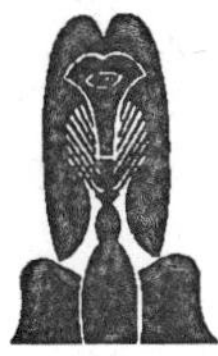

You've already got lots of contacts

Networking paid off for Liz, a young woman eager to make her way in banking or a related industry. She told us why she's glad she took the time to talk with her friends and neighbors about her job search.

"I was having dinner with close friends and telling them about my job search," says Liz. "During the conversation, they mentioned a banker friend they thought might be hiring. As it turned out, the friend didn't have a job for me. But he suggested I come in, meet with him, and discuss some other possibilities. He put me in touch with an independent marketing firm, servicing the publishing industry. The owner of the firm was looking for someone with my exact qualifications. One thing led to another, and pretty soon I had landed exactly the position I wanted."■

Keeping Yourself Organized

The most difficult part of any job search is getting started. A pocket calendar or engagement diary that divides each work day into hourly segments will come in handy.

You will also want to keep a personal log of calls and contacts. You may want to develop a format that's different from the one shown here. Fine. The point is to keep a written record of every person you contact in your job search and the results of each contact.

Your log (it can be a notebook from the dime store) will help keep you from getting confused and losing track of the details of your search. If you call someone who's out of town until Tuesday, say, your log can flag this call so it won't fall between the cracks. It may also come in handy for future job searches.

Your log's "disposition" column can act as a reminder of additional sources of help you'll want to investigate. You'll also have a means of timing the correspondence that should follow any interview.

CALLS AND CONTACTS

Date	Name & Title	Company	Phone	Disposition
2/10	Chas. Junior, V.P. Sales	Top Parts	(312) 689-5562	Interview 2/15
2/10	E. Franklin Sls. Mgr.	Frameco	(708) 876-0900	Out of town until 2/17
2/10	L. Duffy Dir. Mktg	Vassar Inc.	(708) 744-8700	Out of office Call in aft
2/10	P. Lamm Sls. Dir.	Golfco Ent	(312) 834-3000	Busy to 2/28 Call then.
2/10	E. Waixel, VP Mktg. & sales	Half'n'Half Foods	(312) 342-1200	Call after 2

If you're unemployed and job hunting full time, schedule yourself for three exploratory interviews a day for the first week. Each of these meetings should result in at least three subsequent leads. Leave the second week open for the appointments you generated during the first. Maintain this pattern as you go along in your search.

We can't emphasize too strongly how important it is that you put yourself on a job-searching schedule, whether or not you're currently employed. A schedule shouldn't function as a straitjacket, but it ought to serve as a way of organizing your efforts for greatest efficiency. Much of your job-hunting time will be devoted to developing your network of contacts. But you should also set aside a certain portion of each week for doing your homework on companies that interest you (see Chapter 4) and for pursuing other means of contacting employers (we'll get to these in a minute).

As you go through your contacts and begin to research the job market, you'll begin to identify certain employers in which you're interested. Keep a list of them. For each one that looks particularly promising, begin a file that contains articles about the company, its annual report, product brochures, personnel policy, and the like. Every so often, check your "potential employer" list against your log to make sure that you're contacting the companies that interest you most.

Go for the Hiring Authority

The object of your job search is to convince the person who has the power to hire you that you ought to be working for him or her. The person you want to talk to is not necessarily the president of the company. It's the person who heads the department that could use your expertise. If you're a salesperson, you probably want to talk with the vice president of sales or marketing. If you're in data processing, the vice president of operations is the person you need to see.

How do you find the hiring authority? If you're lucky, someone you know personally will tell you whom to see and introduce you. Otherwise, you'll have to do some homework. Some of the directories listed in Chapter 4 will name department heads for major companies in the Chicago area. If you cannot otherwise find out who heads the exact department that interests you, call the company and ask the operator. (It's a good idea to do this anyway, since directories go out of date as soon as a department head leaves a job.)

Use an introduction wherever possible when first approaching a company—that's what networking is all about, anyway. For those companies that you must approach "cold," use the phone to arrange a meeting with the hiring authority beforehand. Don't assume you can drop in and see a busy executive without an appointment.

And don't assume you can get to the hiring authority through the personnel department. If at all possible, you don't want to fill out any personnel forms until you have had a serious interview. The same goes for sending resumes (see Chapter 3). In general, resumes are better left behind, *after* an interview, than sent ahead to generate a meeting.

Telephone Tactics

Cold calls are difficult for most job seekers. Frequently, a receptionist or secretary, sometimes both, stands between you and the hiring authority you want to reach. One way around this is to call about a half-hour after closing. There's a good chance that the secretary will be off to happy hour, and the boss will still be finishing up the XYZ project report. Only now there will be no one to run interference for him or her.

Generally, you're going to have to go through a support staffer, so the first rule is to act courteously and accord him or her the same professional respect you'd like to be accorded yourself. This person is not just a secretary. Often, part of his or her job is to keep unsolicited job hunters out of the boss's hair. You want this intermediary to be your ally, not your adversary. If possible, sell what a wonderfully qualified person you are and how it is to the company's advantage to have you aboard.

If you're not put through to the hiring authority, don't leave your name and expect a return call. Instead, ask when there's a convenient time you might call back, or allow yourself to be put on hold. You can read job-search literature or compose cover letters while you wait. Be sure and keep your target's name and title and the purpose of your call on a card before you, however. You don't want to be at a loss for words when you're finally put through.

Other Tactics for Contacting Employers

Direct contact with the hiring authority—either through a third-party introduction (networking) or by calling for an appointment directly—is far and away the most effective job-hunting method. Your strategy and schedule should reflect that fact, and most of your energy should be devoted to direct contact. It's human nature, however, not to put all your eggs in one basket. You may want to explore other methods of contacting potential employers, but they should take up no more than a quarter of your job-hunting time.

Calling or writing to personnel offices may occasionally be productive, especially when you know that a company is looking for someone with your particular skills. But personnel people, by the nature of their responsibility, tend to screen out rather than welcome newcomers to the company fold. You're always better off going directly to the hiring authority.

Consider the case of a company that runs an ad in *The Wall Street Journal*. The ad may bring as many as 600 responses. The head of personnel asks one of the secretaries to separate the resumes into three piles according to age: "under 30," "over 30," and "I don't know." The personnel chief automatically eliminates two of the three stacks. He or she then flips through the third and eliminates all but, say, eight resumes. The personnel specialist will call the eight applicants, screen them over the phone, and invite three for a preliminary interview. Of those three, two will be sent to the hiring authority for interviews. That means that 598 applicants never even got a chance to make their case.

Statistically, fewer than one out of four job hunters succeed by going to personnel departments, responding to ads (either open or blind, as described in Chapter 4), or using various employment services. Some do find meaningful work this way, however. We repeat, if you decide to use a method other than networking or direct contact, don't spend more than 25 percent of your job-hunting time on it.

As you might expect, many books have been written on job-hunting strategy and techniques. Here is a list of selected resources.

SELECTED BOOKS ON JOB-HUNTING STRATEGY

Baker, Nancy C. *The Mid-Career Job Change and How to Make It.* New York: Vanguard Press, 1980.

Bolles, Richard N. *The Three Boxes of Life and How to Get Out of Them.* Berkeley, CA: Ten Speed Press, 1983.

Bolles, Richard N. *What Color Is Your Parachute?* Berkeley, CA: Ten Speed Press, 1990.

Camden, Thomas M. *Get That Job! How to Succeed in a Job Search.* Hinsdale, IL: Camden and Associates, 1981.

Camden, Thomas M. *The Job Hunter's Final Exam.* Chicago: Surrey Books, 1990.

Cowle, Jerry. *How to Survive Getting Fired and Win.* New York: Warner Books, 1980.
Figler, Howard. *The Complete Job Search Handbook.* New York: H. Holt & Co., 1988.
Gerberg, Robert Jameson. *The Professional Job Changing System.* New York: Performance Dynamics, Inc., 1981.
Haldane, Bernard. *Career Satisfaction and Success: A Guide to Job Freedom.* New York: AMACOM, 1982.
Half, Robert. *How to Get A Better Job in This Crazy World.* New York: Crown Publishers, 1990.
Hart, Lois Borland. *Moving Up—Women and Leadership.* New York: AMACOM, 1980.
Higginson, Margaret V., and Thomas L. Quick. *The Ambitious Woman's Guide to a Successful Career.* New York: AMACOM, 1980.
Jackson, Tom, and Davidyne Mayleas. *The Hidden Job Market for the 80's.* New York: Times Books, 1981.
Kennedy, Marilyn Moats. *Career Knockouts: How to Battle Back.* Piscataway, NJ: New Century, 1980.
Kennedy, Marilyn Moats. *Salary Strategies.* New York: Rawson Wade, 1981.
Kisiel, Dr. Marie. *Design for a Change—A Guide to New Careers.* New York: Franklin Watts, 1980.
Kleiman, Carol. *Women's Networks.* New York: Ballantine, 1981.
Moses, Bruce E. *How To Market Yourself...Yourself.* New York: Pro-Search, Inc., 1979.
Peskin, Dean B. *Sacked.* New York: AMACOM, 1979.
Pettus, Theodore. *One On One—Win the Interview, Win the Job.* New York: Random House, 1981.

There follows a selected list of over 200 organized groups, ready-made for networking, forming relationships, and gleaning information about business in the Chicago area.

SELECTED CHICAGO AREA PROFESSIONAL ORGANIZATIONS, NETWORKS, CLUBS, SOCIETIES

Administrative Management Society
P.O. Box A 3842
Chicago, IL 60690
Contact: Ed Ludwig
Professional association for office managers, personnel professionals. Publishes newsletter; holds monthly meetings.

Advertising Agency Production Managers Club
980 N. Michigan Ave.
Chicago, IL 60611
(312) 527-5030
Contact: Cheryl Blockus
Professional group for purchasers of graphic arts. Holds monthly meetings; maintains an employment bureau.

AFTRA
307 N. Michigan Ave., Suite 312
Chicago, IL 60601
(312) 372-8081
Contact: Paul Wagner, Executive Director
Labor union involved with radio and television performers.

Agate Club of Chicago
c/o Bill Youngberg
Newsweek, Inc.
200 East Randolph St., Suite 7948
Chicago, IL 60601
(312) 565-3500
Oldest club in the U.S. for consumer magazine sales reps. Holds meetings throughout the year.

Alliance of American Insurers
1501 Woodfield Road, Suite 400 West
Schaumburg, IL 60173
(708) 330-8500
Trade association for members of property and casualty insurance companies.

American Academy of Physical Medicine and Rehabilitation
122 S. Michigan Ave., Suite 1300
Chicago, IL 60603
(312) 922-9368
Professional association; publishes monthly journal.

American Architectural Manufacturers Association
2700 River Road, Suite 118
DesPlaines, IL 60018
(708) 699-7310
Contact: William J. Anton
Trade association of manufacturers of structural aluminum products and their suppliers.

American Association of Medical Assistants
20 N. Wacker Drive
Chicago, IL 60606
(312) 899-1500
Professional association; publishes educational materials.

American Association of University Women
2335 W. Touhy, #104
Chicago, IL 60645
(312)262-8662
Contact: Inez Macko
National organization open to female college graduates. Engages in advocacy, action, and research; publishes monthly newsletter with job listings; sponsors meetings and seminars.

American Bar Association
750 N. Lake Shore Drive
Chicago, IL 60611
(312) 988-5000
Professional association for attorneys. Publishes magazines, journals, newspapers with want ads; maintains extensive library and research department; sponsors educational and informational seminars.

American Business Women's Association
Contact by phone only
(708) 843-3800
Network group for betterment of women in business, professions, government, education, retailing, manufacturing, or service

companies. Publishes monthly bulletins; holds meetings, seminars; provides scholarships.

American Center for Design
233 E. Ontario St., Suite 500
Chicago, IL 60611
(312) 787-2018
Contact: Jane Dunne
Professional organization of people in creative graphic arts. Publishes *Creative Registry,* a monthly newsletter with job listings.

American Chemical Society
59 E. Van Buren St.
Chicago, IL 60605
(312) 461-9595
Scientific, educational, and professional association of chemists and chemical engineers. Sponsors educational programs; publishes newsletter with employment listings.

American College of Healthcare Executives
840 N. Lake Shore Drive
Chicago, IL 606ll
(312) 943-0544
Professional association for hospital and health service administrators. Publishes journals and newsletters; hosts seminars and educational programs.

American Concrete Pavement Association
3800 N. Wilke, Suite 490
Arlington Heights, IL 60004
(708) 394-5577
Contact: M.J. Knutson
Trade association of concrete paving contractors, suppliers of services to them, and equipment manufacturers. Sponsors courses on quality control, conducts workshops, publishes monthly newsletter.

American Dental Assistants Association
919 N. Michigan Ave., Suite 3400
Chicago, IL 606ll
(312) 664-3327
Professional association of dental assistants. Promotes educational activities; sponsors verification courses; maintains registry of jobs; publishes bi-monthly newsletter.

American Dietetic Association
216 W. Jackson St., Suite 800
Chicago, IL 60606
(312) 899-0040
Contact: Dawn Treadwell, R.D.
Professional association of dieticians in hospitals, colleges, schools, day care centers, business and industry. Holds workshops and seminars, promotes educational opportunities, publishes newsletter.

American Economic Development Council
9801 W. Higgins Rd., Suite 540
Rosemont, IL 60018
(708) 671-5646
Contact: James Ahr

National organization of professional economic and industrial developers. Publishes monthly newsletter with career opportunities.

American Fishing Tackle Manufacturers Association
1250 Grove Ave., Suite 300
Barrington, IL 60010
(708) 381-9490
Contact: Robert Kavanagh
Trade association of fishing tackle manufacturers and their suppliers.

American Hardware Manufacturers Association
931 N. Plum Grove Road
Schaumburg, IL 60173
(708) 605-1025
Contact: William P. Farrell
Trade association of manufacturers of wide range of products distributed through hardware wholesalers and manufacturers' representatives.

American Hospital Association
840 N. Lake Shore Drive
Chicago, IL 60611
(312) 280-6000
Professional association for hospital employees. Hosts seminars and regular meetings; publishes *Hospital Week* and *Guide to the Health Care Field.*

American Institute of Architects
53 W. Jackson Blvd., Suite 350
Chicago, IL 60604
(312) 663-4111
Chicago-area chapter of professional association for architects and associates.

American Institute of Banking
175 W. Jackson St.
Chicago, IL 60604
(312) 347-3400
Contact: Jack Heyden
Professional school for bankers. Sponsors evening courses and seminars leading to a certificate in banking.

American Institute of Real Estate Appraisers
430 N. Michigan Ave.
Chicago, IL 60611
(312) 329-8559
Association open to people with real estate licenses. Sponsors educational courses in all aspects of real estate appraising; publishes newsletter; maintains employment listings.

American Library Association
50 E. Huron St.
Chicago, IL 60611
(312) 944-6780
Contact: Ernest J. Martin
Professional association of librarians, libraries, trustees, and friends. Publishes *Booklist*, professional journals; maintains extensive research and information departments.

American Lighting Association
435 N. Michigan Ave., Suite 1717
Chicago, IL 60611
(312) 644-0828
Contact: James Nicol
Trade association of manufacturers of lamps and residential lighting fixtures and their suppliers. Conducts showroom management seminars; trains lighting consultants; publishes monthly newsletter, "Lightrays."

American Marketing Association
250 S. Wacker Drive, Suite 200
Chicago, IL 60606
(312) 648-0536
Association for marketing and research executives, sales and promotion managers, and advertising specialists. Organizes educational seminars and meetings; publishes monthly newspaper, "Marketing News," which carries employment listings.

American Medical Association
535 N. Dearborn St.
Chicago, IL 60610
(312) 645-5000
Professional association for doctors. Sponsors seminars and conventions; publishes many publications, including *JAMA*.

American Medical Technologists
710 Higgins Road
Park Ridge, IL 60068
(708) 823-5169
Contact: Dr. Gerard P. Boe
Professional association of medical technologists.

American Medical Writers Association
P.O. Box A3945
Chicago, IL 60690
(312) 784-0724
Contact: Don Radcliffe
Chicago chapter of national organization of communicators in the health sciences: PR people, working press, physicians, media professionals. Holds monthly meetings, yearly educational seminars.

American Physical Therapy Association
5801 N. Lincoln Ave.
Chicago, IL 60659
(312) 271-5735
Contact: Susan Lee, Executive Director
Professional organization of qualified physical therapists, working to improve standards. Recruits and trains physical therapy students; aids agencies in securing qualified physical therapists.

American Planning Association
1313 E. 60th St.
Chicago, IL 60637
(312) 955-9100
Contact: Sylvia Lewis
Professional organization of people in urban planning and related fields. Sponsors seminars, educational programs for non-professionals;

publishes reports, newsletters, and monthly magazine with employment listings.

American Production and Inventory Control Society
104 Wilmot St., Suite 201
Deerfield, IL 60015
(708) 940-8800
Technical society of production and inventory control management personnel. Holds monthly meetings; sponsors seminars; publishes newsletter.

American Society of Artists
Box 1326
Palatine, IL 60078
(312)991-4748
Contact: Nancy Fregin
Organization of professional artists and craftspeople. Maintains showroom and information service, sponsors craft festivals, maintains library; publishes "Art Lovers' Arts and Crafts Fair Bulletin."

American Society for Information Science
Call National Headquarters for contact information: (202) 462-1000. Professional organization for people in information processing and management. Holds monthly meetings.

American Society of Interior Designers
620 Merchandise Mart Plaza
Chicago, IL 60654
(312) 467-5080
Professional society for interior designers and associate members in allied design fields. Sponsors educational seminars; publishes newsletter with want ads.

American Society of Journalists & Authors
15 Sheffield Court
Lincolnshire, IL 60015
Contact: David Landman
Professional group of writers published in either national magazines or books. Holds monthly meetings, sponsors educational seminars, publishes directory.

American Society of Personnel Administrators
600 S. Federal, Suite 400
Chicago, IL 60605
(312) 922-6222
Professional society for anyone interested in personnel. Sponsors seminars; holds monthly meetings; publishes newsletter with listings.

American Society for Quality Control
P.O. Box 344
Glenview, IL 60025
(708) 450-3017
Broadly based organization of people working in the field of quality control. Chicago chapter has monthly meetings, extensive training programs in areas of statistics and management accounting; has job placement officer; publishes monthly newsletter.

American Society of Real Estate Counselors
430 N. Michigan Ave., 3rd Floor
Chicago, IL 60611
(312) 329-8427
Trade association for real estate counselors, i.e., those who receive remuneration on a fee, rather than a commission, basis.

American Society of Safety Engineers
1800 E. Oakton St.
DesPlaines, IL 60018
(708) 692-4121
Professional association. Hosts educational seminars; provides executive placement service.

American Society for Training & Development
203 N. Wabash, Suite 1022
Chicago, IL 60601
(312) 236-3327
Society for professionals in training, education, and human resources development.

American Society of Women Accountants
35 E. Wacker Drive, Suite 1068
Chicago, IL 60601
(312) 726-9030
Professional association for women accountants and educators. Holds monthly dinner meetings, maintains job bank, publishes newsletter, "The Coordinator."

American Warehousemen's Association
1165 N. Clark St., Suite 613
Chicago, IL 60610
(312) 787-3377
Contact: Jerry Leatham
Trade association of firms in warehousing. Publishes magazine, monthly newsletter.

American Women in Radio and Television
Contact by phone only
(312) 528-2311, ask for Freeda Day-Paige
Professional group for people in radio and television. Holds monthly meetings; publishes newsletter; holds seminars and workshops; sponsors annual convention.

American Women's Society of Certified Public Accountants
111 E. Wacker Drive
Chicago, IL 60601
(312) 644-6100
Professional association. Holds monthly meetings, offers specialized education, publishes monthly newsletter.

Amusement and Music Operators Association
111 E. Wacker Drive, Suite 600
Chicago, IL 60601
(312) 644-6610
Contact: William Carpenter

Trade association for manufacturers, distributors, and operators of coin-operated amusement devices. Sponsors international exposition, hosts three educational seminars per year, publishes newsletter.

Association for Computing Machinery
P.O. Box 95316
Chicago, IL 60694
(312) 644-6610
Professional group for people working in applications development, system analysis, and programming. Monthly meetings, publishes newsletter, holds professional development seminars.

Association of Home Appliance Manufacturers
20 N. Wacker Drive, Suite 1500
Chicago, IL 60606
(312) 984-5800
Trade association of manufacturers of approximately 90 percent of the major and portable appliances made in the U.S. and their suppliers. Provides market research, public relations, product testing and certification; publishes magazines; hosts annual convention.

Association of Human Resource Systems Professionals
(312) 701-4757
Contact: Alden Briscoe

Association of Information Systems Professionals
104 Wilmot Road
Deerfield, IL 60015
(708) 940-8800
Contact: Connie Allen
Network group of supervisors, managers, vendors, consultants, and educators in the fields of office automation, data processing, word processing, telecommunications. Holds monthly meetings, yearly convention; publishes newsletter with ads.

Association of Legal Administrators
525 W. Monroe, Suite 1600
Chicago, IL 60606
(312) 902-5200
Contact: Rich Koslowski
Organization of administrators of private law firms and corporate and government legal departments. Offers job placement service.

Association for Multi-Image
C/o Gary Balenger
150 E. Ohio St.
Chicago, IL 60611
Contact by mail only.
Chicago chapter of national organization for film producers and dealers. Holds periodic meetings, educational seminars, publishes newsletter.

Association for Women in Science
P. O. Box 13
Lemont, IL 60439
(708) 972-4341
Contact: Marie Louise Sabougni

Automotive Service Industry Association
444 N. Michigan Ave.
Chicago, IL 60611
(312) 836-1300
Contact: John W. Nerlinger
Multiple trade association of manufacturers, remanufacturers, warehouse distributors, and jobbers in the automobile industry. Holds annual trade show; provides career opportunity programs to schools and organizations; publishes "Business Opportunities," a bi-monthly guide to jobs in auto industry, and a booklet, "Automotive Instructional Materials," listing all instructional materials available from auto companies.

Bank Administration Institute
60 Gould Center
Rolling Meadows, IL 60008
(708) 228-6200
Contact: Ronald G. Burke
Organization of bank administrators and their staffs. Hosts educational seminars; publishes magazine with job listings.

Bank Marketing Association
309 W. Washington Blvd.
Chicago, IL 60606
(312) 782-1442
Professional organization for public relations and marketing executives for banks and related institutions. Sponsors workshops and seminars; maintains job search service; publishes "Community Bank Marketing," a newsletter with want ads, and *Bank Marketing Journal*.

Broadcast Advertising Club of Chicago
111 E. Wacker Drive, Suite 600
Chicago, IL 60601
(312) 644-6610
Contact: Mike Quaid
Professional organization of people working in advertising or sales departments of radio and TV stations. Holds monthly luncheon meetings; sponsors seminars; publishes newsletter.

Builders Association of Chicago
1647 Merchandise Mart Plaza
Chicago, IL 60654
(312) 644-6670
Contact: Donald Dvorak
Trade association, representing general contractors in the commercial, institutional, and industrial construction industry. Hosts educational seminars; publishes magazines.

Building Managers Association of Chicago
135 S. LaSalle St., Suite 1011
Chicago, IL 60603
(312) 236-5237
Contact: Llani O'Connor
Professional association of building managers. Hosts meetings, publishes newsletter.

Career Directions
YWCA of Metropolitan Chicago
180 N. Wabash Ave., Suite 301

Chicago, IL 60601
(312) 372-6600
Maintains sources of information on careers and job availabilities.

Career Management
YWCA of Metropolitan Chicago
180 N. Wabash Ave., Suite 301
Chicago, IL 60601
(312) 372-6600, ext. 65
Seminars and workshops for management-oriented women.

Catholic Alumni Club
P.O. Box 41684
Chicago, IL 60641
(312) 726-0735
Social club for single Catholic college grads under 40. Holds meetings; sponsors social events; publishes newsletter.

Center for New Television
912 S. Wabash Ave.
Chicago, IL 60605
(312) 427-5446
Membership group serves independent television producers, media professionals, and video artists.

Chicago Advertising Club
225 N. Michigan Ave., 19th Floor
Chicago, IL 60601
(312) 819-2959
Contact: Sharon Mitchner
Professional group for people in advertising and related fields. Holds monthly meetings; publishes newsletter with want ads; hosts seminars; sponsors charitable and social events.

Chicago Alliance of Business Employment and Training
14 E. Jackson
Chicago, IL 60604
(312) 786-0890
Contact: Tyrone Farris
Organization formed to help minorities and the handicapped find jobs.

Chicago Architecture Foundation
1800 S. Prairie
Chicago, IL 60616
(312) 326-1393
Not-for-profit organization to increase the level of awareness of Chicago area past, present, and future architecture.

Chicago Area Broadcast Public Affairs Association
WGN Radio
435 N. Michigan Ave.
Chicago, IL 60611
(312) 222-4700
Contact: Bob Mannewith
Professional group for people working in public affairs journalism. Holds meetings; publishes newsletter with want ads; hosts seminars.

Chicago Artists Coalition
5 W. Grand Ave.
Chicago, IL 60610
(312) 670-2060
Network of visual artists.

Chicago Association of Commerce and Industry
200 N. LaSalle St.
Chicago, IL 60601
(312) 580-6900
Trade association for business people. Publishes brochures dealing with all aspects of business in Chicago; directory of largest employers; guides, maps. Economic research and statistical division provides data pertaining to Chicago metropolitan area.

Chicago Association of Direct Marketing
600 S. Federal, Suite 400
Chicago, IL 60605
(312) 922-6222
Professional group. Holds monthly meetings; sponsors seminars; holds annual convention; sponsors social programs.

Chicago Association of Women Business Owners
600 S. Federal St., Suite 400
Chicago, IL 60605
(312) 922-6222
Contact: Mary McCurry, President
National network group of women owning their own businesses. Holds monthly meetings, conducts seminars, publishes newsletter.

Chicago Audio Visual Producers Association
C/o Frank Stedronsky, Motivation Media, Inc.
1245 Milwaukee Ave.
Glenview, IL 60025
(708) 297-4740
Organization of people working in the visual arts. Holds quarterly educational meetings, publishes freelance talent directory for members.

Chicago Automobile Trade Association
5600 River Road, Suite 825
Rosemont, IL 60018
(708) 698-6630
Contact: Jerry H. Cizek, III
Trade association of vehicle dealers. Hosts the Chicago Auto Show, educational seminars, and meetings; publishes newsletter with job listings.

Chicago Bar Association
29 S. LaSalle St.
Chicago, IL 60603
(312) 782-7348
Independent local professional association for lawyers.

Chicago Board of Realtors
430 N. Michigan Ave.
Chicago, IL 60611
(312) 329-8500

Professional group of licensed real estate brokers. Holds meetings and educational seminars; publishes newsletter and information brochures; sponsors real estate courses.

Chicago Bond Club
c/o Kevin Burke, Wm. Blair & Co.
135 S. LaSalle St.
Chicago, IL 60603
(312) 236-1600

Chicago Book Clinic
100 E. Ohio, Suite 630
Chicago, IL 60611
(312) 951-8254
Contact: Anthony Chung
Organization of people working in all aspects of book production. Holds monthly meetings, offers courses in book publishing practices conducted with University of Chicago, holds annual exhibit of award-winning book designs.

Chicago Coalition
303 E. Ohio St.
Chicago, IL 60611
(312) 902-2258
Contact: Ted Schulte
Umbrella organization comprised of audio-visual and media groups (talent, union members, producers, broadcasters, etc.) formed to lobby to keep production in Chicago. Periodic meetings.

Chicago Commission for Women
500 N. Peshtigo Court, 6B
Chicago, IL 60611
(312) 744-4427
Managers and advocates of improving the status of women in the Chicago area.

Chicago Computer Society
P.O. Box 8681
Chicago, IL 60680
Hotline number is (312) 794-7737
Networking group for personal computer users. Meetings, special interest seminars, newsletter, private electronic bulletin board.

Chicago Convention and Tourism Bureau
McCormick Place on the Lake
2300 S. Lake Shore Drive
Chicago, IL 60616
(312) 567-8500
Trade association to promote business. Sponsors seminars; maintains listing of scheduled conventions and trade shows in Chicago; publishes guides, maps, brochures about Chicago.

Chicago Cosmetologists Association
111 E. Wacker Drive, Suite 600
Chicago, IL 60601
(312) 644-6610
Contact: Fred Piattoni
Trade association of people working in sales of cosmetics.

Chicago Council on Foreign Relations
116 S. Michigan Ave.
Chicago, IL 60603
(312) 726-3860
Founded to acquaint its membership with American foreign policy, the Council sponsors luncheon and dinner meetings with prominent persons in business and government. Sponsors foreign trips and educational programs; Council Forum group hosts social and educational activities for members under 40.

Chicago Council of Lawyers
220 S. State St., Suite 800
Chicago, IL 60604
(312) 427-0710
Independent professional group for lawyers.

Chicago Finance Exchange
414 Plaza Drive, Suite 209
Westmont, IL 60559
(708) 655-0113
Network group for women in finance.

Chicago Foundation for Women
332 S. Michigan Ave., Suite 840
Chicago, IL 60604
(312) 922-8762
Contact: Marianne Philbin
Professional organization.

Chicago Headline Club
444 N. Michigan, Suite 1070
Chicago, IL 60611
(312) 644-8688
Contact: Gary Ruderman
National group of print and electronic journalists. Holds monthly meetings; sponsors seminars and awards.

Chicago High Tech Association
53 W. Jackson Blvd., Suite 1634
Chicago, IL 60604
(312) 939-5355
Contact: Ken Boyce
Group lends support to the local technical community in industry, academics, service industries, and government.

Chicago Home Economists in Business
Dairy Nutrition Council In Westmont
999 Oakmont Plaza Drive
Westmont, IL 60559
(708) 655-8866
Contact: Sandra Brown
Group of home economists employed in industry. Holds monthly meetings; publishes newsletter.

Chicago Jewelers Association
600 S. Federal St., Suite 400
Chicago, IL 60605
(312) 922-6222

Contact: Mary Meyers
Trade association of Chicago-area jewelers.

Chicago Metropolitan Building Managers Club
H.M. Warken Co.
1 S. Wacker
Chicago, IL 60606
(312) 346-2476
Contact: Robert Taylor, Vice President
Holds meetings, publishes newsletter.

Chicago Midwest Credit Managers Association
c/o Jackie Moore
315 S. Northwest Highway
Park Ridge, IL 60068
(708) 696-3000
Professional organization of commercial credit managers. Holds industry group meetings, seminars; members' job bank.

Chicago Network
5734 S. Kimbark Ave.
Chicago, IL 60637
(312) 324-0202
Contact: Sandy Ostetler
Group of the city's highest-ranking women. Membership by invitation only.

Chicago Network of Insurance Women
1000 Skokie Blvd.
Wilmette, IL 60091
(708) 256-5245
Contact: Marylou V. Gadin
For women in the insurance industry. Holds monthly meetings; publishes newsletter with job listings; hosts seminars.

Chicago Newspaper Reporters
500 N. Michigan Ave.
Chicago, IL 60611
(312) 787-0890

Chicago Press Photographers
WBBM-TV (Channel 2)
630 N. McClurg Court
Chicago, IL 60611
(312) 944-6000
Contact: Steve Lasker, Chairman

Chicago's Fine Dining Association
405 N. Wabash, Suite 3512
Chicago, IL 60611
(312) 467-7142
Contact: Edie Tracer
Organization of 23 of Chicago's top restaurants. Bi-monthly meetings, newsletter, job data.

Chicago Society of Association Executives
20 N. Wacker Drive, Suite 1456
Chicago, IL 60606

(312) 236-2288
Professional group. Holds meetings and seminars; maintains job referral service.

Chicago Teachers' Center
3901 N. Ridgeway St.
Chicago, IL 60618
(312) 478-2506
Resource center for elementary and secondary school teachers and educators.

Chicago Transportation Club
6029 N. Austin Ave.
Chicago, IL 60664
(312) 763-4306
Social organization for anyone involved in transportation business.

Chicago Women in Publishing
2 N. Riverside Plaza, Suite 2400
Chicago, IL 60606
(312) 641-6311
Contact: Liz Babison
Professional group open to women interested in book and magazine publishing. Holds monthly meetings; publishes newsletter with job listings; sponsors educational seminars.

Chicago Women's Club
8 S. Michigan Ave.
Chicago, IL 60603
(312) 372-9443
Network group. Holds weekly meetings.

Chicago Women's Political Caucus
53 W. Jackson Blvd., Room 1015
Chicago, IL 60604
(312) 922-8530
Contact: Cece Lobin

Chicago Women's Travel Club
(312) 321-9800, ask for Jeanette Nicholas
Association for professional women in the travel industry.

Citizen's Information Service
332 S. Michigan
Chicago, IL 60604
(312) 939-4636
Provides information about government and civic concerns.

City Club of Chicago
151 N. Michigan Ave., Suite 2300
Chicago, IL 60601
(312) 565-6500
Group founded 78 years ago to explore community issues. Hosts meetings and debates; sponsors educational seminars.

Executive networking

The higher your rung on the corporate ladder, the greater the chances that networking with executives outside your own field will pay off. If you're looking for a top spot in electronics, don't pass up a chance to discuss your credentials and employment needs with the recruiting executive of an advertising firm. He or she just might have the hidden connection that could land you a great job.

One hiring exec from a large corporation reports: "I network with recruiters from more industries than most people would think, both industries that are related to ours and those that are not. It helps to find out what talent is available. If one of my contacts has someone in a file they don't need and I do, they're happy to tell me about that person. And I work the same way."■

Contract Furnishings Council
1190 Merchandise Mart Plaza
Chicago, IL 60654
(312)321-0563
Contact: Ms. M. B. Gregory, Exec. V.P.
Association of full-service contract furnishings dealers. Specialized education, placement service.

Corporate Responsibility Group of Greater Chicago
2646 Bennett
Evanston, IL 60201
(708)475-5717
Contact: Carol Kurtz
Network group of people active in community affairs. Publishes newsletter; hosts luncheon meetings.

Don't overlook the watering holes

For convivial networking, you can't beat the casual atmosphere of one (or several) of Chicago's saloons on a Friday afternoon. Chicago area professionals helped us with the following suggestions for imbibers and teetotalers alike.

You can meet **architects** at Moonrakers (735 S. Dearborn) and The Berghoff (17 W. Adams). **Politicians** like the Berghoff, too, although politicians can be found everywhere meeting as many people as they can. The general **business crowd** can be found at Harry Caray's (33 W. Kinzie).

People in **advertising, journalism**, or **public relations** meet at the Billy Goat Tavern (430 N. Michigan Ave., lower level), Avanzare (161 E. Huron), Riccardo's (437 N. Rush), and the Wrigley Restaurant bar (410 N. Michigan).

Attorneys frequent Jerome's (2450 N. Clark St.) and Sieben's Brewing Company (436 W. Ontario), while **artists** hang out at gallery openings, which are listed in Friday's *Tribune*. **Interior designers,** members of the furniture trades, and textile manufacturers meet at George's (230 W. Kinzie).

You can meet **financial** wizards at Broker's Inn (326 S. LaSalle St.) or at the Sign of the Trader in the lobby of the Board of Trade building (141 W. Jackson). **Accountants** add up the bills at the City Tavern (33 W. Monroe).

As a safe bet, restaurants or bars on the lower levels of professional buildings are generally good places to meet people from offices in the building, so if all else fails, try those.■

Data Processing Management Association
505 Busse Highway
Park Ridge, IL 60068
(708) 693-5070
Contact: Donni Greene, Education Department
Local chapter of national organization of directors, managers, and supervisors of data processing installations, programmers, systems analysts, research specialists, and educators. Publishes newsletter with job listings.

Decorating Products Association of Chicago
5251 W. 95th St.
Oak Lawn, IL 60453
(708) 424-5300
Contact: Joan Murphy
Organization of retailers and distributors of wallpaper, paint, and other decorating products. Conducts surveys, promotes educational activities, publishes monthly magazine, *Decorating Retailer.*

Dietary Managers Association
400 E. 22nd St.
Lombard, IL 60148
(708) 932-1444
Contact: William St. John

Organization of dietetic assistants and technicians. Sponsors continuing education courses for managers and supervisors; publishes bi-weekly newsletter.

Donors Forum of Chicago
53 W. Jackson, Suite 430
Chicago, IL 60604
(312) 431-0260
Contact: Valerie Lies
Clearinghouse for information on philanthropic and non-profit charitable organizations in Chicago. Maintains research library, sponsors educational seminars, holds five meetings a year, publishes newsletter.

Economic Club of Chicago
20 N. Clark St., Suite 2720
Chicago, IL 60602
(312) 726-1628
Educational group for top executives. Hosts meetings and seminars.

Economic Development Council
150 N. Michigan, Suite 2810
Chicago, IL 60601
(312) 726-8787
Contact: Glenda Mallen, Secretary
Not-for-profit organization that records current events in the Chicago area. Hosts monthly luncheon with a guest speaker; publishes monthly newsletter.

Electronic Industries Association
Contact by phone only
(312) 648-2300, ask for Gerald Newman
Trade association for manufacturers of radio, TV, video systems, and audio equipment. Holds monthly meetings, publishes newsletter, sponsors educational programs.

Executives Club of Chicago
8 S. Michigan, Suite 1604
Chicago, IL 60603
(312) 263-3500
71-year-old club for "executives." Has weekly luncheons, sponsors charitable activities, maintains an informal job bank.

Fashion Group of Chicago
333 N. Michigan Ave., Suite 2032
Chicago, IL 60601
(312) 372-4811
Network group of models, designers, and retailers working in or associated with the fashion industry.

Federal Information Center
(312) 353-4242
Hotline answers questions about 125 government agencies.

Financial Managers Society For Savings Institutions
111 E. Wacker Drive
Chicago, IL 60601
(312) 938-2576
Contact: Delores Valles

Technical information exchange for controllers and chief operations officers of savings institutions. Publishes monthly newsletter, "Printout."

Food Equipment Manufacturers Association
111 E. Wacker Drive, Suite 600
Chicago, IL 60601
(312) 644-6610
Contact: Maxine Couture
Organization of manufacturers of commercial food service equipment and supplies for restaurant, hotel, and industrial use. Publishes monthly newsletter.

Foodservice Equipment Distributors Association
332 S. Michigan Ave.
Chicago, IL 60604
(312) 427-9605
Contact: Ray Herrick
Trade association for distributors of food service equipment such as ovens, ranges, china, silverware, etc., for hotels, restaurants and institutions. Sponsors meetings and conventions; publishes newsletter, "News and Views."

Government Finance Officers Association
180 N. Michigan Ave.
Chicago, IL 60601
(312) 977-9700
Professional association of auditors, comptrollers, treasurers, directors of finance, and accounting officials of federal, state, provincial, and local governments in the U.S. and Canada. Sponsors technical inquiry service, career development seminars; publishes newsletter with job listings.

Greater North Michigan Ave. Association
645 N. Michigan Ave, Suite 610
Chicago, IL 60611
(312) 642-3570
Contact: Executive Director
Provides development, protection, promotion for property owners, retailers, hotels, tenants, restaurants, community residents, and educational institutions located on N. Michigan Ave.

Greater State St. Council
36 S. State St., Suite 902
Chicago, IL 60603
(312) 782-9160
Contact: Sarah Bode, President
Provides development, protection, promotion for property owners, retailers, hotels, tenants, restaurants, and movie theaters located on State St., and sponsors the annual Santa Claus parade.

Healthcare Financial Management Association
2 Westbrook Center, Suite 700
Westchester, IL 60154
(708) 531-9600
Professional association of health care financial managers and those in related fields. Sponsors seminars; publishes newsletter with want ads.

Health Insurance Association of America
1350 E. Touhy Ave., Suite 380 W
DesPlaines, IL 60018
(708) 297-1490
Trade association of accident and health insurance firms. Sponsors meetings and educational seminars.

Home Builders Association of Greater Chicago
1010 Jorie Blvd., Suite 112
Oak Brook, IL 60521
(708) 990-7575
Trade association of persons involved in all phases of the building industry. Hosts seminars; publishes publications with want ads.

Home Economists in Business
M.H.S. Culinary Services
3543 N. Wilton Ave.
Chicago, IL 60657
Contact: Mary Helen Steindler
Professional association of home economists employed in business and industry. Publishes newsletters; holds monthly meetings.

Hotel-Motel Association of Illinois
27 E. Monroe, Suite 700
Chicago, IL 60603
(312) 346-3135
Contact: Arnold F. Karr
Organization of management employees of Chicago-area hostelries.

Hotel Sales & Marketing Association
Lora Chleboun
Ramada Renaissance Hotel
(312) 372-5959
Local branch of international organization of hotel sales & marketing people. Newsletter, meetings.

Human Resources Management Association
100 W. Monroe, Room 705
Chicago, IL 60603
(312) 332-0143
Group of personnel professionals. Meetings, bi-monthly newsletter.

Illinois Arts Council
100 W. Randolph St., Suite 10-500
Chicago, IL 60601
(312) 814-6750
Maintains information on local arts organizations, including the Illinois Creative Artists Registry.

Illinois Association of School Business Officials
NIU Graham 244
DeKalb, IL 60115
(815) 753-1276
Contact: Dr. Ron Everett
Professional organization of college and secondary school business managers and their suppliers. Publishes newsletter with job listings.

Illinois Bankers Association
111 N. Canal St.
Chicago, IL 60606
(312) 876-9900
Professional association for bankers. Sponsors educational seminars; publishes *Illinois Banker* magazine with want ads.

Illinois CPA Society
222 S. Riverside, Suite 1600
Chicago, IL 60606
(312) 993-0393
Professional association. Sponsors educational seminars.

Illinois Creative Artists Registry
c/o Illinois Arts Council
100 W. Randolph St., Suite 10-500
Chicago, IL 60601
(312) 814-6750
List made available to people and organizations interested in hiring people in the arts.

Illinois Food Retailers Association
1919 S. Highland Ave.
Lombard, IL 60148
(708) 627-8100
Contact: Phillip Fazio
Trade association of independent grocers in Illinois. Meetings, newsletter with want ads.

Illinois Hospital Association
1151 E. Warrenville Road
Naperville, IL 60566
(708) 505-7777
Trade association of Illinois hospitals.

Illinois Mortgage Bankers Association
11 S. LaSalle, Suite 2155
Chicago, IL 60603
(312) 236-6208
Contact: Barbara Zajicek
Educational association for mortgage bankers at commercial banks and savings & loans. Seminars, meetings, social events; publishes bi-monthly newsletter with want ads.

Illinois Park and Recreation Association
500 S. Plum Grove Rd.
Palatine, IL 60067
(708) 991-2820
Contact: Kay Kastel Forest
Organization of administrative and recreational programming professionals and students working in park districts. Educational seminars; annual conference; publishes bi-monthly magazine, *Illinois Parks and Recreation,* with want ads.

Illinois Restaurant Association
350 W. Ontario
Chicago, IL 60610
(312) 787-4000

Contact: Erik Jensen
Lobbying organization, serving members of the food service industry in Illinois and their suppliers. Holds seminars and educational programs; publishes legislative newsletter and magazine with want ads.

Illinois Retail Hardware Association
300 W. Edwards, #201
Springfield, IL 62704
(800) 322-4742
Contact: Jay Boor
Trade association for hardware dealers and their suppliers. Sponsors seminars, educational programs; publishes monthly newsletter with want ads.

Illinois Retail Merchants Association
36 S. Wabash Ave.
Chicago, IL 60603
(312) 726-4600
Contact: David Vite
Trade association of small and large retailers located in Illinois. Sponsors seminars, educational programs, sales training course; publishes monthly and weekly newsletters.

Illinois Women's Agenda
6 N. Michigan Ave.
Chicago, IL 60602
(312) 704-1833
Contact: Elaine Weiss
State-wide coalition lobbies for women's issues.

Illinois Women's Press Association
14428 Ellis
Dolton, IL 60419
(708) 849-4000, ext. 27
Contact: Marlene Cook, President

Independent Accountants Association of Illinois
8142 Milwaukee Ave.
Niles, IL 60648
(708) 593-1179
Professional association. Hosts educational seminars and meetings.

Independent Insurance Agents of Illinois
222 N. Riverside Plaza, Suite 1530
Chicago, IL 60606
(312) 236-4888
Contact: Gladys Israel
Professional group of independent insurance agents. Publishes newsletters; hosts seminars; sponsors educational programs and workshops.

Independent Voters of Illinois
220 S. State St., Suite 612
Chicago, IL 60604
(312) 663-4203
Group supports independent politics and participatory democracy.

Independent Writers of Chicago
645 N. Michigan Ave., Suite 1058
Chicago, IL 60611
(312) 951-9114
Contact: Ruth McNitt
Network group for all freelance writers. Holds monthly meetings; sponsors seminars; provides group insurance; has informal job bank.

Institute of Business Designers
341 Merchandise Mart
Chicago, IL 60654
(312) 467-1950
Contact: Jackie Schiewe
Organization of professional interior and furnishings designers actively engaged in the non-residential contract fields and their allied manufacturing sources. Conducts research; holds seminars and workshops; sponsors student programs; maintains job bank.

Institute of Food Technologists
221 N. LaSalle St.
Chicago, IL 60601
(312) 782-8424
Contact: Howard Mattson
Chicago branch of worldwide organization of executives, educators, scientists, and engineers in the food technology industry. Hosts seminars, educational programs; publishes magazine, *Food Technology,* with want ads.

International Association of Business Communicators
203 N. Wabash
Chicago, IL 60601
Contact by phone only
(312) 332-0147
Professional group for people active in the communications industry. Sponsors monthly luncheons and seminars; publishes newsletter; holds annual convention.

International Association of Defense Counsels
20 N. Wacker Drive, Suite 3100
Chicago, IL 60606
(312) 368-1494
Professional association for lawyers in the insurance field. Publishes newsletter.

International Association of Personnel Women
22 W. Monroe St., Suite 904
Chicago, IL 60603
(312) 368-1377
Contact: Geraldine Gist
Networking group of personnel professionals. Monthly meetings, newsletter, in-house job bank.

International Food Service Manufacturers Association
321 N. Clark, Suite 2900
Chicago, IL 60610
(312) 644-8989
Contact: Michael J. Licata

Trade association for leading manufacturers of food products and equipment for the meal-away-from-home market. Holds 10-12 meetings and conferences per year; publishes two newsletters.

International Trade Club of Chicago
203 N. Wabash, Suite 1102
Chicago, IL 60601
(312) 368-9197
Contact: Josie Ritchie
Network group for promotion of international business. Holds meetings; publishes newsletter.

Investment Analysts Society of Chicago
600 S. Federal, Suite 400
Chicago, IL 60605
(312) 922-6222
Network group for financial analysts. Holds weekly meetings; maintains speakers' bureau.

Kiwanis Club, District Office
10220 S. Cicero
Oak Lawn, IL 60453
(708) 857-7910
Federation of business and professional men's civic service clubs. Holds meetings; publishes monthly magazine.

Lawyers for the Creative Arts
213 W. Institute Place, Suite 411
Chicago, IL 60610
(312) 944-2787
Free legal assistance and information to artists and arts groups.

League of Chicago Theaters
67 E. Madison, Suite 2116
Chicago, IL 60603
(312) 977-1730
Support group for Chicago's professional, community, and educational theaters.

League of Women Voters of Illinois
332 S. Michigan Ave., Room 1142
Chicago, IL 60604
(312) 939-5935
Provides information on elections, voting, state and congressional representatives; holds meetings and educational seminars about politics and legal rights.

Lions Club International
300 E. 22nd St.
Oak Brook, IL 60521
(708) 571-5466
Fraternal organization involved in civic and charitable activities. Holds meetings, publishes magazine.

Marketing Research Association
401 N. Michigan Ave., Suite 2100
Chicago, IL 60611
(312) 664-6610

Contact: Marti DeGraaf
Organization of field and executive personnel engaged in market research for advertising agencies, research firms, and industry. Publishes bi-monthly newsletter, "Alert."

Mechanical Contractors Association
1530 Merchandise Mart
Chicago, IL 60654
(312) 670-6740
Contact: Edward Teske
Trade association for contractors who furnish, install, and service piping systems and related equipment for heating, cooling, and ventilating systems. Offers training and certification; seminars; meetings; publications.

Merchandising Executives Club
333 N. Michigan Ave., Suite 800
Chicago, IL 60601
(312)332-1601
Network group of sales executives and retailers, some manufacturers reps. Holds monthly meetings and technical sessions.

Metropolitan Chicago Health Care Council
222 S. Riverside Plaza, 17th Floor
Chicago, IL 60606
(312) 906-6000
Trade association of Chicago-area hospitals.

Midwest Women's Center
53 W. Jackson Blvd., Suite 1015
Chicago, IL 60604
(312) 922-8530
Contact: Phyllis Buntyn
Service agency for women seeking career help. Publishes newsletter and Illinois Women's Directory; maintains job bank; sponsors educational programs and career development seminars.

Million Dollar Round Table
325 W. Touhy Ave.
Park Ridge, IL 60068
(708) 692-6378
Contact: Judy Miluski
Network group of successful insurance agents; publishes newsletter.

Municipal Bond Club of Chicago
c/o Blunt, Ellis & Loewy
333 W. Wacker Drive
Chicago, IL 60606
(312)630-8500
Contact: Mike Gagnon
Holds annual outing, conducts a municipal bond school, publishes directory, holds occasional meetings with speakers.

Municipal Women of Chicago
c/o Bear Stearns, Inc.
3 First National Plaza, 25th Floor
Chicago, IL 60602
(312)580-4479

Professional association of women in municipal finance. Holds outings, has four meetings a year, publishes newsletter.

Music Distributors Association
111 E. Wacker Drive, Suite 600
Chicago, IL 60601
(312) 644-6610
Contact: William Carpenter
Organization of wholesalers and suppliers of musical instruments, sheet music, and manufacturers of musical merchandise.

National Academy of Television Arts & Sciences
c/o WMAQ-TV
Merchandise Mart Plaza, 19th Floor
Chicago, IL 60654
(312) 861-8300
Chicago chapter of the association of persons actively engaged in television. Holds monthly luncheon meetings; sponsors the local Emmy Awards.

National Association of Bank Women
500 N. Michigan Ave., Suite 1400
Chicago, IL 60611
(312) 661-1700
Contact: Phyllis Haeger
Network group for women officers and managers in the banking industry. Holds monthly meetings.

National Association of Floor Covering Distributors
85 N. Algonquin Road
Arlington Heights, IL 60005
(708) 364-9040
Contact: Wade Newman
Trade association of floor covering distributors and manufacturers. Holds regional meetings; publishes newsletter, "News & Views."

National Association of Food Equipment Manufacturers
111 E. Wacker Drive, Suite 600
Chicago, IL 60601
(312) 644-6610
Contact: William Carpenter
Trade association for manufacturers of commercial food-service equipment and supplies for restaurant, hotel, and institutional use. Publishes monthly newsletter.

National Association of General Merchandise Representatives
111 E. Wacker Drive, Suite 600
Chicago, IL 60601
(312) 644-6610
Contact: Jack M. Springer
Organization of manufacturers' agents, specializing in selling drug, health, and beauty aids to food chains and food items to non-food chains and stores. Publishes monthly newsletter.

National Association of Independent Insurance Adjusters
300 W. Washington St., Suite 805
Chicago, IL 60606

(312) 853-0808
Trade association for insurance professionals.

National Association of Realtors
430 N. Michigan Ave.
Chicago, IL 60611
(312) 329-8200
Professional association. Hosts seminars; publishes magazines and educational materials; sponsors conventions.

National Association of Retail Dealers of America
10 E. 22nd St., Suite 310
Lombard, IL 60148
(312)953-8950
Contact: John W. Shields
Organization of retailers and dealers of audio components, kitchen and laundry appliances, and other household equipment. Sponsors sales and management training and advertising workshops; conducts surveys.

National Association of Service Merchandising
118 S. Clinton St., Suite 300
Chicago, IL 60606
(312) 876-9494
Contact: Gary Ebben
Trade organization of service merchandiser and distributor companies and manufacturers of health and beauty aids and general merchandise, including soft goods, toys, stationery, pet supplies, and housewares sold to supermarket, drug, and convenience stores. Holds educational seminar each year; facilities tours; publishes newsletter; informal job bank.

National Association of Women Business Owners
600 S. Federal, Suite 400
Chicago, IL 60605
(312) 922-0465
Contact: Peggy Leonard
Chicago chapter of national organization founded to provide guidance, information, and referrals to women business owners.

National Association of Women in Construction
Kelso-Burnett Company, Electrical Contractors
233 W. Jackson St., Suite 1216
Chicago, IL 60606
(312) 922-2610
Contact: Marjorie Homer
Professional association for women actively working in the construction industry. Holds monthly meetings; sponsors seminars and educational programs; publishes newsletter.

National Association of Word Information Processing Specialists
P.O. Box 6442
Broadview, IL 60153
(708) 343-2463
Contact: Connie Allen

National Black MBA Association
111 E. Wacker Drive, Suite 600
Chicago, IL 60601
(312) 644-6610
Contact: Dorothy Davenport
Group for minority MBAs. Holds monthly meetings; sponsors seminars; publishes newsletter.

National Council of Jewish Women
53 W. Jackson Blvd., Room 835
Chicago, IL 60604
(312) 987-1927
Contact: President

National Dairy Council
6300 N. River Road
Rosemont, IL 60018
(708) 696-1020
Trade association. Holds meetings; publishes promotional materials.

National Electronic Distributors Association
35 E. Wacker Drive, Suite 3202
Chicago, IL 60601
(312) 558-9114
Contact: Dean Cobble
Trade organization of wholesale distributors of electronic parts, components, and consumer products. Conducts research programs; offers specialized education. Publishes monthly newsletter.

National Employee Services and Recreation Association
2400 S. Downing Ave.
Westchester, IL 60154
(708)562-8130
Contact: Patrick B. Stinson

National Family Business Council
60 Revere Drive, Suite 500
Northbrook, IL 60062
(708) 480-9574
Contact: John Messervey
Open to all owners of family businesses. Holds monthly meetings; publishes newsletter.

National Futures Association
200 W. Madison St., Suite 1600
Chicago, IL 60606
Contact: Gerald Byrne

National Housewares Manufacturers Association
1324 Merchandise Mart Plaza
Chicago, IL 60654
(312) 644-3333
Trade association of manufacturers and distributors of housewares. Publishes directories, educational and promotional materials; sponsors trade shows and annual convention.

National Network of Women in Sales
National Office: (800) 321-6697
Network group for women pursuing sales careers. Hosts meetings.

Northshore Chapter
7855 Gross Point Road, Unit G-4
Skokie, IL 60077
(708) 673-6697

Northwest Suburban Chapter
P.O. Box 1611
Arlington Heights, IL 60006
(708)253-2661

West Suburban Chapter
P.O. Box 1286
Oak Brook, IL 60522
(708) 462-5255

National Organization for Women
53 W. Jackson Blvd.
Chicago, IL 60604
(312) 922-0025
Chicago chapter of national women's organization does electoral work; fund-raising; sponsors educational seminars; publishes local and national newsletters.

National PTA
700 N. Rush St.
Chicago, IL 60611
(312) 787-0977
Contact: Pamela Grotz
Organization of parents, teachers, students, principals interested in uniting the forces of home, school, and community on behalf of children. Conducts research, maintains standing committees and extensive publications list.

National Restaurant Association
150 N. Michigan, Suite 2000
Chicago, IL 60601
(312) 853-2525
Trade association of restaurants, cafeterias, clubs, contract feeders, drive-ins, caterers, and institutional food services. Sponsors national convention, meetings, and management courses; publishes magazines and promotional materials.

National Society of Fund-Raising Executives
414 Plaza Drive, Suite 209
Westmont, IL 60559
(708) 655-0134
Contact: Linda Diehl
Professional organization of fund-raising and public relations personnel, working in non-profit organizations. Holds monthly meetings; educational seminars; publishes newsletter.

National Sporting Goods Association
1699 Wall St.
Mt. Prospect, IL 60056
(708) 439-4000
Trade association. Publishes newsletter with job listings.

National Wine Distribution
10400 S. Roberts Road
Palos Hills, IL 60465
(708) 598-7070
Contact: Bud Rebedeau
Organization of independent wine distributors and their suppliers. Sponsors seminars; produces educational materials, research, and statistics. Publishes monthly magazine.

Newspaper Representatives Association of Chicago
500 N. Michigan Ave.
Chicago, IL 60611
(312) 787-0890
Professional association of national advertising sales representatives.

North Business & Industrial Council of Chicago
3920 N. Rockwell
Chicago, IL 60618
(312) 588-5855
Contact: Carl Bufalini
Free job referral service to general public, including placement not only among member firms but to other selected employers. Sponsors workshops for member firms; operates a clerical training program.

North Side Real Estate Board
2625 W. Peterson Ave.
Chicago, IL 60659
(312) 769-3888
Professional group for people in real estate. Publishes monthly periodical.

Pharmaceutical Advertising Council
Contact by phone only
(312) 943-6666
Contact: Kay Ross
Membership consists of manufacturers, product managers, ad agency people, marketing firms, and magazine space reps. Meetings, newsletter.

Professional Career Counselors Network
c/o Jack Chapman, Bernard Haldane & Associates
307 N. Michigan, Suite 2001
Chicago, IL 60601
(312) 332-4516
Organization of private and retail career counselors, outplacement specialists, college placement directors, and test administrators. Meetings, annual seminars, newsletter.

Professional Photographers of America
1090 Executive Way
Des Plaines, IL 60018
(708) 299-8161
Professional association of over 16,000 photographers and photography-related companies. Publishes a membership directory, *Who's Who in Professional Photography* ($110, free to members). Holds annual international convention and regional seminars.

Publicity Club of Chicago
1163 Shermer Road
Northbrook, IL 60062
(708) 564-8180
Professional association for people in the communications industry. Holds monthly meetings, educational seminars; maintains job listings; publishes monthly newsletter and annual *Chicago Media Directory.*

Public Relations Society of America
30 N. Michigan Ave., Suite 508
Chicago, IL 60602
(312) 372-7744
Professional association for public relations practitioners. Holds monthly luncheon meetings; sponsors educational seminars; provides certification; publishes newsletter with want ads.

Purchasing Management Association of Chicago
201 N. Wells St.
Chicago, IL 60606
(312) 782-1940
Professional association. Sponsors seminars and courses; maintains job placement bureau.

Radio Advertising Bureau
333 N. Michigan Ave., Suite 816
Chicago, IL 60601
(312) 372-4620
Trade association for developing sales leads. Sponsors seminars and meetings.

Retail Advertising Conference
500 N. Michigan Ave., Suite 600
Chicago, IL 60611
(312) 245-9011
President: Douglas Raymond
International association devoted exclusively to retail advertising and marketing professionals.

Retail Merchants Association
36 S. Wabash Ave., Suite 1226
Chicago, IL 60603
(312) 726-4600
Trade association of department, chain and mass merchandising, and specialty stores. Sponsors educational seminars, workshops; provides extensive educational service on all phases of retailing. Publishes monthly newsletter.

Rotary Club of Chicago
12 S. Michigan Ave.
Chicago, IL 60603
(312) 372-3900
Professional businessmen's club. Promotes civic and charitable activities among members; holds monthly meetings; maintains job listings for vets.

Sales & Marketing Executives Association of Chicago
1411 Peterson Ave.
Park Ridge, IL 60106

(708) 696-0028
Contact: Steve Cartozian
Professional organization for executives in sales and marketing. Publishes newsletters; sponsors workshops; holds monthly dinner meetings.

Service Corps of Retired Executives (SCORE)
219 S. Dearborn
Chicago, IL 60604
(312) 353-7723
Free counseling to existing or projected businesses.

Social Service Communicators
32 W. Randolph St., Suite 1331
Chicago, IL 60601
(312) 248-5915
Contact: Deborah Easley
Professional group of writers and PR people working in areas of social service.

Society of Architectural Administrators
Perkins & Will
123 N. Wacker Drive
Chicago, IL 60606
(312) 977-1100
Contact: Diane Breman
Professional administrators of architectural and construction firms. Holds meetings and publishes bi-monthly newsletter.

Society of Broadcast Engineers
65 E. Wacker Drive
Chicago, IL 60601
(312) 332-0936
Organization of people working in technical jobs in radio and television.

Society of Human Resource Professionals
8 S. Michigan Ave.
Chicago, IL 60603
(312) 922-6222
Professional organization.

Society of Manufacturing Engineers
Contact by phone only
(708) 668-1600, contact Ruth Swan
Professional group of engineers. Publishes newsletter; holds monthly meetings; sponsors educational programs.

Society of Professional Business Consultants
8 S. Michigan Ave.
Chicago, IL 60603
(312) 922-6222
Professional group.

Society of Professional Journalists
53 W. Jackson, Suite 731
Chicago, IL 60604
(312) 922-7424
Professional organization.

Society of Real Estate Appraisers
225 N. Michigan Ave., Suite 724
Chicago, IL 60601
(312) 819-2400
Professional organization.

Society of Women Engineers
c/o Kathy Cunningham
(312) 727-7536
Professional organization for women in all areas of engineering. Meetings; educational programs; publishes newsletter; informal job bank.

Suburban Press Club of Chicago
Northern Illinois Gas
P.O. Box 190
Aurora, IL 60507
(708) 983-8888
Contact: Carol Anderson
Professional organization of journalists covering suburban areas, PR professionals, suburban media. Holds monthly meetings; sponsors yearly professional development seminar, internships, and awards; publishes monthly newsletter.

Western Society of Engineers
176 W. Adams St., Suite 1734
Chicago, IL 60603
(312) 372-3760
Umbrella organization of engineering associations located in the Chicago area.

West Suburban YWCA
739 Roosevelt Road
Bldg. 8, Suite 210
Glen Ellyn, IL 60137
(708) 790-6600
Contact: Kit Mathey
Community organization.

Women Employed
22 W. Monroe St., Suite 1400
Chicago, IL 60603
(312) 782-3902
Organization of working women that has helped thousands of women find jobs and develop short- and long-term career plans. Monthly seminars on essential career skills; monthly program meetings on topics of concern to working women.

Women Health Executives Network
c/o Judy Hicks
3233 N. Arlington Heights Road, Suite 208
Arlington Heights, IL 60004
(708) 253-2420

Professional group of health care executives, from department managers to presidents. Monthly meetings, newsletter with job listings.

Women in Cable
500 N. Michigan Ave., Suite 1400
Chicago, IL 60611
(312) 661-1700
Network group for women working in cable TV. Holds meetings; conducts speakers bureau; publishes newsletter.

Women in Communications
100 E. Ohio, Suite 630
Chicago, IL 60611
(312) 642-4331
Chicago chapter of national professional group for women in all areas of communications. Publishes newsletter with job listings; hosts seminars; holds monthly meetings.

Women in Design/Chicago
2 N. Riverside Plaza, Suite 2400
Chicago, IL 60606
(312) 648-1874
Network group of professional graphic designers.

Women in International Trade
180 N. LaSalle St., Suite 2920
Chicago, IL 60601
(312) 641-1466
Group for management-level women who work in aspects of international trade. Educational programs, speakers, newsletter, special events.

Women in Management
P.O. Box 11268
Chicago, IL 60611
(708) 359-6110
Contact: Jean Waldorf
Support group for professional women in management. Publishes newsletters; holds monthly meetings; sponsors seminars and workshops.

Women's Advertising Club of Chicago
30 N. Michigan Ave., Suite 508
Chicago, IL 60602
(312) 263-2215
Professional group for women in advertising and allied fields. Holds monthly meetings; sponsors seminars; publishes monthly newsletter.

Women's Bar Association of Illinois
11 E. Hubbard St.
Chicago, IL 60611
(312) 527-9227
Professional association open to all women lawyers. Sponsors seminars and meetings.

Women's Council of Realtors
430 N. Michigan Ave.
Chicago, IL 60611

(312) 329-8569
Contact: Catherine Collins
Support system for women in real estate within the National Association of Realtors, dedicated to preparing women for leadership roles in business and community service through its network of active state and local chapters. Hosts seminars, educational workshops; publishes newsletter, "Communique."

Women's Direct Response Group of Chicago
c/o Mail Well Envelopes
5445 N. Elston Ave.
Chicago, IL 60630
(312)286-6400
Members work in all phases of the direct marketing industry. Monthly meetings; newsletters.

Young Democrats of Cook County
134 N. LaSalle, Suite 1119
Chicago, IL 60602
(312) 263-0575
Political group meets on the 3rd Wednesday of each month.

Young Executives Club of Chicago
53 W. Jackson Blvd., Suite 1663
Chicago, IL 60604
(312) 853-0186
Network group for Chicago's future business leaders. Monthly luncheons with captains of industry.

Young Leadership Division
Jewish United Fund
1 S. Franklin St.
Chicago, IL 60606
(312) 346-6700, ext. 7626
Educational and social programs for adults under 40.

Young Republican Organization of Illinois
2258 N. Orchard
Chicago, IL 60614
(312) 477-6443
Contact: Suzanne Davis
Holds political meetings on the last Wednesday of the month.

YWCA of Metropolitan Chicago
180 N. Wabash, Suite 301
Chicago, IL 60601
(312) 372-6600
Career program features management seminars for women on the way up. Hosts "View from the Top," monthly breakfast seminars with successful business people.

6

Using Professional Employment Services

Conducting a job search is no easy task. When the pressure is on, many a job seeker's first instinct is to turn to professional employment services for relief. "After all," he or she reasons, "everyone knows that professional services have all the job listings." Wrong!

It's smart to use every available resource to generate leads and interviews. But professional employment services vary from agencies that specialize in temporary clerical help to executive recruiters who deal primarily with top-management types. Employment agencies, career consultants, and executive recruitment firms differ greatly in the kinds of services they offer and in how—and by whom—they get paid. You can save yourself a lot of time, effort, and perhaps even money and anguish by informing yourself about the advantages and disadvantages of the various kinds of professional employment services. One handbook that might prove useful is the *Directory of Approved Counseling Services* (American Personnel and

Guidance Assn., 5201 Leesburg Pike 400, Falls Church, VA 22041).

Employment Agencies

The thousands of employment agencies that have succeeded through the years have done so by acting as intermediaries in the job market between buyers (companies with jobs open) and sellers (people who want jobs). An employment agency obtains a fee when a person it refers to a company is hired by that company. The fee may be paid by the company, but in some cases it is paid by the worker. Agencies that specialize in restaurant and domestic help, for example, often charge the worker a fee. Usually the placement fee amounts to a certain percentage of the worker's annual salary.

Seldom will an employment agency place a candidate in a job that pays more than $50,000 a year. Most employment agencies concentrate on support jobs. Supervisory openings also may be listed, but employment agencies usually don't handle middle or upper management positions. In the computer field, for example, computer operators, programmers, and perhaps systems analysts could find work through an agency. But directors of data processing or MIS (management information systems) would go to an executive search firm or would job-hunt on their own.

A company that's looking for a secretary gains certain advantages by going to a reputable agency. It doesn't have to advertise or screen the hundreds of resumes that would probably pour in from even a small want ad in the Sunday *Chicago Tribune*. A good employment agency will send over only qualified applicants for interviews. Referrals are made quickly, and there is no cost to the company until it hires the secretary. For many companies, it's worth it to pay an agency fee to avoid the hassle of prescreening dozens, if not hundreds, of applicants.

The advantage to the agency of a successful placement (besides the fee) is repeat business. After two or three referrals work out well, an employment agency can generally count on receiving future listings of company vacancies.

The value to the job seeker of using an employment agency depends on a number of factors, including the quality of the agency, the kind of work you're looking for, how much experience you have, and how broad your network of personal and business contacts is.

In general, an agency's loyalty will be to its source of income. Agencies are more interested in making placements than in seeing to it that applicants land in jobs that are really fulfilling. An agency is likely to put pressure on its applicants to accept jobs that they don't really want, just so it can collect its fee. With certain exceptions, unless you're just starting out, new in town, or switching to a field in which you have no experience, an agency probably can't do much more for you than you could do for yourself in an imaginative and energetic job search. If a company has to pay a fee to hire you, you're at a disadvantage compared with applicants who are "free." Also, giving an employment agency your resume could be a serious mistake if you're trying to conduct a confidential job search.

On the other hand, a good agency can help its candidates develop a strategy and prepare for employment interviews. This training can be very valuable to people who are inexperienced in job-hunting techniques. Agency pros know the market, screen well, and provide sound advice. A secretary who tries to investigate the Chicago market on his or her own will take up to six times longer to get the "right" job than someone who uses a quality agency.

Historically, certain employment agencies engage in practices that can only be called questionable at best, and the field as a whole is trying to polish up a somewhat tarnished image. In Illinois, all employment agencies must be licensed by the state. There are many highly respected and successful employment agencies able and willing to help qualified job seekers. But, as in any profession, there are also crooks. It's still a practice in some agencies to advertise nonexistent openings to attract applicants for other, less desirable positions.

So much for the pros and cons of employment agencies. If you decide to try one, be sure it's a reputable firm. Ask people in your field to recommend a quality agency, and consult the Better Business Bureau and other resources listed below (in sidebar) to see if there have been any complaints about the agency you're considering.

Most important, *be sure to read the contract thoroughly, including all the fine print, before you sign it.* If you have any questions, or if there's something you don't understand, don't be afraid to ask. It's your right. Make sure you know who is responsible for paying the fee, and what the fee is. Remember that in some cases *an agency's application form is also the contract.*

Here, then, is a selective listing of Chicagoland employment agencies, including their areas of specialty.

EMPLOYMENT AGENCIES

Accountants Center Ltd.
5 N. Wabash St., Suite 1410
Chicago, IL 60602
(312) 782-3960
Specialty: accounting

Accountants on Call
200 N. LaSalle St., Suite 2830
Chicago, IL 60601
(312) 782-7788

Accountants on Call
3400 Dundee Road, Suite 260
Northbrook, IL 60062

(708) 205-0800
Specialty: accounting/financial

Accountemps
35 E. Wacker Drive
Chicago, IL 60601
(312) 263-8367
Specialty: accounting

Adams Personnel
Options Exchange Building
400 S. LaSalle St.
Chicago, IL 60605
(312) 922-3344
Specialty: financial

American Engineering Consultants
5234 W. Diversey
Chicago, IL 60639
(312) 286-1451
Specialty: engineering, technical

American Medical Personnel
612 N. Michigan Ave., Suite 714
Chicago, IL 60611
(312) 337-4221
Specialty: health care

Ball Personnel Services
11 E. Adams St.
Chicago, IL 60603
(312) 663-1040
Specialty: word processing

Bankers' Personnel
327 S. LaSalle St., Suite 1720
Chicago, IL 60604
(312) 786-1274
Specialty: banking

Britt Associates
53 W. Jackson Blvd.
Chicago, IL 60604
(312) 427-9450
Specialty: distribution and materials management

B-W Associates
4415 W. Harrison St.
Hillside, IL 60162
(312) 449-5400
Specialty: engineering, technical

Career counselors network, too!

The Professional Career Counselor's Network (PCCN) is a professional association of career counselors. It was incorporated in 1984 as a not-for-profit organization formed to be a professional association of career development specialists; to promote the public awareness of career counseling services; and to encourage and sponsor programs for professional development of counselors in the field.

PCCN is located at 36 S. Wabash Ave., Room 1202, Chicago, IL 60603. They can be used to select a career consultant and provide the guidelines for what constitutes quality career counseling. They will advise consumers about what to expect from career counseling services. Approximately 50 professional counselors are members of PCCN and are dedicated to high quality, ethical work in the field.■

Bob Canyon & Associates
55 E. Washington St., Suite 515
Chicago, IL 60602
(312) 332-2288

Casey Services
600 N. McClurg Court
Chicago, IL 60611
(312) 649-0755
Specialty: accounting

CEMCO Systems
2015 Spring Road
Oak Brook, IL 60521
(708) 573-5050
Specialty: data processing

Central Clearing
10031 Roosevelt Road
Westchester, IL 60153
(708) 450-2660
Specialty: engineering, technical, chemical

Compupro, Inc.
312 W. Randolph St., Suite 250
Chicago, IL 60606
(312) 263-5507
Specialty: data processing

Corporate Organizing and Research Services
One Pierce Place, Suite 300 East

Itasca, IL 60143
(800) 323-1352
The nation's largest recruitment research firm

Cox Engineering Recruiters
2 S. 855 Hickory Lane, Box 544
Batavia, IL 60510
(708) 879-2830
Specialty: engineering

CPS, Inc.
1 Westbrook Corporate Center, Suite 425
Westchester, IL 60153
(708) 531-8367
Specialty: technical and professional

Data Career Center
2008 Prudential Plaza
Chicago, IL 60601
(312) 565-1060
Specialty: data processing, telecommunications

DataPath 2000
6170 N. LeMont Ave.
Chicago, IL 60646
(312) 725-1505
Specialty: data processing

Dunhill, Inc.
230 N. Michigan Ave., 30th Floor
Chicago, IL 60601
(312) 346-0933
Specialty: marketing, financial

Edwards, Swanston, Fox
20 N. Wacker Drive, Suite 1745
Chicago, IL 60606
(312) 899-9080
Specialty: financial

Electronic Engineering Group
9944 Roberts Road
Palos Hills, IL 60465
(708) 430-4222
Specialty: electronics

Esquire Personnel Service
222 S. Riverside Plaza
Chicago, IL 60605
(312) 648-4600
Specialty: financial

Fardig Associates
176 W. Adams St., Suite 1611
Chicago, IL 60603
(312) 332-1480
Specialty: financial

Dale Fels, Inc.
333 N. Michigan Ave., Suite 2900
Chicago, IL 60601
(312) 263-6025
Specialty: advertising

Financial Search
2720 Des Plaines Ave., Suite 154
Des Plaines, IL 60018
(708) 297-4900
Specialty: financial

First Personnel Service
28 E. Jackson Blvd.
Chicago, IL 60604
(312)939-7544
Specialty: general

Karen Gillick & Associates
980 N. Michigan Ave., Suite 1060
Chicago, IL 60611
(312) 337-0345
Specialty: advertising

Robert Half of Chicago
35 E. Wacker Drive
Chicago, IL 60601
(312) 782-6930
Specialty: financial

Shirley Hamilton, Inc.
333 E. Ontario
Chicago, IL 60611
(312) 787-4700
Specialty: models and talent

Insurance Register
4N 171 Thornapple Road
St. Charles, IL 60174
(708) 377-2738
Specialty: insurance

Kresin-Wingard
333 N. Michigan Ave., Suite 622
Chicago, IL 60601
(312) 726-8676
Specialty: graphic design

Management Recruiters
2 N. Riverside Plaza, Suite 1815
Chicago, IL 60606
(312) 648-1800
Specialty: data processing

Midwest Technical Search
1420 Kensington Road
Oak Brook, IL 60521

(708) 571-4100
Specialty: design

National Metal Services Corp.
P.O. Box 39
Dyer, IN 46311
(219) 322-4664
Specialty: metals industry

National Search
1752 D Plymouth Court
Wheaton, IL 60187
(708) 665-8026
Specialty: outside sales and marketing

O'Meara & Associates
166 E. Superior St., Suite 212
Chicago, IL 60611
(312) 337-6211
Specialty: advertising

O'Shea Employment Systems
209 W. Jackson Blvd., Suite 401
Chicago, IL 60606
(312) 987-2669
Specialty: accounting

Plaza Inc.
55 E. Monroe St., Suite 3834
Chicago, IL 60603
(312) 263-0944
Specialty: advertising, marketing

Retail Recruiters of Chicago
9701 W. Higgins Road, Suite 240
Rosemont, IL 60018
Chicago number: (312) 693-5716
Specialty: retail sales

Ritt-Ritt & Associates
1400 E. Touhy Ave.
Des Plaines, IL 60018
(708) 298-2510
Specialty: hospitality, food

John M. Ruh Personnel
27 E. Monroe St.
Chicago, IL 60602
(312) 332-6900
Specialty: law

Sales & Management Search
10 S. Riverside Plaza, Suite 1424
Chicago, IL 60606
(312) 930-1111
Specialty: banking; computer sales

Sales Consultants
420 N. Wabash
Chicago, IL 60611
(312) 836-9100
Specialty: sales

Snelling & Snelling
999 E. Touhy Ave.
Des Plaines, IL 60018
(708)296-1026

Star Personnel
333 N. Michigan Ave.
Chicago, IL 60601
(312) 726-6100

Stone Enterprises, Ltd.
405 N. Wabash Ave., Suite 1702
Chicago, IL 60611
(312) 836-0470
Specialty: sales, accounting, data processing, human resources

Technical Resources
2221 Camden Court
Oak Brook, IL 60521
(708) 574-0200
Specialty: engineering, technical

Sandy Wade & Co.
101 E. Ontario, Suite 500
Chicago, IL 60611
(312) 280-9036
Specialty: advertising

Career Consultants

If you open the employment section of the Sunday *Chicago Tribune* or the Midwest edition of *The Wall Street Journal,* you'll see several ads for career consultants (also known as career counselors or private outplacement consultants). The ads are generally directed to "executives" earning yearly salaries of anywhere between $20,000 and $300,000. Some ads suggest that the consultants have access to jobs that are not listed elsewhere. Others claim, "We do all the work." Most have branch offices throughout the country.

Career consultants vary greatly in the kind and quality of the services they provide. Some may offer a single service, such as vocational testing or resume preparation. Others coach every aspect of the job search and stay with you until you accept an offer. The fees vary just as broadly and range from $100 to several thousand dollars. *You,* not your potential employer, pay the fee.

A qualified career consultant can be a real asset to your job search. But *no consultant can get you a job.* Only you can do that. You are the one who will participate in the interview, and you are the one who must convince an employer to hire you. A consultant can help you focus on an objective, develop a resume, research the job market, decide on a strategy, and train you in interviewing techniques. But you can't send a consultant to interview in your place. It just doesn't work that way.

Don't retain a career consultant if you think that the fee will buy you a job. The only reason you should consider a consultant is that you've exhausted all the other resources we've suggested here and still feel you need expert and personalized help with one or more aspects of the job search. The key to choosing a career consultant is knowing what you need and verifying that the consultant can provide it.

There are many reputable consulting firms in the Chicago area. But as is true of employment agencies, some career consultants have been in trouble with the law. Before engaging a career consultant, check with the Better Business Bureau and other resources listed below (in sidebar). Are there an unusual number of complaints against the firm you're considering?

Check references. A reputable firm will gladly provide them. Before you sign anything, ask to meet the consultant who will actually provide the services you want. What are his or her credentials? How long has the consultant been practicing? Who are the firm's corporate clients?

Read the contract carefully before you sign it. Does the contract put the consultant's promises in writing? Has the consultant told you about providing services that are not specified in the contract? What does the firm promise? What do you have to promise? Are all fees and costs spelled out? What provisions are made for refunds? For how long a time can you use the firm's or the consultant's services? Be sure to do some comparison shopping before you select a consultant.

CAREER CONSULTANTS

Thomas Camden
3 Westbrook Corporate Center, Suite 420
Westchester, IL 60154
(708) 449-4020

Career Path
3033 Ogden Ave.
Lisle, IL 60532
(708) 369-3390

Career Strategies
1153 Wilmette Ave.
Wilmette, IL 60091
(708) 251-1661

Career Woman
3 Westbrook Corporate Center, Suite 425
Westchester, IL 60154
(708) 449-4025

Derson Group
332 S. Michigan Ave.
Chicago, IL 60604
(312) 663-4179

Drake Beam Morin
1011 E. Touhy Ave.
Des Plaines, IL 60018
(708) 299-2286

Hay Career Consultants
205 N. Michigan Ave., Suite 4000
Chicago, IL 60601
(312) 819-2100

Bernard Haldane & Associates
307 N. Michigan Ave., Suite 2001
Chicago, IL 60601
(312) 332-4516

David P. Helfand
Career Planning Consultant
230 Ridge #3E
Evanston, IL 60202
(708) 328-2787

Adrienne Hochstedt
9729 Lowell
Skokie, IL 60076
(708) 679-5835

Lansky Career Consultants
233 E. Erie St.
Chicago, IL 60611
(312) 642-5738
Specialty: midlife career change

Marcia Medema
Midwest Women's Center
53 W. Jackson Blvd., Room 1015
Chicago, IL 60604
(312) 922-8530

Paul J. Reibman
1030 Indian Road
Glenview, IL 60025
(708) 729-2117

Eugene B. Shea Associates
800 Enterprise Drive
Oak Brook, IL 60521
(708) 573-4266

Robin Sheerer
Career Enterprises
225 W. Ohio
Chicago, IL 60611
(312) 670-4370

The Charles Stuart Group
20 N. Wacker Drive
Chicago, IL 60606
(312) 641-1646

Diane G. Wilson
Career Development
55 E. Washington, Suite 1221
Chicago, IL 60602
(312) 524-8113

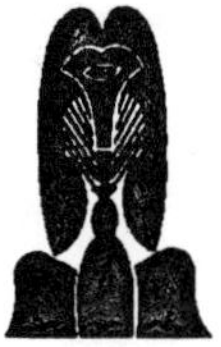

Who's good?
Who's not?

A listing in this book does not constitute an endorsement of an employment agency or career consultant. Before engaging these professional services, check with one or more of the following resources. Employment agencies (except those listing temporary positions only) must be licensed by the State of Illinois. Career consultants, however, do not have to be licensed.

Better Business Bureau
(between 10 a.m. and 2:30 p.m.):
Inquiries: (312) 444-1188
Complaints: (312) 346-3313

City of Chicago Office of Consumer Complaints:
(312) 744-9400

City of Chicago Office of Consumer Services:
(312) 744-4091

Governor's Office of Consumer Affairs:
(312) 917-2754

Illinois Dept. of Labor, Private Employment Agencies Div.:
(312) 793-2810

If you have a complaint about a licensed employment agency, contact the **Illinois Department of Labor, Bureau of Employment Security:** (312) 744-9400.■

Executive Search Firms

An executive search firm is one that is compensated by a company to locate a person with specific qualifications that meet a precisely defined employment need. Most reputable executive search firms belong to an organization called the Association of Executive Recruiting Consultants (AERC). The association publishes a code of ethics for its membership.

A search firm never works on a contingency basis. Only employment agencies do that. The usual fee for a search assignment is 30 percent of the first year's salary of the person to be hired, plus out-of-pocket expenses. These are billed on a monthly basis. During hard times, most companies forgo retaining search firms because it's so expensive.

It's difficult to get an appointment to see a search specialist. Executive search consultants have only their time to sell. If a specialist spends time with you, he or she can't bill that time to a client. If you can use your personal contacts to meet a search professional, however, by all means do so. Executive specialists know the market and can be very helpful in providing advice and leads.

Search firms receive dozens of unsolicited resumes every day. They seldom acknowledge receipt and usually retain only a small portion for future search needs or business development. They really can't afford to file and store them all. Sending your resume to every search firm in the Chicago area will be useful only if one firm coincidentally has a search assignment to find someone with *exactly* your background and qualifications. It's a long shot, similar to answering blind want ads.

The following is a selected list of executive search firms in the Chicago area.

EXECUTIVE SEARCH FIRMS

Accountants on Call
200 N. LaSalle St., Suite 2830
Chicago, IL 60601
(312) 782-7788
Contact: Michael Parbs, Branch Manager

Billington, Fox & Ellis
20 N. Wacker Drive
Chicago, IL 60606
(312) 236-5000

Bools & Associates
35 E. Wacker Drive, 26th Floor
Chicago, IL 60601
(312) 372-1777
Specialty: advertising

Dorothea Bowlby & Associates
P. O. Box 347
Winnetka, IL 60093
(708) 263-5293
Specialty: medical

Robert Campbell Associates
18 S. Michigan Ave., Room 1120

Chicago, IL 60603
(312) 263-0234

Central Clearing
10031 W. Roosevelt Road
Westchester, IL 60153
(708) 450-2660
Specialty: engineering, technical

Chicago Search Group
1110 Lake Cook Road, Suite 375
Buffalo Grove, IL 60089
(708)520-7800

William H. Clark Associates
29 S. LaSalle St.
Chicago, IL 60601
(312) 263-0830

Coopers & Lybrand
203 N. LaSalle
Chicago, IL 60601
(312) 701-5500

Ernst & Whinney/Executive Search
150 S. Wacker Drive
Chicago, IL 60606
(312) 368-1800

Heidrick & Struggles
125 S. Wacker Drive, Suite 2800
Chicago, IL 60606
(312) 372-8811

A.T. Kearney, Inc.
222 S. Riverside Plaza
Chicago, IL 60606
(312) 648-0111

KGPM Peat Marwick
303 E. Wacker Drive
Chicago, IL 60601
(312) 938-1000

Korn/Ferry International
120 S. Riverside Plaza, Suite 918
Chicago, IL 60606
(312) 726-1841

Paul R. Ray & Co.
200 S. Wacker Drive, Suite 3820
Chicago, IL 60606
(312) 876-0730

Research Alternatives
782 Industrial Drive
Elmhurst, IL 60126
(708) 941-0000

Russell Reynolds Associates
200 S. Wacker Drive, Suite 3600
Chicago, IL 60606
(312) 993-9696

Witt Associates
1211 W. 22nd St.
Oak Brook, IL 60521
(708) 574-5070

Social Service Agencies

Unlike professional employment agencies, career consultants, and executive search firms, social service agencies are not-for-profit. They offer a wide range of services, from counseling and vocational training to job placement and follow-up—and their services are usually free.

American Indian Business Association
4753 N. Broadway, Suite 700
Chicago, IL 60640
(312) 784-2434
Offers services, including job counseling, referral, and placement.

American Indian Center
1630 W. Wilson Ave.
Chicago, IL 60640
(312) 275-5871
Placement services for on-the-job training programs. Not limited to American Indians.

American Spanish Institute
2619 W. Armitage Ave.
Chicago, IL 60647
(312) 278-5130
Job placement agency with emphasis on Spanish-speaking people.

Casa Central
1401 N. California Ave.
Chicago, IL 60622
(312) 276-1902
Social service agency serving the Hispanic community.

Chicago Urban League
4510 S. Michigan Ave.
Chicago, IL 60653
(312) 285-5800
Counseling, job placement, and follow-up. Not limited to blacks.

Forty Plus
53 W. Jackson Blvd.
Chicago, IL 60604
(312) 922-0285
Organization aids middleaged people in their job search.

Jewish Vocational Service
1 S. Franklin St.

Chicago, IL 60606
(312) 346-6700
Provides vocational counseling, guidance, testing, job placement to persons of all religious faiths.

Minority Economic Resources Corp.
15605 Ellenwood
Des Plaines, IL 60016
(708) 297-4705
Assists minorities and women in finding employment in the northwest suburbs.

Operation Able
180 N. Wabash Ave.
Chicago, IL 60603
(312) 782-3335
Network of over 30 social agencies that address the employment problems of people over 55. Operates a free job hotline, provides technical assistance and training, teaches job-finding skills to older adults.

Government Agencies

Most job seekers do not take advantage of the free employment listings available through the city and state because the caliber of jobs is often disappointing. These government agencies are free, however, and if you are near one of the following offices, you may as well stop in and see what is available.

The Mayor's Office of Employment and Training
500 Peshtigo Court
Chicago, IL 60611
(312) 744-8787
Vocational counseling and referral, direct job placement. Administers the Mayor's Summer Youth Employment Program.

Illinois Dept. of Labor
Register for a job in the bureau closest to your home:

1751 W. 47th St.—(312) 254-2769
1514 W. Division St.—(312) 489-6262
8516 S. Commercial Ave.—(312) 374-8410
4809 N. Ravenswood Ave.—(312) 334-6646
9415 S. Western Ave.—(312) 881-6830

For professional, sales, and clerical jobs:
29 E. Congress Parkway—(312) 793-4900

Networking at the "YW"

The Career Management Department of the Loop Center YWCA, 180 N. Wabash Avenue, offers a number of programs and services for job hunters and people who need help planning their careers. According to Lisa Goodale, Director of Career Management at Loop Center, the department's programs serve a wide range of people.

"We serve women in mid- to upper-level management, as well as women who aspire to such positions," says Lisa. "We also serve a variety of women who are looking for jobs, including many who have been out of the work force for some time—displaced homemakers, mothers who have been raising children, and so on.

"One of our programs is a Job Resource Group, held every Wednesday from 12 to 1 p.m. It's a very informal open forum, in which we explore any topic of interest to the people in attendance. We may share contacts in the job market or discuss how to develop such contacts. Other topics that come up include resumes and women's professional organizations.

"On the first Tuesday of every month we hold a networking breakfast that we call `A View from the Top.' It begins at 7:45 a.m., and the fee is $5. The breakfast features a prominent Chicago-area woman who discusses her career, followed by an informal question-and-answer period."

The Loop Center YWCA's Career Management Department also offers classes and workshops dealing with such topics as stress management, developing self-esteem, writing resumes, and job interview techniques. In addition, the department offers an annual career conference. "The topic of the conference changes each year," says Lisa, "but is always useful to people who are job hunting."

For more information about Loop Center YWCA career management programs, call **(312) 372-6600.**

The South Suburban YWCA in Olympia Fields also has a career development program that offers career counseling and career-related conferences and workshops. For information, call Joyce A. Short, Director of Career Development, at **(312) 748-6600.**

The West Suburban YWCA in Lombard offers a program called TARGET, which serves women who are reentering the work force. "We also recently expanded our services to include an employment center," says Kit Mathey, Director of TARGET. "We will be offering a job bank, job-hunting workshops, and support groups." For more information, call **(312) 629-0170.**■

7 How To Succeed In an Interview

If you've read straight through this book, you already know that networking (see Chapter 5) is one of the most important and useful job-hunting techniques around. Networking is nothing more or less than using personal contacts to research the job market and to generate both exploratory and formal job interviews.

Networking and interviewing go hand-in-hand; all the contacts in the world won't do you any good if you don't handle yourself well in an interview. No two interviews are ever identical, except that you always have the same goal in mind: to convince the person to whom you're talking that he or she should help you find a job or hire you personally. An interview is also an exchange of information. But you should never treat it as you would a casual conversation, even if the "interviewer" is an old friend.

Preparing for the Interview: The 5-Minute Resume

Whether you're talking to the housewife next door about her brother-in-law who knows someone you want to meet or going through a final, formal interview with a multinational corporation, you are essentially making a sales presentation—in this case, selling yourself. Your goal is to convince the interviewer that you have the ability, experience, personality, maturity, and other characteristics required to do a good job and to enlist the interviewer's help in getting you that job.

In an informal interview you'll be talking first to friends and acquaintances. Most of the people you'll be talking to will want to help you. But they need to know who you are, what you've done, what you want to do, and most important, *how they can help you.*

To prepare for any interview, first perfect what we like to call the five-minute resume. Start by giving a rough description, not too detailed, of what you're doing now (or did on your last job) so that when you're telling your story, the listener isn't distracted by wondering how it's going to end.

Then go all the way back to the beginning—not of your career, but of your life. Talk about where you were born, where you grew up, what your folks did, whether or not they're still living, what your brothers and sisters do, and so on. Then trace your educational background briefly and, finally, outline your work history from your first job to your latest.

"What!" say many of our clients. "Drag my PARENTS into this? Talk about my crazy BROTHER and the neighborhood where we grew up?"

Yes, indeed. You want to draw the listener into your story, to make him or her interested enough in you to work for you in your search. You want the interviewer to know not only who you are and what you have achieved but also what you are capable of. You also want to establish things in common with the listener. The more you have in common, the harder your listener will work for you.

Co-author Tom Camden, we are not ashamed to admit, is a master of the five-minute resume. Here's how he would begin a presentation to someone like the neighbor down the street:

"Would it be all right with you if I gave you a broad-brush review of my background? Let you know what I've done, what I'd like to do? That'll give us some time to talk about how I should go about this job search. Maybe I could pick your brain a little about how you can help me. OK?

"Currently, I'm vice president of EnterChange, a national career transition management consulting firm.

"Originally, I'm from the Southwest Side of Chicago, near Midway Airport. I'm 54 years old, married with five grown children.

"My father was a security guard at IIT Research Institute; my mother is retired. She used to work for Walgreens—made aspirins, vitamins, and other pills. I'm the oldest of four children. My brother John does the traffic 'copter reports for a Chicago radio station. My sister Connie is a consultant for an industrial relations firm.

"I went to parochial schools. When I was 14, I left home and went into a monastery. I stayed there until I was 19. Then I went to Loyola University, studied psychology, got my degree in '59. I was also commissioned in the infantry.

"I started my graduate work in Gestalt psychology. In 1960 Kennedy called up troops for the Berlin crisis. That included me, so I spent a year on active duty. Following that, I came back and continued my graduate work in industrial relations..."

Tom took exactly a minute and a half to make this part of his presentation, and he's already given his neighbor several areas in which they may have something in common. He's volunteered enough information not only to get the neighbor interested in his story but to let the neighbor form judgments about him. People don't like to play God, says Tom. Yet it's a fact of life that we constantly form judgments about each other. In an interview—even an exploratory, informal one—you may as well provide enough information to be judged on who you are rather than on what someone has to guess about your background. What does it mean to be the oldest of four kids? What can you deduce from Tom's middle-class background?

The typical personnel professional will tell you that the number of brothers and sisters you have has nothing to do with getting a job. Technically, that's true. The law says that an employer can't ask you how old you are, your marital status, and similar questions. Yet anyone who's considering hiring you will want to know those things about you.

The typical applicant begins a presentation with something like, "I graduated from school in June, nineteen-whatever, and went to work for so-and-so." Our task in this book is to teach you how *not* to be typical. Our experience has convinced us that the way to get a job offer is to be *different* from the rest of the applicants. You shouldn't eliminate the first 20 years of your life when someone asks you about your background! That's the period that shaped your basic values and personality.

Neither should you spend too much time on your personal history. A minute or two is just about right. That gives you from three to eight minutes to narrate your work history. Most exploratory interviews, and many initial employment interviews, are limited to half an hour. If you can give an oral resume in 5 to 10 minutes, you have roughly 20 minutes left to find out what you want to know (more on that shortly).

The five-minute resume revisited

Psychologist and career expert Gayle Roberts has her own slant on the five-minute resume. She believes that "while nothing works every time, you should try to emphasize those aspects of your personal history that have a bearing on your current qualifications for the job you're seeking.

"For example, I am one of those rare creatures who always liked school. I got along fine with the teachers. I even liked studying and taking tests. I liked to learn, and I still do. That's part of why I choose to work in an academic setting. I think it's helpful to mention my long history as a book worm any time I'm applying for a position that requires research, writing, or critical thinking skills. I don't think I'd mention it if I were going for a sales position.

"I personally wouldn't recommend saying too much about your past unless you can connect it to the present in a way that makes you look like a better job candidate. Everybody has a number of revealing personal anecdotes. The trick is to pick the right ones."■

A word about your work history. If you've done the exercises in Chapter 2, or written your own resume, you ought to be able to rattle off every job you've had, from the first to the latest, pretty easily. In the oral resume you want especially to *emphasize your successes and accomplishments* in each job. This will take some practice. We are not accustomed to talking about ourselves positively. From childhood we're conditioned that it's not nice to brag. Well, we are here to tell you that if you *don't* do it in the interview, you *won't* get the offer.

We repeat: *the interview is a sales presentation.* It's the heart of your job search, your effort to market yourself. In an exploratory interview, the listener will be asking, "Should I help this person?" In a formal interview, the employer will be asking, "Should I hire this person?" In either case, the answer will be "yes" only if you make a successful presentation, only if you convince the interviewer that you're worth the effort.

So, the first step in preparing for any interview, formal or informal, is to *practice your five-minute resume.* Go through it out loud enough times so that you're comfortable delivering it. Then work with a tape recorder and critique yourself. Try it out on a couple of friends.

When you're preparing for a formal employment interview, *do your homework* on the company. This advice is merely common sense. But it's surprising how many candidates will ask an interviewer, "What does this company do?" Don't be one of them. Before you go in for an employment interview, find out everything you can about the company—its history, organization, products and services, and growth expectations. Get hold of the company's annual report, catalogs, and brochures. Consult your networking contacts, and use the resources in Chapter 4.

Steps to a Successful Interview

Before the Interview

- Self-assessment: identify strengths, goals, skills, etc.
- Research the company.
- Rehearse what you plan to say. Practice answers to common questions.
- Prepare questions to ask employer.

During the Interview

- Make sure you arrive a few minutes early.
- Greet the interviewer by his/her last name; offer a firm handshake and a warm smile.
- Be aware of non-verbal communication. Wait to sit until you are offered a chair. Sit up straight, look alert, speak clearly and forcefully but stay relaxed. Make good eye contact, avoid nervous mannerisms, and try to be a good listener as well as a good talker. Smile.
- Follow the interviewer's lead, but try to get the interviewer to describe the position and duties to you fairly early in the interview so you can then relate your background and skills in context.
- Be specific, concrete, and detailed in your answers. The more information you volunteer, the better the employer gets to know you.
- Offer examples of your work that document your best qualities.
- Answer questions as truthfully and as frankly as you can. Do not appear to be "glossing over" anything. On the other hand, stick to the point and do not over-answer questions. The interviewer may steer the interview into ticklish political or social questions. Answer honestly, trying not to say more than is necessary.

Closing the Interview

- Don't be discouraged if no definite offer is made or specific salary discussed.
- If you get the impression that the interview is not going well and that you have already been rejected, do not let your discouragement show. Once in a while, an inter-

viewer who is genuinely interested in you may seem to discourage you to test your reaction.

- A typical interviewer comment toward the close of an interview is to ask if you have any questions. Prepare several questions in advance, and ask those that weren't covered during the interview.
- At the conclusion of your interview, ask when a hiring decision will be made. Also thank your interviewer for his or her time and express your interest in the position.

After the interview

- Take notes on what you feel you could improve upon for your next interview.
- If you are interested in the position, type a brief thank-you letter to the interviewer, indicating your interest.
- If offered the position, one to two weeks is a reasonable amount of time to make a decision. All employment offers deserve a written reply whether or not you accept them.

How to dress

A young friend of ours who wanted to break into real estate finally landed her first big interview—with Coldwell Banker. It was fairly easy for her to do her homework on a company of that size. Two days before the interview, however, it suddenly dawned on her that she had no idea how to dress. How did she solve her problem?

"It was pretty easy, actually, and fun, too," says Susan. "All I did was go and hang around outside the office for 15 minutes at lunchtime to see what everyone else was wearing."

However, we recommend that even if the office attire is casual, one should still dress professionally. One career counselor recommends that one should "always dress one step above the attire of those in the office where you are interviewing."■

What Interviewers are Looking For

- **General Personality:** Ambition, poise, sincerity, trustworthiness, articulateness, analytical ability, initiative, interest in the firm. (General intelligence is assumed.) Different firms look for different kinds of people—personalities, style, appearance, abilities, and technical skills. Always check the job specifications. Don't waste time talking about a job you can't do or for which you do not have the minimum qualifications.

- **Personal Appearance:** A neat, attractive appearance makes a good impression and demonstrates professionalism.

- **Work Experience:** Again, this varies from job to job, so check job specifications. If you've had work experience, be able to articulate the importance of what you did in terms of the job for which you are interviewing and in terms of your own growth or learning. Even if the work experience is unrelated to your field, employers look upon knowledge of the work environment as an asset.

- **Verbal Communication Skills:** The ability to express yourself articulately is very important to most interviewers. This includes the ability to listen effectively, verbalize thoughts clearly, and express yourself confidently.

- **Skills:** The interviewer will evaluate your skills for the job, such as organization, analysis, and research. It is important to emphasize the skills that you feel the employer is seeking and to give specific examples of how you developed them. This is the main reason why it is important to engage in self-assessment prior to the interview.

- **Goals/Motivation:** Employers will assess your ability to articulate your short-term and long-term goals. You should seem ambitious, yet realistic about the training and qualifications needed to advance. You should demonstrate interest in the functional area or industry and a desire to succeed and work hard.

- **Knowledge of the Interviewer's Company and Industry:** At a minimum, you really are expected to have done some homework on the company. Don't waste interview time asking questions you could have found answers to in printed material. Know the firm's position and character relative to others in the same industry. General awareness of media coverage of a firm and its industry is usually expected.

Handling the Interview

In an exploratory, or informal, interview most of the people you'll talk with will want to help you. But they need to know *how*. After you've outlined your personal and work history, ask your contact how he or she thinks your experience fits into today's market. What companies should you visit? Specifically, what people should you contact?

When someone gives you advice or a recommendation to call someone else, do it! Few things can be more irritating than to provide free counsel to someone who then ignores it. If your contact suggests that you call Helen Smith, call her!

In a formal employment interview, there are several typical questions you can expect to encounter, though not necessarily in this order:

Tell me about yourself. (This is your cue for the five-minute resume.)

Why do you want to change jobs?

What kind of job are you looking for now?

What are your long-range objectives?

What are your salary requirements?

When could you be available to start here?

Tell me about your present company.

What kind of manager are you?

How would you describe yourself?

What are your strengths and weaknesses?

(In the course of his career, Tom Camden has posed this last question to untold numbers of applicants. "They'll list two or three strengths," he says, "and then can't wait to tell me about their weaknesses." Don't be one of those people! Accentuate the positive. Remember, this is a competitive interview.)

Describe your present boss.

To whom can I talk about your performance?

Are you open to relocation?

How long have you been looking for a new job?

Why are you interested in this company? (This is your golden opportunity to show the interviewer that you've done your homework on the company.)

Practice your answers to these questions *before* you go in for the interview. Anticipate other questions you might be asked, and develop answers for them. In general, keep your responses positive. Never volunteer a negative about yourself, another company, or a former employer. Even if you hate your present boss, describe your areas of disagreement in a calm, professional manner. You are selling *yourself,* not downgrading others. Even if you're not particularly interested in the company, always conduct the interview as if you were dead set on getting the job.

The interviewer will apply your responses to the questions he or she *really* wants answered:

Does the applicant have the ability to do the job?

Can he or she manage people?

How does he or she relate to people?

What kind of person is this? A leader? A follower?

What strengths does he or she have that we need?

Why the number of job changes so far?

Where is he or she weak?

How did the applicant contribute to present and past companies?

What are his or her ambitions? Are they realistic?

Is he or she too soft or too tough on subordinates?

What is this person's standard of values?

Does he or she have growth potential?

Is there a health problem anywhere?

What is the nature of the "chemistry" between us?

What will the department manager think of this applicant as opposed to the others?

Should this person get an offer?

The interview should not be a one-sided affair, however. Questions that you should ask the interviewer are equally important in this exchange of information. For example, you have to know about the job, the company, and the people in your future employment situation. It's necessary to use your judgment to determine how and when to ask questions in an interview. But without the answers, it will be next to impossible for you to make a sound decision if you receive an offer. Some of the questions you want answered are:

What are the job's responsibilities?

What is the company's recent history? Its current objectives? Its market position?

Where are its plants located? What distribution systems does it use?

To whom will I report? What's his or her background?

How much autonomy will I have to get the job done?

Why is the job available?

Where does the job lead?

What about travel requirements?

Where is the job located?

Are there any housing, school, or community problems that will develop as a result of this job?

What is the salary range? (Do not raise the question of explicit salary at this point.)

What is the detailed benefit picture?

What is the company's relocation policy?

When will an offer decision be made?

What references will be required?

When would I have to start?

What is the personality of the company?

Do the job and company fit my plan for what I want to do now?

What's the next step?

Career guides

Some companies administer standardized tests to see if applicants are qualified for certain kinds of work, such as secretarial, data processing, and the like.

The Chicago Public Library's Business Information Center (400 N. Franklin St., 4th Floor) has an impressive number of workbooks to help you prepare for the most common tests. These include study guides for elevator operators, computer programmers, women in the armed forces, law and court stenographers, laboratory aides, supervisory engineers, even mortuary caretakers! Reviews for state board exams for nurses and certified public accountants are also available.■

Following the Interview

Many job seekers experience a kind of euphoria after a good interview. Under the impression that a job offer is imminent, a candidate may discontinue the search. This is a serious mistake. The decision may take weeks, or may not be made at all. On the average, about six weeks elapse between the time a person makes initial contact with a company and when he receives a final answer. If you let up on the search, you will prolong it. Maintain a constant sense of urgency. Get on with the next interview. Your search isn't over until an offer is accepted and you actually begin the new job.

Always follow up an interview with correspondence. The purpose of the letter is to supplement the sales presentation you made. Thank the interviewer for his or her time and hospitality. Express interest in the position (ask for the order). Then mention three additional points to sell yourself further. Highlight how your specific experience or knowledge is directly applicable to the company's immediate needs. Try to establish a date by which a decision will be made.

If you think you could benefit from professional counseling in interviewing skills, consider the resources suggested in Chapter 2 and in Chapter 6. You may also find it helpful to refer to some of the following books.

BOOKS ON INTERVIEWING

Allen, Jeffrey. *How to Turn an Interview Into a Job.* New York: Simon & Schuster, 1988.

Biegelein, J.I. *Make Your Job Interview a Success.* New York: Arco, 1987.

Danna, Jo. *Winning the Job Interview Game: Tips for the High-Tech Era.* Briarwood, NY: Palomino Press, 1986.

Goodale, James G. *The Fine Art of Interviewing.* Englewood Cliffs, NJ: Prentice-Hall, 1982.

Krannich, Caryl R. *Interview for Success.* San Luis Obispo, CA: Impact, 1982.

Marcus, John J. *The Complete Job Interview Handbook.* 2nd ed. New York: Harper & Row, 1988.

Medley, H. Anthony. *Sweaty Palms: The Neglected Art of Being Interviewed.* Berkeley: Ten Speed Press, 1984.

Pell, Arthur R. *How to Sell Yourself in an Interview.* New York: Monarch Press, 1982.

Smart, Bradford D. *The Smart Interviewer.* New York: John Wiley & Sons, 1989.

How to get the most from your references

References should be kept confidential and never revealed until a company is close to making you an offer, and you want to receive one.

Always brief your references before you supply an interviewer with their names and numbers. Tell the references what company you're interviewing with and what the job is. Give them some background on the company and the responsibilities you'll be asked to handle.

Your references will then be in a position to help sell your abilities. Finally, don't abuse your references. If you give their names too often, they may lose enthusiasm for your cause.■

8

What To Do If Money Gets Tight

Any job search takes time. One particularly pessimistic career counselor we know suggests you plan to spend about two weeks of search time for every thousand dollars you want to earn per year. (Pity the poor soul who wants to make $60,000!) A more optimistic estimate for a job search is around three months, provided the search is conducted full time.

If you already have a full-time job, it will take you longer to find a new one. But at least you will be receiving a paycheck while you're looking. This chapter is intended for those who are unemployed and facing the prospect of little or no income during the search.

When the financial squeeze is on, the first thing to do is make a thorough review of your liquid assets and short-term liabilities. Ask yourself how much cash you can expect to receive during the next three months from the following sources, plus any others you might come up with:

Savings
Securities
Silver and gold
Insurance loan possibilities
Second mortgage possibilities
Unemployment compensation
Severance pay
Accrued vacation pay
Personal loan sources (relatives, friends)
Sale of personal property (car, boat, stamp collections, etc.)

Then you should consider exactly what bills absolutely *must* be paid. Don't worry about your total outstanding debt. Many creditors can be stalled or might be willing to make arrangements to forgo principal as long as interest payments are made. Talk to each of your creditors to see if something can be worked out.

The final step is easy—if sometimes painful. You compare the amount of money you have on hand or expect to receive with the amount you know you'll have to spend. The difference tells you exactly what kind of financial shape you're in.

The old adage has it that it's better to be unemployed than underemployed. If you can afford it, it's wise not to take a part-time or temporary job. The more time you spend looking for a good full-time position, the sooner you're likely to succeed. But if the cupboard looks pretty bare, it may be necessary to supplement your income any way legally possible in order to eat during the search.

Fast talk nets big part-time $$$

People who need to earn money while job hunting might consider the telemarketing, or telephone sales, industry. Debra Schwartz, who has worked as a telemarketing manager, feels that the field offers a variety of challenges and rewards.

"Being a telemarketer is almost like being an actor in a radio play," says Debra. "Your success depends on how well you control your voice. You also have to be able to receive feedback from people without the benefit of eye contact or body language."

We asked Debra what telemarketing managers look for in the people they hire. "The crucial element is the person's voice. Telemarketers must speak clearly and have pleasing voices. They also must use standard English grammar. Previous sales experience is a plus, although it's not necessary. Managers also look for people who can handle rejection. A person might get rejected 25 or 30 times before making a sale."

According to Debra, most telemarketers work in four-hour shifts. "You can't work on the phone for more than four hours without becoming ineffective. Also, many firms operate only in the afternoons and evenings. But some firms do have morning hours—those involved in corporate sales, for example."

How much can a telemarketer expect to make?

"Top people can make over $10 per hour," says Debra. "The average telemarketer makes about $4-$8 per hour. The pay varies, depending on whether you are working on a straight commission basis or are being paid a base hourly wage plus commissions."

Debra suggests investigating a telemarketing firm carefully before accepting a job since there are quite a few fly-by-night operations. But she emphasizes the many benefits of working for a reputable firm: "Telemarketing is a great experience for job hunters. Many of the basic sales techniques that you learn are usable when promoting yourself to a potential employer."

Getting a part-time job in telemarketing requires persistence since managers receive hundreds of calls and applications. "Don't give up," advises Debra. "Have your sales pitch ready when you call. Sell yourself on the phone in the same way that you would sell a product once you're hired."■

Try to find part-time or temporary work that leaves you as free as possible to interview during the day. For this reason, many people choose to drive a cab at night or work in a bar or restaurant during the evenings. This kind of job gives you the advantage of flexible hours, but the pay is not always desirable. Commissioned sales positions abound in almost every industry. But if your personality isn't suited to sales work, don't pursue it. You'll find it very frustrating.

It's best if you can locate part-time work in your chosen field. The pay is usually more attractive, and you can continue to develop your network of contacts. Many professionals can freelance. An administrative assistant, for example, might be able to find part-time work at a law firm. An accountant might be able to do taxes on a part-time basis and still gain access to new referrals.

Here are some additional sources to consider when the money is really tight and you need part-time or temporary work.

SELECTED SOURCES FOR PART-TIME WORK

Advanced Temporary Office Services
4777 N. Harlem Ave., Suite 5
Howard Heights, IL 60656
(708) 867-4171
Contact: Laura Svihula, Personnel Dir.
Supplier of temporary office help.

American United Cab Co.
2353 W. Belmont Ave.
Chicago, IL 60618
(312) 248-7600
Cab leasing.

Checker Taxi Co.
845 W. Washington Blvd.
Chicago, IL 60607
(312) 421-1314
Cab leasing.

Good advice from a bartender

One of our friends, a successful freelance television producer, spent several years tending bar part time in various popular Mid-north saloons to support his television habit.

"The best places to look for part-time work," he says, "are those where you're already known. Bar owners will rarely hire a bartender who walks in off the street or fresh out of Famous Bartending School's two-week course. That's because it's very easy for bartenders to steal. An owner wants to know someone, to have a sense of a person's character, before he hires a bartender.

"So if you're looking for part-time work—and this goes for waiters and waitresses, too—spend some time in the place for a couple of weeks. Get to know the people who work there and the regular customers, and become one of the regulars yourself. Learn how the place operates. Every bar or restaurant has its own way of doing things, from handling special orders to taking care of rowdy customers. The more you know about a place, the easier it is to step in when somebody calls in sick or quits."■

Chicago Europe Language Center
1220 N. Hoyne Ave.
Chicago, IL 60622
(312) 372-5922
Translating; need to know a foreign language.

Flash Cab Co.
4747 N. Clark St.
Chicago, IL 60640
(312) 561-1444
Cab leasing.

Andy Frain, Inc.
310 W. Chicago Ave.
Chicago, IL 60610
(312) 266-6900
Contact: Matthew Vail, Personnel Dir.
Security guard and usher service.

Helpmate, Inc.
8 S. Michigan Ave.
Chicago, IL 60603
(312) 372-6875
Suppliers of temporary office help.

Just Jobs
4753 N. Broadway, Suite 1010
Chicago, IL 60640
(312) 784-0455
Contact: Ellen O'Reilly Garcia, Personnel Dir.
General labor and factory work assigned on a daily basis.

The Kane Service
6325 N. Avondale Ave.
Chicago, IL 60631
(312) 775-1118
Security guard service.

Kelly Services
2625 Butterfield Road
Oak Brook, IL 60521
(708) 571-4060
Contact: Tony Zahn, Regional Mgr.
Suppliers of temporary office help.

Manpower, Inc.
500 Park Blvd., Suite 154
Itasca, IL 60143
(708) 773-0042
Contact: Warren Rosenow, Area Mgr.
Temporary office, warehouse, and factory help.

Norrell, Inc.
55 W. Monroe St., Suite 3355
Chicago, IL 60603
(312) 782-4181
Contact: Denise Hunt, Office Mgr.
Suppliers of temporary office help.

Olstens of Chicago
123 W. Madison St.
Chicago, IL 60602
(312) 782-1014
Contact: (Mr.) B. J. Dolan, Office Mgr.
Suppliers of temporary office help; offer word processing training.

Personnel Pool
1200 Harger Road, Suite 217
Oak Brook, IL 60521
(708) 571-3900
Contact: Suzanne Clem, Employee Relations Consultant
Supplier of temporary office help.

Profile Temporary Services
55 W. Wacker Drive
Chicago, IL 60603
(312) 641-1920
Contact: Cheryl Davis, Executive Dir.
Providers of temporary office help.

Revell Temporary Services
7506 N. Harlem Ave.
Harwood Heights, IL 60656
Chicago No.: (312) 774-0808
Contact: Brian Hampton, Personnel Dir.
Supplier of temporary office help; offers word processing training.

Right Temporaries
53 W. Jackson Blvd., Suite 1320
Chicago, IL 60604
(312) 427-3136
Contact: Nancy Barth, Branch Mgr.
Suppliers of temporary office help.

RRS Security Service
1601 N. Bond Ave.
Naperville, IL 60540
(708) 369-6761
Contact: Pat Somers, Personnel Mgr.
Security guard service.

Servicemaster Industries
2300 Warrenville Road
Downers Grove, IL 60515
(708) 964-1300
Contact: William Hargreaves, Asst. V.P., Personnel
Supplies management support personnel to hospitals, households, plants.

Stivers Temporary Personnel
200 W. Monroe St. Suite 1100
Chicago, IL 60606
(312) 558-3550
Contact: Wilma J. Schroeder, V.P. Personnel
Suppliers of temporary office services.

Western Services
2225 Enterprise Drive Center, Suite 2515
Westchester, IL 60154
(708) 562-7474
Contact: Betty Brown, Branch Mgr.
Suppliers of temporary office and factory help.

Yellow Cab Co.
1730 S. Indiana Ave.
Chicago, IL 60616
(312) 225-7440
Cab leasing.

SELECTED BOOKS ON PART-TIME AND FLEXIBLE EMPLOYMENT

Alter, Joanne. *A Part-Time Job for a Full-Time You.* Boston: Houghton Mifflin Co., 1982.
Anderson, Joan. *The Best of Both Worlds: A Guide to Home-Based Careers.* White Hall, VA: Betterway Publications, Inc., 1982.
Arden, Lynie. *The Work-at-Home Sourcebook.* Boulder, CO: Live Oak Publications, 1987.
Lowman, Kaye. *Of Cradles and Careers.* Franklin Park, IL: La Leche League, 1984.
Magid, Renee Y. *When Mothers and Fathers Work: Creative Strategies for Balancing Career and Family.* New York, NY: AMACOM, 1987.
O'Hara, Bruce. *Put Work in Its Place.* Victoria, BC, Canada: Work Well, 1988.
Olmsted and Smith. *The Job Sharing Handbook.* Walnut Creek, CA: Ten Speed Press, 1983.
Rothberg and Cook. *Part-Time Professional.* Washington, DC: Acropolis Books, 1985.
Sernaque, V. *Part-Time Jobs.* New York, NY: Ballantine Books, 1982.

Government and Private Assistance Programs

If you've exhausted all your resources and can't find part-time or temporary work, you might consider local, state, federal, or private assistance. Many people bridle at the mere mention of "charity" or "welfare." But if the help you receive is needed—and temporary—it's a way of bridging the gap until you land a job. More people take advantage of these sources of assistance than you might imagine. In the case of state and federal aid, your tax dollars have helped to provide the benefits. Your taxes have also paid for the salaries of the people distributing the benefits.

Don't pass judgment on the merits of the following sources until you talk with the professionals who administer their respective programs. Pros can advise you on eligibility, benefits, and also provide you with other ideas and resources.

The following organizations represent some major sources of aid available in the Chicago area.

GOVERNMENT PROGRAMS

City of Chicago: Dept. of Consumer Services
Counseling Service for Debt Control
121 N. LaSalle
The Loop Family Center
Chicago, IL 60602
(312) 744-4090
Offers money-management counseling, can arrange with creditors for reduced monthly payments, and can often stop a wage assignment. Has a consumer education library with educational materials.

City of Chicago: Dept. of Housing
Neighborhood Housing Support Program
318 S. Michigan
Chicago, IL 60604
(312) 922-8275
Offers counseling for homeowners facing default and possible foreclosure on their property.

City of Chicago: Dept. of Human Services
500 N. Peshtigo Court
Chicago, IL 60611
(312) 744-8111
The city, through 14 Community Service Centers, offers emergency services on the local level, including emergency shelter for victims of evictions.

City of Chicago: Dept. of Human Services
Low Income Energy Assistance Program
(312) 744-6717
Emergency help in payment of energy bills for indigent or near-indigent families.

City of Chicago: Mayor's Office of Employment and Training
121 N. LaSalle
Chicago, IL 60602
(312) 744-8787
Offers vocational counseling and referral services; some job placement.

Cook County: Energy Assistance Program
224 N. DesPlaines St.
Chicago, IL 60606
(312) 207-5444
Provides service for payment of past-due heating and utility bills.

State of Illinois: Dept. of Public Aid
624 S. Michigan Ave.
Chicago, IL 60605

(312) 793-4706
Administers the state-funded public aid programs.

State of Illinois: Dept. of Registration & Education
100 W. Randolph, Suite 9-300
Chicago, IL 60601
(312) 815-4500
Call them if you are being threatened by a debt-collection agency, and they may be able to help.

State of Illinois: Dept. of Unemployment Insurance
401 S. State St.
Chicago, IL 60605
(312) 793-4240
Administers the Unemployment Insurance Act of Illinois. This is the place to call to find out if you are eligible to collect unemployment payments.

University of Illinois Cooperative Extension Service
17722 Oak Park Ave.
Tinley Park, IL 60477
(708) 532-4369
The urban gardening program offers gardening plots in the city to those who want to grow their own.

PRIVATE CHARITABLE ORGANIZATIONS

Austin People's Action Center
5929 W. Lake St.
Chicago, IL 60644
(312) 921-2122
Emergency clothing, food pantry, legal aid clinic.

Catholic Charities of Chicago
Dept. of Social Development Services
721 N. LaSalle St.
Chicago, IL 60610
(312) 266-6100
Provides legal assistance to the indigent; financial assistance counseling; emergency food, clothing, and furniture.

Emergency Fund for Needy People
150 N. Michigan Ave.
Chicago, IL 60601
(708) 534-9097
Small financial grants for emergency needs.

Hinsdale Community Service
19 E. Chicago Ave.
Hinsdale, IL 60521
(708) 323-2500
Short-term financial counseling; emergency financial assistance; operates food pantry, used clothing service; conducts "Stretching Your Food Dollar" workshops.

Hull House Association
Jane Addams Center
800 S. Halsted

Chicago, IL 60607
(312) 549-1631
Provides legal aid, emergency food, consumer credit union, consumer debt counseling.

Jewish Family & Community Service
1 S. Franklin St.
Chicago, IL 60606
(312) 346-6700
Offers assistance on financial management problems; non-interest-bearing loans for economic readjustment and vocational training; consultation on legal problems.

Legal Assistance Foundation of Chicago
343 S. Dearborn St.
Chicago, IL 60604
(312) 341-1070
Provides free legal services in all civil areas such as landlord-tenant relations, public aid benefits, social security, consumer contracts.

Northwestern University Legal Assistance Clinic
357 E. Chicago Ave.
Chicago, IL 60611
(312) 908-8576
Provides legal assistance.

Society of St. Vincent de Paul of Chicago
126 N. DesPlaines
Chicago, IL 60606
(312) 236-5172
Provides unrestricted cash grants upon investigation by volunteer.

United Charities of Chicago
Family Financial Counseling
14 E. Jackson Blvd.
Chicago, IL 60604
(312) 461-0800
Offers debt management program and budget counseling.

Young Women's Christian Association (YWCA)
180 N. Wabash, Suite 301
Chicago, IL 60601
(312) 372-6600
Offers financial and legal counseling to women.

Unemployment compensation

If you have been fired or laid off and your former employer has paid the unemployment tax, you may be entitled to collect unemployment insurance.

Call the **Illinois Dept. of Employment Security** at (312) 793-8138 and ask for the office closest to your home. They will tell you to bring your Social Security card and another piece of identification with you so you can file for benefits, which should begin arriving within two weeks if you are eligible.■

9

Where To Turn If Your Confidence Wilts

Recently a bank fired a loan officer who had worked there for more than ten years. The employee was 58 years old, about 5'6", weighed almost 300 pounds, and did not have a college degree. His written communication skills were negligible. His poor attitude and appearance, lack of enthusiasm, and dismal self-esteem suggested he would be unemployed a long time.

The bank decided to use Camden & Associates outplacement service to help the person get another job. "There wasn't much we could do about changing his age, education, size, or communication skills," Tom Camden recalls. "But we certainly could—and did—work with him on improving his self-esteem and changing his attitude toward interviewing for new jobs."

After a four-month search, the loan officer succeeded in landing a position that exactly suited his needs. His new job even was located in the neighborhood where he lived. It seemed like a typical success story—until the bank informed Tom Camden how dissatisfied the person was with the counsel he had received. The man told the bank that they would have been better off paying *him* the consulting fee instead of retaining outside help.

"He was really angry," Tom recalls. "And also full of stress, guilt, fear, anxiety, desire for vengeance, and a host of other emotions."

Such feelings, unfortunately, are not at all unusual. In fact, they're a *normal* part of any job search, particularly for those who have been laid off or fired. That's because rejection, unfortunately, is inevitable in any job search.

If you've read Chapter 5, you know that you may speak with up to 300 people on a formal or informal basis while you're looking for suitable work—and a healthy percentage of those people will be unable or unwilling to help you. Every job seeker must anticipate rejection—it comes with the territory. Being turned down in an interview is a painful experience, and it's normal to feel hurt. The trick is to keep those hurt and angry feelings from clouding your judgment or affecting your behavior.

What To Do If You Get Fired

Being fired ranks just after the death of someone you love or divorce when it comes to personal traumas. If it should happen to you, *take time to evaluate the bad news before accepting a settlement offer.* If you quickly accept what your employer has to offer, it will be much more difficult to change your situation later. Tell the boss you want some time to think about a settlement. Then go back in a day or two and negotiate.

Stay on the payroll as long as you can, even if your pride hurts. Find out if you are eligible for part-time work or consulting jobs to tide you over until you find your new job. You may be able to hang on to insurance and other benefits until you've found new employment.

Try to negotiate a generous severance payment. In the last five years, severance agreements have risen dramatically in some industries. What the company offers at first may not be the maximum. Negotiation doesn't always work, but you certainly ought to try to get the most for your years of service.

Check with your personnel office to make sure you're getting all the benefits to which you are entitled, such as vacation pay and profit sharing. Check your eligibility for unemployment compensation before you accept an offer to resign instead of being terminated.

Don't attack management during your termination interview. It may cost you good references and hurt your chances of finding a new job.

Take advantage of any placement assistance that's offered. Don't reject the company's offer to help even if your pride has been stung.

Dealing with Emotional Stress

If you're beginning to feel your confidence wilt, reread the tips for treating yourself well in Chapter 5. Put yourself on a regular schedule. Make sure you're eating healthy foods and getting enough rest and exercise. Don't punish yourself for being unemployed or losing a job offer.

One of the worst things that can happen in any job search is to let rejection undermine your self-confidence. Like the little boy at the door who asks, "You don't want to buy a magazine, do you?" A person who doesn't feel good about himself will not easily convince an employer that he should be hired. Each new rejection further erodes self-esteem, and the job search stalls or takes a nosedive: "Maybe I *am* a loser. Perhaps I was lucky to have had my old job as long as I did. Maybe my sights are set too high. I suppose I should look for something less responsible at a lower salary."

Thoughts such as these cross most people's minds at some time or other in the job search. As we've said, it's normal to feel hurt, angry, and depressed after a series of rejections. It's important, however, to recognize these feelings and learn to work them out in some non-destructive way. It is *not* normal to let such feelings sabotage your job search. Just because you're unemployed or looking for a new job doesn't mean you're a bad or worthless person. The only thing "wrong" with you is that you haven't found the offer that you want.

When your confidence starts to wilt, turn to a trusted friend or relative. Talk about your feelings frankly. Get mad or sad or vengeful. Then get back to work on your job search. Don't let fear of rejection keep you from making that next call. It may be just the lead you're looking for.

There are no hard and fast rules on when to seek professional counseling and emotional support, but we can offer certain guidelines. If you seriously think you need professional help, you ought to investigate two or three sources. Besides the ones we've listed below, check with your minister, priest, or rabbi. Many clerics are trained counselors, and their help is free.

If you feel you have nowhere else to turn, or if you don't want to share your feelings with anyone you know, you should consider psychiatric or psychological counseling. If you're not making calls or not preparing for interviews or not doing what you know you have to do to get the job you want, you could probably use some counseling.

Everybody feels bad about being rejected. But if you allow those feelings to overwhelm you, or if they're interfering with finding a job, it's probably time to talk with a professional. Another sure sign of the need for help is to wake up most mornings too sick or lethargic from overeating, overdrinking, or abusing some other substance to do what you have to do.

A listing in this book does not constitute an endorsement of any institution, therapist, or school of therapy. Therapy depends a great deal on the "chemistry" between therapist and patient—something only you can evaluate. A basic rule of thumb is that if you're not comfortable with or confident in a particular therapist, it may not be wise to continue seeing him or her.

Therapy is offered by quite a variety of people, from psychiatrists and psychologists with years of post-graduate training to those with considerably lower levels of education and experience. Before engaging a therapist, check his or her credentials. Where was the therapist trained? What degrees does the therapist hold? How long has the therapist been practicing? Does he or she belong to any professional associations?

SELECTED CRISIS CENTERS AND INSTITUTIONS

Adult Community Outreach Network
926 Foster St.
Evanston, IL 60201
(708) 866-7186
Community drop-in center offers support to individuals who are coping with social, emotional, and economic difficulties.

Alcoholics Anonymous
205 W. Wacker Drive
Chicago, IL 60606
(312) 346-1475
People helping themselves and others to recover from alcoholism.

All About Women
637 E. Golf Road, Suite 201
Arlington Heights, IL 60005
(708) 952-1300
Career, personal, alcohol abuse, and family counseling.

Chicago Counseling and Psychotherapy Center
5711 S. Woodlawn Ave.
Chicago, IL 60637
(312) 684-1800
Individual therapy or support groups.

Fox Valley Mental Health Center
Ecker Center
384 Division St.
Elgin, IL 60120
(708) 695-1115
Psychological support groups.

Health Evaluation and Referral Services
1954 W. Irving Park Road
Chicago, IL 60613
(312) 781-9560

24-hour health referral service; provides general information on health issues.

Hinsdale Community Service Center
19 E. Chicago Ave.
Hinsdale, IL 60521
(708) 323-2500
Short-term counseling.

Institute for Psychoanalysis
180 N. Michigan Ave.
Chicago, IL 60601
(312) 726-6300
Offers psychoanalytic therapy, diagnostic consultations, and referral service.

Michael Reese Hospital and Medical Center
Dept. of Psychiatry
Wexler Pavilion
2960 S. Lake Park Ave.
Chicago, IL 60616
(312) 791-3900
Offers psychiatric evaluation and treatment; community mental health services; consultation.

Northwestern Memorial Hospital
Institute of Psychiatry
320 E. Huron St.
Chicago, IL 60611
(312) 908-8100
Offers outpatient and community psychiatric services.

People's Resource Center
107 W. Indiana Ave.
Wheaton, IL 60187
(708) 682-3844
Short-term psychiatric and stress counseling.

Project Hope
Northeastern Illinois University
5500 N. St. Louis Ave.
Chicago, IL 60625
(312) 583-4050
Self-help counseling groups.

Re-entry Center
1017 Central Ave.
Wilmette, IL 60091
(708) 251-9320
Individual counseling, seminars, support groups.

Rush Presbyterian St. Luke's Medical Center
Dept. of Psychiatry
1720 W. Polk St.
Chicago, IL 60612
(312) 942-5380
Psychoanalytic and supportive therapy; alcoholic treatment program.

The Self-Help Center
1600 Dodge Ave., Suite 5122
Evanston, IL 60201
(708) 328-0470
Aids people in finding support groups.

University of Chicago Hospitals & Clinics
Dept. of Psychiatry Services
5841 S. Maryland Ave.
Chicago, IL 60637
(312) 702-1000
Diagnostic psychiatric evaluation and treatment available on a fee basis.

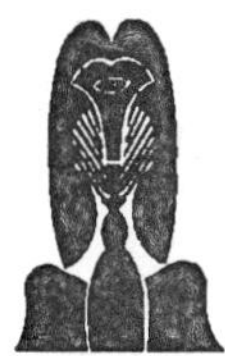

Who's good? Who's not?

You can call the **Illinois Department of Registration and Education** at (312) 917-4900 to find out if a therapist is licensed and, if so, whether any complaints have ever been proven against the therapist. Not all therapists have to be licensed, however. Only psychiatrists, psychologists, and certain kinds of social workers must be licensed in Illinois. So consumer, beware.

The **Institute for Psychoanalysis** at (312) 726-6300 maintains extensive referral files on therapists in Illinois and elsewhere in the country. Therapists don't *have* to register with the Institute, but chances are that if your therapist is registered, he or she is reputable. You can also call the **Mental Health Association of Greater Chicago** at (312) 922-0703 for referral to a therapist or to check on a clinic's professional reputation.■

Risk and Opportunity: Career Transition Issues

Any job search is going to involve risk and opportunity, according to a notable career counselor. If you are autonomous, you are able to view the risk as opportunity and to come up with creative ideas for changing jobs. However, many job searchers begin to lose their sense of independence and control after some setbacks. They start believing that nothing they do will help lift them out of their situation.

An autonomous person is "self-governing" and believes that his actions will have a definite effect on his or her life. One of the most important aspects of finding or changing a job is to keep believing that you can control your life. When this belief begins to falter, many people slip into some of the traps of self-doubt and loss of independence.

Seven key issues that most people confront during a job hunt are:

Self-esteem: Do you feel good about yourself, your daily life, and your future? Are you self-accepting? Do you have a positive self-image?

Self-validation: Do you validate yourself both from without and within? Do you have an inner sense of your own worth? Are you able to learn from the feedback you get from others during the job hunt?

Risk-taking: Are you willing to take the risks needed to get what you want? Are you willing to reveal yourself even in a situation such as a job interview when you're not completely in control?

Sadness or depression: Can you feel sad about loss but still bounce back? Can you learn from failure even as you feel good about success?

Internalized anger: Can you recognize when you feel angry? If you are angry, can you identify which of your needs are not being met? Can you discover effective and appropriate ways to express anger?

Goal setting: Are your goals appropriate to who you are and what you need? Are your goals and expectations realistic in terms of the current job market and your own training and expertise?

Phase of life issues: How have your goals changed over time? Has your self-image changed as you have changed and grown? Are you flexible enough to change as your life changes?

Selecting the Right Job for You

Welcome to the most pleasant chapter of this book—and the one that's the most fun. You've figured out what you want to do, developed an acceptable resume, and used your contacts and other resources to research the job market and generate all sorts of interviews. At this point in the process you've probably received or are pretty close to landing at least a couple of offers that come fairly close to your objective.

You have a problem if one of your possibilities becomes a firm offer that demands an immediate response while you're still investigating other promising leads. The employer making this offer is essentially telling you, "We think you have everything we're looking for, and we want you to start as soon as possible." It is difficult to stall or delay your acceptance just because other promising leads still haven't yielded firm offers. You have to use your best judgment in such a case, but try to delay a final decision until all likely offers are in. Unless you're absolutely desperate, there's no reason to jump at the first offer you receive.

You owe it both to yourself and the people who interviewed you to consider all outstanding possibilities and *then* make your decision. Tell the employer who gave you the offer the truth—that you need more time to review the offer against all the situations that are outstanding and pending—that a decision can't be made for at least two weeks. If the offering company refuses to wait, that tells you a great deal about the atmosphere in which you'd be working.

If a company wants you badly enough, they'll wait a reasonable length of time for you to decide. In the meantime, use your offer to "encourage" other companies to reach a decision about your candidacy. We're not suggesting that you play hardball. That probably won't work and might even work against you. But it makes perfect sense to inform other companies who are interested in you that you have an offer. If you're sure you'd rather work for them, say so. But also say that you'll have to accept the first offer if you don't hear from them within the allotted time. Don't lie about your intentions. If you don't intend to accept the first offer, don't say that you do. Otherwise, the second (and perhaps better) company might write you off, assuming that you won't be available by the time they're ready to decide.

A job involves much more than a title and base salary. For any firm offer, be sure you understand what your responsibilities will be, what benefits you'll receive besides salary (insurance, vacation, profit sharing, training, tuition reimbursement, and the like), how much overtime is required (and whether you'll be paid for it), how much travel is involved in the job, who your superior will be, how many people you'll be supervising, and where the position might lead. (Is it a dead-end job or are people in this slot often promoted?) In short, find out anything and everything you need to know to evaluate the offer.

For many positions, especially those requiring several years' experience, it's appropriate to ask for an offer in writing. Such a document would specify the position's title, responsibilities, reporting relationship, and compensation and include a statement of company benefits.

At the very least, before you make a firm decision, be sure to obtain a copy of the company's personnel policy. It will fill you in on such details as the number of paid sick days, overtime and vacation policy, insurance benefits, and profit sharing. These so-called fringe benefits can really add up. It's not a bad idea to try to assign a dollar value to them to help you evaluate the financial pros and cons of each offer.

It seems obvious to us that it's unwise to choose a job exclusively on the basis of salary and benefits. Don't condemn yourself to working with people you can't stand, doing work you find boring, to accomplish goals you don't believe in.

Finding the Right Culture

Career counselors often warn that you ignore a company's "culture" at your own peril. You can find a position that suits you to a "T" but still be unhappy if you don't fit the culture of the company that hires you. It takes some doing to assess an organization's culture, but it's worth your while.

Some signs are fairly obvious: What do people wear? What is the furniture like? Are office doors kept open or closed? Are there any minorities or women in positions of power? How friendly are people to you? To each other? Does anybody laugh? A very important question to ask—Do I feel comfortable here?

There are five aspects of an organization's culture to consider. Try to find out as much as you can about each.

1. What is the relationship between a company and its environment? Does it control its own destiny or must it depend on the mood of an adversarial home office? You probably wouldn't be wise to work for the Department of Defense under a pacifist administration.

2. How does a company view human nature? Good or evil? Changeable or immutable? Answers to these questions determine how employees are treated, how much supervision and control is exerted. How openly will employees communicate? Will there be opportunities for training and development?

3. What are the philosophy and mission of a company? Printed brochures are often good indicators. A good company is clear on what business it's in.

4. How do people relate to each other in a company? Is there a formal flow chart? Are there many vertical levels (the military)? Or is power more evenly and horizontally spread out (some new high-tech firms)? The more horizontal, the more informal and the easier it is to get things done, generally through relationships.

5. How are decisions made, who makes them, and upon what basis? Facts and reason? Politics? Ideology? Good-old-boy network? The whims of an autocrat at the top?

The answers to these questions will determine the working atmosphere for most companies.

Salary Strategy

Before you accept an offer—or bicker about salary—you need to know what other people who fill similar positions are making. The *Occupational Outlook Handbook,* put out by the U.S. Department of Labor every two years, cites salary statistics by field. Probably a better source of information is *The American Almanac of Jobs and Salaries* by John Wright, published by Avon. What you really need to know is what other people with your qualifications and experience are making in the Chicago area for working the job you're considering. Professional societies and associations frequently provide this sort of information. It's one more good reason to belong to one. Probably the best source of all for salary orientation is—you guessed it—your network of contacts.

For advice on how to get the salary you want, we recommend these books:

Chapman, Jack. *How to Make $1000 a Minute.* Berkeley, CA: Ten Speed Press, 1987.

Cohen, Herb. *You Can Negotiate Anything.* New York: Bantam Publishing Co., 1982.

Fisher, Roger, and William Ury. *Getting to Yes.* New York: Penguin Books, 1983.

Kennedy, Marilyn Moats. *Salary Strategies: Everything You Need to Know to Get the Salary You Want.* New York: Rawson Wade, 1982.

Compare the Offers on Paper

You've talked with each employer and taken notes about the responsibilities and compensation being offered. Where possible, you've obtained a job offer in writing. You have also read through the company's personnel policy. Next, draw up a checklist for comparing the relative merits of each offer. We've provided a sample here, but if another format suits your purposes better, use it. The idea is to list the factors that you consider important in any job and then assign a rating for how well each offer fills the bill in each particular area.

We've listed some of the factors that we think ought to be considered before you accept any offer. Some may not be relevant to your situation. Others that we've left out may be of great importance to you. So feel free to make any additions, deletions, or changes you want.

Once you've listed your factors, make a column for each job offer you're considering. Assign a rating (say, 1 to 5, with 1 the lowest and 5 the highest) for each factor and each offer. Then, total the scores for each offer.

The offer with the most points is not necessarily the one to accept. The chart doesn't take into account the fact that "responsibilities" may be more important to you than "career path," or that you promised yourself you'd never punch a time clock again. Nevertheless, looking at the pros and cons of each offer in black and white should help you make a much more methodical and logical decision.

Factor	**Offer A**	**Offer B**	**Offer C**
Responsibilities	______	______	______
Company reputation	______	______	______
Salary	______	______	______

Insurance	______	______	______
Paid vacation	______	______	______
Pension	______	______	______
Profit sharing	______	______	______
Tuition reimbursement	______	______	______
On-the-job training	______	______	______
Career path (where can you go from this job?)	______	______	______
Company future	______	______	______
Quality of product or service	______	______	______
Location (housing market, schools, transportation)	______	______	______
Boss(es)	______	______	______
Other workers	______	______	______
Travel	______	______	______
Overtime	______	______	______
Other	______	______	______
______________	______	______	______
______________	______	______	______
TOTAL POINTS	______	______	______

A Final Word

Once you have accepted a job, it's important that you notify each of the people in your log of your new position, company, address, and phone number. Be sure to thank these people; let them know you appreciated their assistance. After all, you never know when you may need to ask them to help you again. *Keep your network alive!*

On each anniversary date of your new job, take the time to run through the self-appraisal process to evaluate your situation and the progress you are making (as measured by increased responsibilities, salary, and abilities). Compare your progress against the objectives you set at the start of your search. Although you may be completely satisfied in your new assignment, remember that circumstances can change overnight, and you must always be prepared for the unexpected. So make an employment "New Year's resolution" to weigh every aspect of your job annually and compare the result with what you want and expect from your life's work.

We hope that you have made good use of the job-search techniques outlined in this book. Indeed, we hope that the resulting experiences not only have won you the job you want but—equally important—also have made you a better person. Perhaps the next time you talk to an unemployed person or someone who is employed but seeking a new job, you will look at that person with new insight gained from your own search experiences. We hope you'll gladly share what you've learned about how to get a job in Chicago.

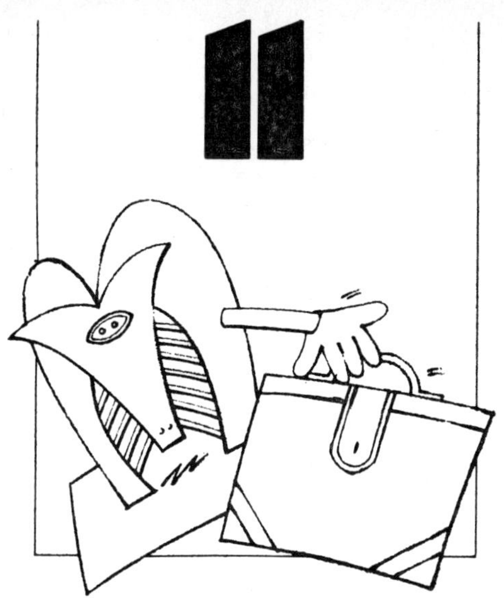

Where Chicago Works

This chapter contains the names, addresses, and phone numbers of the Chicago area's top 1,500 employers of white-collar workers. The companies are arranged in categories according to the major products and services they manufacture or provide. Where appropriate, entries contain a brief description of the company's business and the names of the personnel director or other contact.

This listing is intended to help you survey the major potential employers in fields that interest you. It is selective, not exhaustive. We have not, for example, listed all the advertising agencies in the area as you can find that information in the Yellow Pages. We have simply listed the top 25 or so, that is, the ones with the most jobs.

The purpose of this chapter is to get you started, both looking and thinking. This is the kickoff, not the final gun. Browse through the whole chapter, and take some time to check out areas that are unfamiliar to you. Many white-collar skills are transferable. People with marketing, management, data processing, accounting, administrative, secretarial, and other talents are needed in a huge variety of businesses.

Ask yourself in what areas your skills could be marketed. Use your imagination, especially if you're in a so-called specialized field. A dietician, for instance, might look first under Health Care, or perhaps Hospitality. But what about Insurance Agencies, Museums, Banks, or the scores of other places that run their own dining rooms for employees or the public? What about Food and Media? Who invents all those recipes and tests those products?

The tips and insider interviews that are scattered throughout this chapter are designed to nudge your creativity and suggest additional ideas for your job search. Much more detailed information on the area's top employers and other, smaller companies can be found in the directories and other resources suggested in Chapter 4. We can't stress strongly enough that you have to do your homework when you're looking for a job, both to unearth places that might need a person with your particular talents and to succeed in the interview once you've lined up a meeting with the hiring authority.

A word about hiring authorities: if you've read Chapter 5, you know that the name of the game is to meet the person with the power to hire you, or to get as close to that person as you can. You don't want to go to the chairman or the personnel director if the person who actually makes the decision is the marketing manager or customer service director.

Obviously, we can't list every possible hiring authority in the area's "Top 15,000." If we tried, you'd need a wagon to haul this book around. Besides printed directories go out of date—even those that are regularly and conscientiously revised. So always double-check a contact whose name you get from a book or magazine, including this one. If necessary, call the company's switchboard to confirm who heads a particular department or division.

Here, then, are Chicago's greatest opportunities. Happy hunting!

The Chicago area's top 1,500 employers are arranged in the following categories:

Accounting/Auditing
Advertising and Marketing
Architecture Firms
Auto/Truck/Transportation Equipment
Banks/Savings and Loans
Book Publishers and Distributors
Broadcasting
Chemicals, Paints, and Coatings
Computers: Data Processing

Computers: Hardware, Software, Technical Services, Telecommunications
Construction and Engineering
Drugs/Pharmaceuticals/Medical Supplies
Educational Institutions
Electrical Equipment and Supplies
Electronics and Communications Equipment
Entertainment: Theaters and Talent Agents
Fashion/Clothing/Cosmetics
Foods and Beverages
Furniture/Fixtures/Household Textiles
Government: City, County, State, Federal
Health Care
Hospitality: Hotels/Restaurants/Exposition Planners
Housewares
Human Services
Insurance/Benefits Consultants
Investment Institutions/Stock Brokers
Law Firms
Management Consultants
Manufacturers
Media: Newspapers and Magazines
Metals and Minerals
Museums and Galleries
Office Equipment and Supplies
Paper/Packaging
Petroleum/Rubber/Plastics
Printers
Public Relations
Real Estate Developers and Brokers
Recreation/Sports
Retailers/Wholesalers
Steel Manufacturing
Travel/Transportation/Shipping
Utilities

Accounting/Auditing

For networking in **Accounting** and related fields, check out these professional organizations listed in Chapter 5:

PROFESSIONAL ORGANIZATIONS:

American Women's Society of Certified Public Accountants
Chicago Finance Exchange
Illinois CPA Society
Independent Accountants Association of Illinois
National Black MBA Association

For additional information, you can write to:

American Institute of CPA's
1455 Pennsylvania Ave., N.W.
Washington, DC 20004

American Society of Women Accountants
35 E. Wacker Drive
Chicago, IL 60601

National Association of Accountants
10 Paragon Drive
Montvale, NJ 07645-1760

National Association of Black Accountants
900 Second St., N.E. Suite 205
Washington, DC 20002

National Association of Minority CPA's
1625 I St., N.W.
Washington, DC 20006

National Society of Public Accountants
1010 N. Fairfax St.
Alexandria, VA 22314

PROFESSIONAL PUBLICATIONS:

Cash Flow
The CPA Journal
Journal of Accountancy
Management Accounting
National Public Accountant

DIRECTORIES:

Accounting Firms and Practitioners (American Institute of Certified Public Accountants, New York, NY)
Emerson's Directory of Leading U.S. Accounting Firms (Emerson's, Seattle, WA)
National Directory of Certified Public Accountants (Peter Norback Publishing Co., Princeton, NJ)
Who Audits America (Data Financial Press, Menlo Park, CA)

EMPLOYERS:

Altschuler, Melvoin & Glasser
30 S. Wacker Drive, Suite 2600
Chicago, IL 60606

(312) 207-2800
Managing Partner: Howard Stone

Arthur Andersen & Co.
33 W. Monroe St., 8th Floor
Chicago, IL 60603
(312) 580-0033
Managing Partner: John Oltman

Bansler & Kiener
300 W. Washington St.
Chicago, IL 60606
(312) 263-2700
Managing Partner: Bernard J. Sullivan

BDO Seidman
205 N. Michigan Ave., Suite 2100
Chicago, IL 60601
(312) 856-9100
Managing Partner: Scott Elsasser

Berger Goldstein & Co.
510 Lake Cook Road
Deerfield, IL 60015
(708) 948-7700
Managing Partner: Robert Goldstein

Blackman, Kallick, Bartelstein
300 S. Riverside Plaza, Suite 660
Chicago, IL 60606
(312) 207-1040
Managing Partner: R. Kallick

Blumenfeld, Weiser, Friedman & Co.
8707 Skokie Blvd., Suite 106
Skokie, IL 60077
(708) 675-0211

Checkers, Simon & Rosner
1 S. Wacker Drive, Suite 1700
Chicago, IL 60606
(312) 346-4242
Managing Partner: Jerome A. Harris

Coopers & Lybrand
203 N. LaSalle St.
Chicago, IL 60601
(312) 701-5550
Managing Partner: Ernest R. Wish

DeLoitte and Touche
2 Prudential Plaza

180 N. Stetson St.
Chicago, IL 60601
(312) 946-3000
Managing Partner: Thomas Flanagan

Ernst & Young
150 S. Wacker Drive
Chicago, IL 60606
(312) 368-1800
Managing Partner: Jack Staley

Friedman, Eisenstein Raemer & Schwartz
401 N. Michigan Ave.
Chicago, IL 60611
(312) 644-6000
Managing Partner: Irwin Friedman

Grant Thornton
700 Prudential Plaza
130 E. Randolph Drive
Chicago, IL 60601
(312) 856-0200
Managing Partner: John C. Burke

Thomas Havey & Co.
30 N. LaSalle St., Suite 4200
Chicago, IL 60602
(312) 368-0500
Managing Partner: Thomas W. Havey

KGPM Peat Marwick
303 E. Wacker Drive
Chicago, IL 60601
(312) 938-1000
Managing Partner: James Brocksmith

Kupferberg, Goldberg & Neimark
111 E. Wacker Drive, Suite 1400
Chicago, IL 60601
(312) 819-4300
Managing Partner: Stanley Neimark

Laventhol & Horwath
300 S. Riverside Plaza
Chicago, IL 60606
(312) 648-0555
Managing Partner: Kenneth I. Solomon

McGladrey & Pullen
1699 E. Woodfield Road, Suite 300
Schaumburg, IL 60173

(708) 517-7070
Managing Partner: Bob Jensen

Miller, Cooper and Co., Ltd.
650 Dundee Road, Suite 250
Northbrook, IL 60052
(708) 205-5000
Managing Partner: Neal S. Fisher

Spicer & Oppenheim
222 S. Riverside Plaza, Suite 800
Chicago, IL 60606
(312) 648-1211
Managing Partner: Emanuel Katten

Ostrow, Reisin, Berk & Abrams, Ltd.
676 St. Clair St.
Chicago, IL 60611
(312) 440-3600
Managing Partner: Herbert Ostrow

Auditing a candidate's prospects

Touche Ross & Co. is one of the so-called Big Eight accounting firms. We asked Dick Jensen, Director of Human Resources at the company's Chicago office, what he looks for in an interview.

"A combination of things," says Jensen. "Intelligence, of course. Also business presence, by which I mean not only appearance and communication skills but listening skills as well. We try to get a sense of a person's judgment, maturity, and independence. Then there's leadership potential—how well is this person respected by his or her peers?

"It's not just what a person says in an interview that counts. We try to tie what they say to what they've done. I look for patterns of success and try to get a sense of the history of a person's accomplishments, sometimes going all the way back to grammar school. I'm likely to ask questions that don't seem at first to relate to working at a large accounting firm—such as, 'What was your standing in the Eagle Scouts?'" ■

Petty's Accounting Service
1528 S. Pulaski Ave.
Chicago, IL 60623
(312) 277-4488
Contact: Ammit Petty, Sr.

Price Waterhouse & Co.
200 E. Randolph St.
Chicago, IL 60601
(312) 565-1500
Managing Partner: Thomas Donahoe

Rome Associates
40 E. Huron St., Suite 700
Chicago, IL 60611
(312) 280-9151
Personnel Director: Eileen Zaba

Philip Rootberg & Co.
250 S. Wacker Drive, Suite 800
Chicago, IL 60606
(312) 930-9600
Personnel Director: Terry Stabiner

Washington, Pittman & McKeever
819 S. Wabash, Suite 600
Chicago, IL 60605
(312) 786-0330
Contact: Personnel
Managing Partner: Lester McKeever

Wolf & Co.
2100 Clearwater Drive
Oak Brook, IL 60521-1927
(708) 574-7800

Advertising and Marketing

For networking in **advertising** and related fields, check out the following professional organizations listed in Chapter 5:

PROFESSIONAL ORGANIZATIONS:

Advertising Agency Production Managers Club
Agate Club of Chicago
American Marketing Association
Bank Marketing Association
Broadcast Advertising Club of Chicago
Chicago Advertising Club
Chicago Association of Commerce and Industry
Chicago Association of Direct Marketing
Chicago Coalition
International Association of Business Communicators
Marketing Research Association
Newspaper Representatives Association of Chicago

Radio Advertising Bureau
Retail Advertising Conference
Sales and Marketing Executives Association of Chicago
Women in Design/Chicago
Women's Advertising Club of Chicago
Women's Direct Response Group of Chicago

For additional information, you can write to:

The Advertising Council
825 Third Ave.
New York, NY 10022

American Advertising Federation
1400 K St., N.W.
Washington, DC 20005

American Association of Advertising Agencies
606 Third Ave.
New York, NY 10017

Direct Marketing Association
6 E. 43rd St.
New York, NY 10017

PROFESSIONAL PUBLICATIONS:

Advertising Age
Adweek
American Demographics
Business Marketing
Direct Marketing Magazine
Journal of Advertising Research
Journal of Marketing Research
Madison Avenue
Marketing/Communications
Marketing & Media Decisions
Marketing News
Potentials in Marketing

DIRECTORIES:

Bradford's Directory of Marketing Research Agencies (Bradford Publishing Co., Fairfax, VA)
Handbook of Independent Advertising and Marketing Services (Executive Communications, Inc., New York, NY)
International Membership Directory and Marketing Services Guide (American Marketing Association, Chicago, IL

Multinational Marketing and Employment Directory (World Trade Academy Press, Inc., New York, NY)
Standard Directory of Advertising Agencies (National Register Publishing Co., Skokie, IL)

EMPLOYERS, AD AGENCIES:

Abelson-Taylor Inc.
35 E. Wacker Drive
Chicago, IL 60601
(312) 781-1700
President: Dale Taylor

Bayer Bess Vanderwarker
225 N. Michigan Ave.
Chicago, IL 60601
(312)861-3800
Director, Creative Services: Mary Thompson

BBDM, Inc.
444 N. Michigan Ave.
Chicago, IL 60611
(312) 644-9600
Creative Director: Dennis Gillespie

BBDO-Chicago
410 N. Michigan Ave.
Chicago, IL 60611
(312) 337-7860
Personnel Director: Michelle Shotts

Bently Barnes & Lynn
420 N. Wabash
Chicago, IL 60611
(312) 467-9350
President: Paul Oleff

Bozell, Jacobs, Kenyon & Eckhardt
625 N. Michigan Ave.
Chicago, IL 60611
(312) 988-2000
President: Rick Cooper

Leo Burnett Company
35 W. Wacker Drive
Chicago, IL 60601
(312) 220-5959
Account Manager: Kathy Hoppe

Burrell Advertising
20 N. Michigan Ave.
Chicago, IL 60602
(312) 443-8600
Creative Director: Anna Morris

Campbell-Mithun, Inc.
737 N. Michigan Ave.
Chicago, IL 60611
(312) 266-5100
Creative Manager: Jordie Krimstein

Frank J. Corbett, Inc.
211 E. Chicago Ave.
Chicago, IL 60611
(312) 664-5310
Creative Director: Dick Jacob

Cramer-Krasselt
225 N. Michigan Ave.
Chicago, IL 60601
(312) 977-9600
President: Peter Krivkovich

D'Arcy, Masius, Benton & Bowles
200 E. Randolph St.
Chicago, IL 60606
(312) 861-5000
Personnel Director: Rebecca Price

DDB Needham Worldwide
303 E. Wacker Drive
Chicago, IL 60601
(312) 861-0200
Account Manager: Kathy McCurdy

della Femina, McNamee WCRS
500 N. Michigan Ave.
Chicago, IL 60611
(312)222-1313
President: Geoffrey Charleton-Perrin

A. Eicoff & Co.
401 N. Michigan Ave.
Chicago, IL 60611
(312) 527-7100
Creative Director: Sandy Stern

Flair Communications
214 W. Erie St.
Chicago, IL 60610

(312) 943-5959
President: Allyn Miller

Foote, Cone & Belding Communications
101 E. Erie St.
Chicago, IL 60611
(312) 751-7000
Creative Manager: Lou Centlivre

Garfield-Linn & Co.
142 E. Ontario
Chicago, IL 60611
(312) 943-1900

Grant/Jacoby, Inc.
737 N. Michigan Ave.
Chicago, IL 60611
(312) 664-2055
Chairman: Bruce Carlson

Haddon Advertising
919 N. Michigan Ave.
Chicago, IL 60611
(312) 943-6266

HCF & Lois/GGK
2300 Merchandise Mart Plaza
Chicago, IL 60654
(312) 527-5030
Personnel Manager: Billie Royek

Huwen & Davies
311 W. Superior St.
Chicago, IL 60610
(312) 440-9500
President: Lewis P. Hayhurst

Kobs & Draft Advertising
142 E. Ontario
Chicago, IL 60611
(312) 944-3500
President: Howard Draft

Ketchum/Mandabach & Simms
111 N. Canal St., Suite 1150
Chicago, IL 60606-7272
(312) 902-1300
Vice President: Kevin Beauseigneur

Jack Levy & Associates
222 N. Michigan Ave.
Chicago, IL 60611

(312) 332-7540
President: Jack Levy

McCann-Erickson
625 N. Michigan
Chicago, IL 60611
(312) 642-4429

McCann Healthcare Advertising
625 N. Michigan Ave.
Chicago, IL 60611
(312) 266-9200
Creative Director: Pricilla Kozel

Noble and Associates
500 N. Michigan Ave., 7th Floor
Chicago, IL 60611
(312) 644-4600
President: Bob Noble

Ogilvy & Mather
676 St. Clair St.
Chicago, IL 60611
(312) 988-2500
Personnel Director: Wendy Shields

Playboy Enterprises
680 N. Lake Shore Drive
Chicago, IL 60611
(312) 751-8000
Personnel Director: Margot Bennett
Video production, magazine publishing, cable TV.

Proctor & Gardner Advertising
111 E. Wacker Drive, Suite 321
Chicago, IL 60601
(312) 565-5400
President: Barbara Proctor

Hal Riney & Partners
54 W. Hubbard St.
Chicago, IL 60610
(312) 644-0220
Creative Director: Jonathan Harries

Schawk, Inc.
1695 River Road
Des Plaines, IL 60018
(312) 694-9080
Personnel Director: Robert Drew

Stern Walters Partners
150 E. Huron St., 12th Floor
Chicago, IL 60611
(312) 642-4990
Personnel Director: Audrey Happe

Stone & Adler
1 E. Wacker Drive
Chicago, IL 60601
(312) 346-6100
President: Craig Thomas

Tatham, Laird & Kudner
980 N. Michigan Ave.
Chicago, IL 60611
(312) 337-4400
Personnel Director: Eileen Haggerty

J. Walter Thompson Co.
900 N. Michigan Ave.
Chicago, IL 60611
(312) 951-4000
Personnel Director: Barbara Lewis

Wells Rich & Greene
111 E. Wacker Drive
Chicago, IL 60601
(312) 938-0900
President: Larry Singer

Arthur E. Wilk, Inc.
1 S. Wacker Drive
Chicago, IL 60601
(312) 828-9500
Dir., Client Services: Richard Kaplan

Young & Rubicam
1 S. Wacker Drive, Suite 1800
Chicago, IL 60606
(312) 845-4000
Contact: Personnel

Zechman & Associates
333 N. Michigan Ave.
Chicago, IL 60601
(312) 346-0551
Creative Director: Jan Zechman

Zwiren, Collins, Karo, Trusk, and Ayer
211 E. Ontario St., 4th Floor
Chicago, IL 60611

(312) 280-0830
Creative Partner: John Trusk

Breaking into film production

Tracy Barnett was working in public relations when she decided to break into film production in Chicago. Although she didn't know anyone in the industry when she began, today she is a successful freelance production manager, working on commercials, training films, and industrial films. We asked her how she did it.

"Most important was that I had the desire to do it," says Tracy, "and I didn't get discouraged. I began by making a few contacts in the industry through people I knew in related fields. Then I set up interviews with these contacts. At the end of each interview, I asked for the names of three to five other contacts in the industry. This strategy opened a lot of doors for me. I followed up each interview with a phone call. I also kept in touch with my contacts on a monthly basis."

We asked Tracy what jobs are available for beginners in the film business and what qualifications are needed for these jobs.

"Entry-level positions include production assistant, assistant prop manager, assistant stylist, assistant wardrobe manager, and grip," says Tracy. "There are no special requirements for these jobs. You don't need a degree in film to work in the business. In fact, people with film degrees begin at the same level as everybody else. What does count is intelligence and the ability to get things done quickly and efficiently. You need to think on your feet and be able to anticipate what needs to be done."

According to Tracy, freelance production assistants begin at about $75-$100 per day. More experienced production assistants can make as much as $175 per day. "But keep in mind that as a freelancer, you don't have the security of a regular paycheck," says Tracy. "You may not work every day." She advises those who need a more reliable income to look for a staff position in the industry.■

EMPLOYERS, PRODUCTION HOUSES:

AGS&R Communications
314 W. Superior St.
Chicago, IL 60610
(312) 649-4500
President: Paul Chapman

Coronet MTI Film & Video Distribution
108 Wilmot Road
Deerfield, IL 60015
(708) 940-1260

The Creative Works
650 N. Dearborn, Suite 200
Chicago, IL 60610
(312) 649-6555

Filmfair Inc.
22 W. Hubbard St.
Chicago, IL 60610
(312) 822-9200
Executive Producer: Joanne Bittman

Richard Foster Studios
157 W. Ontario St.
Chicago, IL 60610
(312) 943-9008
President: Rich Foster

Hagmann, Impastato, Stephens & Kerns
111 E. Chestnut St., #30D
Chicago, IL 60611
(312) 280-9177

Motivation Media
1245 Milwaukee Ave.
Glenview, IL 60025
(708) 297-4740

Fred A. Niles Communications
1028 W. Washington Blvd.
Chicago, IL 60607
(312) 738-4181
Executive Producer: Fred Niles

Polycom Teleproductions
142 E. Ontario

Chicago, IL 60611
(312) 337-6000
Executive Producer: Carmen Trombetta

Sedelmaier Film Productions
221 W. Ohio
Chicago, IL 60601
(312) 822-0110
President: Joe Sedelmaier

Telemation Productions
100 S. Sangamon
Chicago, IL 60607
(312) 421-4111
President: Jim Hartzer

EMPLOYERS, MARKET RESEARCH FIRMS:

Adler-Weiner Research Co.
6336 N. Lincoln
Chicago, IL 60659
(312) 463-5552
President: Betty Weiner

B. Angell & Associates
1 E. Superior St.
Chicago, IL 60611-2509
(312) 943-4400
Contact: Personnel

Arbitron Rating Co.
211 E. Ontario
Chicago, IL 60611
(312) 454-3444

Georgia Bender Research
867 N. Dearborn St., 2nd Floor
Chicago, IL 60610
(312) 642-0961
President: Georgia Bender

The Chicago Group
744 N. Wells St.
Chicago, IL 60610
(312) 751-0303
President: Lester Teichner

Conway-Millikan Corporation
875 N. Michigan Ave., Suite 4060
Chicago, IL 60611
(312) 787-4060
President: Roger Ehle

Elrick & Lavidge
10 S. Riverside Plaza
Chicago, IL 60606
(312) 726-0666
Contact: Personnel

Goldring & Co.
820 N. Orleans
Chicago, IL 60610
(312) 440-5252
President: Robert Kaden

Heakin Research
3615 Park Drive, Suite 101
Olympia Fields, IL 60461
(708) 503-0100
President: Patricia Heakin

Home Arts Guild Research Center
35 E. Wacker Drive
Chicago, IL 60601
(312) 726-7406
President: Roy Roberts

IDC Services
303 E. Ohio St., 25th Floor
Chicago, IL 60611
(312) 943-7500

Information Resources
150 N. Clinton St.
Chicago, IL 60606
(312) 726-1221
Computerized marketing research firm.

Kapuler & Associates
3436 N. Kennicott Ave.
Arlington Heights, IL 60004
(708) 870-6700
President: Stanley Kapular

Kennedy Research
70 W. Hubbard
Chicago, IL 60610
(312) 222-9400
President: Gail Kennedy

Luhrs Marketing Research Corporation
150 E. Huron, Suite 1000
Chicago, IL 60611
(312) 944-5279
President: Gay Luhrs

Market Facts
676 N. St. Clair St.
Chicago, IL 60611
(312) 280-9100
President: Thomas Payne

Market Research Corp. of America
2215 Sanders Road
Northbrook, IL 60062
(708) 480-9600

Mid-America Research
Randhurst Center
999 N. Elmhurst Road, Suite 17
Mount Prospect, IL 60056
(708) 394-1500
Contact: Personnel

National Opinion Research Center
1125 E. 25th St.
Chicago, IL 60637
(312) 702-1200
Research Director: Norman Bradburn

A.C. Nielsen Co.
Nielsen Plaza
Northbrook, IL 60062
(708) 498-6300
Research Director: Travis Wetlow

Opinion Research Corporation
500 N. Michigan Ave., Suite 2040
Chicago, IL 60611
(312) 828-9780

Social Research
945 Sheridan Road
Evanston, IL 60202
(708) 726-5981
Contact: Personnel

Statistical Tabulating Corporation
2 N. Riverside Plaza
Chicago, IL 60606
(312) 454-8000

Viewpoint, Inc.
3059 W. Palmer Square
Chicago, IL 60647
(312) 276-3900
President: Felix Burrows

EMPLOYERS, MEDIA REPRESENTATIVES:

ABC-TV Spot Sales
190 N. State, 10th Floor
Chicago, IL 60601
(312) 899-4200

Blair TV
455 N. Cityfront Plaza Drive
Chicago, IL 60611
(312) 321-6600

CBS Spot Sales
630 N. McClurg Court
Chicago, IL 60611
(312) 944-6000

Fox Television
35 E. Wacker Drive, Suite 1234
Chicago, IL 60611
(312) 372-1589

Group W Television Sales
455 N. Cityfront Plaza Drive, 6th Floor
Chicago, IL 60611
(312) 245-4830

Katz Agency
444 N. Michigan Ave., Suite 3200
Chicago, IL 60611
(312) 836-0500

Major Market Radio
205 N. Michigan Ave., Suite 2015
Chicago, IL 60601
(312) 938-0999

MGM-UA
333 N. Michigan Ave., Suite 1634
Chicago, IL 60601
(312) 263-1490

NBC Spot Sales
NBC Tower
454 N. Columbus Drive
Chicago, IL 60611
(312) 836-5555

Petry Television
410 N. Michigan Ave.
Chicago, IL 60611
(312) 644-9660

Tele Rep
401 N. Michigan Ave., Suite 3300
Chicago, IL 60611
(312) 329-1515

United Stations Radio Networks
401 N. Michigan Ave., Suite 3100
Chicago, IL 60611
(312) 836-8300

Architecture Firms

For networking in **architecture** and related fields, check out the following professional organizations listed in Chapter 5:

PROFESSIONAL ORGANIZATIONS:

American Architectural Manufacturers Association
American Institute of Architects, Chicago Chapter
Builders Association of Chicago
Chicago Architecture Foundation
Home Builders Association of Greater Chicago
Society of Architectural Administrators

For additional information, you can write to:

American Institute of Architects
1735 New York Ave., N.W.
Washington, DC 20006

Society of American Registered Architects
600 S. Michigan Ave.
Chicago, IL 60601

PROFESSIONAL PUBLICATIONS:

AIA Journal
Architectural Forum
Architectural Record
Building Design & Construction
Inland Architect
Progressive Architecture

DIRECTORIES:

AIA Membership Directory (American Institute of Architects, New York, NY)

EMPLOYERS:

Balsamo/Olson Group
1 S. 376 Summit Ave.
Oakbrook Terrace, IL 60181
(708) 629-9800
Managing Partner: Salvatore J. Balsamo

Barancik Conte & Associates
211 E. Ontario St.
Chicago, IL 60611
(312) 939-4500

Anthony Belluschi Architects
30 W. Monroe, Suite 500
Chicago, IL 60603
(312) 236-6751
Managing Partner: Anthony Belluschi

Bernheim, Kahn & Brimm
211 W. Wacker Drive, Suite 1200
Chicago, IL 60606
(312) 236-1333
Managing Partner: Fred Bernheim

Booth & Hansen
555 S. Dearborn St.
Chicago, IL 60605
(312) 427-0300
Managing Partner: Laurence Booth

Eichstaedt Architects/Planners
100 E. Irving Park Road
Roselle, IL 60172
(708) 529-3131
Managing Partner: Albert Eichstaedt

Ellerbe Becket, Inc.
200 W. Adams St., Suite 2900
Chicago, IL 60606
(312) 346-4460
Managing Partner: Stanley E. Pochron

A. Epstein & Sons International
600 W. Fulton St.
Chicago, IL 60606-1199
(312) 454-9100
Managing Partner: Sidney Epstein

Fujikawa Johnson & Associates
111 E. Wacker Drive, Suite 3015
Chicago, IL 60601

(312) 565-2727
Managing Partner: Joe Fujikawa

Gelick Foran, Ltd.
180 N. Wabash
Chicago, IL 60601
(312) 606-0646
Managing Partner: Walter Foran

Bertrand Goldberg Associates
800 Wells, Suite 180
Chicago, IL 60607
(312) 431-5200
Managing Partner: Bertrand Goldberg

Green Hiltscher Shapiro
1021 W. Adams, Suite 300
Chicago, IL 60607
(312) 243-8230

Hansen, Lind, Meyer
35 E. Wacker Drive, Suite 1600
Chicago, IL 60601
(312) 609-1300
President: James E. Zajac

Holabird & Root
300 W. Adams St.
Chicago, IL 60606
(312) 726-5960
Managing Partner: Jeff Case

Lester B. Knight & Associates
549 W. Randolph St.
Chicago, IL 60606
(312) 346-2100

Architects—getting in on the ground floor

Mary Jo Graf is Director of Communications for Loebl, Schlossman & Hackl, an architectural firm, and a former executive director of the Chicago chapter of the American Institute of Architects (AIA). We asked for her advice on how to go about getting that all-important first architectural job.

"Move to the Sun Belt," she laughed. "Chicago is a tough job market. When you're in school, do whatever you can to form good working relationships with faculty members, particularly those who also have practices. Get involved with student activities, such as your local student AIA chapter. Get as much visibility as possible.

"You have to be willing to do grunt work on your first job or jobs. Realize that you're not going to become Frank Lloyd Wright overnight—or a design partner, for that matter. You have to pay dues in this profession as in any other. How long depends on how much working experience you amass, especially part-time experience while you're still in school.

"Architecture is particularly sensitive to waves in the economy. If you get laid off, try not to be bitter. Remember that an opportunity may open up tomorrow in a firm where no job exists today."■

Legat Architects
24 N. Chapel St.
Waukegan, IL 60085
(708) 662-3535
Managing Partner: Michael Gilfillan

Loebel, Schlossman & Hackl
130 E. Randolph, Suite 3400
Chicago, IL 60601
(312) 565-1800
President: Donald Hackl

Loewenberg/Fitch Partnership
1 E. Erie St., Suite 600
Chicago, IL 60611
(312) 440-9600
Managing Partner: James R. Loewenberg

Lohan Associates
225 N. Michigan Ave.
Chicago, IL 60601
(312) 938-4455
President: Dirk Lohan

McClier
401 E. Illinois St., Suite 625
Chicago, IL 60611
(312) 836-7700
Managing Partners: Grant G.McCullagh, Frank N. Cavalier

Murphy/Jahn
35 E. Wacker Drive, Suite 300
Chicago, IL 60601

(312) 427-7300
President: Helmut Jahn

Nagle & Hartray
230 N. Michigan Ave.
Chicago, IL 60601
(312) 263-6990
President: James Nagle

O'Donnell Wicklund Pigozzi & Peterson Architects
570 Lake Cook Road
Deerfield, IL 60015
(708) 940-9600
Managing Partner: Leonard A. Peterson

Otis Associates
1450 E. American Lane, Suite 1300
Schaumburg, IL 60173
(708) 517-7100
President: Mark Hopkins

Perkins & Will
123 N. Wacker Drive
Chicago, IL 60606
(312) 977-1100
Managing Partner: Bob Barnes

Schipporeit, Inc.
351 W. Hubbard St.
Chicago, IL 60610
(312) 670-4480
President: George Schipporeit

Schmidt, Garden & Erickson
104 S. Michigan Ave.
Chicago, IL 60603
(312) 332-5070
Managing Partner: Robert Lange

Shaw & Associates
55 E. Monroe St.
Chicago, IL 60603
(312) 263-4077
Personnel: Dorothy Wilson

Skidmore, Owings & Merrill
33 W. Monroe St.
Chicago, IL 60603
(312) 641-5959
Managing Partner: Tom Eyerman

Solomon, Cordwell, Buenz & Associates
57 Grand Ave.
Chicago, IL 60610
(312) 245-5250
Managing Partner: Tom Humes

STS Consultants
111 Pfingston Road
P.O Box 10019
Northbrook, IL 60652
(708) 272-6520

Vickrey/Ovresat/Awsumb Associates
435 N. Michigan Ave., Suite 1515
Chicago, IL 60611
(312) 644-3464
President: Michael A. Toolis

VOA Associates
224 S. Michigan Ave., Suite 1400
Chicago, IL 60604
(312) 554-1400
Managing Partner: Michael A.Toolis

Harry Weese & Associates
10 W. Hubbard St.
Chicago, IL 60610
(312) 467-7030
President: Stan Allan

Wight & Co.
814 Ogden Ave.
Downers Grove, IL 60515
(708) 969-7000
Managing Partner: R.B. Wight

Wilson/Jenkins & Associates
300 Park Blvd., Suite 250
Itasca, IL 60143
(708)250-9100

Auto/Truck/Transportation Equipment

For networking in the **automotive** and related industries, check out the following professional organizations listed in Chapter 5:

PROFESSIONAL ORGANIZATIONS:

Automotive Service Industry Association
Chicago Automobile Trade Association

For additional information, you can write to:

Society of Automotive Engineers
400 Commonwealth Drive
Warrendale, PA 15096

PROFESSIONAL PUBLICATIONS:

Automotive Industries
Automotive News
Jobber Topics
Motor
Motor Age
Truck and Off Highway Industries

DIRECTORIES:

ASIA Membership Directory (Automotive Service Industries Association, Chicago, IL)
Automotive Age, Buyer's Guide Issue (Freed-Crown Publishing Co., Van Nuys, CA)
Automotive News, Market Data Book (Crain Publishing, Detroit, MI)
Directory of Automobile Aftermarket Supplies (Business Guides, New York)
Jobber Topics, Annual Marketing Directory (Irving Cloud Publishing Co., Chicago, IL)
Ward's Automotive Yearbook (Ward's Communications, Inc., Detroit, MI)

EMPLOYERS:

Ammco Tools
Wacker Park
North Chicago, IL 60064
(708) 689-1111
President: Lou Alvarez
Manufactures automotive service tools and equipment.

Amsted Industries
Boulevard Towers South, 44th Floor
205 N. Michigan Ave.
Chicago, IL 60601-5914
(312) 372-5384

Director of Personnel: Arthur M. Meske
Manufactures a wide range of products for general industry, construction, and railroads.

Atlas Lift Truck Rental & Sales
5050 N. River Road
Schiller Park, IL 60176
(708) 678-3450
Contact: Personnel
Distributes lift trucks and construction equipment.

Barco
A Subsidiary of Marison Industries
500 N. Hough St.
Barrington, IL 60010
(708) 381-1700
Human Resources Manager: Karen Borre
Manufacturers of rotary ball and swivel joints for railroad cars and engines, hydraulic hoses and fittings, and measurement devices.

Borg-Warner Corporation
200 S. Michigan Ave.
Chicago, IL 60604
(312) 322-8500
Director of Personnel: Angela D'Aversa
Widely diversified company whose principal operations are environmental control equipment for homes, industry, and transportation; chemicals; power transmission components, pumps, valves; transportation equipment; and a finance company, the Borg-Warner Acceptance Corporation.

BWD Automotive Corporation
11045 Gage Ave.
Franklin Park, IL 60131
(708) 455-3120
Personnel Director: Connie Lewis
International supplier of aftermarket parts for cars and trucks, including electrical parts, brake systems, fuel pumps, and turbochargers.

Champion Parts
2525 22nd St.
Oak Brook, IL 60521
(708) 573-6600
Human Resources Manager: Fred Pochowicz
Nation's largest remanufacturer of functional automotive, truck, and tractor parts.

C.R. Industries
900 N. State St.
Elgin, IL 60123

(708) 742-7840
Contact: Personnel
Diversified manufacturer of automotive sealing devices and other products.

Fansteel, Inc.
One Tantalum Place
North Chicago, IL 60064
(708) 689-4900
Director of Personnel: Robert Nelson
Manufacturer of refractory metals; fabricator of high-technology products for the automotive, appliance, metalworking, aerospace, recreational, electronic, and chemical industries.

Federal Signal Corporation
Regency Towers
1415 W. 22nd St.
Oak Brook, IL 60521
(708) 954-2000
Contact: Personnel
Manufacturer and worldwide supplier of signaling and communication equipment, fire trucks, parking gate signs, and electronic message displays.

Fel-Pro Inc.
7450 N. McCormick Blvd.
P.O. Box 1103
Skokie, IL 60076
(708) 674-7700
Director of Personnel: Steve Bloomfield
Major manufacturer of automotive gaskets and sealing compounds.

Firestone, Inc.
205 N. Michigan Ave.
Chicago, IL 60601-5965
(312) 819-0001
Personnel Director: Alex Kolosiwsky
Major manufacturer of industrial products; also provides automotive services.

Ford Motor Company
Chicago Automotive Assembly Division
12600 S. Torrence Ave.
Chicago, IL 60633
(312) 646-3100
Plant Manager: Joseph E. Bobnar
One of the largest manufacturers of automobiles, trucks, and heavy-duty vehicles in the world.

Ford Motor Company
Chicago Stamping Plant
1000 E. Lincoln Highway
Chicago Heights, IL 60411
(708) 756-6600
Plant Manager: Ronald G. Wallace

Furnas Electric Co.
1000 McKee St.
Batavia, IL 60510
(708) 879-6000
Director of Personnel: Gary Gardner
Manufacturer of motor controls and starters.

GATX Corporation
120 S. Riverside Plaza
Chicago, IL 60606
(312) 977-3247
Director of Personnel: J. Chris Sprung
Manufactures, leases, and sells railroad tank and freight cars and specialized motor equipment; owns and operates tank storage terminals; participates in Great Lakes and ocean shipping and capital equipment financing.

Goodyear Tire & Rubber Co.
1501 Nicholas Blvd.
Elk Grove Village, IL 60007
(708) 640-5000
Contact: Personnel
World's largest manufacturer of tires and rubber products.

Gould, Inc.
10 Gould Center
Rolling Meadows, IL 60008
(708) 640-4040
Contact: Personnel
Manufactures and sells electrical products and batteries.

Ingersoll Products Corporation
1000 W. 120th St.
Chicago, IL 60643
(312) 264-7800
President: Jose Marchesan
Manufactures agricultural disc blades.

ITEL
200 S. Michigan Ave.
Chicago, IL 60604
(312) 322-7070
Director of Personnel: Diane Kreja
Manufacturer of railway freight cars.

Joslyn Corporation
30 S, Wacker Drive
Chicago, IL 60606
(312) 454-2900
Director of Personnel: Louis Jacobson
Diversified company operating in the fields of transportation, real estate, graphic arts, hobby and household products, mechanical contracting, heating and air conditioning.

Libby-Owens-Ford
799 Roosevelt Road
Glen Ellyn, IL 60137
(708) 861-5811
District Manager: Thomas Ruppee
Manufacturer of rotary ball and swivel joints for railroad cars and engines, hydraulic hoses and fittings, and measurement devices.

Maremont Corporation
250 E. Kehoe
Carol Stream, IL 60188
(708) 861-4000
Director of Personnel: Chris Dodge
Major manufacturer of auto exhaust systems, shock absorbers, and mufflers.

Midas International Corporation
225 N. Michigan Ave.
Chicago, IL 60601
(312) 565-7500
Director, Professional Recruitment: Mose Glynn
Manufactures and markets automobile exhaust systems and mufflers.

Navistar International Transportation Co.
455 N. Cityfront Plaza Drive
Chicago, IL 60611
(312) 836-2000
Personnel Manager: Bob Goldie
One of the world's largest manufacturers of trucks, tractors, and farm equipment.

Parker-Hannifin
501 S. Wolf Road
Des Plaines, IL 60016
(708) 298-2400
Contact: Personnel
Manufacturer of components and replacement parts for hydraulic and pneumatic power systems for the industrial, automotive, aviation, space, and marine industries.

Pettibone Corporation
2700 River Road, Suite 302
Des Plaines, IL 60018
(708) 390-7840
Manufactures railway and industrial equipment.

Portec, Inc.
300 Windsor Drive
Oak Brook, IL 60521
(708) 573-4600
Personnel Director: Pat Riccio
Manufactures railroad and construction products.

Raybestos Corporation
10 N. Church St.
Elmhurst, IL 60126
Contact: Personnel
(708) 455-2662
Manufacturer of brakes.

Rockwell International
8425 S. Lamont Road
Downers Grove, IL 60515
(708) 985-9000
Contact: Personnel
Automotive Products Division manufactures leaf springs.

Scully-Jones Corporation
1901 S. Rockwell Ave.
Chicago, IL 60608
(312) 247-5900
Contact: Personnel
Manufactures parts for the auto industry such as brakes, steering systems, electronic controls, air cleaner assemblies; manufactures equipment used in the aerospace and oil drilling industries; develops forest products for the housing industry.

Sun Electric Co.
One Sun Parkway
Crystal Lake, IL 60014
(815) 459-7700
Personnel Director: Jim Nugent
Develops, manufactures, and sells diagnostic test equipment for the transportation industry.

Trailer Train Co.
101 N. Wacker Drive
Chicago, IL 60606
(312) 853-3223
Personnel Director: Jim Chandler
Maintains railroad freight car pools.

Trans Union Corporation
11 W. Jackson Blvd.
Chicago, IL 60604
(312) 431-0144
Director, Industrial Recruiting: Jane Watson
Tank car leasing; water and waste management.

Turtle Wax
5655 W. 73rd St.
Bedford Park, IL 60638
(708) 563-3600
President: Denis J. Healy
Produces waxes, polishes, and vinyl protectants.

Western Engine Co.
500 S. Lombard Road
Addison, IL 60101
(708) 620-2000
Personnel Director: Jennifer Mason
Distributes diesel products and parts.

Banks/Savings and Loans

For networking in the **banking industry** and related fields, check out the following professional organizations listed in Chapter 5:

PROFESSIONAL ORGANIZATIONS:

American Institute of Banking
Bank Administration Institute
Bank Marketing Association
Chicago Finance Exchange
Financial Managers Society for Savings Institutions
Government Finance Officers Association
Illinois Bankers Association
Investment Analysts Society of Chicago
Municipal Bond Club of Chicago
Municipal Women of Chicago
National Association of Bank Women

For additional information, you can write to:

American Bankers Association
1120 Connecticut Ave., N.W.
Washington, DC 20036

Bank Marketing Association
309 W. Washington Blvd.
Chicago, IL 60606

Mortgage Bankers Association of America
1125 15th St., N.W.
Washington, DC 20005

National Bankers Association
122 C St., N.W.
Washington, DC 20001

National Council of Savings Institutions
1101 15th St., N.W.
Washington, DC 20005

United States League of Savings Institutions
1709 New York Ave., N.W., Suite 801
Washington, DC 20006

PROFESSIONAL PUBLICATIONS:

ABA Banking Journal
American Banker
Bank Administration
Bank Marketing
Bankers Magazine
Bankers Monthly
Banking Magazine
Savings Institutions
Savings & Loan News

DIRECTORIES:

American Bank Directory (McFadden Business Publications, Norcross, GA)
American Banker's Guide to the First 5,000 U.S. Banks (American Banker, New York, NY)
Callahan's Credit Union Directory (Callahan and Associates, Washington, DC)
Directory of American Savings and Loan Associations (T.K. Sanderson, Baltimore, MD)
Money Market Directory (Money Market Directories, Charlottesville, VA)
Moody's Bank and Finance Manual (Moody's Investor Services, New York, NY)
Polk's Bank Directory (R.L. Polk, Nashville, TN)
Rand McNally Bankers Directory (Rand McNally, Chicago, IL)
U.S. Savings and Loan Directory (Rand McNally, Chicago, IL)

EMPLOYERS:

Affiliated Bank/North Shore
4747 Dempster Ave.
Skokie, IL 60076
(708) 674-3600
Personnel Director: Barbara Buscemi

Amalgamated Trust & Savings
1 W. Monroe St.
Chicago, IL 60603
(312) 822-3030

American National Bank of Arlington Heights
1 N. Dunton Ave.
Arlington Heights, IL 60005
(708) 632-8900

American National Bank & Trust Co. of Chicago
33 N. LaSalle St.
Chicago, IL 60690
(312) 661-5000
V.P. Human Resources: Ron Majka

American Trust & Savings Bank
1321 119th St.
Whiting, IN 46394
(219) 659-0850

AmeriFed Federal Savings Bank
120 N. Scott St.
Joliet, IL 60431
(815) 727-2601
Personnel Director: Robert Biedron

Arlington Heights Federal Savings & Loan
25 E. Campbell St.
Arlington Heights, IL 60005
(708) 255-9000
Personnel Director: Marlene Kusera

Avondale Federal Savings Bank
20 N. Clark St.
Chicago, IL 60602
(312) 782-6200
Personnel Director: Charles Viskocil

Bank of Ravenswood
1825 W. Lawrence Ave.
Chicago, IL 60640
(312) 989-3000

Baxter Credit Union
1425 Lake Cook Road
Deerfield, IL 60015
(708) 940-6300

Bell Federal Savings & Loan
79 W. Monroe St.
Chicago, IL 60603
(312) 346-1000
Personnel Director: Nancy Owens

Boulevard Bank
410 N. Michigan Ave.
Chicago, IL 60611
(312) 836-6500
Personnel Director: Lies Vander Ark

Calumet National Bank
5231 Hohman Ave.
Hammond, IN 46320
(219) 932-6900
Personnel Director: Barbara Linos

Chicago Title & Trust Co.
111 W. Washington Blvd.
Chicago, IL 60602
(312) 630-2400
Director of Operations: Caroline Carter

Chicago-Tokyo Bank
40 N. Dearborn St.
Chicago, IL 60602
(312) 236-1200
Personnel Director: Kathleen Spellacy

Citicorp of Chicago
1 S. Dearborn St.
Chicago, IL 60603
(312) 977-5000
Personnel Director: Timothy F. Burns

Clyde Federal Savings & Loan
7222 W. Cermak Road
North Riverside, IL 60546
(708) 442-6700
Personnel Director: Maryann Penczak

Cole Taylor Bank/Drovers
1542 W. 47th St.
Chicago, IL 60609
(312) 927-7000
Director of Human Resources: Judy Bunting

Cole Taylor Bank/Ford City
7601 S. Cicero Ave.
Chicago, IL 60652
(312) 284-3500
Personnel Director: Marcy Ryder

Commercial National Bank
4800 N. Western Ave.
Chicago, IL 60625
(312) 989-5100
Personnel Director: Cindy Neil

Concordia Federal Savings & Loan
2320 Thornton Road
Lansing, IL 60438
(708) 474-1600
Personnel Director: Barbara Gardner

Continental Illinois National Bank & Trust Co.
231 S. LaSalle St.
Chicago, IL 60697
(312) 828-2345
V.P., Personnel: Michael Timley

Corporate America
970 Oaklawn Ave.
Elmhurst, IL 60126
(708) 681-7300

Cragin Federal Savings & Loan
5200 W. Fullerton Ave.
Chicago, IL 60639
(312) 889-1000
Personnel Director: Anna Leal

Des Plaines National Bank
678 Lee St.
Des Plaines, IL 60016
(708) 296-5000
Personnel Representative: Michelle Berg

Edison
300 W. Adams St., Suite 330
Chicago, IL 60606
(312) 332-6357

Enterprise Savings Bank
200 S. Wacker
Chicago, IL 60606
(312) 930-0900
Personnel Director: Diane Caprio

Exchange National Bank of Chicago
120 S. LaSalle St.
Chicago, IL 60603
(312) 781-8000
Personnel Director: John Scully

Federal Reserve Bank of Chicago
230 S. LaSalle St., P.O. Box 834
Chicago, IL 60604
(312) 322-5322
Personnel Administrator: Bob DiCosola

Financial Federal Savings & Loan
21110 Western Ave.
Olympia Fields, IL 60461
(708) 747-2000
Personnel Director: Kay Wing

First Chicago Bank of Mount Prospect
111 E. Busse Ave.
Mount Prospect, IL 60056
(708) 398-4000
Director of Human Resources: James J. Smith

First Chicago Bank of Oak Park
1048 W. Lake St.
Oak Park, IL 60301
(312) 626-9400
Personnel Director: Terry Moore

You have to work to keep banker's hours

We asked the Executive Vice President of a major bank if there were any tricks to succeeding in banking.

"Yeah. You work hard," said the executive. "You have to realize that banking is a sales job. A banker is essentially a salesperson in a service business. If you don't like the idea of selling a service—and sometimes being treated like a servant, which is all part of the business—then you really shouldn't be in banking. But the people who succeed do very well indeed."■

First Illinois Corporation
800 Davis St.
Evanston, IL 60204
(708) 273-4200
Personnel Director: Sharon Kawasaki

First Midwest Bank
214 Washington St.

Waukegan, IL 60085
(708) 623-1250
Personnel Director: D. Langher

First Midwest Bank/Illinois
50 W. Jefferson St.
Joliet, IL 60431
(815) 727-5222
Vice President, Personnel: Diane Mill

First National Bank of Chicago
One First National Plaza
Chicago, IL 60670
(312) 732-4000
V. P., Management & Professional Development: Lucinda Smith

First National Bank of Cicero
6000 W. Cermak Road
Cicero, IL 60650
(708) 656-3000

First National Bank of Des Plaines
701 Lee St.
Des Plaines, IL 60016
(708) 827-4411
Personnel Director: Katie Speth

First National Bank of Elgin
6 Fountain Square Plaza
Elgin, IL 60120
(708) 697-1100
Personnel Director: Mary Ann Meyers

First National Bank of Evergreen Park
3101 W. 95th St.
Evergreen Park, IL 60642
(708) 779-6700
Personnel Director: Gaines Wilson

First National Bank of Joliet
78 N. Chicago St.
Joliet, IL 60431
(815) 726-4371

First Nationwide Bank
281 Lawrencewood
Niles, IL 60648
(708) 990-8844
Personnel Director: Karen Antink

Gainer Bank of Indiana
P.O. Box 209
Gary, IN 46404
(219) 465-9700

Gainer Bank of Indiana
479 State St.
Hammond, IN 46320
(219) 933-6240

Gary-Wheaton Bank
120 W. Wesley
Wheaton, IL 60187
(708) 665-2600
Human Resources: Jodi Benware

Glenview State Bank
800 Waukegan Road
Glenview, IL 60025
(708) 273-5166
Personnel Director: Joan Cantrell

Great American Federal Savings & Loan
1001 Lake St.
Oak Park, IL 60301
(708) 383-5000
V. P., Personnel: Richard Klancer

Great Lakes Credit Union
Building 290
Great Lakes, IL 60088-8290
(708) 689-1510

Harris Bank Barrington, NA
201 S. Grove
Barrington, IL 60010-4493
(708) 381-4000

Harris Trust & Savings Bank
P.O. Box 765
Chicago, IL 60690
(312) 461-2121
V. P., Personnel: David S. Finch

Hinsdale Federal Savings & Loan
Grant Sq., P.O. Box 386
Hinsdale, IL 60522
(708) 323-1776
Personnel Director: Helen Bentel

Home Federal Savings & Loan
16 N. Spring St.

Elgin, IL 60120
(708) 742-3800
Personnel Director: Pat Lenard

Horizon Federal Savings
825 Green Bay Road
Wilmette, IL 60091
(708) 251-7200
Personnel Director: Linda Sepp

Household Bank
6655 W. Cermak Road
Berwyn, IL 60402
(708) 749-1900
Personnel Director: Lisa Granger

Household International
2700 Sanders Road
Prospect Heights, IL 60070
(708) 564-5000
Personnel Director: Shayon Kvam

Indiana Federal Savings & Loan
6760 Broadway
Merrillville, IN 46410
(219) 769-3481

LaGrange Federal Savings & Loan
1215 E. 31st St.
LaGrange Park, IL 60525
(708) 354-6000

Lake Shore National Bank
605 N. Michigan Ave.
Chicago, IL 60611
(708) 787-1900
Personnel Director: Richard Nevell

LaSalle Bank, Lake View
3201 N. Ashland Ave.
Chicago, IL 60657
(312) 525-2180
Personnel Director: Martin Quinn

LaSalle National Bank
135 S. LaSalle St.
Chicago, IL 60603
(312) 443-2000
Human Resources Coordinator: MaryAnn Hagerty

Lincoln National Bank
3959 N. Lincoln Ave.

Chicago, IL 60613
(312) 549-7100

Lyons Savings & Loan
440 Ogden Ave.
Hinsdale, IL 60521
(708) 323-2900

Manufacturers Bank
1200 N. Ashland Ave.
Chicago, IL 60622
(312) 278-4040

Marquette National Bank
6316 W. Western Ave.
Chicago, IL 60636
(312) 476-5100

Merchandise National Bank
Merchandise Mart Plaza
Chicago, IL 60654
(312) 836-8000

Mid-America Federal Savings & Loan
5900 W. Cermak Road
Cicero, IL 60650
(708) 242-2646

Mid-America Federal Savings & Loan
55th & Holmes
Clarendon Hills, IL 60514
(708) 325-7300
Personnel Development and Compliance Manager: Theresa Colson

Mid City National Bank
801 W. Madison St.
Chicago, IL 60607
(312) 421-7600

National Boulevard Bank of Chicago
410 N. Michigan Ave.
Chicago, IL 60611
(312) 836-6500
Personnel Director: Jack Stocky

NBD Bank Evanston, NA
1603 Orrington Ave.
Evanston, IL 60204
(708) 273-5000
Personnel Director: Sandra Byrnes

NBD Highland Park Bank NA
513 Central Ave.
Highland Park, IL 60035
(708) 432-1800
Personnel Director: Barbara Greenberg

NBD Park Ridge Bank
1 S. Northwest Hwy.
Park Ridge, IL 60068
(708) 399-4100
Personnel Officer: Patricia A. Kosla

NBD/Skokie
8001 Lincoln Ave.
Skokie, IL 60077
(708) 673-2500
Personnel Director: Jason Grade

North Shore National Bank
1737 W. Howard St.
Chicago, IL 60626
(312) 743-2112
Personnel Director: Ruth Christianson

Northern Trust Bank/Lake Forest
265 E. Deerpath Road
Lake Forest, IL 60045
(708) 234-5100
Personnel Director: Mrs. Pat O'Malley

Northern Trust Bank, O'Hare
8501 W. Higgins Road
Chicago, IL 60631-2801
(312) 693-5555
Personnel Director: Shirley Shipp

Northern Trust Corporation
50 S. LaSalle St.
Chicago, IL 60675
(312) 630-6000
Senior V. P., Human Resources: William Setterstrom

Northwest National Bank of Chicago
4747 W. Irving Park Road
Chicago, IL 60641
(312) 777-7700
V.P., Personnel: Elizabeth Croft

Northwestern Savings & Loan
2300 N. Western Ave.
Chicago, IL 60647
(312) 489-2300

Old Kent Bank
105 S. York Ave.
Elmhurst, IL 60126
(708) 941-5200
Personnel Director: James Bristow

Old Kent Bank Chicago
233 S. Wacker Drive
Chicago, IL 60606
(312) 876-4200
Personnel Recruiter: Carolyn Reed

Olympic Federal
6201 W. Cermak Road
Berwyn, IL 60402
(708) 795-8700

Pathway Financial
99 W. Washington St.
Chicago, IL 60602
(312) 346-4200

Pioneer Bank & Trust Co.
4000 W. North Ave.
Chicago, IL 60639
(312) 772-8600
Personnel Director: Donna Evinger

St. Paul Federal Savings & Loan
6700 W. North Ave.
Chicago, IL 60635
(312) 622-5000
Employment Manager: Robert Pfeiffer

South Holland Trust & Savings Bank
16178 S. Park Ave.
South Holland, IL 60473-1524
(708) 333-2600
Personnel Director: Kevin Botma

Suburban Bancorp
50 N. Brockway
Palatine, IL 60067
(708) 359-1077
Bank holding company.

Talman Home Savings & Loan
5501 S. Kedzie Ave.
Chicago, IL 60629
(312) 434-3322
Human Resources Director: Kris Nelson

United Air Lines Credit Union
P.O. Box 66100
Chicago, IL 60666
(312) 956-2336

United Federal Savings & Loan
4192 S. Archer Ave.
Chicago, IL 60632
(312) 847-1140
Personnel Director: Patricia Barrera

United Savings of America
3335 N. Ashland Ave.
Chicago, IL 60657
(312) 477-7770

Book Publishers and Distributors

For networking in **book publishing** and related fields, check out the following professional organizations listed in Chapter 5:

PROFESSIONAL ORGANIZATIONS:

American Library Association
American Society of Journalists and Authors
Chicago Book Clinic
Chicago Women in Publishing
Independent Writers of Chicago
Lawyers for the Creative Arts

For additional information, you can write to:

American Booksellers Association
122 E. 42nd St.
New York, NY 10017

Association of American Publishers
1718 Connecticut Ave., N.W., Suite 700
Washington, DC 20009-1148

PROFESSIONAL PUBLICATIONS:

American Bookseller
Editor and Publisher
Library Journal
Publishers Weekly
Small Press

DIRECTORIES:

American Book Trade Directory (R.R. Bowker, New York, NY)
Literary Market Place (R.R. Bowker, New York, NY)

EMPLOYERS:

Academy Chicago, Ltd.
213 W. Institute Place
Chicago, IL 60610
(312) 644-1723
Vice President: Jordan Miller
Book publisher.

Baker & Taylor Co.
501 S. Gladiolus St.
Momence, IL 60954
(815) 472-2444
General Manager: Richard L. Porter
Book wholesaler.

Caroline House Publishers
5S 250 Frontenac Road
Naperville, IL 60563
(708) 983-6400
President: Art Soderlund
Book publisher.

Chicago Review Press
814 N. Franklin St.
Chicago, IL 60610
(312) 337-0747
Publisher: Curt Matthews
Book publisher.

Children's Press
5440 N. Cumberland
Chicago, IL 60656
(312) 693-0800
Personnel Director: Carol Werkmeister
Book publisher.

Computer Book Service
4201 Raymond Drive
Hillside, IL 60162
(708) 547-4400
Asst. Vice President: Carol Kloster
Distributor.

Contemporary Books
180 N. Michigan Ave.

Chicago, IL 60601
(312) 782-9181
President: Harvey Plotnick
Book publisher.

D. C. Cook Co.
850 N. Grove Ave.
Elgin, IL 60120
(708) 741-2400
Product Manager: Bruce Adair
Religious book publisher.

Dartnell Corporation
4660 N. Ravenswood Ave.
Chicago, IL 60640
(312) 561-4000
President: Clark W. Fetridge
Business book publisher.

DBI Books
4092 Commercial Ave.
Northbrook, IL 60062
(312) 272-6310
President: Charles T. Hartigan
Book publisher.

Dearborn Financial Publishing
520 N. Dearborn St.
Chicago, IL 60610
(312)836-4400
Personnel Director: Gwen Collins
Trade, reference, and business books.

Reuben H. Donnelley Corporation
205 N. Michigan Ave.
Prudential Plaza
Chicago, IL 60601
(312) 861-3500
Yellow Pages publisher.

Dow Jones- and
Richard D. Irwin
1818 Ridge Road
Homewood, IL 60430
(708) 798-6000
Human Resources Director: Wendy Poppers
Book publisher.

Encyclopedia Britannica
310 S. Michigan Ave.
Chicago, IL 60604
(312) 347-7000

Personnel Manager: Joan Downey
Encyclopedia publisher.

Follett Corporation
1000 W. Washington Blvd.
Chicago, IL 60607
(312) 666-4300
Personnel Director: Carl Dickes
Wholesaler.

Great Books of the Western World
310 S. Michigan Ave.
Chicago, IL 60604
(312) 347-7000
Anthology publisher.

Johnson Publishing
820 S. Michigan Ave.
Chicago, IL 60605
(312) 322-9200
Personnel Director: LaDoris Foster
Publishes books and magazines.

Charles Levy Circulating Co.
1200 N. North Branch St.
Chicago, IL 60622
(312) 440-4400
Employment Manager: Terri Umland
Book and periodical distributor.

McDougall Littel & Co.
1560 Sherman Ave.
Evanston, IL 60201
(708) 869-2300
President: Alfred McDougall
Educational publisher.

National Textbook Co.
4255 W. Touhy Ave.
Lincolnwood, IL 60646
(708) 679-4210
President: S. William Pattis
Educational and trade book publisher.

Nelson-Hall Publishers
111 N. Canal St.
Chicago, IL 60606
(312) 930-9446
Vice President: Steve Ferrara
Book publisher.

North Shore Distributors
411 N. Wolf Road
Wheeling, IL 60090
(708) 537-6900
President: James A. Levy
Book and periodical distributor.

Official Airline Guides
2000 Clearwater Drive
Oak Brook, IL 60521
(708) 574-6000
Employment Manager: Mike Roberts
Directory publisher.

Open Court Publishing Co.
407 S. Dearborn, Suite 600
Chicago, IL 60604
(312) 939-1500
Personnel Director: Madeline Dupys
Book and magazine publisher.

Publications International
7373 N. Cicero Ave.
Lincolnwood, IL 60646
(708) 676-3470
President: Louis Weber
Book and periodical publisher.

Quality Books
918 Sherwood Drive
Lake Bluff, IL 60044
(708) 295-2010
President: Tom Drewes
Book distributor.

Rand McNally & Co.
8255 N. Central Park Ave.
Skokie, IL 60680
(708) 267-6868
V.P. Industrial Relations: Don Helm
Book and map publisher.

Science Research Associates
155 N. Wacker Drive
Chicago, IL 60606
(312) 984-7000
Contact: Personnel Director
Educational publisher.

Scott, Foresman & Co.
1900 E. Lake St.
Glenview, IL 60025

(708) 729-3000
Human Resource Manager: Stuart Cone
Educational publisher.

Scripture Press
1825 College Ave.
Wheaton, IL 60187
(708 668-6000
Religious book publisher.

Standard Rate & Data Co.
3004 Glenview Road
Wilmette, IL 60091
(708) 256-6067
Personnel Director: Dennis Kave
Directory publisher.

Surrey Books, Inc.
230 E. Ohio, Suite 120
Chicago, IL 60611
(312) 751-7330
Book publisher.

University of Chicago Press
5801 S. Ellis Ave.
Chicago, IL 60637
(312) 702-8878
Head Administrator: Morris Phillipson
Book and periodical publisher.

Vance Publishing Corporation
400 Knightsbridge Parkway
Lincolnshire, IL 60069
(708) 634-2600
Personnel Direstor: Ann O'Neil

World Book Encyclopedia
510 Merchandise Mart Plaza
Chicago, IL 60654
(312) 245-3456
Editorial Director: Robert O. Veleny
Encyclopedia publisher.

Yearbook Medical Publishers
200 N. LaSalle
Chicago, IL 60601
(312) 726-9733
Director, Human Resources: Susan Price
Directory publisher.

Broadcasting

For networking in **TV, radio, cable,** and related fields, check out the following professional organizations listed in Chapter 5:

PROFESSIONAL ORGANIZATIONS:

AFTRA
American Women in Radio and Television
Association for Multi-Image
Broadcast Advertising Club of Chicago
Center for New Television
Chicago Area Broadcast Public Affairs Association
National Academy of Television Arts and Sciences
Radio Advertising Bureau
Social Service Communicators
Society of Broadcast Engineers
Women in Cable
Women in Communications

For additional information, you can write to:

American Women in Radio and Television
1101 Connecticut Ave.
Washington, DC 20036

Broadcast Promotion Association
P.O. Box 5102
Lancaster, PA 17601

National Academy of Television Arts and Sciences
110 W. 57th St.
New York, NY 10019

National Association of Broadcasters
1771 N St., N.W.
Washington, DC 20036

National Association of Television Program Executives
P.O. Box 5272
Lancaster, PA 17601

National Cable Television Association
1724 Massachusetts Ave., N.W.
Washington, DC 20036

National Radio Broadcasters Association
2033 M St., N.W.
Washington, DC 20036

Radio-Television News Directors Association
1735 DeSales St., N.W.
Washington, DC 20036

Television Information Office
745 Fifth Ave.
New York, NY 10022

PROFESSIONAL PUBLICATIONS:

Billboard
Broadcast Communications
Broadcasting Magazine
Cable Television News
Communications News
Variety

DIRECTORIES:

Broadcasting Cable Source Book (Broadcasting Publishing Co., Washington, DC)
Broadcasting Yearbook (Broadcasting Publishing Co., Washington, D.C.)
Cable/Radio/Television Contacts (Larimi Media Directories, Billboard Publications, New York)
Television Fact Book (Television Digest, Washington, DC)
TV/Radio Age Ten-City Directory (TV Editorial Corp., New York, NY)

EMPLOYERS:

American Broadcasting Companies
190 N. State St.
Chicago, IL 60601
(312) 750-7777
V. P. & General Manager: Joseph Ahern
Owns and operates WLS-TV, WLS-AM radio, WLS-FM radio, WYTZ-FM radio; local and network news bureaus; local, network, and spot sales offices.

Bonneville International Corporation
8833 Gross Point Road
Skokie, IL 60077
(708) 677-5900

V. P. & General Manager: Chet Redpath
Owns and operates WCLR-FM radio.

Burnham Broadcasting
980 N.Michigan Ave., Suite 1200
Chicago, IL 60611
(312) 787-9800
Managing General Partner: Peter Desnoes
Owns and operates various network affiliates.

Cablevision of Chicago
820 Madison St.
Oak Park, IL 60302
(708) 383-9110
Cable TV outlet.

CBS, Inc.
630 N. McClurg Court
Chicago, IL 60611
(312) 944-6000
V.P. & General Manager: William Applegate
Owns and operates WBBM-TV, WBBM-AM radio, WBBM-FM radio; local and network news bureaus; local, network, and spot sales offices.

Century Broadcasting Corporation
875 N. Michigan Ave., Suite 4145
Chicago, IL 60611
(312) 922-1000
President: George Collias
Owns and operates WLOO-FM and WCZE-AM.

Chicago Educational Television Association
303 E. Wacker Drive
3 Illinois Center
Chicago, IL 60601
(312) 565-5000
President: Al Antlitz
Operates WTTW-TV and WFMT-FM radio.

Colby Broadcast Corporation
6405 Olcott Ave.
Hammond, IN 46320
(219) 844-1230
General Manager: Judy Grambo
Owns and operates WJOB-AM radio.

Combined Broadcasting
541 N. Fairbanks, Suite 1100
Chicago, IL 60611
(312) 751-6666

General Manger: Steve Friedheim
Owns and operates WGBO-TV.

Continental Cablevision
1575 Rohlwing Road
Rolling Meadows, IL 60008
(708) 577-1818
Cable TV outlet.

Cox Enterprises
150 N. Michigan Ave., Suite 1040
Chicago, IL 60601
(312) 781-7300
General Manager: Marc Morgan
Owns and operates WCKG-FM radio.

Evergreen Media
875 N. Michigan Ave., Suite 3650
Chicago, IL 60611
(312) 440-5270
General Manager: Larry Wert
Owns and operates WLUP-FM radio and WLUP-AM radio.

First Media of Illinois
875 N. Michigan Ave., Suite 1310
Chicago, IL 60611
(312) 649-0099
General Manager: Steve Ennen
Owns and operates WUSN-FM radio.

Fox Television Stations
205 N. Michigan Ave.
Chicago, IL 60601
(312) 565-5532
General Manager: Stuart Powell
Owns and operates WFLD-TV, a UHF television station.

Gannett Media Sales
444 S. Michigan Ave.
Chicago, IL 60604
(312) 527-0552
General Manager: Marv Dyson
Owns and operates WGCI-FM radio; WVON-AM radio.

Illiana Broadcasters
2915 Bernice Road
Lansing, IL 60438
(708) 895-1400
Attention: Program Director
Operates WLNR-FM radio.

Infinity Broadcasting Co.
180 N. Michigan Ave., Suite 1200
Chicago, IL 60601
(312) 977-1800
General Sales Manager: Louis Gredell
Owns and operates WJJD-AM radio and WJMK-FM radio.

Jones Intercable
8 E. Galena Blvd., #302
Aurora, IL 60506
(708) 897-0440
Personnel Director: John Savas
Cable TV outlet.

Metrovision Southwest Cook County
10335 S. Roberts Road
Palos Hills, IL 60465
(708) 430-4840
Contact: Personnel Director
Cable TV outlet.

Metrowest Corporation
2151 N. Elston Ave.
Chicago, IL 60614
(312) 276-5050
Program Manager: Neal Sabin
Owns and operates WPWR-TV.

Midway Broadcasting Corporation
3350 S. Kedzie Ave.
Chicago, IL 60623
(312) 247-6200
President, C.E.O. & General Manager: Wesley South

National Broadcasting Co.
NBC Tower
454 N. Columbus Drive
Chicago, IL 60611
(312) 836-5555
Employee Relations: William Fallon
Owns and operates WMAQ-TV and WKQX-FM radio; local and network news bureaus; local, network, and spot sales offices.

New Age Broadcasting Inc. of Illinois
2400 E. Devon Ave.
Des Plaines, IL 60018
(708) 297-8430
President: Jeff Crabtree
Owns and operates WTWV-FM radio.

Northern Illinois Broadcasting Co.
1140 W. Erie St.

Chicago, IL 60622
(312) 633-9700
General Manager: Sonia Florian
Owns and operates WNIB-FM radio.

Pyramid West Associates
444 N. Michigan Ave., Suite 300
Chicago, IL 60611
(312) 645-9550
General Manager: John Gehron
Owns and operates WNUA-FM radio.

RKO General
130 E. Randolph, Suite 2303
Chicago, IL 60601
(312) 861-8100
General Manager: Kelly Seaton
Owns and operates WFYR-FM radio.

Sonderling Radio Corporation
408 S. Oak Park Ave.
Oak Park, IL 60302
(708) 524-3200
General Manager: Barry Mayo
Owns and operates WBMX-FM radio.

Telecommunications, Inc., of Illinois
1201 Feehanville Drive
Mt. Prospect, IL 60056
(708) 299-9220
Cable TV outlet.

Tichenor Media Systems
625 N. Michigan Ave., 3rd Floor
Chicago, IL 60611
(312) 649-0105
General Manager: Chuck Brooks
Owns and operates WOJO-FM radio and WIND-AM radio.

Tribune Broadcasting Co.
2501 W. Bradley Place
Chicago, IL 60618
(312) 528-2311
Contact: Personnel
Owns and operates WGN-TV and WGN-AM radio.

United Cable TV of Northern Illinois
300 Carpenter Blvd.
Carpentersville, IL 60110
(708) 428-6161
Contact: Personnel
Cable TV outlet.

United Cable TV of Northern Indiana
844 169th St.
Hammond, IN 46320
(219) 932-4111
Contact: Personnel

U.S. Cable of Northern Indiana
6161 Cleveland St.
Merrillville, IN 46410
(219) 887-6008
Contact: Personnel

Viacom International
150 N. Michigan Ave., Suite 1135
Chicago, IL 60601
(312) 329-8840
General Manager: Phil Redo
Owns and operates WLAK-FM radio.

WCFC-TV
Christian Communications of Chicagoland
20 N. Wacker Drive, Suite 2000
Chicago, IL 60606
(312) 977-3838
President: Jerry Rose

WCIU-TV
141 W. Jackson Blvd., Suite 3200
Chicago, IL 60604
(312) 663-0260
General Manager: Howard Shapiro
Owns and operates WCIU-TV, a UHF television station.

Breaking into broadcasting

Susan Eggleton is an executive at a Chicago radio station. We asked her how to get started in broadcasting.

"Persevere," she says. "One of my first interviews was with the personnel director of a television station in Cleveland. 'Do you realize,' he said, 'that Ohio State University graduated 600 communications majors this year alone? There aren't that many jobs in the whole state.'

"That was a sobering thought. It discourages a lot of people. But you have to keep in there. Send out resumes, read the trades, see who's switching formats, and all that. Do anything on the side that might result in a good lead.

The year after I graduated from college, I took a news writing course that was taught by the producer of 'Two on Two' at WBBM-TV. In Chicago there are a lot of broadcasting professionals teaching all over the city—at Columbia, Loyola, Northwestern. Taking a course from a working professional can lead to valuable contacts.

"Another important thing is to treat your contacts with respect. Broadcasting is a volatile business. You can't afford to burn a lot of bridges or alienate a lot of people. Somebody can be your assistant one day and your boss the next." ■

Westinghouse Broadcasting Co.
NBC Tower
455 N. Cityfront Plaza Drive
Chicago, IL 60611
(312) 670-6767
General Manager: Rick Starr
Owns and operates WMAQ-AM radio.

Windy City Broadcasting Co.
4949 W. Belmont Ave.
Chicago, IL 60641
(312) 777-1700
President: Daniel Lee
Owns and operates WXRT-FM and WSBC-AM.

WSNS-TV
430 W. Grant Pl.
Chicago, IL 60614
(312) 929-1200
Contact: Personnel
Owns and operates WSNS-TV, a UHF television station.

WTTW Television
5400 N. St. Louis Ave.
Chicago, IL 60625
(312) 583-5000
President: William J. McCarter
Operates WTTW-TV, PBS television station.

WXEZ Radio
875 N. Michigan Ave., Suite 3201
Chicago, IL 60611
(312) 440-8200
General Manager: Jim Haviland
Owns and operates WXEZ-AM/FM radio.

WYCC-TV
7500 S. Pulaski Road

Chicago, IL 60652
(312) 838-4853
General Manager: Elynne Chaplik
Operates Channel 20 for the City Colleges of Chicago.

Chemicals, Paints, and Coatings

For additional information, you can write to:

PROFESSIONAL ORGANIZATIONS:

American Chemical Society
1155 16th St., N.W.
Washington, DC 20036

Chemical Specialties Manufacturers Association
1913 I St., N.W.
Washington, DC 20006

PROFESSIONAL PUBLICATIONS:

Chemical and Engineering News
Chemical Marketing Reporter
Chemical Week

DIRECTORIES:

Chemical and Engineering News, Career Opportunities issue (American Chemical Society, Washington, DC)
Chemical Week, Buyer's Guide issue (McGraw Hill, New York, NY)

EMPLOYERS:

Allied Signal Chemical Corporation
1701 E. Woodfield Road
Schaumburg, IL 60173
(708) 517-4832
Contact: Personnel
Diversified manufacturer of industrial and specialty chemical products.

American Cyanamid Co.
1100 E. Business Center Drive
Mount Prospect, IL 60056
(708) 827-8871
Contact: Personnel

A diversified corporation with several divisions: Agricultural Div., Cyanamid Americas Div., Cyanamid Europe Div., Fibers Div., Formica Corp., Household Products Div., Industrial Chemicals Div., Organic Chemicals Div., Plant Food Div., Jacqueline Cochran Div., and Lederle Laboratories Div.

Amsted Industries
205 N. Michigan Ave., 44th Floor
Chicago, IL 60601
(312) 645-1700
Manager of Personnel: Shirley Whitesell
Manufactures a wide range of products for general industry, construction, and railroads.

Binks Manufacturing Co.
9201 W. Belmont Ave.
Franklin Park, IL 60131
(708) 671-3000
Personnel Director: Hank Binder
Manufactures spray equipment.

CF Industries
Salem Lake Drive
Long Grove, IL 60047
(708) 438-9500
Contact: Personnel
Manufactures chemical fertilizers; operates petroleum refinery.

Chemcentral Corporation
P.O.Box 730
Bedford Park, IL 60499-0730
(708) 594-7000
President: H. D. Wenstrup
Wholesale distributor of chemical raw materials.

Chemical Waste Management
3001 Butterfield Road
Oak Brook, IL 60521
(708) 218-1500
Vice President: Victor J. Barnhart
Provides treatment and disposal of hazardous waste.

Culligan International Co.
One Culligan Parkway
Northbrook, IL 60062
(708) 267-1330
Personnel Director: Dave Horsley
Manufacturer and distributor of water treatment products and systems.

Daubert Industries
1 Westbrook Corporate Center, Suite 1000
Westchester, IL 60514
(708) 409-5000
Personnel Director: William Gaeth

DeSoto, Inc.
1700 S. Mount Prospect Road
Des Plaines, IL 60017
(708) 391-9000
Contact: Personnel
Diversified manufacturer of chemical coatings, furniture, household cleaning products, and Sears paints.

Eastman Kodak Co.
Midwest Marketing & Distribution
1901 W. 22nd St.
Oak Brook, IL 60522
(708) 954-6000
Midwest marketing and distribution center for the photography giant.

Farley Industries
6300 Sears Tower
233 S. Wacker Drive
Chicago, IL 60606
(312) 876-7000
Corporate Staff Personnel Manager: Sherry Mc Creary
A management and holding company that manufactures and markets industrial, chemical, and consumer products through its subsidiaries.

FMC Corporation
200 E. Randolph Drive
Chicago, IL 60601
(312) 861-6000
V. P., Human Resources: Lawrence P. Holleran
Manufactures broad range of chemicals and machinery in the following areas: industrial chemicals, energy equipment & services, military equipment and systems.

Great American Management & Investment
2 N. Riverside Plaza, 7th Floor
Chicago, IL 60606
(312) 648-5656
Personnel Director: Carol Reinhart
Manufactures agricultural chemicals.

Great Lakes Terminal & Transports Corporation
1750 N. Kingsbury St.
Chicago, IL 60614
(312) 664-3500

President: Louis Dehmlow
Distributes raw materials for solvents, industrial chemicals, plastics, and rubber.

Handschy Industries
120 25th Ave.
Bellwood, IL 60104
(708) 276-6400
Contact: Personnel
Produces a wide range of chemicals for the graphic arts industry, including printers' inks; owns St. Clair Manufacturing Co., maker of decorative papers, and Pak-Well Paper Products, maker of specialty packaging.

Industrial Coatings Group
2141 S. Jefferson St.
Chicago, IL 60616
(312) 421-4030
Personnel Director: George Pentaris
Produces coated fabrics for book industry.

International Minerals and Chemical Corporation
310 Heuhl Road
Northbrook, IL 60062
(708) 564-2600
Recruitment Manager: Tom Miller
World's largest producer of fertilizer materials.

Lawter International
990 Skokie Blvd.
Northbrook, IL 60062
(708) 498-4700
Contact: Personnel
Manufactures and markets printing inks and thermographic compounds.

Lever Brothers Co./ Cheesborough Ponds
6901 W. 65th St.
Chicago, IL 60638
(312) 735-6800
Personnel Manager: Mary Ellen Bilotta
Leading manufacturer of soaps and household products.

Liquid Air Corporation
5230 S. East Ave.
Countryside, IL 60525
(708) 482-8400
Contact: Personnel
Manufacturer of dry ice and fire protection equipment.

Material Sciences Corporation
2300 E. Pratt Blvd.

Elk Grove Village, IL 60007
(708) 439-8270
Personnel Director: John Schram
Coated materials company.

Morton International
110 N. Wacker Drive
Chicago, IL 60606
(312) 807-2000
Vice President, Human Resources: John C. Hedley
Manufacturer of salt and chemicals.

Nalco Chemical Co.
Nalco Center
Naperville, IL 60563
(708) 305-1000
Employment Manager: Karen Nordquist
Manufacturer of specialized industrial chemicals.

Proctor & Gamble Mfg. Co.
1232 W. North Ave.
Chicago, IL 60622
(312) 258-8872
Contact: Personnel
Manufactures and markets household products including Tide, Zest soap, Pampers, Crest toothpaste, and other well-known brands.

Purex Corporation, Ltd.
Chicago District Office
2500 S. 25th Ave.
Broadview, IL 60153
(708) 344-0088
District Sales Manager: Ron Illian
Manufactures and distributes toiletries, chemicals, and medicines.

Rhone-Poulenc Basic Chemicals Co.
1245 E. Deihl Road, Suite 303
Naperville, IL 60563
(708) 505-1450
Director of Personnel: Glen Hanson
Manufacturer of phosphate chemicals.

Rust-Oleum Corporation
11 Hawthorne Parkway
Vernon Hills, IL 60061
(708) 367-7700
Contact: Personnel
Leading manufacturer of rust preventatives and paints.

Safety-Kleen Corporation
777 Big Timber Road
Elgin, IL 60123
(708) 697-8460
Contact: Personnel
Provider of automotive and industrial cleaners.

Sherwin-Williams Co.
11541 S. Champlain Ave.
Chicago, IL 60628
(312) 821-3000
Personnel Director: Henry Murphy
Manufacturer of paints and varnishes.

A. E. Staley Manufacturing Co.
2200 E. Eldorado St.
Decatur, IL 62525
(217) 423-4411
Contact: Personnel
Manufacturer of food, animal feeds, and household products.

Stepan Company
Edens and Winnetka Aves.
Northfield, IL 60093
(708) 446-7500
President: F. Quinn Stepan
Manufactures and markets chemicals used in the personal care, household, agricultural, and petroleum industries.

Sun Chemical Corporation
135 W. Lake St.
Northlake, IL 60164
(708) 562-0550
Director of Personnel: Nick Heller
Manufacturer of graphic arts equipment, dyes, and printing inks; paper packaging.

Union Carbide Corporation
120 S. Riverside Plaza
Chicago, IL 60606
(312) 454-2000
Director Employee Relations: David Gardner
Manufacturer of chemicals, plastics, and gases.

Union Oil Co. of California
Union 76 Division Office
1650 E. Golf Road
Schaumburg, IL 60196
(708) 330-0076
Manager, Employment and Recruiting: Joyce Rodgers
Distributor of petroleum products and chemicals.

United Coatings
875 N. Michigan Ave., Suite 1360
Chicago, IL 60611
(312) 944-5400
Personnel Director: Jody Mascolino
Manufactures paint and equipment.

United Laboratories
955 Hawthorne
Itasca, IL 60143
(708) 773-0252
Contact: Personnel
Manufactures and distributes chemical products.

USG Corporation
101 S. Wacker Drive
Chicago, IL 60606
(312) 606-4000
Senior VP, Human Resources: Harold E. Pendexter, Jr.
Nation's largest producer of gypsum products; also produces carpeting, adhesives, and paint for the construction industry.

Vulcan Materials Co.
500 W. Plainfield Road
Countryside, IL 60525
(708) 482-7000
Personnel Director: Wayne Houston
One of the nation's largest producers of construction aggregates, chemicals, and secondary (scrap) aluminum.

Waste Management
3003 Butterfield Road
Oak Brook, IL 60521
(708) 572-8800
Director of Personnel: Dave Rogers
Provides recycling and disposal of solid and chemical wastes.

Witco Chemical Corporation
2701 Lake St.
Melrose Park, IL 60160
(708) 344-4300
Personnel Director: Dorothy Thoren
Manufacturer of chemicals and petroleum products.

Computers: Data Processing

For networking in **data processing** and related fields, check out the following professional organizations listed in Chapter 5:

PROFESSIONAL ORGANIZATIONS:

American Society for Information Science
Association of Information Systems Professionals
Data Processing Management Association
National Association of Word Information Processing Specialists
Women in Information Processing

PROFESSIONAL PUBLICATIONS:

Data Communications
Datamation

DIRECTORIES:

Datamation 100 (Datamation, Newton, MA)
Data Communications Buyers Guide (McGraw-Hill, New York, NY)
Data Processing Equipment Directory (American Business Directories, Omaha, NE)
Data Processing Services Directory (American Business Directories, Omaha, NE)
Data Sources (Ziff-Davis, Cherry Hill, NY)
Engineering, Science and Computer Jobs (Peterson's Guides, Princeton, NJ)
IWP Word Processing Directory (International Word Processing Association, Willow Grove, PA)
PC Tech Journal Directory (Ziff-Davis, Cherry Hill, NY)
Thomas Register's Mid-Year Guide to Data/Information Processing (Thomas Publishing Co., New York)

EMPLOYERS:

Applied Learning
1751 W. Diehl Road
Naperville, IL 60563
(708) 369-3000

Automatic Data Processing
7350 W. Lawrence Ave.
Harwood Heights, IL 60656
(708) 867-6400

Centel Corporation
8725 W. Higgins
Chicago, IL 60631
(312) 399-2500

Central Computing Co.
P.O. Box 681
Decatur, IL 62525
(217) 424-2221

Control Data Business Management Services
1030 W. Higgins Road
Park Ridge, IL 60068
(708) 693-3021

CRC
70 E. Lake St.
Chicago, IL 60601
(312) 443-1120

Data Mark Corporation
3700 W. Devon, Suite E
Lincolnwood, IL 60659
(708) 673-1700

Distribution Sciences
1700 Higgins Road, Suite 280
Des Plaines, IL 60018
(708) 699-6620

Hartley Data Services
1807 Glenview Road
Glenview, IL 60025
(708) 724-9280

Information Resources
150 N. Clinton St.
Chicago, IL 60606
(312) 726-1221
Computerized marketing research firm.

Robert J. Irmen Associates
1491 Circle Court
Elk Grove Village, IL 60007
(708) 325-8220

May & Speh Data Processing
1501 Opus Pl.
Downers Grove, IL 60515
(708) 964-1501

Merchants Data Processing Center
9944 Roberts Road, Suite 707
Palos Hills, IL 60465
(708) 430-7700

National Computer Network of Chicago
1929 N. Harlem Ave.
Chicago, IL 60635
(312) 622-6666

Oak Brook Data Center/American Drugstores
2107 Swift Drive
Oak Brook, IL 60521
(708) 572-5400

Pansophic Systems
2400 Cabot Drive
Lisle, IL 60532
(708) 572-6000

Byte into data processing management

Jim Larson, director of computer services for Homewood/Flossmoor School District #233, works with students and professionals alike. He tracks movement in the field and says, "For a recent graduate to get a first job as a computer center manager would take luck. A manager needs not only technical expertise but competence with budgetary matters and with handling money—some accounting is extremely beneficial. A manager is also responsible for personnel and needs those skills.

"To get a foot in the door generally means starting out as a programmer or operator, moving into systems analysis and then manager. And this would likely be in a small- to medium-size installation," Jim continues.

"Turnover is high in data processing, and more often than not, a person is expected to step in and take over. There's not much on-the-job training. I advise young people to have a good, strong resume and to take sample programs they've written to the interview."■

Phoenix Data Processing
645 Blackhawk Drive
Westmont, IL 60559-1198
(708) 654-4400

RJE Data Processing Business Systems
2513 W. Peterson Ave.
Chicago, IL 60659
(312) 561-6966

Safe Pay
444 N. Wabash
Chicago, IL 60611
(312) 527-1077

SEC Cos. of the USA
1333 Butterfield Road, Suite 200
Downer's Grove, IL 60615
(708) 515-0500

Statistical Tabulating Co.
2 N. Riverside Plaza
Chicago, IL 60606
(312) 454-8000
President: Michael Natow
Financial turnkey systems, data processing, timesharing, remote data entry, electronic printing.

R. F. White & Co.
209 W. Jackson, 11th Floor
Chicago, IL 60606
(312) 322-9600

Mark Williams Company
1601 Skokie Highway
North Chicago, IL 60064
(708) 689-2300

Computers: Hardware, Software, Technical Services, Telecommunications

For networking in the **computer hardware and software industries,** check out the following professional organizations listed in Chapter 5:

PROFESSIONAL ORGANIZATIONS:

Administrative Management Society
American Production and Inventory Control Society
Association for Computing Machinery
Chicago Computer Society
Chicago High Tech Association
Electronic Industries Association
National Association of Word Information Processing Specialists

For additional information, you can write to:

ADAPSO—The Computer Software and Services Industry Association
1300 N. 17th St.
Arlington, VA 22209

Association for Computer Sciences
P.O. Box 19027
Sacramento, CA 95819
(916)421-9149

IEEE Computer Society
345 E. 47th St.
New York, NY
(212)705-7900

Semiconductor Industry Association
10201 Torre Ave., #275
Cupertino, CA 95014
(408)973-9973

PROFESSIONAL PUBLICATIONS:

Byte
Computer World
Design News
Electronic Business
Electronic Products
Electronics Distributor
Electronics News
Electronics Week
Microtimes
MIS News
PC Computing
PC Week
PC World
Personal Computing
Semiconductors International

DIRECTORIES:

Data Sources (Ziff-Davis, New York, NY)
Design News Electronic Directory (Cahners Publishing Co., Boston, MA)
Directory of Computer Software and Services Companies (ADAPSO, Arlington, VA)
EIA Trade Directory (Electronic Industries Association, Washington, DC)

Engineering, Science, and Computer Jobs (Peterson's Guides, Princeton, NJ)
Who's Who in Electronics (Harris Publications, Twinsburg, OH)
Yearbook/Directory (Semiconductor Industry Association, San Jose, CA)

EMPLOYERS:

AG Communications Systems
400 N. Wolf Road
Northlake, IL 60164
(708) 681-7100
Employment Manager: Pat Murphy
Manufacturers of communications systems and equipment.

A T & T
3800 Golf Road
Rolling Meadows, IL 60008
(708) 981-2000
Personnel Manager: Judy Dagoda
Manufacturer of communications systems.

Bell & Howell Company
6800 McCormick Road
Chicago, IL 60645-2797
(312) 539-7300
Director of Human Resources: Joanne Zimo
Information systems company. Information Storage and Retrieval division produces computer-related microimagery products, systems, and services.

Bio-logic Systems Corporation
One Bio-logic Plaza
Mundelein, IL 60060
(708) 949-5200
Personnel Director: Faith Curtis
Manufactures computers for medical diagnosis.

Business Systems
9845 Roosevelt Road
Westchester, IL 60153
(708) 681-6060
Personnel Director: Zale Scott
Computer programming services.

Cincom Systems
500 Park Blvd., Suite 575
Itasca, IL 60143

(708) 250-8383
Software, programming, consulting.

Codex Corporation
854 E. Algonquin Road
Schaumburg, IL 60173
(708) 576-2036
Personnel Director: Tom Fordonski
Sales and service of modems, multiplexers, network processors, and intelligent terminals.

Comdisco, Inc.
611 N. River Road
Rosemont, IL 60018
(708) 698-3000
Programming.

Compaq Computer Corporation
425 N. Martingale Road
Schaumburg, IL 60173
(708) 240-2030
Personnal Director: Mike Coombs
Computer manufacturer.

Compumat, Inc.
17 W. 220 22nd St., Suite 300
Oakbrook Terrace, IL 60181
(708) 617-4400
Vice President: Stuart E. Schwartz
Markets computer hardware and software.

Computer Task Group
1000 E. 80th Place, Suite 325N
Merrillville, IN 46410
(219) 738-1908
Computer programming service.

Concepts Dynamic
9200 Calumet Ave., Suite 103E
Munster, IN 46321
(219) 836-9090
Personnel Director: Louis Noe
Computer programming service.

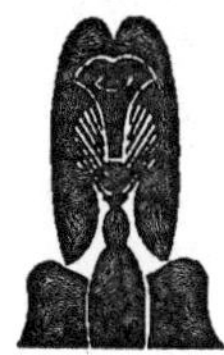

Closing the deal on sales

Jerry Packer put in a long and successful stint as a salesman for Xerox, then got an MBA and went to work as district manager for Paradyne Corporation in DesPlaines, a comparatively risky, aggressive new computer company. We asked him about the differences between selling for a giant and taking a risk with a relatively unknown firm.

"Xerox is probably fairly typical of any large corporation," says Jerry, "in that they are very structured. It was a good place to work, but it didn't provide much opportunity for individual decision making. A company like Paradyne offers a fantastic chance to exercise some entrepreneurial skills. The corporation sets general goals, but it's up to me how I meet them. I can try out different marketing techniques, divide up the territory in new ways, create teams, whatever. It's neat to be able to exercise that kind of flexibility."

We asked Jerry what it takes to be a good salesperson.

"A lot of people think that salesmen are forever buying people lunches and playing golf," says Jerry. "But in order to be really successful, you have to work hard. I don't necessarily mean 80 hours a week. But you need to put in sufficient time to do the things that are necessary. A second important requirement is an absolutely thorough understanding of the products you're selling. Not only your own products but also your competitors'.

"In high-level selling, sales people have to be especially sharp in terms of interpersonal skills. There's an old saying, and it's true: people don't buy from companies, they buy from people. When you're selling systems that range upward of $5 million, you're also selling yourself. It's important that your clients feel you'll be around even after the sale to handle any problems that might come up. To establish that kind of rapport, you have to look presentable and be very articulate. It also helps if you have good written communication skills." ■

Control Data Corporation
300 S. Riverside Plaza, Suite 1950 South
Chicago, IL 60606
(312) 454-6800
Computer manufacturer; software developer.

Dialcom, Inc.
1011 E. Touhy Ave.
Des Plaines, IL 60018
(708) 292-6408
Contact: Beverly Hextall
Programming.

Digital Equipment Corp.
100 Northwest Point Blvd.
Elk Grove Village. IL 60007
(708) 806-0200

Ernst & Young
150 S. Wacker Drive
Chicago, IL 60606
(312) 368-1800
Partner in Charge: Jack Staley
Furnishes computer and consulting services to hospitals.

Forsythe McArthur Associates
7500 Frontage Road
Skokie, IL 60077
(708) 675-8000
Personnel Director: Diane Thilmany
Computer brokers.

G.E. Computer Service
224 James St.
Bensenville, IL 60106
(708) 595-1050
Operations Manager: Brian Joyce
Hardware; systems analysis.

David Groth & Associates
200 E. Howard St., Suite 264
Des Plaines, IL 60018
(708) 296-9675
Programming and systems.

Hartley Data
1807 Glenview Road
Glenview, IL 60025
(708) 724-9280
Personnel Manager: Dan Koolish
Programming.

Honeywell, Inc.
1500 W. Dundee Road
Arlington Heights, IL 60004
(708) 394-4000
Personnel Director: Wanda Tanner
Manufacturer and marketer of high-technology products in the fields of information processing, automation, and controls.

IBM Corporation
One IBM Plaza, 26th Floor
Chicago, IL 60611
(312) 245-2000
Corporate Employment Manager: Don Folkl
World's largest manufacturer and marketer of information technology.

Illinois Computer Cable Corporation
1404 Sherman Road
Lemont, IL 60439
(708) 810-0200
Personnel Director: Jennifer Miller
Custom cable assemblers.

Memo-Tech
2800 N. River Road, Suite 290
Des Plaines, IL 60018
(708) 298-9383
Personnel Manager: Jennifer Nowicki
Computer programmer.

Meridian Group
570 Lake Cook Road, Suite 300
Deerfield, IL 60015
(708) 940-1200
Personnel Director: Roy Vaks
Computer and telecommunications services.

National Computer Network of Chicago
1929 N. Harlem Ave.
Chicago, IL 60635
(312) 622-6666
Personnel Director: Sally Nowotarski
Software, timesharing, consulting.

NCR Corporation
7400 N. Caldwell
Niles, IL 60648
(708) 775-0500
District Manager: J.J. Derkos
Manufactures, sells, and services data-entry equipment terminals, computers, EDP, and supplies.

North American Computer Consultants
28835 N. Herky Drive, Suite 212
Lake Bluff, IL 60044
(708) 234-7212
Personnel Director: Ron White
Software, timesharing, consulting.

Nuclear Data
1300 Golf Road
Schaumburg, IL 60196
(708) 884-3600
Human Resources Director: Judy Fairfield
Principal business is the design, manufacture, and marketing of computer systems.

Paradyne Corporation
2800 River Road, Suite 475
Des Plaines, IL 60018
(708) 699-6040
Manufacturer of computer hardware and accessories.

PC Quote
401 S. LaSalle St.
Chicago, IL 60605
(312) 786-5400
Senior Vice President: James E. Vath
Provides financial information and software services.

Racal-Milgo Information Systems
939 N. Plum Grove Road, Suite F
Schaumburg, IL 60173
(708) 605-8720
Data communications systems.

Reuters Information Services
141 W. Jackson St., Suite 2900
Chicago, IL 60604
(312) 294-9005
Software, timesharing, programming.

A.O. Smith Corporation
7250 S. Cicero Ave.
Chicago, IL 60629
(708) 496-2500
Personnel Director: John Dwyer
Software.

Sorkin-Enenstein Research Service
500 N. Dearborn St.
Chicago, IL 60610
(312) 828-0702
Software.

Statistical Tabulating Co.
2 N. Riverside Plaza
Chicago, IL 60606
(312) 454-8000
Software consulting.

System Software Associates
500 W. Madison St., Suite 3200
Chicago, IL 60606
(312) 641-2900
Develops and markets business application software for IBM.

Time Sharing Business Applications
5647 W. Diversey Pkwy.
Chicago, IL 60639
(312) 889-9393
Programming.

Unisys Corporation
324 S. Michigan Ave.
Chicago, IL 60604
(312) 322-2440
Contact: Personnel
Manufacturer of computers.

Wallace Computer Services
4600 W. Roosevelt Road
Hillside, IL 60162
(708) 626-2000
V.P., Human Resources: Anthony M. Grassi
The Business Data division markets accounting, inventory control, and fleet management computer software systems; other divisions market computer and business forms and catalogs.

Xerox Corporation
3000 Des Plaines Ave.
Des Plaines, IL 60018
(709) 297-3600
Regional Personnel Manager: Ralph Volpe
One of the world's largest manufacturers of computers, copiers, and duplication equipment.

XL/Datacomp
908 N. Elm St., 4th Floor
Hinsdale, IL 60521
(708) 323-1200
Personnel Director: Cathy Baker
Markets computer equipment.

Zenith Radio Corporation
1000 Milwaukee Ave.

Glenview, IL 60025
(312) 391-7000
Director of Organizational Development: Mike Kaplan

Construction and Engineering

To network in the **construction and engineering** industry and related fields, check out the following professional organizations listed in Chapter 5:

PROFESSIONAL ORGANIZATIONS:

American Concrete Pavement Association
American Planning Association
American Society of Safety Engineers
Builders Association of Chicago
Home Builders Association of Greater Chicago
National Association of Women in Construction
Society of Women Engineers
Western Society of Engineers

For additional information, you can write to:

American Society of Civil Engineers
345 E. 47th St.
New York, NY 10017

Construction Products Manufacturers Council
1600 Wilson Blvd.
Arlington, VA 22209

National Asphalt Pavement Association
6811 Kenilworth Ave.
Riverdale, MD 20840

National Association of Home Builders
15th and M Sts.
Washington, DC 20005

National Association of Minority Contractors
806 15th St., N.W., Suite 340
Washington, DC 20005

National Construction Industry Council
2000 L St., N.W., Suite 612
Washington, DC 20036

Society of Women Engineers
345 E. 47th St., #305
New York, NY 10017

PROFESSIONAL PUBLICATIONS:

Building Design and Construction
Civil Engineering
Construction Review
ENR (Engineering News Record)
Glass Industry
Pit and Quarry

DIRECTORIES:

Blue Book of Major Homebuilders (CMR Associates, Inc., Crofton, MD)
Construction Equipment, Construction Giants (Cahners Publishing, Des Plaines, IL)
Directory of Contract Service Firms (C.E. Publications, Kenmore, WA)
ENR Directory of Contractors (McGraw-Hill, New York, NY)
ENR Directory of Design Firms (McGraw Hill, New York, NY)
Guide to Information Sources in the Construction Industry (Construction Products Manufacturers Council, Arlington, VA)
Peterson's Guide to Careers (Peterson's Guides, Princeton, NJ)
Who's Who in Engineering (Engineers Joint Council, New York, NY)
Who's Who in Technology Today (Technology Recognition Corporation, Pittsburgh, PA)

EMPLOYERS:

Amsted Industries
Boulevard Towers South, 44th Floor
205 N. Michigan Ave.
Chicago, IL 60601
(312) 645-1700
Personnel Manager: Shirley Whitesell
Manufactures a wide range of products for general industry, construction, and railroads.

Austin Co.
401 S. La Salle St., Suite 1500
Chicago, IL 60605
(312) 786-5200
Vice President: Sergio de los Reyes

Bartkus & Associates
819 S. Wabash
Chicago, IL 60605
(312) 663-4141

President: Eugene Bartkus
Engineers.

Barton-Aschman Associates
820 Davis St.
Evanston, IL 60204-1381
(708) 491-1000
Engineers.

Alfred Benesch & Co.
233 N. Michigan Ave.
Chicago, IL 60601
(312) 565-0450
President: Louis Bowman
Engineers.

Ragnar Benson
250 S. Northwest Highway
Park Ridge, IL 60068
(708) 698-4900
President: James Bergstrom

Brand Insulations
1420 Renaissance Drive
Park Ridge, IL 60068
(708) 298-1200
Personnel Director: Nancy Zielinski

Bulley & Andrews
1755 W. Armitage Ave.
Chicago, IL 60622
(312) 235-2433
President: Allan E. Bulley

CBI Industries
800 Jorie Blvd.
Oak Brook, IL 60521
(708) 654-7000
President: John E. Jones

Ceco Corporation
1 Tower Lane
Oakbrook Terrace, IL 60181
(708) 242-2000
Contact: Personnel

Crane Construction Co.
343 Wainwright Drive
Northbrook, IL 60062
(312) 291-3400
President: Jeffrey Crane
Engineers.

Crane/Fiat
1235 Hartrey Ave.
Evanston, IL 60202
(312) 864-7600
Contact: Corporate Personnel

CRS Sirrine
8700 W. Bryn Mawr Ave.
Chicago, IL 60631
(312) 693-1030
Personnal Director: Betty Latham
Engineers.

Joseph J. Duffy Co.
4994 N. Elston Ave.
Chicago, IL 60630
(312) 777-6700
President: James M. Mann

Envirodyne Engineers
168 N. Clinton St.
Chicago, IL 60606
(312) 648-1700
President: Dr. Ronald K. Linde
Engineers.

A. Epstein & Sons, International
600 W. Fulton St.
Chicago, IL 60606
(312) 454-9100
President: Melvin Kupperman
Engineers.

Fluor Daniel
200 W. Monroe St.
Chicago, IL 60606
(312) 368-3500
General Manager: Don Huston

Graycor, Inc.
640 N. La Salle St.
Chicago, IL 60610-3767
(312) 943-9100
President: Melvin Gray

Greeley & Hansen
222 S. Riverside Plaza, Room 900
Chicago, IL 60606
(312) 648-1155
Managing Partner: Allan B. Edwards
Engineers.

Harbour Contractors
701 Harger Road, Suite 100
Oak Brook, IL 60521
(708) 572-2200
President: Patrick C. Harbour

Harza Engineering Co.
150 S. Wacker Drive
Chicago, IL 60606
(312) 855-7000
President: Walter Bogbovitz
Engineers.

Hyre Electric Co.
2320 W. Ogden Ave.
Chicago, IL 60608
(312) 738-7200
President: A. J. Pavlick
Engineers.

J.A. Jones Construction Co.
550 W. Jackson Blvd., Suite 419
Chicago, IL 60606
(312) 902-1666
Vice President: Paul Nelson

George A. Kennedy & Associates
6 N. Michigan Ave., Suite 806
Chicago, IL 60602
(312) 332-7060
President: George A. Kennedy
Engineers.

Lester B. Knight Associates
549 W. Randolph St.
Chicago, IL 60606
(312) 346-2100
President: DeForest P. Davis, Jr.
Engineers.

Lombard Co.
4245 W. 123rd St.
Alsip, IL 60658
(708) 389-1060
President: George Lombard

Materials Service Corporation
222 N. LaSalle
Chicago, IL 60601-1090
(312) 372-3600
Employment Representative: Lauren Nessler
Makers and distributors of ready-mix concrete.

Mayfair Construction Co.
5660 N. Jersey Ave.
Chicago, IL 60659
(312) 588-7600
President: Paul Cocose

McDonough Engineering
224 S. Michigan Ave., Suite 500
Chicago, IL 60604
(312) 922-2100
President: James McDonough
Engineers.

Mellon Stuart Co.
118 S. Clinton St., Suite 350
Chicago, IL 60606
(312) 876-1444
Vice President of Operations: Laurence Buchman

Gerhardt F. Meyne Co.
345 N. Canal St.
Chicago, IL 60606
(312) 207-2100
President: John Aberson

Miller Building Systems
102 Wilmont Road, Suite 390
Deerfield, IL 60015
(708) 945-3222
Produces moveable commercial structures.

Morse/Diesel, Inc.
547 W. Jackson Blvd., Suite 1100
Chicago, IL 60606
(312) 341-0600
Territorial Vice President: David L. Hoffman

L.E. Myers Co. Group
1010 Jorie Blvd.
Oak Brook, IL 60521
(708) 990-4666
Constructs electric utility projects.

Nichols-Homeshield, Inc.
1470 N. Farnsworth Ave.
P.O. Box 1617
Aurora, IL 60507
(708) 851-5430
Personnel Director: Lou Bennett
Manufactures aluminum products for home construction and remodeling.

O'Donnell Wicklund Pigozzi & Peterson
570 Lake Cook Road
Deerfield, IL 60015
(708) 940-9600
President: Leonard Peterson
Engineers.

W.E. O'Neil Construction Co.
2751 N. Clybourn Ave.
Chicago, IL 60614
(312) 327-1611
President: Michael Faron

Opus North Corporation
9700 W. Higgins Road, Suite 900
Rosemont, IL 60018
(312) 318-1600
Executive Vice President: Jim Nygaard

Paschen Contractors
739 N. Elston Ave.
Chicago, IL 60647
(312) 278-4700
Managing Partner: Henry Paschen
Engineers.

Peck/Jones Construction Corporation
P.O. Box 66501
A.M.F. O'Hare
Chicago, IL 60666
(312) 686-4356
President: Terry Jackson

Pepper Companies
643 N. Orleans St.
Chicago, IL 60610
(312) 266-4703
President: Geoffrey Knudson

Power Contracting & Engineering Corporation
3205 N. Wilke Road
Arlington Heights, IL 60004
(708) 259-1100
President: Alvin Gorman

Process Design Associates
300 W. Adams St., Suite 510
Chicago, IL 60606
(312) 977-4200
Personnel Manager: Tom O'Leary
Engineers.

Professional Service Industries
510 E. 22nd St.
Lombard, IL 60148
(708) 691-1490
Vice President: Blaine Kincaid
Engineers.

Sargent & Lundy
55 E. Monroe St.
Chicago, IL 60603
(312) 269-2000
Senior Partner: William Chittenden
Engineers.

Schal Associates
200 W. Hubbard St.
Chicago, IL 60610
(312) 245-1000
Chief Executive Officer: Richard Halpern

Soil Testing Services
111 Pfingston Road
Northbrook, IL 60062
(708) 272-6520
President: Doug Keats
Engineers.

George Sollitt Construction Co.
790 N. Central Ave.
Wood Dale, IL 60191
(708) 860-7333
President: Don Maziarka

Turner Construction Co.
55 W. Monroe St.
Chicago, IL 60603
(312) 558-7600
Group Manager and Vice President: Joe McCullough

Walsh Construction Co. of Illinois
3710 S. Western Ave.
Chicago, IL 60609
(312) 927-4131
President: Daniel Walsh

Drugs/Pharmaceuticals/Medical Supplies

For networking in the **drug industry** and related fields, you can contact the following professional organization listed in Chapter 5:

PROFESSIONAL ORGANIZATIONS:

Pharmaceutical Advertising Council

Or you can write to:

American Pharmaceutical Association
2215 Constitution Ave., N.W.
Washington, DC 20037

Association of Biotechnology Companies
1220 L St., N.W.
Washington, DC 20005

National Association of Chain Drug Stores
1911 Jefferson Davis Highway
Alexandria, VA 22209

National Association of Pharmaceutical Manufacturers
747 Third Ave.
New York, NY 10017

National Association of Retail Druggists
205 Daingerfield Road
Alexandria, VA 22314

National Wholesale Druggist Association
105 Oronoco St.
Alexandria, VA 22314

Pharmaceutical Manufacturers Association
1155 15th St., N.W.
Washington, DC 20005

PROFESSIONAL PUBLICATIONS:

American Druggist
Biotechnology

Cosmetics and Toiletries
Drug Store News
Drug Topics
Soap/Cosmetics/Chemical Specialties

DIRECTORIES:

Biotechnology Directory (Stockton Press, New York, NY)
Blue Book American Druggist (Hearst Corp., New York, NY)
Drug Topics Red Book (Litton Publications, Oradell, NJ)
Health Care Directory (Litton Publications, Oradell, NJ)
NACDS Membership Directory (National Association of Chain Drugstores, Alexandria, VA)
NWDA Membership Directory (National Wholesale Druggists Association, Alexandria, VA)
Pharmaceutical Manufacturers of the U.S. (Noyes Data Corporation, Park Ridge, NJ)
Soap/Cosmetics/Chemical Specialities Blue Book (MacNair Publications, New York, NY)

EMPLOYERS:

Abbott Laboratories
One Abbott Park Road
Abbott Park, IL 60064-3500
(708) 937-7000
Mgr. of Corporate Placement: Mike Omelanuk
Diversified manufacturer of health care products, including pharmaceuticals, hospital products, diagnostic products, chemicals, and nutritional products.

Alva-Amco Pharmacal
6625 N. Avondale Ave.
Chicago, IL 60631
(312) 792-0200
Personnel Director: Nancy Dahlstrom
Manufacturer and distributor of pharmaceuticals.

American Home Products
Ayerst Laboratories Division
745 N. Gary Ave.
Carol Stream, IL 60188
(708) 462-7200
Personnel Director: Judy Contoro
Manufacturer of laboratory equipment and supplies.

Armour Pharmaceutical Co.
P.O. Box 511
Kankakee, IL 60901
(815) 932-6771

Personnel Director: Mike Johnson
Pharmaceuticals manufacturer.

Associated Mills/Pollenex
165 N. Canal St.
Chicago, IL 60606
(312) 454-5400
Personnel Director: George Becella
Manufactures health care appliances.

Baxter Hospital Supplies
1450 Waukegan Road
McGaw Park, IL 60085
(708) 473-0400
Vice President, Human Resources: Bob Rook
Manufacturer and distributor of equipment, supplies, and services to the health care industry.

Baxter Travenol Laboratories
One Baxter Parkway
Deerfield, IL 60015
(708) 948-2000
Contact: Human Resources
Develops, manufactures, and distributes a diversified line of medical care products in the U.S. and 17 countries.

Beltone Electronics Corporation
4201 W. Victoria St.
Chicago, IL 60646
(312) 583-3600
Personnel Director: Robert Riefke
Manufactures and distributes hearing aids and test equipment.

John O. Butler Co.
4635 W. Foster Ave.
Chicago, IL 60630
(312) 777-4000
Personnel Director: Mark Dugan

Ciba-Geigy Corporation
900 Corporate Grove Drive
Buffalo Grove, IL 60089
(708) 763-8700
Contact: Personnel
Manufacturer of pharmaceuticals and ethical drugs.

Dial Corporation
2500 S. 25th Ave.
Broadview, IL 60153
(708) 344-0088
Personnel Manager: Richard Haggerty

Manufactures and distributes toiletries, chemicals, and medicines.

Evron Industries
2159 W. Pershing Road
Chicago, IL 60609
(312) 847-1000
Personnel Director: Ella Woods
Pharmaceuticals manufacturer.

General Drug Co.
200 N. Fairfield Ave.
Chicago, IL 60612
(312) 826-4242
President: Julius Sarnat
Drug wholesaler.

Humiston-Keeling, Inc.
233 E. Erie St., Suite 200
Chicago, IL 60611
(312) 943-6066
Chairman: Burton H. Olin
Full-line wholesale drug distributor.

Lederle Laboratories/American Cyanimid
1100 E. Business Center Drive
Mount Prospect, IL 60056
(708) 827-8871
Pharmaceuticals manufacturer.

Eli Lilly, Inc.
8735 W. Higgins Road, Suite 270
Chicago, IL 60631
(312) 693-8740
Contact: Personnel
Pharmaceuticals manufacturer.

Lindberg Corporation
6133 N. River Road, Suitc 700
Rosemont, IL 60018
(708) 823-2021
Contact: Corporate Pesonnel
Manufactures metal surgical products.

Lypho-Med, Inc.
2020 N. Ruby St.
Melrose Park, IL 60160
(708) 345-6170
Director, Human Resources: Nancy Straka
Manufacturer of pharmaceuticals.

Medline Industries
1200 Townline Road
1 Medline Place
Mundelein, IL 60060
(708) 949-5500
Contact: Employee Services
Manufactures and distributes hospital supplies.

Merck Sharp & Dohme
2010 Swift Drive
Oak Brook, IL 60522
(708) 521-0800
Contact: Personnel
Pharmaceuticals manufacturer.

Morton International
110 N. Wacker Drive
Chicago, IL 60606
(312) 807-2000
Vice President, Human Resources: John C. Hedley
Manufacturer of salt and chemicals and Norwich-Eaton pharmaceuticals.

Pfizer, Inc.
2400 W. Central Road
Hoffman Estates, IL 60196
(708) 381-9500
Personnel Manager: Brian Rafferty
Pharmaceuticals manufacturer.

Plough, Inc.
12900 S. Crawford Ave.
Alsip, IL 60658
(708) 597-5000
Contact: Personnel
Manufacturer of pharmaceuticals and toiletries.

Rugby Labs—Midwest
3400 W. Lake St.
Glenview, IL 60025
(800) 447-8429
Drug wholesaler.

G. D. Searle & Co.
4711 Gold Road
Skokie, IL 60076
(708) 982-7000
Contact: Personnel
Researches, develops, and markets consumer pharmaceutical products, medical products, and prescription eyewear.

Smith Laboratories
300 Tri-State International Center, Suite 200
Linconshire, IL 60069
(708) 405-7400
V.P. Sales and Marketing: John Fowler
Pharmaceutical and medical products.

E.R. Squibb & Sons
3200 Squibb Ave.
Rolling Meadows, IL 60008
(708) 439-4900
Contact: Personnel
Pharmaceuticals manufacturer.

Upjohn Co.
303 E. Wacker Drive
Chicago, IL 60601
(312) 565-1714
Contact: Personnel
Pharmaceuticals manufacturer.

Louis Zahn Drug Co.
1930 George St.
Melrose Park, IL 60160
(708) 921-5100
Contact: Personnel
Wholesale distributer of ethical drugs and medical supplies.

Educational Institutions

For networking in **education** and related fields, check out the following professional organizations listed in Chapter 5:

PROFESSIONAL ORGANIZATIONS:

American Association of University Women
Chicago Teachers' Center
Donors Forum of Chicago
Illinois Park and Recreation Association
National PTA
National Society of Fund-Raising Executives

For additional information, you can write to:

American Association of School Administrators
1801 N. Moore St.
Arlington, VA 22209

Association of Independent Colleges and Universities
One DuPont Circle
Washington, DC 20036

Association of School Business Officials
1760 Reston Ave.
Reston, VA 22090

Council for Educational Development and Research
1201 16th St., N.W.
Washington, DC 20036

National Association of College and University Business Officials
One DuPont Circle, #510
Washington, DC 20036

National Education Association
1201 16th St., N.W.
Washington, DC 20036

PROFESSIONAL PUBLICATIONS:

The Chronicle of Higher Education
Education Week
Instructor
Teaching Pre-K-8
Technology and Learning
Today's Catholic Teacher

DIRECTORIES:

Bricker's International Directory of University Executive Programs (Peterson's Guides, Princeton, NJ)
Consumer's Guide to Chicago Public Elementary Schools (Citizen's School Committee, Chicago, IL)
Directory of Education Associations (Marquis Publishing Co., Chicago, IL)
Patterson's American Education (Educational Directories Inc., Mt. Prospect, IL)
QED's School Guide (Quality Education Data, Denver, CO)
Training Marketplace Directory (Lakewood Publications, Minneapolis, MN)
Yearbook of Higher Education (Marquis Publishing Co., Chicago, IL)

EMPLOYERS:

American Academy of Art
122 S. Michigan Ave., 16th Floor

Chicago, IL 60603
(312) 939-3883
Junior college, offering two-year program in commercial art. Approx. enrollment: 1,000.

American Conservatory of Music
17 N. State St., Suite 1800
Chicago, IL 60602
(312) 263-4161
Professional school, offering undergraduate, master's, and doctoral degrees in music. Approx. enrollment: 400.

American Learning Corporation
200 S. Michigan Ave., Suite 800
Chicago, IL 60604
(312) 939-0303
Operates a network of private after-school reading centers.

Applied Learning
1751 W. Diehl Road
Naperville, IL 60563
(708) 369-3000
Personnel Director: Nora McCarthy
Leading producer and distributor of technology-related training courses.

Aurora University
347 S. Gladstone Ave.
Aurora, IL 60506
(708) 892-6431
Independent four-year liberal arts college, offering bachelor's degrees in 30 areas. Approx. enrollment: 1,000.

Barat College
700 E. Westleigh Road
Lake Forest, IL 60045
(708) 234-3000
Private four-year college. Approx. enrollment: 600.

Bell & Howell Company
6800 McCormick Road
Chicago, IL 60645-2797
(312) 539-7300
Human Resources Director: Joanne Zimo
Information systems company. Career Education Division markets educational programs in electronics and computer science.

Board of Education, City of Chicago
Superintendent's Office
1819 W. Pershing Road

Chicago, IL 60609
(312) 890-8000

Calumet College
2400 New York Ave.
Whiting, IN 46394
(219) 473-7770

Chicago College of Osteopathic Medicine
5200 S. Ellis Ave.
Chicago, IL 60615
(312) 947-3000
Professional medical college, offering comprehensive training in the field of osteopathic medicine. Approx. enrollment: 400.

Chicago State University
95th St. at King Drive
Chicago, IL 60628
(312) 995-2000
A member of the state university system, offering bachelor's and master's degrees in every field of humanities, natural and social sciences. Approx. enrollment: 7,000.

City College of Chicago
226 W. Jackson Blvd.
Chicago, IL 60606
(312) 641-0808
System composed of nine junior colleges located in Chicago communities: Kennedy-King College, Chicago Loop College, Malcolm X College, Olive-Harvey College, Truman College, Wright Junior College, Richard J. Daley College, Chicago Urban Skills Institute, and Chicago City-Wide College. Approx. enrollment: 45,000.

College of DuPage
425 W. 22nd St.
Glen Ellyn, IL 60137
(708) 858-2800
Community junior college; part of the state university system. Approx. enrollment: 17,000.

College of Lake County
19351 W. Washington St.
Grayslake, IL 60030
(708) 223-6601
Community junior college, offering general education in the liberal arts and sciences, continuing education, and career development. Approx. enrollment: 10,000.

Columbia College
600 S. Michigan Ave.
Chicago, IL 60605

(312) 663-1600
Private four-year college, offering bachelor's degrees, with an emphasis on communications, arts, film, dance, drama, and photography within a structure of liberal arts education. Approx. enrollment: 3,000.

Concordia University
7400 Augusta St.
River Forest, IL 60305
(708) 771-8300
University offering bachelor's and master's degrees in liberal arts and teacher education. Approx. enrollment: 1,100.

De Paul University
25 E. Jackson Blvd.
Chicago, IL 60604
(312) 321-8000
Private Catholic university, offering bachelor's, master's, and doctoral degrees through the Colleges of Arts and Sciences, College of Commerce, School of Music, Goodman School of Drama, School of Education, School for New Learning, and the Graduate College. Approx. enrollment: 11,000.

Devry, Inc.
2201 W. Howard St.
Evanston, IL 60202
(708) 328-8100
V. P., Personnel: Edward Cabot
Operates technical schools, offering programs in electronics and computer science.

Elgin Community College
1700 Spartan Drive
Elgin, IL 60123
(708) 697-1000
Junior college; part of the Illinois community college system. Approx. enrollment: 5,000.

Elmhurst College
190 Prospect St.
Elmhurst, IL 60126
(708) 617-3500
Private four-year college, offering bachelor's degrees in liberal arts areas. Approx. enrollment: 3,300.

Governor's State University
University Park
Park Forest South, IL 60466
(708) 534-5000
Part of the state university system; offers bachelor's and master's degrees through liberal arts and professional schools. Approx. enrollment: 4,000.

William Rainey Harper College
1200 W. Algonquin Road
Palatine, IL 60067
(708) 397-3000
Public community junior college, offering associate's degrees in arts, sciences, and applied sciences. Approx. enrollment: 16,000.

Illinois Benedictine College
5700 College Road
Lisle, IL 60532
(708) 960-1500
Private independent university, offering bachelor's degrees in 27 different undergraduate majors. Approx. enrollment: 2,000.

Illinois College of Optometry
3241 S. Michigan Ave.
Chicago, IL 60616
(312) 225-1700
Private school, offering graduate and undergraduate degrees in the visual sciences. Approx. enrollment: 600.

Illinois College of Podiatric Medicine
1001 N. Dearborn St.
Chicago, IL 60610
(312) 280-2880
Four-year professional program prepares students to be doctors of podiatry. Approx. enrollment: 650.

Illinois Institute of Technology
3300 S. Federal St.
Chicago, IL 60616
(312) 567-3000
Diverse institution, offering graduate and undergraduate degrees through the Armour College of Engineering; Lewis College of Sciences and Letters; the College of Architecture, Planning & Design; the Stuart School of Management & Finance; the Chicago-Kent College of Law; and the Institute for Advanced Studies. Approx. enrollment: 7,000.

Indiana University Northwest
3400 Broadway
Gary, IN 46408
(219) 980-6500

Keller Graduate School of Management
10 S. Riverside Plaza
Chicago, IL 60606
(312) 454-0880
Privately operated graduate school, offering programs leading to MBA degree. Approx. enrollment: 1,000.

Kendall College
2408 Orrington Ave.
Evanston, IL 60201
(708) 866-1300
Private four-year liberal arts college. Approx. enrollment: 400.

Lake Forest College
College & Sheridan Roads
Lake Forest, IL 60045
(708) 234-3100
Private college, offering graduate and undergraduate programs in liberal arts areas. Approx. enrollment: 1,000.

Loyola University
820 N. Michigan Ave.
Chicago, IL 60611
(312) 670-3000
Private university, offering a wide range of graduate and undergraduate programs in the following areas: arts and sciences, business administration, education, nursing, and University College. Approx. enrollment: 15,000.

MacCormac Junior College
327 S. LaSalle St.
Chicago, IL 60604
(312) 922-1884
Privately operated junior college, offering courses in departments of Business Administration, Secretarial Studies, Court Reporting, Paralegal Studies, Professional Art and Design, and Audio-Visual Design. Approx. enrollment: 500.

John Marshall Law School
315 S. Plymouth Court
Chicago, IL 60604
(312) 427-2737
Private law school offers three-year full time and four-year evening courses leading to Juris Doctor degree. Approx. enrollment: 1,500.

McCormick Theological Seminary
5555 S. Woodlawn Ave.
Chicago, IL 60637
(312) 241-7800
Private seminary, offering bachelor's, master's and doctoral degrees in theological studies.

Moody Bible Institute
820 N. LaSalle Drive
Chicago, IL 60610
(312) 329-4000
Private four-year college provides education and training to Christian workers. Approx. enrollment: 1,600.

Moraine Valley Community College
10900 S. 88th Ave.
Palos Hills, IL 60465
(708) 974-4300
Junior college, offering Associate in Arts and Associate in Science degrees in science and the humanities. Approx. enrollment: 9,500.

Morton College
3801 S. Central Ave.
Cicero, IL 60650
(708) 656-8000
Junior college offers a wide range of continuing education courses, career programs, and university transfer courses in most areas of the humanities, arts, and sciences. Approx. enrollment: 3,300.

Mundelein College
6363 N. Sheridan Road
Chicago, IL 60660
(312) 262-8100
Private women's institution, offering extensive courses in liberal arts areas leading to bachelor's and master's degrees. Operates a "weekend college" for working men and women. Approx. enrollment: 1,500.

National College of Chiropractic Medicine
200 E. Roosevelt Road
Lombard, IL 60148
(708) 629-2000
Four-year program covers all phases of chiropractic medicine leading to Doctor of Chiropractic degree. Approx. enrollment: 1,000.

National Lewis University
2840 Sheridan Road
Evanston, IL 60201
(708) 256-5150
Private college offers graduate and undergraduate programs in special and general fields of teaching and business careers. Approx. enrollment: 1,200.

North Central College
30 N. Brainard St.
P.O.Box 3036
Naperville, IL 60566
(708) 420-3400
Private liberal arts college. Approx. enrollment: 1,000.

North Park College
3225 W. Foster
Chicago, IL 60625

(312) 583-2700
Private four-year liberal arts college. Approx. enrollment: 1,400.

Northeastern Illinois University
5500 N. St. Louis Ave.
Chicago, IL 60625
(312) 583-4050
University, offering graduate and undergraduate programs through the College of Arts and Sciences, the Graduate College, and the College of Education. Approx. enrollment: 10,000.

Northwestern University
633 Clark Street
Evanston, IL 60208
(708) 491-3714
Private university, offering degrees at all levels through the College of Arts and Sciences, the School of Speech, the School of Music, the Medill School of Journalism, the School of Education, and others. The Law, Business Administration, Medical, and Dental schools are located at the downtown campus at 339 E. Chicago Ave., Chicago, IL 60611. Approx. enrollment: 10,766.

Oakton Community College
1600 E. Golf Road
Des Plaines, IL 60016
(708) 635-1739
Junior college; part of the state community college system. Offers associate's degrees in business administration, education, engineering, humanities, fine arts, science, and other fields. Approx. enrollment: 10,000.

Prairie State College
202 S. Halsted St.
Chicago Heights, IL 60411
(708) 756-3110
Part of the state community college system. Offers associate's degrees in a wide range of transfer, occupational, and general educational fields. Approx. enrollment: 5,500.

Purdue University Calumet
2233 171st St.
Hammond, IN 46323
(219) 844-0520

Roosevelt University
430 S. Michigan Ave.
Chicago, IL 60605
(708) 341-3500

Private institution, offering degrees at all levels through the following divisions: the College of Arts and Sciences, Walter E. Heller College of Business Administration, College of Education, and the Graduate Division. Approx. enrollment: 7,000.

Rosary College
7900 W. Division St.
River Forest, IL 60305
(708) 366-2490
Private university, offering undergraduate and graduate degrees in most fields in the sciences and humanities. Approx. enrollment: 1,500.

Rush University
600 S. Paulina St.
Chicago, IL 60612
(312) 942-7120
Private medical school. Approx. enrollment: 1,000.

Saint Xavier College
3700 W. 103rd St.
Chicago, IL 60655
(312) 779-3300
Private four-year college, offfering bachelor's and master's degrees in most fields. Approx. enrollment: 2,000.

School of the Art Institute of Chicago
37 S. Wabash
Chicago, IL 60603
(312) 443-3700
Private school, offering undergraduate and master's degrees in all fields of fine arts. Approx. enrollment: 1,700.

South Suburban College
15800 S. State St.
South Holland, IL 60473
(708) 596-2000
Junior college; part of the state community college system. Offers associate's degrees in general education, transfer education, and occupational fields. Approx. enrollment: 10,000.

Triton College
2000 Fifth Ave.
River Grove, IL 60171
(708) 456-0300
Junior college; part of the Illinois community college system. Approx. enrollment: 18,000.

University of Chicago
5801 S. Ellis St.

Chicago, IL 60637
(312) 753-1234
Private university, offering degrees at all levels in the following departments: Humanities, Social Sciences, Biological Sciences, Physical Sciences, and the New Collegiate Division. Offers advanced degrees in the School of Medicine, the Law School, and the Graduate School of Business. Approx. enrollment: 9,000.

University of Health Sciences/The Chicago Medical School
200 E. Randolph Drive
Chicago, IL 60601
(312) 856-1100
Private medical school with approximate enrollment of 700. Also has a School of Graduate and Postdoctoral Studies and School of Related Health Sciences.

University of Illinois
Chicago Circle Campus
P.O. Box 4348
Chicago, IL 60680
(312) 996-3000
Part of the state university system. Offers degrees at all levels in every field of the natural and social sciences and humanities. Approx. enrollment: 20,000.

University of Illinois Medical Center
1740 W. Taylor St.
Chicago, IL 60612
(312) 996-7000
Part of the state university system, the medical school offers degrees from the associate to the doctoral level in medicine and affiliated fields. Approx. enrollment: 4,000.

Valparaiso University
Valparaiso, IN 46383
(219) 464-5000

Waubonsee Community College
Rt. 47 at Harter Road
Sugar Grove, IL 60554
(708) 466-4811
Junior college; part of the state community college system. Approx. enrollment: 5,000.

Wheaton College
501 E. Seminary Ave.
Wheaton, IL 60187
(708) 260-5000

Private undergraduate college, offering courses in the following divisions: Biblical Studies, Humanities, Science and Mathematics, Social Sciences, and Music. Approx. enrollment: 2,500.

George Williams College
Box 1476
1315 Butterfield Road, Suite 218
Downers Grove, IL 60515
(708) 964-3100
Four-year private university, offering bachelor's and master's degrees in liberal arts areas. Approx. enrollment: 1,600.

Electrical Equipment and Supplies

For industry information, you can write:

PROFESSIONAL ORGANIZATIONS:

National Electrical Manufacturers Association
821 15th St., N.W.
Washington, DC 20005

PROFESSIONAL PUBLICATIONS:

EC&M (Electrical, Construction, and Maintenance)
Electrical World
Merchandising Week

DIRECTORIES:

Directory of Electrical Wholesale Distributors (McGraw-Hill, New York, NY)

EMPLOYERS:

Advance Ross Corporation
111 W. Monroe St., Suite 2100 E
Chicago, IL 60603
(312) 346-9126
Contact: Personnel
Provides products for the transportation and pollution control industries.

Altair Corporation
350 Barclay Blvd.

Lincolnshire, IL 60069
(708) 634-9540
Contact: Personnel
Manufactures printing and packaging control systems, controlled-air processing equipment for food, pharmaceutical, and hospital-supply manufacturers, and magnetic cores for use in communications equipment.

Amphenol Corporation
4300 Commerce Court
Lisle, IL 60532
(708) 983-3500
Contact: Personnel
Producer of electronic connectors and interconnection devices, information systems, and deep-pile textiles through its Borg Textiles division.

Anixter Brothers
4711 Golf Road
Skokie, IL 60076
(708) 677-2600
Contact: Personnel Director
Manufactures and distributes wire and cable used in the transmission of electric, telephone, and television signals.

Atcor, Inc.
16100 S. Lathrop Ave.
Harvey, IL 60426
(708) 339-1610
V.P., Human Resources: Dennis Matha
Manufacturer of electrical products.

Bally Manufacturing Co.
8700 W. Bryn Mawr Ave.
Chicago, IL 60631
(312) 399-1300
Contact: Personnel
Principally engaged in the design, manufacture, distribution, and renting of slot machines, pinball machines, and amusement arcade games; operates 450 Aladdin's Castle amusement centers; owns theme parks, resort hotels, casinos, and health & fitness clubs.

Cherry Electrical Products Corporation
3600 Sunset Ave.
Waukegan, IL 60087
(708) 662-9200
Personnel Director: Gary Claypool
One of the largest producers of precision snap-action switches and electronic keyboards; also manufactures electrical components, gas discharge displays, and semiconductor devices.

Circuit Systems
2350 E. Lunt Ave.
Elk Grove Village, IL 60007
(708) 439-1999
Personnel Director: Dilip Vyas
Manufactures and sells printed circuit boards.

Corcom, Inc.
1600 Winchester Road
Libertyville, IL 60048
(708) 680-7400
Personnel Director: Sherril Bishop
Manufactures electronic filters.

DuKane Corporation
2900 Dukane Drive
St. Charles, IL 60174
(708) 584-2300
Employment Manager: Robert Scarlett
Manufacturer of electronic communications.

Dwyer Instruments
P. O. Box 373
Michigan City, IN 46360
(219) 872-9141
Personnel Manager: Gregg Miller
Manufacturer of controls, gauges, meters, and switches.

Dynacircuits, Inc.
11230 Addison St.
Franklin Park, IL 60131
(708) 451-1700
Human Resources: Ivonno Alzate
Manufactures circuit boards.

Dynascan Corporation
6470 W. Cortland St.
Chicago, IL 60635
(312) 889-8870
Contact: Micki Monroe
Leading producer of electronic systems for industrial control, CB radios, and portable telephones.

Eaton Corporation
191 E. North Ave.
Carol Stream, IL 60187
(708) 260-3000
Contact: Personnel
Highly diversified manufacturer of consumer durables, including sewing products; aerospace and marine electronics systems for government and industry; educational products and services; and furniture.

Echo Inc.
400 Oakwood Road
Lake Zurich, IL 60047
(708) 540-8400
Contact: Personnel
Manufacturer and marketer of outdoor power equipment.

Fansteel, Inc.
One Tantalum Plaza
North Chicago, IL 60064
(708) 689-4900
Manager of Personnel: Earl Legler
Manufacturer of refractory metals; fabricator of high-technology products for the automotive, appliance, metalworking, aerospace, recreational, electronic, and chemical industries.

Furnas Electric Co.
1000 McKee St.
Batavia, IL 60510
(708) 879-6000
Personnel Director: Gary Gardner
Manufacturer of motor controls and starters.

Furnas Electric Co.
1500 Harvester
West Chicago, IL 60185
(708) 231-6200
President: R. W. Hansen
Manufactures and markets electrical controls.

W. W. Grainger, Inc.
5500 W. Howard St.
Skokie, IL 60077
(708) 982-9000
Contact: Personnel
Nationwide distributor of electric motors, controls, fans, blowers, pumps, compressors, office maintenance equipment, and products for industrial lighting and gardening equipment.

Health-Mor, Inc.
151 E. 22nd St.
Lombard, IL 60148
(708) 953-9770
Contact: Personnel
Manufactures the Filter Queen brand of household, institutional, and industrial vacuum cleaners.

Howe Richardson
403 Washington Blvd., Suite 15
Mundelein, IL 60060
(708) 223-4801

Contact: Personnel
Manufactures and sells a single product line of electronic measuring devices.

Illinois Tool Works
8501 W. Higgins Road
Chicago, IL 60631
(312) 693-3040
Personnel Director: Joseph Welcome
Produces and markets engineered fasteners and components; packaging products; electronic keyboards; precision tools and gearing; and instruments.

Joslyn Corporation
Corporate Headquarters
30 S. Wacker Drive
Chicago, IL 60606
(312) 454-2900
Senior Vice President: Alwyn A. DeSouza
Diversified company, operating in the fields of transportation, real estate, graphic arts, hobby and household products, mechanical contracting, heating and air conditioning.

Joslyn Corporation
Chicago Plant
3700 S. Morgan
Chicago, IL 60609
(312) 927-1420
Vice President: James Staulcup

Katy Industries
853 Dundee Ave.
Elgin, IL 60120
(708) 379-1121
Contact: Personnel
The Electrical Equipment Group manufactures and sells testing and measuring instruments for the electronics market;the Transportation Group owns railroad lines; the Financial Services Group operates insurance companies; the Consumer Products Group manufactures and sells Elgin watches; the Industrial Machinery Group manufactures equipment for industry.

Klein Tools
7200 N. McCormick Blvd.
Chicago, IL 60645
(312) 677-9500
Chairman: Mathias Klein

Mark Controls
5202 Old Orchard Road
Skokie, IL 60077

(708) 470-8585
President: William Bendix
Manufactures flow controls and energy management equipment.

McGill Mfg. Co.
909 N. Lafayette St.
Valparaiso, IN 46383
(219) 465-2200
Senior V.P., Industrial Relations: Seth H. Mosley
Manufacturer of electric switches and wiring devices.

Methode Electronics
7444 W. Wilson Ave.
Chicago, IL 60656
(312) 867-9600
Contact: Personnel
Engaged in the development and manufacture of electronic component devices used in computers, communications, industrial, military, and aerospace systems.

Microenergy, Inc.
350 Randy Road
Carol Stream, IL 60188
(708) 653-5900
Executive Vice President: Robert J. Fanella
Produces and markets supplies for the electronics industry.

Molex, Inc.
2222 Wellington Court
Lisle, IL 60532
(708) 969-4550
Vice President: Ronald H.Canaday
Produces and markets a wide range of electronic devices and electrical equipment.

Motorola, Inc.
1303 E. Algonquin Road
Schaumburg, IL 60196
(708) 397-1000
Personnel Director: James Donnely
Manufacturer of radios and electronic components.

Oak Industries
100 S. Main St.
Crystal Lake, IL 60014
(815) 459-5000
Contact: Personnel
Manufacturer of electrical switches, controls, and components for measuring devices; operates a CATV system.

Revere Electric Supply Co.
2501 W. Washington Blvd.
Chicago, IL 60612
(312) 738-3636
Personnel Director: Mary Lawson
Distributes electronic control products and electrical components.

Richardson Electronics
40W267 Keslinger Road
LaFox, IL 60147
(708) 232-6400
Personnel Director: Joe Grill
Manufacturer and distributor of power tubes and semiconductors.

Roper Corporation/Whirlpool
2000 M 63 North
Benton Harbor, MI 49022
(800) 447-6737
Contact: Personnel
Manufactures garden tractors and lawn mowers, snow-throwers, electric ranges, Venetian blinds, luggage, and other products.

Sargent-Welch Scientific Co.
7400 N. Linder Ave.
Skokie, IL 60077
(708) 677-0600
Contact: Personnel
Manufactures and distributes over 55,000 industrial and educational laboratory products to schools, research, and hospital laboratories.

S & C Electric
6601 N. Ridge Blvd.
Chicago, IL 60626
(312) 338-1000
Contact: Personnel
Manufacturer of high-voltage switching gear.

SigmaTron, Inc.
2201 Landmeier Road
Elk Grove Village, IL 60007
(708) 956-8000
Personnel Director: Nancy Geiser
Manufactures printed circuits and electrical connectors.

Square D Co.
Executive Plaza
1415 S. Roselle Road
Palatine, IL 60067
(708) 397-2600

Contact: Personnel
Manufacturer of electrical equipment.

Sun Electric Co.
One Sun Parkway
Crystal Lake, IL 60014
(815) 459-7700
Contact: Personnel
Develops, manufactures, and sells diagnostic test equipment for the transportation industry.

Sunbeam Corporation
1333 Butterfield Road
Downers Grove, IL 60515
(708) 719-4853
Mail Resume to:
P.O. Box 17199
Milwaukee, WI 53217
Attn: Corporate Personnel
The largest manufacturer and marketer of small appliances in the word.

Sunstrand Corporation
P.O. Box 7003
Rockford, IL 61125
(815) 226-6000
Contact: Personnel
Engaged in the design, manufacture, and sale of a broad line of transmissions and hydraulic equipment.

Switchcraft, Inc.
5555 N. Elston Ave.
Chicago, IL 60630
(312) 792-2700
V.P. Human Relations: Richard Dose
Manufacturer of electric components.

Teledyne, Inc.
700 E. Northwest Highway
Des Plaines, IL 60016
(708) 299-1111
Personnel Director: Bob Zimmanck
Diversified, multi-product corporation, consisting of 130 companies operating primarily in the areas of aviation and electronics, machines, metals, engines, energy, and power.

Triangle Home Products
945 E. 93rd St.
Chicago, IL 60619
(312) 374-4400
Contact: Personnel

Manufactures and distributes bathroom cabinets, range hoods, mirrors, ventilators, interior and exterior lighting fixtures.

Union Special Corporation
222 N. LaSalle, Suite 900
Chicago, IL 60601
(312) 606-9500
Director of Human Resources: Charles Sass
Manufacturer of industrial sewing machines.

Weldy/Lamont
1008 E. Northwest Highway
Mt. Prospect, IL 60056
(708) 398-4510
Contact: Personnel
The company's business is in six areas: industrial products for the automotive industry; electrical products such as switches and motors; warehousing and distribution of merchandise; manufacture and sale of light structural steels; manufacture and sale of metallurgical products; and the manufacture of portland cement.

Wells-Gardner Electronics Corporation
2701 N. Kildare Ave.
Chicago, IL 60639
(312) 252-8220
Contact: Personnel
Manufactures video game monitors, intrusion security devices, color TV consoles for private label sale, and data display monitors.

Westinghouse Electric Corporation
10 S. Riverside Plaza, 4th Floor
Chicago, IL 60606
(312) 454-7200
Personnel Manager: Joan Burke
Manufacturer of electrical equipment, nuclear power equipment, systems for cable TV.

Whitman Corporation
111 E. Wacker Drive
Chicago, IL 60601
(312) 565-3000
Assistant Vice President: Don Sulzer
A diversified holding company, operating in three major business areas: consumer products, industrial products, and the Illinois Central Gulf Railroad.

Electronics and Communications Equipment

For networking in **electronics** and related fields, check out the following professional organizations listed in Chapter 5:

PROFESSIONAL ORGANIZATIONS:

National Electronic Distributors Association

For additional information, you can write to:

Communications Equipment Distributors Association
2007 Gray Drive
Carbondale, IL 62901

Electronics Industry Association
2001 I St., N.W.
Washington, DC 20006

Institute of Electrical and Electronics Engineers (IEEE)
345 W. 47th St.
New York, NY 10017

North American Telecommunications Association
2000 M St., N.W.
Washington, DC 20036

United States Telephone Association
900 19th St., N.W.
Washington, DC 20006

PROFESSIONAL PUBLICATIONS:

Communications News
Communication Week
Design News
Electronic Business
Electronic Distributor
Electronic News
Electronic Products
Semiconductors International
Telecommunications
Telephone Engineer & Management
Telephony

DIRECTORIES:

Design News Electronic Directory (Cahner's Publishing Co., Boston, MA)
Directory of Wholesale Distributors (McGraw-Hill, New York, NY)
EIA Trade Directory (Electronics Industry Association, Washington, DC)
SIA Yearbook (Semiconductor Industry Association, Washington, DC)
Telephone Engineer and Management Directory (Edgell Communications, Chicago, IL)
Telephony's Directory & Buyer's Guide (Infertec, Chicago, IL)
Who's Who in Electronics (Harris Publications, Twinsburg, OH)
Who's Who in Technology (Research Publications, Woodbridge, CT)

EMPLOYERS:

AAR Corporation
2100 Touhy Ave.
Elk Grove Village, IL 60007
(708) 439-3939
President: Barton J. Levin
Manufactures navigational instruments for the aerospace industry.

AG Communications
400 N. Wolf Road
Northlake, IL 60164
(708) 681-7100
Employment Manager: Patrick Murphy
Manufacturer of communications systems and equipment.

Allnet Communications Services
100 S. Wacker Drive
Chicago, IL 60606
(312) 269-5725
Personnel Director: Patrick Greene
Interstate long-distance telephone service.

Amphenol Corporation
4300 Commerce Court
Lisle, IL 60532
(708) 983-3500
Contact: Personnel
Producer of electronic connectors and interconnection devices, information systems, and deep-pile textiles through its Borg Textiles division.

Andrew Corporation
10500 W. 153rd St.

Orland Park, IL 60462
(708) 349-3300
Director of Personnel: Rod Moss
Manufactures equipment for the telecommunications industry.

Anixter Bros.
4711 Golf Road
Skokie, IL 60076
(708) 677-2600
Office Manager: Ed O'Donnell
Manufactures products used in the transmission of telephone and cable TV communications.

AT&T
3800 Golf Road
Rolling Meadows, IL 60008
(708) 981-2000
Personnel Manager: Judy Dogoda
Manufacturer of communications systems.

AT&T
5555 Touhy Ave.
Skokie, IL 60077
(708) 676-8000
Contact: Personnel
Manufacturer of communications equipment such as data transmission apparatus and supplies.

Bally Manufacturing Co.
8700 W. Bryn Mawr Ave.
Chicago, IL 60631
(312) 399-1300
Director of Personnel: Lois Balodis
Manufactures electronic games and gaming equipment; operates 450 Aladdin's Castle amusement centers; owns Six Flags theme parks, resort hotels and casinos, health & fitness clubs.

Beatricc Foods
2 N. LaSalle
Chicago, IL 60602
(312) 782-3820
Contact: Personnel
Holding company with major interests in personal products, chemicals and industrial products, foods, high fidelity equipment and automotive products.

Centel Corporation
8725 W. Higgins Road
Chicago, IL 60631
(312) 399-2500

National distributor of telecommunications equipment, services, and supplies.

Cherry Electrical Products Corporation
3600 Sunset Ave.
Waukegan, IL 60087
(708) 662-9200
Personnel Director: Nancy Guarascio
One of the largest producers of precision snap-action switches and electronic keyboards; also manufacturers electrical components, gas discharge displays, and semiconductor devices.

Circuit Sales
650 E. Divan
Itasca, IL 60143
(708) 773-0200
Contact: Personnel Director
Principal business is the design, manufacture, and marketing of computer systems.

Cook Electric Co.
6201 W. Oakton St.
Morton Grove, IL 60053
(708) 967-6600
Manager, Employee & Industrial Relations: Cathy Brosmith
Manufacturer of data-handling systems.

A. B. Dick Co.
5700 W. Touhy Ave.
Chicago, IL 60648
(312) 763-1900
Contact: Personnel
Major manufacturer of duplicating machines, offset printers, and word processors.

DuKane Corporation
2900 DuKane Drive
St. Charles, IL 60174
(708) 584-2300
Employment Manager: Robert Scarlett
Manufacturer of communications equipment.

Eaton Corporation
191 E. North Ave.
Carol Stream, IL 60188
(708) 260-3400
Personnel Director: Nick Blauwiekle
Multi-divisional organization involved in manufacturing and sales of automotive parts, electronic and energy conservation equipment.

Fansteel, Inc.
One Tantalum Place
North Chicago, IL 60064
(708) 689-4900
Personnel Manager: Earl Legler
Manufacturer of refractory metals; fabricator of high-technology products for the automotive, appliance, metalworking, aerospace, recreational, electronic, and chemical industries.

Federal Signal Corporation
1415 W. 22nd St.
Oak Brook, IL 60521
(708) 954-2000
President & Chief Executive Officer: Joseph Ross
Manufacturer and worldwide supplier of signaling and communication equipment, fire trucks, parking gate signs, and electronic message displays.

General Electric Co.
1540 S. 54th Avenue
Cicero, IL 60650
(708) 780-2600
Plant Manager: Jeffrey Svoboda
Manufactures and distributes a broad range of personal and home appliances, industrial products, and aerospace components.

Honeywell, Inc.
1500 W. Dundee Road
Arlington Heights, IL 60004
(708) 394-4000
Contact: Personnel
Diversified electronics company, manufacturing quality products in the fields of temperature control, security devices, and information processing.

IBM Corporation
One IBM Plaza, 26th Floor
Chicago, IL 60611
(312) 245-2000
Corporate Employment Manager: Don Folkl
World's largest manufacturer and marketer of information technology.

IBM Rolm Systems
1100 Woodfield Road
Schaumburg, IL 60173
(708) 330-1600
Manufacturer of telecommunications equipment.

Illinois Tool Works
8501 W. Higgins Road
Chicago, IL 60631
(312) 693-3040
Personnel Director: Joseph Welcome
Produces and markets engineered fasteners and components, packaging products, electronic keyboards, precision tools and gearing, and instruments.

Interand Corp.
3200 W. Peterson Ave.
Chicago, IL 60659
(312) 478-1700
Senior Vice President, Human Resources: Linda Thomas-Phillips
Develops and produces interactive image communications systems.

MCI Telecommunications Corporation
205 N. Michigan Ave., Suite 2600
Chicago, IL 60601
(312) 856-2121
Long-distance telecommunications carrier.

Methode Electronics
7444 W. Wilson Ave.
Chicago, IL 60656
(312) 867-9600
Contact: Personnel
Principally engaged in the manufacture of electronic component devices used in the production of electronic equipment, including computer, communications, industrial, military, and aerospace systems.

Molex, Inc.
2222 Wellington Court
Lisle, IL 60532
(708) 969-4550
Contact: Personnel
Leading worldwide producer of electrical and electronic components and interconnecting systems used in the computer, telecommunications, medical, and household appliance industries.

Motorola, Inc.
1303 E. Algonquin Road
Schaumburg, IL 60196
(708) 397-1000
Staffing: Tom Tobin
Manufacturer of radios and electronic components.

NCR Corporation
7400 N. Caldwell

Chicago, IL 60648
(312) 775-0500
Manager, Personnel: Mike Kieley
Manufactures, sells, and services data-entry equipment terminals, computers, EDP, and supplies.

Northrop Corporation
Defense Systems Division
600 Hicks Road
Rolling Meadows, IL 60008
(708) 259-9600
Contact: Personnel
Researches and develops electronic equipment.

Oak Industries
100 S. Main St.
Crystal Lake, IL 60014
(815) 459-5000
Personnel Director: Marty Davis
Provides over-the-air subscription and cable television services; manufactures equipment for these systems.

Panduit Co.
17301 S. Ridgeland Ave.
Tinley Park, IL 60477
(708) 532-1800
Contact: Personnel
Manufacturer of electronic accessories.

Pittway Corporation
333 Skokie Blvd.
Northbrook, IL 60065
(708) 498-1260
Contact: Personnel
Manufacturer of aerosol products and home burglar and fire alarms.

Prime Capital Corporation
1701 Golf Road
Tower 2, Suite 500
Rolling Meadows, IL 60008
(708) 593-1300
Leases telecommunications materials.

Quasar Company
1325 Pratt Blvd.
Elk Grove Village, IL 60007
(708) 228-6366
Contact: Personnel
Manufacturer of consumer products such as videotape machines, microwave ovens, and televisions.

Quixote Corporation
One E. Wacker Drive
Chicago, IL 60601
(312) 467-6755
Contact: Personnel
Manufactures computer-assisted transcription machines used in court reporting.

Reliance Electric Co.
11333 W. Addison St.
Franklin Park, IL 60131
(708) 455-8010
Contact: Personnel
Manufacturer of connection equipment utilized by communications and power companies.

Richardson Electronics
3030 N. River Road
Franklin Park, IL 60131
(708) 232-6400
Manufactures electron tubes and semiconductors.

Rockwell International
8245 Lemont Road
Downers Grove, IL 60515
(708) 985-9000
Personnel Manager: Dennis Kebrolle
Manufactures telecommunications products such as PBX equipment, switching systems, PCM transmission multiplexers.

Shure Brothers
222 Hartrey Ave.
Evanston, IL 60202-3696
(708) 866-2200
Personnel Director: Jack Shea
Manufacturer of electronic and communications equipment.

Steiner Electronic Co.
1250 Touhy Ave.
Elk Grove Village, IL 60007
(708) 228-0400
Personnel Director: Carol Boling
Electronic and electrical distributing company.

Sun Electric Co.
One Sun Parkway
Crystal Lake, IL 60014
(815) 459-7700
Personnel Director: Betty Zambon
Develops, manufactures, and sells diagnostic test equipment for the transportation industry.

Switchcraft, Inc.
5555 N. Elston Ave.
Chicago, IL 60630
(312) 792-2700
Human Resource Manager: Elaine Lysandrou
Manufacturer of electric components.

Telephone & Data Systems
79 W. Monroe St., Suite 905
Chicago, IL 60603
(312) 630-1900
Provides telecommunications services to local markets.

Telesphere Communications
Two Mid America Plaza, Suite 500
Oakbrook Terrace, IL 60181
(708) 954-7700
Vice President: Robert L. Longhitano
Provides telecommunications and long distance services.

Tellabs, Inc.
4951 Indiana Ave.
Lisle, IL 60532
(708) 969-8800
Manufacturer of a wide variety of communications equipment.

Unisys Corporation
One Unisys Center, Suite 601
Lombard, IL 60148
(708) 969-5550
Director, Human Resources (Public Sector): Denny Hutton
Manufacturer of computational equipment and computers.

US Sprint Communications Corporation
5600 N. River Road
Rosemont, IL 60018
(708) 318-3000
Long-distance telecommunications carrier.

Wells Fargo Alarm Services
230 W. Division St.
Chicago, IL 60610
(312) 337-3100
Director, Personnel: Beverly Owens
Provides burglar and fire alarm systems.

Westinghouse Electric Corporation
10 S. Riverside Plaza
Chicago, IL 60606
(312) 454-7200
Personnel Director: Joan Burke

Manufacturer of electrical equipment, nuclear power equipment, systems for cable TV.

Woodhead Industries
3411 Woodhead Drive
Northbrook, IL 60062
(708) 272-7990
V.P. Human Resources: Robert Jennings
Manufactures computer telecommunications equipment.

Xerox Corporation
3000 Des Plaines Ave.
Des Plaines, IL 60018
(708) 635-2335
Regional Personnel Manager: Ralph Volpe
One of the world's largest manufacturers of copiers and duplication equipment; owns educational publishing company.

Zenith Electronics Corporation
1000 Milwaukee Ave.
Glenview, IL 60025
(708) 391-7000
Vice President, Personnel: Michael Kaplan
Manufacturer of computers, television, and radio equipment.

Entertainment: Theaters and Talent Agents

For networking in the **entertainment business** and related fields, check out the following professional organizations listed in chapter 5:

PROFESSIONAL ORGANIZATIONS:

AFTRA
American Society of Artists
American Women in Radio and Television
Amusement and Music Operators Association
Association for Multi-Image
Center for New Television
Chicago Artists Coalition
Chicago Coalition
Fashion Group of Chicago
Illinois Arts Council
Illinois Creative Artists Registry
Lawyers for the Creative Arts
League of Chicago Theaters

Music Distributors Association
National Academy of Television Arts & Sciences

For additional information, you can write to:

American Federation of Arts
41 E. 65th St.
New York, NY 10021

American Film Institute
Kennedy Center for the Performing Arts
Washington, DC 20566

Amusement and Music Operators Association
1101 Connecticut Ave., N.W.
Washington, DC 20036

Arts and Business Council
130 E. 40th St.
New York, NY 10016

Illinois Arts Council
111 N. Wabash Ave.
Chicago, IL 60601

National Assembly of Local Arts Agencies
1625 I St., N.W., Suite 725 A
Washington, DC 20006

Southern California Motion Picture Council
1922 Western Ave.
Los Angeles, CA 90010

PROFESSIONAL PUBLICATIONS:

Audition News
Backstage
Billboard
Chicago Scene
Performing Arts Journal
Screen
Theater Times
Variety

DIRECTORIES:

Back Stage TV/Film/Tape/Syndication Directory (Back Stage Publications, New York, NY)

How To Get a Job

Blue Book (Hollywood Reporter, Hollywood, CA)
Entertainment Facilities Buyer's Guide (Billboard Publications, Nashville, TN)
Film Producers, Studios, and Agents Guide (Lone Eagle Publishing, Beverly Hills, CA)
Who's Who in the Motion Picture Industry (Packard House, Beverly Hills, CA)
Who's Who in Television (Packard House, Beverly Hills, CA)

EMPLOYERS:

Ambassador Talent Agents
203 N. Wabash Ave., Suite 2210
Chicago, IL 60601
(312) 641-3491
Talent agency.

A Plus Talent Agency
680 N. Lake Shore Drive
Chicago, IL 60611
(312) 642-8151
Talent agency.

Arie Crown Theater
2301 S. Lake Shore Drive
McCormick Place on the Lake
Chicago, IL 60616
(312) 791-6000
Housed in McCormick Place, this is the city's largest theater.

Auditorium Theater
50 E. Congress Parkway
Chicago, IL 60605
(312) 922-4046
Exec. Director: Dulci Gilmore
National historic landmark theater; designed, with near-perfect acoustics, by Louis Sullivan.

Body Politic
2261 N. Lincoln Ave.
Chicago, IL 60614
(312) 871-3000
Managing Director: Nan Charbonneau
Theater.

Mary Boncher Model Management
Presidential Towers
575 W. Madison, Suite 810
Chicago, IL 60606
(312) 902-2400
Talent agency.

Candlelight Dinner Playhouse
5620 S. Harlem Ave.
Summit, IL 60501
(708) 496-3000
Owner/Director: William Pullinsi
Theater.

Chicago Symphony Chorus
122 S. Michigan Ave.
Chicago, IL 60604
(312) 435-8172

Chicago Symphony Orchestra
220 S. Michigan Ave.
Chicago, IL 60604
(312) 435-8122

Cineplex Odeon
70 E. Lake St.
Chicago, IL 60601
(312) 726-5300
Movie theater chain.

City of Chicago Cultural Center
78 E. Washington
Chicago, IL 60602
(312) 744-1742

City of Chicago Department of Special Events
121 N. LaSalle, Room 703
Chicago, IL 60602
(312) 744-3315

Court Theater
5535 S. Ellis Ave.
Chicago, IL 60637
(312) 753-4472
Producer: Nicholas Rudall
Theater.

David & Lee Model Management
70 W. Hubbard, Suite 200
Chicago, IL 60610
(312) 661-0500
Talent agency.

Harrise Davidson Associates
230 N. Michigan Ave.
Chicago, IL 60601
(312) 782-4480
Talent agency.

Drury Lane Theaters
2500 W. 95th St.
Evergreen Park, IL 60642
(708) 779-4000
Owner: John & Ray Lazzarra
Operates dinner theaters in Evergreen Park and Oak Brook.

Durkin Talent Agency
743 N. LaSalle St., Suite 250
Chicago, IL 60610
(312) 664-0045

Elite Model Management
212 W. Superior, Suite 406
Chicago, IL 60610
(312) 943-3226
Talent agency.

ETA, Inc.
7558 S. South Chicago Ave.
Chicago, IL 60619
(312) 752-3955
Talent agency.

Excellent Theaters
231 Westland Road, Suite 2700
Chicago, IL 60606
(312) 332-7465
Movie theater chain.

Ferrer Agency
935 W. Chestnut St.
Chicago, IL 60622
(312) 243-2388
Talent agency.

Geddes Agency
188 W. Randolph Drive, Suite 2500
Chicago, IL 60601
(312) 263-4090
Talent agency.

Goodman Theater
200 S. Columbus Drive
Chicago, IL 60603
(312) 443-3800
Director: Robert Falls
Legitimate theater.

Hall Agency
980 N. Michigan Ave., Suite 1400
Chicago, IL 60611

(312) 280-4784
Send Resume to:
P.O. Box 931
Gaylord, MI 49735
Talent agency.

Shirley Hamilton, Inc.
333 E. Ontario St.
Chicago, IL 60611
(312) 787-4700
Talent agency.

Holiday Star Theater
8001 Delaware St.
Merrillville, IN 46410
(219 769-6600
Managing Director: Dennis Andres
Las Vegas-style theater, booking nationally known, big-name acts.

Jefferson & Associates
1050 N. State St.
Chicago, IL 60610
(312) 337-1930
Talent agency.

Susanne Johnson Talent Agency
108 W. Oak St.
Chicago, IL 60610
(312) 943-8315
Talent agency.

Kordos-Charbonneau Casting
430 Hibbard Road
Wilmette, IL 60091
(708) 251-2072
Talent agency.

Kuumba Theater Company
1900 W. Van Buren St.
Chicago, IL 60604
(312) 461-9000
Producer: Val Ward
Theater company.

League of Chicago Theaters
67 E. Madison, Suite 2116
Chicago, IL 60603
(312) 977-1730
Association of local independent theaters.

Lily's Talent Agency
650 N. Greenwood
Park Ridge, IL 60068
(708) 698-1044
Talent agency.

Emilia Lorence, Ltd.
619 N. Wabash
Chicago, IL 60611
(312) 787-2033
Talent agency.

Lyric Opera of Chicago
20 N. Wacker Drive
Chicago, IL 60606
(312) 332-2244
Director: Ardis Krainek
Chicago's resident opera company.

M & R Amusement Companies
8707 Skokie Blvd.
Skokie, IL 60077
(708) 673-5600
Movie theater chain.

Marriot's Lincolnshire Theater
10 Marriot Ave.
Lincolnshire, IL 60069
(708) 634-0200
Producer: Kary Walker

Medinah Temple
600 N. Wabash Ave.
Chicago, IL 60611
(312) 266-5000
Theatrical facility.

National Jewish Theater
5050 Church St.
Skokie, IL 60077
(708) 675-5070
Artistic Director: Sheldon Patinkin
Theater.

National Talent Network
101 E. Ontario, Suite 760
Chicago, IL 60611
(312) 280-2225
Talent agency.

North Light Repertory Theater, Cornet Theatre
817 Chicago Ave.

Evanston, IL 60201
(708) 869-7278
Repertory company.

Nouvelle Talent Management
703 N. Franklin St., Suite 304
Chicago, IL 60610
(312) 944-1133
Talent agency.

Office of Film and Entertainment Industries-Chicago
174 W. Randolph St., 3rd Floor
Chicago, IL 60601
(312) 744-6415

Orchestral Association
220 S. Michigan Ave.
Chicago, IL 60604
(312) 435-8122
General Manager: Henry Fogel
Manages the Chicago Symphony Orchestra and Orchestra Hall.

Phoenix Talent
332 S. Michigan Ave., Suite 1847
Chicago, IL 60604
(312) 786-2024
Talent agency.

Ravinia Festival Association
P.O. Box 896
Highland Park, IL 60035
(708) 728-4642
Exec. Director: Zarin Mahta
Three-month summer festival, featuring the Chicago Symphony, world-renowned classical and pop artists, dance, and drama.

Remains Theater
1800 N. Clybourne
Chicago, IL 60614
(312) 549-7725
Producer: Larry Sloan

Rosemont Horizon
6920 Mannheim Road
Rosemont, IL 60018
(312) 635-6601
Indoor arena, booking big-name acts and sports events.

Salazar & Navas
367 W. Chicago Ave.
Chicago, IL 60610

(312) 751-3419
Talent agency.

Screen Actors Guild
307 N. Michigan Ave.
Chicago, IL 60601
(312) 372-8081

Second City Theater
1616 N. Wells St.
Chicago, IL 60614
(312) 644-4032
The improvisational troupe that launched the careers of Mike Nichols, David Steinberg, Joan Rivers, John Belushi, and other nationally known performers.

Shubert Theater
22 W. Monroe St.
Chicago, IL 60603
(312) 977-1710
Legitimate theater specializing in musicals.

Shucart Enterprises
1417 Green Bay Road
Highland Park, IL 60035
(708) 433-1113
Talent agency.

State of Illinois Film Office
100 W. Randolph, Suite 3400
Chicago, IL 60601
(312) 814-3600

Steppenwolf Theater
2851 N. Halsted St.
Chicago, IL 60657
(312) 472-4141
Managing Director: Stephen Eich
Innovative off-Loop theatrical company.

Stewart Talent Management Corporation
212 W. Superior, Suite 406
Chicago, IL 60610
(312) 943-3131
Talent agency.

Victory Gardens Theater
2257 N. Lincoln Ave.
Chicago, IL 60614
(312) 871-3000
Artistic Director: Dennis Zacek

Arlene Wilson Talent
414 N. Orleans St., Suite 407
Chicago, IL 60610
(312) 644-6699
Talent agency.

Wisdom Bridge Theater
1559 W. Howard St.
Chicago, IL 60626
(312) 743-6442
Artistic Director: Jeffrey Ortmann

Fashion/Clothing/Cosmetics

For networking in the **fashion industry** and related fields, check out the following professional organizations listed in Chapter 5:

PROFESSIONAL ORGANIZATIONS:

Chicago Cosmetologists Association
Chicago Jewelers Association
Fashion Group of Chicago
Greater North Michigan Avenue Association
Greater State Street Council

For additional information, you can write to:

American Apparel Manufacturers Association
2500 Wilson Blvd., Suite 301
Arlington, VA 22201

Federation of Apparel Manufacturers
225 W. 34th St.
New York, NY 10122

Textile Research Institute
Box 625
Princeton, NJ 08540

PROFESSIONAL PUBLICATIONS:

Apparel Industry
Apparel Merchandising

Cosmetics and Toiletries
Soap/Cosmetics/Chemical Specialties
Textile Industries
Textile Research Journal
Textile World
Women's Wear Daily

DIRECTORIES:

Accessories Resources (Business Journals, Norwalk, CT)
Apparel Industry Sourcebook (Denyse & Co., North Hollywood, CA)
Apparel Trades Book (Dun & Bradstreet, Murray, NJ)
Davison's Textile Blue Book (Davison Publishing, Ridgewood, NJ)
Fairchild's Textile & Apparel Financial Directory (Fairchild Publications, New York, NY)
Household and Personal Products Industry, The Top 50 (Rodman Publishing Co., Ramsey, NJ)
Membership Directory (American Apparel Manufacturer's Association, Arlington, VA)
Models Mart Directory (Peter Glenn Publications, New York, NY)
Textile Blue Book (Davison Publishing, Ridgewood, NJ)

EMPLOYERS:

Alberto-Culver Co.
2525 Armitage Ave.
Melrose Park, IL 60160
(708) 450-3000
Contact: Personnel
Produces and distributes large line of toiletries for men and women; Household/Grocery Products division produces Milani salad dressings, Baker's Joy and Sugar Twin; John A. Frye division produces shoes and boots.

Artra Group
500 Central Ave.
Northfield, IL 60093
(708) 441-6650
Distributor of costume jewelry.

Avon Products
6901 Golf Road
Morton Grove, IL 60053
(708) 966-0200
Human Resources Manager: J.E. Lyons

World's largest distributor of cosmetics, fragrances, and jewelry via in-home sales.

John H. Breck, Inc.
1100 E. Business Center Drive
Mount Prospect, IL 60056
(708) 827-8871
Contact: Personnel
Shampoo and hair products manufacturer.

Chesebrough-Ponds
6901 W. 65th St.
Chicago, IL 60638
(312) 735-6800
Personnel Manager: Mary Ellen Bilotta
Leading manufacturer of soaps and household products.

Cosmetique, Inc.
200 Corporate Woods Parkway
Bergen Hills, IL 60061
(708) 913-9099
President: June Giugni
National beauty continuity club.

Florsheim Shoe Co.
130 S. Canal St.
Chicago, IL 60606
(312) 599-7500
Contact: Personnel
Manufacturer of quality men's and women's shoes and boots; owns retail outlets.

Fruit of the Loom
6300 Sears Tower
233 S. Wacker Drive
Chicago, IL 60606
(312) 876-1724
Vice President: Kenneth Greenbaum
Manufacturer of underwear and activewear.

Albert Given Manufacturing Co.
1301 W. Chicago Ave.
East Chicago, IN 46312
(219) 397-3200
Personnel Manager: Jackie Flores
Manufacturer of men's slacks.

Hartmarx Corporation
101 N. Wacker Drive
Chicago, IL 60606
(312) 372-6300
Contact: Personnel

Manufactures and sells quality clothing under its own and other labels; Retail Stores Group owns and operates 400 apparel stores in the U.S.

Helene Curtis Industries
325 N. Wells St.
Chicago, IL 60610
(312) 661-0222
Vice President: Michael Goldman
Manufacturer of cosmetics and hair preparations.

Jaymar-Ruby, Inc./Hartmarx
5000 S. Ohio St.
Michigan City, IN 46360
(219) 879-7341
Personnel Manager: John Skierkowski
Men's dress slacks, clothing, and sportswear.

Johnson & Johnson
Interstate 55 & Joliet Road
Lamont, IL 60439-9419
(815) 739-1000
Personnel Manager: Dennis Pogany
Manufactures and sells products in the health and personal care fields.

Johnson Products Co.
8522 S. Lafayette Ave.
Chicago, IL 60620
(312) 483-4100
Personnel Manager: Floyd Beverly
Manufactures personal care products for the black ethnic market.

Joy Sportswear
2100 E. 15th Ave.
Gary, IN 46402
(219) 883-9681
Contact: Personnel
Women's sports apparel.

Northwest Industries
6300 Sears Tower
233 S. Wacker Drive
Chicago, IL 60606
(312) 876-7000
V. P., Personnel: Sherry McCreary
Diversified manufacturer whose apparel divisions include Fruit of the Loom, B.V.D., and Screen Stars underwear; Acme, Dingo, and Dan Post boots.

O'Bryan Bros.
4220 W. Belmont Ave.
Chicago, IL 60641
(312) 283-3000
Personnel Director: Janis O'Keefe
Manufactures women's lingerie.

Oxxford Clothes
1220 W. Van Buren St.
Chicago, IL 60607
(312) 829-3600
Treasurer: Robert Steltman
Manufacturer of quality men's suits and coats.

Proctor & Gamble Mfg. Co.
1232 W. North Ave.
Chicago, IL 60622
(312) 252-8872
Contact: Personnel
Manufactures and markets household products including Tide, Zest soap, Pampers, Crest toothpaste, and other well-known brands.

Purex Corporation
2500 S. 25th Ave.
Broadview, IL 60153
(708) 344-0088
Personnel Manager: Richard Haggerty
Manufactures and distributes toiletries, chemicals, and medicines.

Quintessence
980 N. Michigan Ave.
Chicago, IL 60611
(312) 951-7000
Contact: Personnel
Manufacturer of Jovan and other brand-name cosmetics.

Soft Sheen Products
1000 E. 87th St.
Chicago, IL 60619
(312) 978-0700
Personnel Director: Denise Boyd
Manufacturer of hair preparations for the black ethnic market.

Wilson Garment Co.
426 S. Clinton St.
Chicago, IL 60607
(312) 427-1568
Contact: Ted Hymen
Manufacturer of Gino Rossi coats and suits.

Arthur Winer, Inc.
855 Taft St.
Gary, IN 46404
(219) 949-7491
Personnel Director: Beverly Wlordcyzk
Men's and women's trousers and skirts.

Foods and Beverages

For networking in the **food industry** and related fields, check out the following professional organizations listed in Chapter 5:

PROFESSIONAL ORGANIZATIONS:

American Dietetic Association
Dietary Managers Association
Food Equipment Manufacturers Association
Foodservice Equipment Distributors Association
Home Economists in Business
Illinois Food Retailers Association
Illinois Restaurant Association
Institute of Food Technologists
International Food Service Manufacturers Association
National Association of Food Equipment Manufacturers
National Dairy Council
National Restaurant Association
National Wine Distribution

For additional information, you can write to:

Distilled Spirits Council
1250 I St., N.W.
Washington, DC 20005

Food Marketing Institute
1750 K St., N.W.
Washington, DC 20006

National Food Distributors Association
111 E. Wacker Drive
Chicago, IL 60601

National Food Processors Association
1401 New York Ave.
Washington, DC 20005

National Frozen Foods Association
204 E St., N.E.
Washington, DC 20002

National Soft Drink Association
1101 16th St., N.W.
Washington, DC 20036

Wine & Spirits Wholesalers of America
1025 15th St., N.W.
Washington, DC 20005

PROFESSIONAL PUBLICATIONS:

Beverage World
Food and Beverage Marketing
Food Engineering
Food Technology
Forecast for the Home Economist
Institutional Distributor
Institutions
Quick Frozen Foods International

DIRECTORIES:

Directory (National Frozen Foods Association, Hershey, PA)
Frozen Food Fact Book (National Frozen Foods Association, Hershey, PA)
National Beverage Marketing Directory (Beverage Marketing Group, New York, NY)
NFBA Directory (National Food Brokers Association, Washington, DC)
Progressive Grocer's Market Scope (MacLean Hunter, Stamford, CT)
Thomas Grocery Register (Thomas Publishing Company, New York, NY)

EMPLOYERS:

American Home Products Corporation
5151 W. 73rd St.
Chicago, IL 60638
(312) 767-8460
Contact: Personnel
Produces products in food and drug fields, including Anacin, Chef Boy-ar-dee, Brach's candy, Woolite, PAM, and Easy-Off.

American Maize Products Co.
Corn Processing Div.

1100 Indianapolis Blvd.
Hammond, IN 46320
(219) 659-2000
V.P. Human Resources: Jane E. Downing
Corn starches, corn syrups, syrup solids, gluten feed, and gluten meal.

ARA Leisure Services
2000 Spring Road, Suite 300
Oak Brook, IL 60521
(708) 572-2800
Operations Manager: Walter Bucki
Providers of institutional food services;also services vending machines.

Archer Daniels Midland Co.
466 Faries Parkway
Decatur, IL 62526
(217) 424-5200
Personnel Director: Sheila Witts-Mannweiler
Engaged in buying, storing, transporting, processing and merchandising raw agricultural products such as soybean oil and meal, textured vegetable protein, corn sweeteners, and malt products.

Archibald Candy Co./ Fannie May Candies
1137 W. Jackson Blvd.
Chicago, IL 60607
(312) 243-2700
Candy and chocolate retailer and manufacturer.

Armanetti, Inc.
508 W. Lake St.
Addison, IL 60601
(708) 543-9563
Personnel Director: Sylvia Stromberger
Retail liquor store chain.

Barton Brands
55 E. Monroe St., Suite 1700
Chicago, IL 60603
(312) 346-9200
Office Manager: Bob Egan
Distills, blends, bottles, and distributes alcoholic beverages.

Jim Beam Distilling Corporation
510 Lake Cook Road
Deerfield, IL 60015
(708) 948-8888
Personnel Director: Stuart Kauffman
Distills, blends, bottles, and distributes alcoholic beverages.

Beatrice Foods
2 N. LaSalle St.
Chicago, IL 60602
(312) 558-4000
Manager, Corporate Employment: Pam Gehring
Produces, processes, and distributes over 400 brands of food and dairy products, soft drinks, groceries, specialty meats, snack products, citrus products, LaChoy oriental foods, Meadow Gold milk, Aunt Nellie's pickles, etc.

David Berg & Co.
165 South Water Market
Chicago, IL 60608
(312) 738-2200
Personnel Director: Veronica Murray
Manufacturer of hot dogs and other sausage products.

Bernard Food Industries
1125 Hartrey Ave.
Evanston, IL 60204
(708) 273-4497
Personnel Director: John Zabraus
Distributer of retail food products.

Borden, Inc.
2301 Shermer Road
Northbrook, IL 60062
(708) 498-6200
Personnel Director: Daniel Wilde
Manufactures, processes, and distributes grocery items, snacks, refrigerated goods, bakery items, dairy and beverage products including Wylers lemonade mix, Borden milk and cheese, Elmer's Glue, Walltex wall coverings, Cracker Jack snacks, and Mystic Tape.

Campbell Soup Co.
2550 W. 35th St.
Chicago, IL 60632
(312) 376-3700
Contact: Personnel
Manufacturer and marketer of canned soups, beans, and spaghetti.

A.J. Canfield Co.
50 E. 89th Place
Chicago, IL 60619
(312) 483-7000
Vice President, Sales: Gerald Vance
Produces and distributes beverages.

Canteen Company
222 N. LaSalle

Chicago, IL 60601
(312) 701-2000
Personnel Director: Lawrence Wilkas
Services vending machines; operates restaurants.

Central Grocers Cooperative
3701 N. Centrella St.
Franklin Park, IL 60131
(708) 678-0660
General Manager, Accounting: Jane Hidalgo

Certified Grocers of Illinois
4800 S. Central Ave.
Chicago, IL 60638
(312) 585-7000
Director, Human Resources: William Smith
Wholesale grocers.

Charlotte Charles, Inc.
2501 N. Elston Ave.
Chicago, IL 60647
(312) 772-8310
Persoonel Director: Margaret Rich
Manufactures and distributes gourmet and specialty foods.

C&K Snacks
3333 W. 36th St.
Chicago, IL 60632
(312) 376-0700
President: Jerry Campagna
Wholesale beer and snack distributor.

Clark Products
950 Arthur Ave.
Elk Grove Village, IL 60007
(708) 956-1730
Contact: Personnel
Food-service distributor and manufacturer.

Coca-Cola Bottling Co. of Chicago
7400 N. Oak Park Ave.
Niles, IL 60648
(708) 775-0900
V.P. Personnel: Robert T. Palo
Bottler and distributor of carbonated beverages.

Continental Distributing Co.
9800 W. Balmoral Ave.
Rosemont, IL 60018
(708) 671-7700
Sales Manager: Barry Labovitz
Wholesaler of wines and spirits.

Convenient Food Mart
9701 W. Higgins Road, Suite 850
Rosemont, IL 60018
(708) 692-9150
Administrative Manager: Mariann Eder
National franchiser for Convenient food store chain.

Darling & Company
1250 W. 46th St.
Chicago, IL 60609
(312) 927-0500
Personnel Director: Bill Schultz
Producer of poultry by-products and stabilized animal fats.

Dean Foods Company
3600 N. River Road
Franklin Park, IL 60131
(312) 625-6200
Contact: Personnel
Major dairy and specialty foods manufacturer.

DeKalb AgResearch
3100 Sycamore Road
DeKalb, IL 60115
(815) 758-3461
Personnel Director: Cindy Lynch
One of the world's leading developers of hybrid grain seed, hybrid poultry, and swine stock; owns Heinhold Commodities, a commodity brokerage house; owns DeKalb Petroleum Co., producers of natural gas.

Diversifoods, Inc.
910 Sherwood Drive, Suite 13
Lake Bluff, IL 60044
(708) 234-3407
Personnel Director: Meri Bezinski
Fast-food franchiser and restaurant operator, including Burger King, Godfather's Pizza, Chart House restaurants, Luther's Bar-B-Q, and Moxic's.

Mouth-watering opportunities in food service management

Paula Hall, manager of the dietary department of a suburban hospital, sees the food service industry as a growing field with tremendous potential. The many hospitals in the Chicago area offer varied opportunities in food services, according to Paula. Some of the jobs, such as clinical or administrative dietician, require a college degree in nutrition. But many do not.

"Some employees have experience working at a fast-food restaurant," says

Paula. "Others just learn on the job. Still others have completed one- or two-year programs in food service offered by various colleges." Besides registered dieticians, Paula's staff includes food service supervisors, who manage the personnel who prepare food; diet technicians, who prepare and implement menus based on information about the patient; diet aides, who perform such tasks as delivering meals to patients; a chef and cooking staff; and a food purchasing agent.

Paula is optimistic about employment prospects in the food service industry as a whole. "There are tremendous opportunities for those with culinary arts skills, as well as for hotel or restaurant food service managers. Opportunities exist in food equipment companies, public and private schools, contract food companies, and food service consulting firms. Right now the possibilities in food marketing are phenomenal.

"The nutritional needs of the growing elderly population," Paula adds, "will also create many new jobs in the food service business as hospitals and other organizations become involved in the field of long-term care."■

Dominick's Finer Foods
505 Railroad Ave.
Northlake, IL 60164-1696
(708) 562-1000
Contact: Personnel
Retail food store chain.

Edward Don & Company
2500 S. Harlem Ave.
North Riverside, IL 60546
(708) 326-8000
President: Robert Don
Distributor of food service equipment and supplies.

Faber Enterprises
55 E. Monroe St., Suite 3533
Chicago, IL 60603
(312) 558-8989
Contact: Human Resources Department
Owns and operates restaurants and drugstores.

Farley Candy Company
4820 Searle Parkway
Skokie, IL 60077
(708) 673-7200
Personnel Director: Bernie Panocha
Manufactures candy.

Federated Distributors
4130 S. Morgan St.
Chicago, IL 60609
(312) 254-3600
Vice President: Jim Keating
Wholesale liquor distributer.

General Foods Corporation
Beverage & Breakfast Foods Division
7400 S. Rockwell St.
Chicago, IL 60629
(312) 471-7500
Contact: Personnel
Producer and marketer of packaged grocery products including Maxwell House coffee, Jell-o, Kool-Aid, and Birdseye frozen foods.

Gonnella Baking Co.
2002-14 W. Erie St.
Chicago, IL 60612
(312) 733-2020
Supervisor: Theodore Pasquesi
Hearth-baked bread products and frozen dough.

Harvest Industries
350 Barclay Blvd.
Lincolnshire, IL 60069
(708) 634-1870
Contact: Personnel
A diversified agribusiness company that manufactures, sells and distributes animal feed and feed supplements and animal health care products.

Hollymatic Corporation
600 E. Plainsfield Road
Countryside, IL 60525
(708) 579-3700
Personnel Director: Marilyn Krische
World's largest producer of food processing and portioning equipment.

Illini Beef Packers
P.O. Box 28
Geneseo, IL 61254
(309) 658-2291

Personnel Director: Tom Udell
Principally engaged in the slaughtering and dressing of beef cattle and in marketing beef and beef by-products to wholesalers, jobbers, restaurants, grocery stores, and meat markets.

Interstate Brands Corporation
40 E. Garfield Blvd.
Chicago, 60615
(312) 536-7700
Contact: Personnel
Manufactures and markets bread and cake products.

Interstate United Corporation
222 N. LaSalle
Chicago, IL 60601
(312) 701-2000
Personnel Director: Howard McGuire
Provider of food service management to institutions and industry.

Jays Foods
825 E. 99th St.
Chicago, IL 60628
(312) 731-8400
Personnel Director: Louis Baker
Manufacturer and marketer of snack products.

Jel Sert Co.
P.O. Box 261
West Chicago, IL 60185
(708) 231-7590
President: Charles T. Wenger IV
Food and snack products manufacturer.

Jewel Companies
1955 W. North Ave.
Melrose Park, IL 60160
(708) 531-6000
V.P. Human Resources: Ed Buron
Retail supermarket chain.

Katy Industries
853 Dundee Ave.
Elgin, IL 60120
(708) 379-1121
Contact: Human Resources
Multi-industry corporation with interests in food processing, testing and measuring equipment, oil and gas exploration, industrial machinery, and consumer items such as jewelry, silver flatware, and clocks.

Keebler Company
One Hollow Tree Lane
Elmhurst, IL 60126
(708) 379-1525
V.P. Human Resources: John J. Kelley
Major producer and marketer of cookies, biscuits, and other bakery goods.

Kraft, Inc.
Kraft Court
Glenview, IL 60025
(708) 998-2000
Contact: Corporate Staffing
Manufacturer and marketer of Kraft and other brand food and dairy products.

Kraft/Holleb & Co.
800 Supreme Drive
Bensenville, IL 60106
(708) 569-3790
Sales Manager: Debbie Oler
Wholesale food distributor.

Leaf, Inc.
1155 N. Cicero Ave.
Chicago, IL 60651
(312) 745-6200
V.P. Personnel: Paul Serff
Manufacturer of gum and candy.

Lifesavers Planters Company
3401 Mount Prospect Road
Franklin Park, IL 60131
(708) 766-7850
Contact: Personnel
Diversified manufacturer and marketer of food and liquor products including Fleischmann's beverages, Chase & Sanborn coffee, Planter's nuts, Curtiss candy, and Melville confections.

W. E. Long Co.
300 W. Washington St.
Chicago, IL 60606
(312) 726-4606
V. P., Human Resources: Helen Mayberry
Cooperative for wholesale bakery members.

Oscar Mayer & Co.
1241 N. Sedgewick
Chicago, IL 60610
(312) 642-1200
Personnel Director: Connie Steffanus
Manufacturer and marketer of meat and meat products.

M&M Mars Candy Co.
2019 N. Oak Park Ave.
Chicago, IL 60635
(312) 637-3000
Contact: Personnel
Manufacturer of a broad range of candy and confectionery products.

Ed Miniat, Inc.
945 W. 38th St.
Chicago, IL 60609
(312) 927-9200
Personnel Director: Michael Broderick
Manufactures wholesale meats and oils.

Morton Intenational
110 N. Wacker Drive
Chicago, IL 60606
(312) 807-2000
V.P. Human Resources: John C. Hedley
Manufacturer of salt and chemicals.

Nabisco, Inc.
7300 S. Kedzie Ave.
Chicago, IL 60629
(312) 925-4300
Personnel Manager: Mike Southard
Producer of cookies, crackers, and cereals.

National Tea Co.
9701 W. Higgins Road
Rosemont, IL 60018
(708) 693-5100
President: Sheldon Durtsche
Supermarket chain; wholesale food distributors.

Orval Kent Food Co.
120 W. Palatine Road
Wheeling, IL 60090
(708) 459-9000
Personnel Director: Don Koop
Largest manufacturer and distributor of refrigerated perishable salads.

Orville Redenbacher Popcorn
Div. Hunt-Wesson Foods
463 U.S. Highway 30 East
Valparaiso, IN 46383
(219) 464-9602
Personnel Director: Bob LeSage
Gourmet popcorn manufacturer.

Pepsi-Cola General Bottlers
3 Crossroads of Commerce
1501 Algonquin Ave.
Rolling Meadows, IL 60008
(708) 253-1000
Personnel Manager: Gary Hansen

Pepsi-Cola General Bottlers
9300 Calumet Ave.
Munster, IN 46321
(219) 836-1800
Human Resources Manager: Tom Regeskie
Bottler and distributor of carbonated beverages.

Quaker Oats Co.
321 N. Clark St.
Chicago, IL 60610
(312) 222-7111
Contact: Corporate Personnel
Manufacturer and marketer of foods, pet foods, toys; owns and operates specialty restaurants.

Rose Packing Co.
65 S. Barrington Road
Barrington, IL 60010
(708) 381-5700
Personnel Director: Howard Liu
Manufactures and sells pork products.

Rymer Food
4600 S. Packers Ave.
Chicago, IL 60609
(312) 254-7591
Owns specialty food store chain.

John B. Sanfilippo & Son
2299 Busse Road
Elk Grove Village, IL 60007
(708) 593-2300
Personnel Director: Wanda Cecchini
Processes and packages nuts and candy.

Sara Lee Corporation
3 First National Plaza
Chicago, IL 60602
(312) 726-2600
V.P. Human Resources: Philip P. Temple
Manufacturer and marketer of consumer packaged goods including foods and candies; owns Booth Fisheries and Kitchens of Sara Lee.

Scot Lad Foods
P.O.Box 1246
Lansing, IL 60438
(708) 895-2300
Contact: Human Resources
Wholesaler of grocery products.

Seven-Up/Joyce Beverages
777 Joyce Road
Joliet, IL 60436
(815) 741-7777
Personnel Director: Peg Duchene
Bottler and distributor of 7-Up.

Shurfine-Central Corporation
2100 N. Mannheim Road
Northlake, IL 60164
(708) 681-2000
Personnel Director: Carol Lemmel
Food distributor to independent grocers.

Specialty Equipment Companies
5700 McDermott Drive
Berkley, IL 60153-1102
(708) 449-2920
Designs, manufactures, and markets food service equipment.

A. E. Staley Manufacturing Co.
2200 E. Eldorado St.
Decatur, IL 62525
(217) 423-4411
Personnel Director: David Pritts
Manufacturer of food, animal feeds, and household products such as Sno-Bol bathroom cleaner, Sta-Puf fabric softener, and Staley syrup.

Superior Tea & Coffee Co.
990 Supreme Drive
Bensenville, IL 60106
(312) 489-1000 (Chicago number)
Contact: Personnel
Producer and distributor of coffee, salad dressings, syrups, and vending machine products.

Sysco Food Services, Chicago
250 Weiboldt Drive
Des Plaines, IL 60016
(708) 699-5400
Contact: Personnel
Distributes products to the food-service industry.

Tootsie Roll Industries
7401 S. Cicero Ave.
Chicago, IL 60629
(312) 838-6100
Contact: Personnel
Major domestic candy producer.

Vienna Sausage Manufacturing Co.
2501 N. Damen Ave.
Chicago, IL 60647
(312) 278-7800
President: James Bodman
Manufactures hot dogs, delicatessen-style meats, cheesecake, pickles, soups, and institutional foods.

Vincent Foods
135 S. LaSalle
Chicago, IL 60603
(312) 782-1838
Contact: Personnel
Diversified food specialty company engaged in the manufacture and distribution of food and food service products.

White Hen Pantry
660 Industrial Drive
Elmhurst, IL 60126
(708) 833-3100
Senior Vice President: Robert C. Smith
Operates a chain of convenience stores, specializing in deli/bakery products.

Whitman Corporation
111 E. Wacker Drive
Chicago, IL 60601
(312) 565-3000
Senior V. P., Human Resources: Ronald Wright
A diversified holding company, operating in three major business areas: consumer products, industrial products, and the Illinois Central Gulf Railroad.

Wilton Enterprises
2240 W. 75th St.
Woodridge, IL 60517
(780) 963-7100
Personnel Director: Ruth Ann Miller
Develops and markets foods and kitchen products.

Wm. Wrigley, Jr., Co.
410 N. Michigan Ave.
Chicago, IL 60611

(312) 644-2121
World's largest producer of chewing gum.

Furniture/ Fixtures/ Household Textiles

For networking in the **furniture industry,** check out the following professional organizations listed in Chapter 5:

PROFESSIONAL ORGANIZATIONS:

American Lighting Association
American Society of Interior Designers
Decorating Products Association of Chicago
Institute of Business Designers
National Association of Floor Covering Distributors

For more information, you can write to:

American Furniture Manufacturers Association
918 16th St., N.W., Suite 402
Washington, DC 20006

International Home Furnishings Representatives Association
209 S. Main St.
High Point, NC 27260

National Home Furnishings Association
P.O. Box 2396
High Point, NC 27261

Textile Research Institute
601 Prospect Ave.
Princeton, NJ 08540

PROFESSIONAL PUBLICATIONS:

Furniture Design and Manufacturing
HFD—Retail Home Furnishings
Home Improvement Center
Textile Products and Processes
Textile World

DIRECTORIES:

Davidson's Textile Blue Book (Davison's, Ridgewood, NJ)
Professional Furniture Merchant Resource Directory (Gralla Publications, Dallas, TX)
Who's Who in the Furniture Industry (American Furniture Manufacturers Association, High Point, NC)

EMPLOYERS:

All-Steel Inc.
All-Steel Drive
P.O. Box 871
Aurora, IL 60507-0871
(708) 859-2600
Contact: Personnel
Manufacturer of metal office furniture.

Harry Alter Co.
337 N. Bell St.
Chicago, IL 60612
(312) 243-4133
President: Dave Blons
Distributes air conditioning, heating, and refrigeration products.

Beatrice Foods, Inc.
2 N. LaSalle St.
Chicago, IL 60602
(312) 588-4000
Personnel Director: Lee Keenan
Produces, processes, and distributes over 400 brands of food and dairy products; soft drinks, grocery, and snack products; medical supplies through its Brunswick Labs division; and fabricated metal products through its Chicago Specialty Manufacturing Co. division.

Brunswick Corporation
One Brunswick Plaza
Skokie, IL 60077
(708) 470-4700
Contact: Personnel
Consumer Division manufactures pool tables and other leisure products.

Business Interiors
2250 Mannheim Road
Des Plaines, IL 60017
(708) 298-2140

Personnel Director: Sue Clark
Contract furniture dealership.

DeSoto, Inc.
1700 S. Mount Prospect Road
Des Plaines, IL 60017
(708) 391-9000
Personnel Director: Dan Zacharski
Manufacturer of furniture and chemical products.

Elkay Manufacturing Co.
2222 Camden Court
Oak Brook, IL 60521
(708) 574-8484
President: David Craigmile
Manufactures sinks, water coolers, and faucets.

Franklin Picture Co.
4300 N. Knox Ave.
Chicago, IL 60641
(312) 286-9070
Vice President: Frank Hirsch
Manufacturer and distributor of framed pictures to retail and wholesale outlets.

Intercraft Industries
10 S. Riverside Plaza
Chicago, IL 60606
(312) 930-2500
Contact: Personnel
World's largest manufacturer of picture frames and framed artwork.

Interlake, Inc.
701 Harger Road
Oak Brook, IL 60521
(708) 572-6600
Personnel Manager: Sharon Bufton
A diversified manufacturer of metals and material-handling products.

Intermatic, Inc.
Intermatic Plaza
7777 Winn Road
Spring Grove, IL 60081
(815) 675-2321
President: Leann Vinyard
Manufactures heaters.

Joanna Western Mills
2141 S. Jefferson St.
Chicago, IL 60616

(312) 226-3232
Contact: Personnel
Manufacturer of window shades and window treatments.

Juno Lighting
P.O. Box 5065
Des Plaines, IL 60017
(708) 827-9880
Personnel Manager: Anna Rivera
Track lighting.

Kraft, Inc.
2211 Sanders Road
Northbrook, IL 60062
(708) 498-8000
Contact: Personnel
One of the largest food (Kraft Foods), consumer (Tupperware), and industrial products manufacturers in the world.

Leider Companies
855 E. Aptakisic Road
Buffalo Grove, IL 60089
(708) 634-4060
Personnel Director: Carie Bertrand
Provides horicultural ornaments.

Lyon Metal Products
P.O. Box 671
Aurora, IL 60507
(708) 892-8941
Employment Manager: Carol Stathis
Manufacturer of steel shop equipment.

Marden Manufacturing Co.
Merchandise Mart Plaza
Chicago, IL 60654
(312) 527-2574
Contact: Personnel
Furniture manufacturer.

Newell Companies
29 E. Stephenson St.
Freeport, IL 61032
(815) 235-4171
Contact: Corporate Personnel
Manufacturer of drapery hardware, accessories, window shades, shelving systems, and bathroom hardware.

QST Industries
231 S. Jefferson St.
Chicago, IL 60606
(312) 930-9400

Personnel Director: Andrea Glovak
Textile manufacturing.

Reflector Hardware Corporation
1400 N. 25th Ave.
Melrose Park, IL 60160
(708) 345-2500
Contact: Personnel
Manufacturer of store fixtures, office and library furniture.

St. Charles Manfacturing
1611 E. Main St.
St. Charles, IL 60174
(708) 584-3800
Contact: Personnel
Manufacturer of St. Charles custom kitchens.

Schnadig Corporation
4820 W. Belmont Ave.
Chicago, IL 60641
(312) 545-2300
Contact: Personnel
Manufacturer of upholstered furniture for home and industry.

Sealy Mattress Co.
111 N. Canal St.
Chicago, IL 60606
(312) 559-0500
Contact: Personnel
Manufacturer of bedding.

Serta, Inc.
2800 River Road, Suite 300
Des Plaines, IL 60018
(708) 699-9300
President: Zenon Nie
Headquarters of international group of mattress manufacturers.

Shelby Williams Industries
1348 Merchandise Mart
P.O. Box 3442
Chicago, IL 60654
(312) 527-3593
Contract furniture manufacturer.

Spring Air Co.
2980 N. River Road
DesPlaines, IL 60018
(708) 297-5577
President: Donald Pellegrini
Mattress manufacturer.

Triangle Home Products
945 E. 93rd St.
Chicago, IL 60619
(312) 374-4400
Contact: Personnel
Manufactures and distributes bathroom cabinets, range hoods, mirrors, ventilators, and interior and exterior lighting fixtures.

Wells-Gardner Electronics Corporation
2701 N. Kildare Ave.
Chicago, IL 60639
(312) 252-8220
Contact: Personnel
Manufactures video game monitors, intrusion security devices, color TV consoles for private-label sale, and data display monitors.

Government: City, County, State, Federal

For networking in **government** and related fields, check out the following professional organizations listed in Chapter 5:

PROFESSIONAL ORGANIZATIONS:

Chicago Council on Foreign Relations
Chicago Women's Political Caucus
Citizen's Information Service
City Club of Chicago
Federal Information Center
Independent Voters of Illinois
League of Women Voters of Illinois
Midwest Women's Center
Young Democrats of Cook County
Young Republican Organization of Illinois

PROFESSIONAL PUBLICATIONS:

Bureaucrat
City and State
Government Executive
Public Works Magazine

EMPLOYERS, CITY OF CHICAGO:

City Clerk
Administration

121 N. LaSalle St.
Chicago, IL 60602
(312) 744-4000

Consumer Services
Administration
121 N. LaSalle St., Room 808
Chicago, IL 60602
(312) 744-4091

Controller's Office
Administration
121 N. LaSalle St., Room 501
Chicago, IL 60602
(312) 744-7100

Corporation Counsel
Administration
121 N. LaSalle St., Room 511
Chicago, IL 60602
(312) 744-6942

Health, Dept. of
Director's Office
50 W. Washington
Chicago, IL 60602
(312) 744-8500

Housing, Dept. of
Director's Office
318 S. Michigan Ave.
Chicago, IL 60604
(312) 922-8275

Human Services, Dept. of
Director's Office
500 N. Peshtigo Court
Chicago, IL 60611
(312) 744-8111

Inspectional Services, Dept. of
Administration
121 N. LaSalle St., Room 900
Chicago, IL 60602
(312) 744-3400

Park District
Administration
425 E. McFetridge Drive
Chicago, IL 60605
(312) 294-2200

Police Dept. of Chicago
Superintendent's Office
1121 S. State St., Room 400
Chicago, IL 60605
(312) 744-5501

Public Works Dept.
Superintendent's Office
121 N. LaSalle St., Room 406
Chicago, IL 60602
(312) 744-3647

Sanitary District, Metropolitan
Commissioner's Office
100 E. Erie St.
Chicago, IL 60611
(312) 751-5600

The art of getting a job in government

Dorothy Miaso is an administrative assistant in the governor's office. We asked her how one goes about getting a job with the state government.

"Actually," says Dorothy, "there are two kinds of state jobs—civil service jobs and positions to which you're appointed by an elected official. To get an appointment to a personal staff or other position, the best way is to work in a political campaign. You get to know the elected official and become associated with that person's administration. Those jobs are subject to the whims of your constituency. If the official gets voted out of office, you're probably out of a job.

"Today, civil service covers virtually every department except for the top administrators. To get a civil service job, you apply through the Department of Central Management Services. They have postings of what jobs are open and when tests will be given. You go in and apply for a certain test—for instance, Revenue Agent 1, which is an entry-level position in tax collection at the Department of Revenue. Several weeks after you take the test, you receive your score. Generally, you have to have an A to be considered; certainly a B.

"But even if you get a good score, it doesn't mean you have the job. You're notified when a position you've applied for opens up, and then you have to go through the whole interview process. One job may have as many as a hundred qualified applicants. But once you get a civil service job, you're generally pretty secure." ■

Senior Citizens and Handicapped, Office for
Director's Office
510 N. Peshtigo Court
Chicago, IL 60611
(312) 744-5784

Streets and Sanitation, Dept. of
Administration
121 N. LaSalle St., Room 700
Chicago, IL 60602
(312) 744-4611

Water Dept.
Administration
1000 E. Ohio
Chicago, IL 60611
(312) 744-7001

EMPLOYERS, COOK COUNTY:

Bureau of Administration
118 N. Clark St.
Chicago, IL 60602
(312) 443-4660

Circuit Court
Administration
Richard J. Daley Center, Room 2600
50 W. Washington
Chicago, IL 60602
(312) 443-5500

Corrections, Dept. of
Administration
2600 S. California Blvd.
Chicago, IL 60608
(312) 890-7100

County Clerk
Administration
118 N. Clark St., Room 434
Chicago, IL 60602
(312) 443-5500

Forest Preserve District
Administration
536 N. Harlem Ave.
River Forest, IL 60305
(708) 261-8400

Sheriff
Administration
Richard J. Daley Center, Room 704
Chicago, IL 60602
(312) 443-5500

EMPLOYER, DU PAGE COUNTY:

Du Page County Administration
130 N. County Farm Road
Wheaton, IL 60187
(708) 682-7318

EMPLOYER, LAKE COUNTY:

Lake County Administrative Offices
18 N. County Road
Waukegan, IL 60085
(708) 360-6600

EMPLOYERS, STATE OF ILLINOIS:

Attorney General
Administration
100 W. Randolph St.
Chicago, IL 60601
(312) 814-7086

Children & Family Services, Dept. of
Director's Office
100 W. Randolph St.
Chicago, IL 60601
(312) 793-4650

Commerce & Community Affairs, Dept. of
Director's Office
100 W. Randolph St., Suite 3400
Chicago, IL 60601
(312) 917-2354

Courts
Administration
30 N. Michigan Ave., Room 2010

Chicago, IL 60602
(312) 793-3250

Governor's Office
100 W. Randolph St.
Chicago, IL 60601
(312) 814-2121

Insurance, Dept. of
Administration
100 W. Randolph St., Suite 15-100
Chicago, IL 60601
(312) 917-2427

Labor, Dept. of
Personnel Office
100 S. Michigan Ave.
Chicago, IL 60604
(312) 793-2800

Public Aid, Dept. of
Administration
624 S. Michigan Ave.
Chicago, IL 60605
(312) 793-4706

Public Health, Dept. of
Director's Office
100 W. Randolph St., 6th Floor
Chicago, IL 60601
(312) 917-2793

Revenue, Dept. of
Administration
100 W. Randolph St.
8th Floor, Room 100
Chicago, IL 60601
(800) 624-2459

Secretary of State
Administration
100 W. Randolph St.
Chicago, IL 60601
(312) 814-2262

EMPLOYERS, UNITED STATES GOVERNMENT:

Agriculture, Dept. of
Regional Office
165 N. Canal St., Suite 1400 S.C.
Chicago, IL 60606
(312) 353-3903

Air Force, Dept. of
Recruiting Office
536 S. Clark St., Room 279
Chicago, IL 60605
(312) 663-1640

Army, Dept. of
Recruiting Office
536 S. Clark St.
Chicago, IL 60605
(312) 922-5925

Central Intelligence Agency
Regional Director
P. O. Box 2144
Chicago, IL 60690
(312) 353-0311

Commerce, Dept. of
Office of the Secretary
55 E. Monroe, Suite 1440
Chicago, IL 60604
(312) 353-0182

Defense, Dept. of
Office of the Secretary
527 S. LaSalle St.
Chicago, IL 60605
(312) 353-6305

Education, Dept. of
Office of the Secretary
401 S. State St., Suite 700A
Chicago, IL 60605
(312) 353-5215

Environmental Protection Agency
Administration
230 S. Dearborn St.
Chicago, IL 60604
(312) 353-2000

Federal Bureau of Investigation
Regional Office
219 S. Dearborn St., Room 905
Chicago, IL 60604
(312) 431-1333

Federal Communications Commission
Regional Office
1550 Northwest Highway, Room 306

Park Ridge, IL 60068
(708) 353-0195

Federal Trade Commission
Regional Office
55 E. Monroe St., Suite 1437
Chicago, IL 60603
(312) 353-4423

General Accounting Office
Regional Office
200 W. Adams, Suite 700
Chicago, IL 60606
(312) 220-7600

General Services Administration
Regional Office
230 S. Dearborn St., Room 3730
Chicago, IL 60604
(312) 353-5398

Health & Human Services, Dept. of
Regional Office
105 W. Adams St.
Chicago, IL 60603
(312) 353-5175

Housing & Urban Development, Dept. of
Regional Office
326 W. Jackson Blvd.
Chicago, IL 60606
(312) 353-5682

Interior, Dept. Of
Office of Environment
230 S. Dearborn, Room 3422
Chicago, IL 60604
(312) 353-6612

Internal Revenue Service
Regional Office
230 S. Dearborn
Chicago, IL 60604
(312) 435-1040

Justice, Dept. of
Administration
219 S. Dearborn St., Room 1500
Chicago, IL 60604
(312) 353-5300

Labor, Dept. of
Regional Office
230 S. Dearborn St.
Chicago, IL 60604
(312) 353-2220

Marine Corps
Recruiting Office
209 W. Jackson Blvd., Suite 804
Chicago, IL 60606
(312) 353-6578

Navy, Dept. of
Recruiting Office
536 S. Clark St., Room 277
Chicago, IL 60605
(312) 939-3167

Postal Service
Regional Chief
433 W. Van Buren St.
Chicago, IL 60607
(312) 765-5626

Securities & Exchange Commission
219 S. Dearborn St., Room 1204
Chicago, IL 60604
(312) 353-7390

Small Business Administration
Administration
219 S. Dearborn St., Room 437
Chicago, IL 60604
(312) 353-4528

State, Dept. of
230 S. Dearborn St.
Chicago, IL 60604
(312) 353-6163

Transportation, Dept. of
Regional Office
300 S. Wacker Drive, Room 700
Chicago, IL 60606
(312) 353-4000

Treasury, Dept. of
Regional Office
901 Warrenville Road
Lisle, IL 60532
(708) 971-8422

Health Care

For networking in **health care** and related fields, check out the following professional organizations listed in Chapter 5:

PROFESSIONAL ORGANIZATIONS:

American Academy of Physical Medicine and Rehabilitation
American Association of Medical Assistants
American College of Healthcare Executives
American Dental Assistants Association
American Dietetic Association
American Hospital Association
American Medical Association
American Medical Technologists
American Medical Writer's Association
American Physical Therapy Association
Association for Women in Science
Illinois Hospital Association
Metropolitan Chicago Health Care Council
Women Health Executives Network

For additional information, you can write to:

American Health Care Association
1200 15th St., N.W.
Washington, DC 20005

American Public Health Association
1015 18th St., N.W.
Washington, DC 20036

National Council of Community Mental Health Centers
12300 Twinbrook Parkway, Suite 320
Rockville, MD 20852

PROFESSIONAL PUBLICATIONS:

American Journal of Nursing
Contemporary Administration
Health Care Financial Management
Hospital and Health Services Administration
Hospital Purchasing News
Hospitals
Modern Healthcare

DIRECTORIES:

Guide to the Health Care Field (American Hospital Association, Chicago, IL)
Saunders Health Care Directory (W.B. Saunders, Philadelphia, PA)

EMPLOYERS:

Anchor Organization for Health Maintenance
1700 W. Van Buren
Chicago, IL 60612
(312) 666-7600
Contact: Personnel
Major health maintainance organization.

Chicago HMO Ltd.
540 N. LaSalle St.
Chicago, IL 60610
(312) 751-4460
Major health maintainance organization.

Chicago Reed Mental Health Center
4200 N. Oak Park Ave.
Chicago, IL 60634
(312) 794-4000
Contact: Personnel
Psychiatric hospital.

Children's Memorial Hospital
2300 Children's Plaza
Chicago, IL 60614
(312) 880-4000
Human Resources Manager: Alice Spann
General facility for children.

Christ Hospital and Medical Center
4440 W. 95th St.
Oak Lawn, IL 60453
(708) 425-8000
Human Resources Director: Craig Morgan

Columbus-Cuneo-Cabrini Medical Center
467 W. Deming Pl., #500
Chicago, IL 60614
(312) 883-8333
Personnel Director: Kurt Vining

Cook County Hospital
1835 W. Harrison St.
Chicago, IL 60612

(312) 633-6006
Personnel Director: Lou Watson

Edgewater Hospital
5700 N. Ashland Ave.
Chicago, IL 60660
(312) 878-6000
Personnel Director: Gwendolyn Rodriguez

Evanston Hospital Corporation
2650 Ridge Ave.
Evanston, IL 60201
(708) 570-2000
Personnel Director: Bob Warner

Forest Hospital
555 Wilson Lane
Des Plaines, IL 60016
(708) 635-4100
Personnel Administrator: Fritz Baumgartner
Psychiatric hospital.

Grant Hospital of Chicago
550 W. Webster Ave.
Chicago, IL 60614
(312) 883-2000
V. P., Personnel: Fred Konopasek

HealthCare Compare Corporation
3200 Highland Ave.
Downers Grove, IL 60515-1223
(708) 719-9000
Personnel Director: Joan Mason
Provides health care utilization review.

Highland Park Hospital
718 Glenview Ave.
Highland Park, IL 60035
(708) 432-8000
Personnel Director: Tom Roerich

Hines Veterans Administration Hospital
Hines, IL 60141
(708) 261-6700
Contact: Personnel

Hinsdale Hospital
120 N. Oak St.
Hinsdale, IL 60521
(708) 887-2400
Employment Director: Carol Serle

HMO Illinois
2001 Midwest Road
Oak Brook, IL 60521
(708) 620-3000
Major health maintainance organization.

Illinois Masonic Medical Center
836 Wellington Ave.
Chicago, IL 60657
(312) 975-1600
Personnel Director: Carol Natschke

Ingalls Memorial Hospital
One Ingalls Drive
Harvey, IL 60426
(708) 333-2300
Professional Recruiter: Jan Haddon

John F. Kennedy Hospital
5645 W. Addison St.
Chicago, IL 60634-4455
(312) 282-7000
Personnel Director: Bill Dwyer

La Rabida Children's Hospital
East 65th St. at Lake Michigan
Chicago, IL 60649
(312) 363-6700
Contact: Personnel
Children's hospital.

Little Company of Mary Hospital
2800 W. 95th St.
Evergreen Park, IL 60642
(708) 422-6200
Personnel Director: Peter Rzeminski

Loyola University Medical Center
2160 S. First Ave.
Maywood, IL 60153
(708) 531-3000
Director of Hospital Administration: Robert S. Condry

Lutheran General Hospital
1775 Dempster St.
Park Ridge, IL 60068
(708) 696-2210
Personnel Director: John M. Eiden

John J. Madden Mental Health Center
1200 S. First Ave.
Hines, IL 60141

(708) 531-7000
Contact: Personnel
Psychiatric hospital.

Marianjoy Rehabilitation Hospital
P.O. Box 795
26 W. 171 Roosevelt Road
Wheaton, IL 60187
(708) 462-4000
Personnel Director: Marylin Mathe
Rehabilitation hospital.

Maxicare Illinois
P.O. Box 2942
Chicago, IL 60690
(312) 220-9830
Personnel Director: Denine Hammonds

MedCare HMO
1701 S. First Avenue
Maywood, IL 60153
(708) 865-7700
Personnel Director: Rebecca Montalto
Major health maintenance organization

Memorial Hospital
515 Pine St.
Michigan City, IN 46360
(219) 879-0202
Contact: Personnel

Mercy Hospital & Medical Center
Stevenson at King Drive
Chicago, IL 60616
(312) 567-2000
Human Resource Director: Ellen Arens

Michael Reese Health Plan
2545 S. Dr. Martin Luther King Drive
Chicago, IL 60616
(312) 842-7117
Contact: Personnel
Major health maintenance organization.

Michael Reese Hospital and Medical Center
Lake Shore Drive at 31st St.
Chicago, IL 60616
(312) 791-2000
Human Resources Director: Steve Moody

Mount Sinai Hospital & Medical Center
1500 S. Fairfield

Chicago, IL 60608
(312) 542-2000
Human Resources Director: S. Hulsh

Munster Community Hospital
901 MacArthur Blvd.
Munster, IN 46321
(219) 836-1600
Contact: Personnel

Northwestern Memorial Hospital
Superior at Fairbanks Court
Chicago, IL 60611
(312) 908-2000
Vice President, Personnel: John Loyla

Oak Forest Hospital
159th Street
Oak Forest, IL 60452
(708) 687-7200
Contact: Personnel
Chronic disease hospital.

Our Lady of Mercy Hospital
U.S. 30
Dyer, IN 46311
(219) 865-2141
V.P., Human Resources: Rick Tolson

Palos Community Hospital
12251 W. 80th Ave.
Palos Heights, IL 60463
(708) 361-4500
Employment Manager: Linda Nealis

PruCare of Illinois
9450 Bryn Mawr Ave.
Rosemont, IL 60018
(708) 671-8700
Contact: Personnel
Major health maintenance organization.

Rehabilitation Institute of Chicago
345 E. Superior St.
Chicago, IL 60611
(312) 908-6290
Contact: Personnel
Rehabilitation hospital.

Riveredge Hospital
8311 Roosevelt Road
Forest Park, IL 60130

(708) 771-7000
Director of Human Resources: Tina Gutekanst
Psychiatric hospital.

Rush Presbyterian St. Luke's Medical Center
1653 W. Congress Parkway
Chicago, IL 60612
(312) 942-5000
Human Resources Director: James Hill

St. Anthony Medical Center
Main St. at Franciscan Drive
Crown Point, IN 46307
(219) 663-8120
Contact: Personnel

St. Catherine Hospital
4321 Fir St.
East Chicago, IN 46312
(219) 392-1700
Human Resources Director: Susan Bodenhorn

St. Francis Hospital
355 Ridge Ave.
Evanston, IL 60202
(708) 492-4000
Personnel Director: Dorothy Klegerman

St. James Hospital Medical Center
Chicago Road at Lincoln Highway
Chicago Heights, IL 60411-3482
(708) 756-1000
V.P. Human Resources: John Kirk

St. Joseph Hospital
2900 N. Lake Shore Drive
Chicago, IL 60657
(312) 975-3000
V.P. of Human Resources: David Murray

St. Margaret Hospital
5454 Hohman Ave.
Hammond, IN 46320
(219) 932-2300
Human Resources Director: Ron Jerzyk

St. Mary Medical Center
540 Tyler St.
Gary, IN 46402
(219) 882-9411
Contact: Personnel

Schwab Rehabilitation Center
1401 S. California Ave.
Chicago, IL 60608
(312) 522-2010
Contact: Personnel
Rehabilitation hospital.

Share Health Plans of Illinois
1 Pierce Place, Suite 600
Itasca, IL 60143
(708) 250-3200
Major health maintenance organization.

Shriners Hospital for Crippled Children
2211 N. Oak Park Ave.
Chicago, IL 60635
(312) 622-5400
Personnel Director: Sally Bittenbinder
Children's orthopedic hospital.

Tinley Park Mental Health Center
7400 W. 183rd St.
Tinley Park, IL 60477
(708) 614-4000
Contact: Personnel
Psychiatric hospital.

Trans Leasing International
3000 Dundee Road
Northbrook, IL 60062
(708) 272-1000
Personnel Director: Terri Frey
Leases equipment to health care professionals.

University of Chicago Hospitals and Clinics
P.O.Box 247
Chicago, IL 60637
(312) 947-1000
Human Resources Director: James Johnson

University of Illinois Hospitals and Clinics
840 S. Paulina St.
Chicago, IL 60612
(312) 996-6816
Personnel Director: Richard Hanneman

Veterans Administration Hospital
3001 Green Bay Road
North Chicago, IL 60064
(708) 688-1900
Personnel Director: Robert Grant

Veterans Administration Lakeside Medical Center
333 E. Huron St.
Chicago, IL 60611
(312) 943-6600
Personnel Director: Mary Sherril

Veterans Administration West Side Medical Center
820 S. Damen Ave.
Chicago, IL 60612
(312) 666-6500
Personnel Officer: Joseph Bell

Victory Memorial Hospital
1324 N. Sheridan Road
Waukegan, IL 60085
(708) 360-3000
Vice President: Sue Geiger

Louis A. Weiss Memorial Hospital
4646 N. Marine Drive
Chicago, IL 60640
(312) 878-8700
Human Resources Director: Evelyn Schnitzer

West Suburban Hospital
Erie at Austin Blvd.
Oak Park, IL 60302
(708) 383-6200
Human Resources Director: Jeff Johanson

Hospitality: Hotels/ Restaurants / Exposition Planners

For networking in the **hospitality industry** and related fields, check out the following organizations listed in Chapter 5:

PROFESSIONAL ORGANIZATIONS:

Chicago Association of Commerce and Industry
Hotel-Motel Association of Illinois
Hotel Sales & Marketing Association
Illinois Restaurant Association
National Restaurant Association

For more information, you can write to:

Hospitality Lodging & Travel Research Foundation
888 7th Ave.
New York, NY 10106

Hotel Sales Marketing Association
1400 K St., N.W.
Washington, DC 20005

National Restaurant Association
311 First St., N.W.
Washington, DC 20001

PROFESSIONAL PUBLICATIONS:

Foodservice Product News
Hotel and Motel Management
Meetings & Conventions
Restaurant Hospitality
Restaurants & Institutions
Successful Meetings

DIRECTORIES:

Directory, Meetings and Conventions Magazine (Murdoch Magazines, Secaucus, NJ)
Hotel and Motel Redbook (American Hotel & Motel Association, New York, NY)
Meetings and Conventions Magazine, Directory issue (Ziff Davis Publishing Co., New York, NY)
Restaurant Hospitality—500 Issue (Penton/IPC, Cleveland, OH)
Restaurants & Institutions—400 Issue (Cahners Publishing, Des Plaines, IL)

EMPLOYERS:

Ambassador East Hotel
1301 N. State Parkway
Chicago, IL 60610
(312) 787-7200
Personnel Manager: Brian Wode

Ambassador West Hotel
1300 N. State Parkway
Chicago, IL 60610
(312) 787-7900
Personnel Manager: Bill Torres

Americana Hotels, Inns, and Resorts
520 S. Michigan Ave.
Chicago, IL 60605
(312) 427-3800
Personnel Manager: Joe Pines

Barclay Chicago Hotel
166 E. Superior St.
Chicago, IL 60611
(312) 787-6000
Personnel Manager: Tom Hollowed

Best Western Hotels
Regional Sales Office
2340 S. Arlington Heights Road
Arlington Heights, IL 60005
(708) 437-1550
Contact: Personnel

Bismarck Hotel
171 W. Randolph St.
Chicago, IL 60601
(312) 236-0123
Contact: Employment

Blackstone Hotel
636 S. Michigan Ave.
Chicago, IL 60605
(312) 427-4300
Personnel Manager: Bobby Pathan

Brown's Fried Chicken
Regional Headquarters
377 E. Butterfield Road
Lombard, IL 60148
(708) 960-5200
Controller: Mike Mengarelli

Burger King
Regional Headquarters
3051 Oak Grove Road
Downers Grove, IL 60515
(708) 969-5150
Human Resources Manager: Doug Hinderer

Chicago Hilton & Towers Hotel
720 S. Michigan Ave.
Chicago, IL 60605
(312) 922-4400
Personnel Manager: Sheila O'Keefe

Chicago Marriott Hotel
540 N. Michigan Ave.
Chicago, IL 60611
(312) 836-0100
Personnel Director: Bill Georgia

Days Inn Lake Shore Drive
644 N. Lake Shore Drive
Chicago, IL 60611
(312) 943-9200
Contact: Personnel

Dell Displays
2701 United Lane
Elk Grove Village, IL 60007
(708) 595-0610
Personnel Director: Robert Dell
Exposition service contractor.

Drake Hotel
140 E. Walton Place
Chicago, IL 60611
(312) 787-2200
Personnel Director: Leslie Bodell

Drake Oak Brook Hotel
2301 York Road
Oak Brook, IL 60521
(708) 574-5700
Personnel Director: Maureen Callan

Executive House Hotel
71 E. Wacker Drive
Chicago, IL 60601
(312) 346-7100
Personnel Manager: Margaret Lord

Fairmont Hotel
200 N. Columbus Drive
Illinois Center
Chicago, IL 60601
(312) 565-8000
Personnel Director: Bruce Stone

Four Seasons Hotel
120 E. Delaware Place
Chicago, IL 60611
Personnel Director: Meg Fisher
(312) 280-8800

General Exhibits & Displays
4925 W. Lawrence Ave.

Chicago, IL 60630
(312) 736-6699
Exposition contractor.

Giltspur Exposition Services
3225 S. Western Ave.
Chicago, IL 60608-6091
(312) 376-3000

Greyhound Exhibit Group, Chicago
2800 Lively Blvd.
Elk Grove Village, IL 60007
(708) 595-2000
Exhibition contractors.

Hilton Hotels Corporation
27 E. Monroe
Chicago, IL 60603
(312) 443-5100

Holiday Inn
Chicago City Center
300 E. Ohio St.
Chicago, IL 60611
(312) 787-6100
Personnel Manager: Danella Walker

Holiday Inn Mart Plaza
350 N. Orleans St.
Chicago, IL 60654
(312) 836-5000
Contact: Personnel

Holiday Inn O'Hare
5440 N. River Road
Rosemont, IL 60018
(708) 671-6350
Contact: Personnel

Hotel Nikko Chicago
320 N. Dearborn
Chicago, IL 60610
(312) 744-1900
Personnel Director: Dick Burkett

Hyatt Hotels, Hyatt International & Hyatt Development
Corporate Offices
200 W. Madison
Chicago, IL 60606
(312) 750-1234
V.P., Human Resources: Myrna Hellerman

Hyatt Regency Chicago
151 E. Wacker Drive
Chicago, IL 60601
(312) 565-1234
Personnel Manager: Carla Thomas

Hyatt Regency O'Hare
9300 W. Bryn Mawr Ave.
Rosemont, IL 60018
(708312) 696-1234
Manager: John Orr

Intercontinental Forum Hotels
505 N. Michigan Ave.
Chicago, IL 60611
(312) 944-4101
Contact: Personnel Manager

Kentucky Fried Chicken
District Headquarters
2 Westbrook Center
Westchester, IL 60154
(708) 449-2820
Personnel Director: John Malloy

Kitzing, Inc.
1323 W. Carrol Ave.
Chicago, IL 60607
(312) 243-1220
Exhibition contractors.

Knickerbocker-Chicago Hotel
163 E. Walton Place
Chicago, IL 60611
(312) 751-8100
Contact: Executive Office

Lane Industries
1 Lane Center
1200 Shermer Road
Northbrook, IL 60062
(708) 498-6789
President: William N. Lane III
Holding company for interests in hotels and ranching.

Lettuce Entertain You Enterprises
5419 N. Sheridan Road
Chicago, IL 60640
(312) 878-7340
Executive Director, Personnel: Loret Carbone
Headquarters of the multi-restaurant organization.

The Levy Organization
980 N. Michigan Ave.
Chicago, IL 60611
(312) 664-8200
Personnel Director: Margie Mintz
Headquarters of the restaurant and real estate organization.

Management Group
1300 N. State St.
Chicago, IL 60610
(312) 787-2235
Develops, operates, manages, and consults about hotels, including the Ambassador West.

Marriott Hotels Corporation
National Sales Office
6250 River Road, Suite 4020
Rosemont, IL 60018
(708) 318-0500
National Sales Director: Brian Dietmeyer

Marriott's Lincolnshire Resort
1 Marriott Drive
Lincolnshire, IL 60015
(708) 634-0100
Personnel Director: Wiliam Buikema

Mayfair Regent Hotel
181 N. Lake Shore Drive
Chicago, IL 60611
(312) 787-8500
Personnel Manager: Leslie Bodell

McCormick Center Hotel
451 E. 23rd St.
Chicago, IL 60616
(312) 791-1900
Personnel Manager: Stacey Small

McDonald's Corporation
McDonald's Plaza
Oak Brook, IL 60521
(708) 575-3000
Sr. V. P., Personnel: Stanley Stein
National headquarters for the fast-food chain.

MG Design Association
824 W. Superior St.
Chicago, IL 60622
(312) 243-3661
Exhibition contractor.

Midland Hotel
172 W. Adams St.
Chicago, IL 60603
(312) 332-1200
Contact: Personnel

North Shore Hilton
9599 Skokie Blvd.
Skokie, IL 60077
(708) 679-7000
General Manager: Norman Kuka

Palmer House
17 E. Monroe St.
Chicago, IL 60690
(312) 726-7500
Director of Human Resources: James Woods

Park Hyatt
800 N. Michigan Ave.
Water Tower Square
Chicago, IL 60611
(312) 280-2222
Personnel Manager: Bea Hardman

Pheasant Run Lodge
P.O. Box 64
St. Charles, IL 60174
(708) 584-6300
Director of Operations: Pierre DuBose

Pizza Hut
Regional Office
1100 W. 31st St., Suite 130
Downer's Grove, IL 60515
(708) 963-0900
Personnel Manager: Tom Weidenkopf

Popeye's Famous Fried Chicken Restaurants
Midwest Regional Office
10600 W. Higgins Road, Suite 512
Rosemont, IL 60018
(708) 699-9980
Contact: Personnel

Ramada Inn O'Hare
6600 N. Mannheim Road
Rosemont, IL 60018
(708) 827-5131
Personnel Director: Jan Hartzler

Raphael Hotel
201 E. Delaware Place
Chicago, IL 60611
(312) 943-5000
Personnel Manager: Mark Pistilli

Hotel management: more than puttin' on the Ritz

With a little more than two years' experience in the hotel business, Nancy Nachman landed a job as sales manager for the Ritz-Carlton Hotel. We asked her for an overview of the hospitality industry.

"If you want to move up quickly," says Nancy, "this industry is the place to be. It's anything but a dead-end business. Some people stay with the same organization for most of their careers. But I'd say the average is probably around five years with any given company. People are constantly calling and making job offers.

"I studied hotel management and general business. But you can't just walk out of college and into a middle management position. I started as a receptionist at the Ritz-Carlton. Then I became a secretary. I don't know anyone who hasn't paid dues for a year or two. If you're interested in food or beverages, you might move up to dining room assistant. Essentially, you'd be doing the same thing as a secretary—typing up contracts or menus, that sort of thing. You really have to learn the business from the bottom up.

"In sales you move from secretarial work to a full-fledged sales position. I was a sales representative, then was promoted to sales manager. The next step might logically be director of sales or marketing, where I'd be responsible for advertising and marketing strategies, developing budgets, and so on. An equivalent position would be director of food and beverages, the person who's responsible for all the food and drink served in the hotel, room service, all the dining rooms, special banquets, everything. After director of sales or of food and beverages, you go on to general manager.

"I'd say the competition is about average—not nearly as fierce as the advertising industry, for example. Earning potential is pretty good, too, depending, of course, on the size of the hotel, the city you're in, and what kind of company you're working for. You start out pretty low, maybe around $15,000 or $16,000 a year. But each time you move up, you get a hefty raise, or ought to."■

Red Lobster
5201 S. Pulaski
Chicago, IL 60632
(312) 284-7000
For management training, call:
(800) 562-7837

Richmont Hotel
162 E. Ontario St.
Chicago, IL 60611
(312) 787-3580
General Manager: Frances Monteith

Ritz-Carlton Hotel
160 E. Pearson St.
Chicago, IL 60611
(312) 266-1000
Personnel Manager: Susan Pollack

Sheraton North Shore Inn
933 Skokie Blvd.
Northbrook, IL 60062
(708) 498-6500
Front Office Manager: Diana Atkins

Sheraton Plaza
160 E. Huron St.
Chicago, IL 60611
(312) 787-2900
Contact: Personnel Director

Swiss Grand Hotel
323 E. Wacker Drive
Chicago, IL 60601
(312) 565-0565
Personnel Director: Tina Beverly

Tremont Hotel
100 E. Chestnut St.
Chicago, IL 60611

(312) 280-1300
Personnel Manager: Mike Mason

United Exposition Services, Co.
1555 W. 44th St.
Chicago, IL 60609
(312) 376-9400
Exposition contractors.

Wendy's International
2 Trans Am Plaza Drive, Suite 330
Oakbrook Terrace, IL 60181
(708) 932-9400
Contact: Human Resources

Westin Chicago
909 N. Michigan Ave.
Chicago, IL 60611
(312) 943-7200
Personnel Director: Jeffrey Sablick

Westin Hotel O'Hare
6100 N. River Road
Rosemont, IL 60018
(708) 698-6000
Personnel Director: Karen Crouch

White Castle System
Regional Office
4900 W. 73rd St.
Chicago, IL 60638
(312) 582-7373

Whiteco Hospitality Corporation
Radisson Hotel at Star Plaza
I 65 & U.S. 30
Merrillville, IN 46410
(219) 769-6311
President: Bruce White

Whitehall Hotel
105 E. Delaware Place
Chicago, IL 60611
(312) 944-6300
Director of Human Resources: Mike Mason

Housewares

For networking in **housewares** and related fields, check out the following professional organizations listed in Chapter 5:

PROFESSIONAL ORGANIZATIONS:

Association of Home Appliance Manufacturers
National Electronic Distributors Association
National Housewares Manufacturers Association

EMPLOYERS:

Admiral Group/ Magic Chef
1701 E. Woodfield Road
Schaumburg, IL 60196
(708) 706-2600
Personnel Director: Lynn Major
Cooking equipment.

Anchor-Hocking Corporation
1955 N. Delaney Road
Gurnee, IL 60031
(708) 244-1000
Personnel Director: Rade Dimitrijevic
Major manufacturer of glassware, chinaware, decorative hardware, and glass containers.

Ball Glass Container Group
13850 Cottage Grove Ave.
Dolton, IL 60419
(708) 468-7800
Contact: Personnel
Manufacturer of packaging products for food and beverages.

Dresher, Inc.
7200 S. Mason
Chicago, IL 60638
(312) 928-8585
Personnel Director: John Deacy
Manufactures brass beds.

Ecko Products
1949 N. Cicero Ave.
Chicago, IL 60639
(312) 237-2979
Contact: Personnel
Manufacturer of cookware and utensils.

Environdyne Industries
142 E. Ontario, 10th Floor
Chicago, IL 60611
(312) 649-0600
Manufactures plastic dinnerware.

General Electric Co.
300 S. Riverside, Suite 900N
Chicago, IL 60606
(312) 781-7811
Regional Area Manager: Barbara Cresswell
Manufactures and distributes a broad range of personal and home appliances, industrial products, and aerospace components.

Georgia-Pacific Corporation
2nd Place & Waite St.
Gary, IN 46404
(219) 882-1640
Personnel Manager: RoseMary Rivera
Toweling manufacturer.

Globe Glass and Mirror Co.
1880 W. Fullerton Ave.
Chicago, IL 60614
(312) 278-7800
President: Joseph Kellman

Hako Minuteman
111 S. Route 53
Addison, IL 60101
(708) 627-6900
Human Resources Manager: Phyllis Gillam
Manufactures industrial and commercial cleaning equipment.

Health-Mor, Inc.
151 E. 22nd St.
Lombard, IL 60148
(708) 953-9770
Personnel Director: Jo Ann Althoff
Manufacturer of Filter Queen brand household, institutional, and commercial vacuum cleaners; sells machine-tool products and plumbing supplies.

Helene Curtis Industries
325 N. Wells St.
Chicago, IL 60610
(312) 661-0222
Vice President: Michael Goldman
Produces a wide variety of appliances and products in the cosmetics and toiletry industries.

Intermatic, Inc.
7777 Winn Road
Spring Grove, IL 60081
(815) 675-2321
President: Lee Vinyard
Manufactures heaters.

Kerr Glass Mfg. Co.
1500 N. Route 59
Plainfield, IL 60544
(708) 242-4592
Director: Charles Worden
Manufacturer and marketer of glass containers.

Owens-Illinois, Inc.
Libby Glass Division
2200 E. Devon Ave., Suite 358
Des Plaines, IL 60018
(708) 694-0440
Personnel Manager: Lucy Lee
Manufactures and sells glass tableware and stemware.

Ozite Corporation
1755 Butterfield Road
Libertyville, IL 60048
(708) 362-8210
Personnel Director: Kathleen Fox
Manufactures indoor and outdoor carpeting for boats, recreational vehicles, and wall coverings.

Roper Corporation/Whirlpool
2000M 63 North
Benton Harbor, MI 49022
(800) 447-6737
Personnel Director: Ray Warmoth
Manufactures garden tractors and lawn mowers, snow-throwers, electric ranges, Venetian blinds, luggage, and other products.

Sara Lee Corporation
3 First National Plaza
Chicago, IL 60602
(312) 726-2600
V.P. Human Resources: Philip P. Temple
Diversified company involved in the processing of a variety of foods and beverages such as Sara Lee cakes, Popsicles, and Shasta beverages; and non-food items such as Electro-Lux vacuum cleaners, Hanes hosiery, and Fuller brushes.

Sunbeam Corporation
1333 Butterfield Road
Downers Grove, IL 60515
(708) 719-4864
Contact Corporate Hiring at: (414) 719-4864
Manufactures and markets small electric appliances.

Triangle Home Products
945 E. 93rd St.
Chicago, IL 60619

(312) 374-4400
Personnel: Terry Varga
Manufactures and distributes vanities, cabinets, and light fixtures.

White Consolidated Industries
174 3rd St.
Aurora, IL 60507
(708) 892-7696
Contact: Personnel
Engaged in the manufacture of products for the home sold under names such as Kelvinator, White-Westinghouse, and Fridgidaire; also machine tools machinery, food and chemical processing equipment, valves, controls, and instrumentation.

Windsor Industries
1304 S. Indiana Ave.
Chicago, IL 60605
(312) 294-7300
Personnel Director: Lonnie Gleimi
Manufactures lamps and lamp shades.

Human Services

For networking in **human services** and related fields, check out the following professional organizations listed in Chapter 5:

PROFESSIONAL ORGANIZATIONS:

Chicago Foundation for Women
Chicago Society of Association Executives
Corporate Responsibility Group of Greater Chicago
Donors Forum of Chicago
Human Resources Management Association
Illinois Women's Agenda
Lions Club International
Midwest Women's Center
National Society of Fund-Raising Executives
Professional Career Counselors Network
Rotary Club of Chicago
Service Corps of Retired Executives
Social Service Communicators
YMCA of Metropolitan Chicago

For more information, you can write to:

National Association of Social Workers
7981 Eastern Ave.
Silver Spring, MD 20910

PROFESSIONAL PUBLICATIONS:

Children and Youth Services
The Nonprofit Times
Society

DIRECTORIES:

Greater Chicago Religious Directory and Buyer's Guide (Church Federation of Greater Chicago, Chicago, IL)
Hotline: Crisis Intervention Directory (Facts on File, New York, NY)
National Directory of Children and Youth Services (Marion Peterson, Longmont, CO.)
National Directory of Private Social Agencies (Croner Publications, Queens Village, NY)

EMPLOYERS:

Catholic Charities
721 N. LaSalle
Chicago, IL 60610
(312) 266-6100
Contact: Personnel
Provides a wide range of social services to the general public.

Chicago Commons Association
915 N. Wolcott Ave.
Chicago, IL 60622
(312) 342-5330
Personnel Director: Shirley Castanuela
Maintains centers where people with the fewest alternatives meet for community, recreational, and educational activities.

Chicago Youth Centers
231 S. Jefferson, 6th Floor
Chicago, IL 60606
(312) 648-1550
Executive Director: Delbert Arsenault
Provides recreational and educational opportunities to lower income neighborhoods.

Community & Economic Development Association of Cook County
224 N. Des Plaines St.
Chicago, IL 60606
(312) 207-5444
Personnel Director: Jarret DuBois
Social services organization serving suburban Cook County in areas of housing, counseling, day care, senior activities, nutrition, and employment.

Hull House Association
118 N. Clinton St.
Chicago, IL 60606
(312) 726-1526
Personnel Director: Sandra Haynes
Provides recreational and social services through 24 neighborhood locations.

Jewish Federation of Metropolitan Chicago
1 S. Franklin St.
Chicago, IL 60606
(312) 346-6700
Executive Director: Allan Goldstein
Provides a wide range of social services, including vocational guidance, to all segments of the public.

United Charities
14 E. Jackson Blvd.
Chicago, IL 60604
(312) 461-0800
Personnel Director: Evelyn Engler
Provides social services to all segments of the public.

YMCA of Metropolitan Chicago
755 W. North Ave.
Chicago, IL 60610
(312) 280-3400
Director of Personnel: Charlaine Robinson
Provides a wide range of social, educational, and recreational services to all segments of the public.

YWCA of Metropolitan Chicago
180 N. Wabash, Suite 301
Chicago, IL 60601
(312) 372-6600
Executive Director: Audrey R. Peeples
Operates recreational, educational, and social programs primarily for women and girls.

Insurance/ Benefits Consultants

For networking in **insurance** and related fields, check out the following professional organizations listed in Chapter 5:

PROFESSIONAL ORGANIZATIONS:

Alliance of American Insurers
American Society of Safety Engineers
Chicago Network of Insurance Women
Health Insurance Association of America
Independent Insurance Agents of Illinois
Million Dollar Round Table
National Association of Independent Insurance Adjusters

For additional information, you can write to:

American Council of Life Insurance
1001 Pennsylvania Ave., N.W.
Washington, DC 20004

American Insurance Association
85 John St.
New York, NY 10038

National Association of Independent Insurers
2600 River Road
Des Plaines, IL 60018

National Association of Life Underwriters
1922 F St., N.W.
Washington, DC 20006

PROFESSIONAL PUBLICATIONS:

Best's Review
Business Insurance
National Underwriter

DIRECTORIES:

Best's Directory of Recommended Insurance Adjusters (A. M. Best Co., Oldwick, NY)
Insurance Almanac (Underwriter Publishing Co., Englewood, NJ)

Who Writes What in Life and Health Insurance (National Underwriter Co., Cincinnati, OH)

EMPLOYERS:

T.J. Adams & Associates
2001 Spring Road, Suite 630
Oak Brook, IL 60521-1812
(708) 572-1550
Personnel Director: Christine Gruden

Administrative Management Group
3800 N. Wilke Road, Suite 250
Arlington Heights, IL 60004
(708) 577-6000
Personnel Director: Dave Goldenberg
Benefits consultants.

Affiliated Insurance Consultants
1023 Burlington Ave.
Western Springs, IL 60558
(708) 246-1234
Personnel Director: Dee Albrecht

Alexander & Alexander
225 N. Michigan
Chicago, IL 60601
(312) 565-6000
Managing Vice President: Robert Hughes
Insurance and benefits consultants.

Allstate Insurance Co.
Allstate Plaza
Northbrook, IL 60062
(708) 402-6953
Employment Manager: Rich Warren

Alper Services
60 W. Superior St.
Chicago, IL 60610
(312) 642-1000
Contact: Personnel

Arthur Andersen & Co.
33 W. Monroe
Chicago, IL 60603
(312) 580-0033
Personnel Director: Jim Dublin
Benefits consultants.

Aon Corporation
123 N. Wacker Drive

Chicago, IL 60606
(312) 701-3000

Associated Agencies
651 W. Washington
Chicago, IL 60606-2193
(312) 707-9000
Personnel Director: Bonnie Jochem
Insurance and benefits consultants.

Bankers Life & Casualty Co.
4444 W. Lawrence Ave.
Chicago, IL 60630
(312) 777-7000
Personnel Director: Frank Lucchesi

Blue Cross/Blue Shield
233 N. Michigan Ave.
Chicago, IL 60601
(312) 938-6000
Contact: Personnel

Boockford & Co.
22nd St. & Butterfield Road
One Oakbrook Terrace
Oakbrook Terrace, IL 60181
(708) 932-4000
Personnel Director: Lois Vesley

Buck Consultants
55 W. Monroe St., Suite 1700
Chicago, IL 60603
(312) 332-2285
Contact: Personnel
Benefits consultants.

CCC Information Services
640 N. LaSalle St.
Chicago, IL 60610
(312) 787-2640
Personnel Director: Claudia Hoffman
Provides financial data and services to automobile insurance companies.

CNA Financial Corporation
CNA Plaza
Chicago, IL 60685
(312) 822-5000
Personnel Administrator: Lynn Dragisic

Combined Insurance Corporation
5050 N. Broadway

Chicago, IL 60640
(312) 275-8000
Contact: Employment Representative

Complete Equity Markets
1098 S. Milwaukee Ave.
Wheeling, IL 60090
(708) 541-0900
Personnel Director: Theresa Mikosz

Connecticut Mutual Insurance Co.
180 N. LaSalle St., Suite 1700
Chicago, IL 60601
(312) 984-5700
Contact: Personnel

Continental Insurance Co.
200 S. Wacker Drive
Chicago, IL 60606
(312) 876-5000
V.P. Human Resources: Joyce Heidemann

Coopers & Lybrand
203 N. LaSalle
Chicago, IL 60601
(312) 701-5500
Personnel Director: Pat Jones
Benefits consultants.

Corroon & Black of Illinois
135 S. LaSalle St., Suite 1800
Chicago, IL 60603
(312) 621-4700
Personnel Director: Angie Garafalo
Benefits consultants.

Dann Brothers
650 Dundee Road
Northbrook, IL 60062
(708) 564-8700
Contact: Personnel

Deloitte & Touche
2 Prudential Plaza
180 N. Stetson St.
Chicago, IL 60601
(312) 946-3000
Managing Partner: Thomas P. Flanagan
Benefits consultants.

Engler, Zoglin, Mann
1000 Skokie Blvd.

Wilmette, IL 60091
(708) 256-5500
Head of Employee Benefits: Coleen Foley
Benefits consultants.

Equitable Life Assurance Society
401 N. Michigan Ave., Suite 1400
Chicago, IL 60611
(312) 836-1000
Contact: Personnel

Euclid Insurance Agencies
977 N. Oaklawn Ave., Suite 300
Elmhurst, IL 60126
(708) 833-1000
Manager of Commercial Lines: Colleen Lacina

Financial Insurance Service
210 W. 22nd St., Suite 128
Oak Brook, IL 60521
(708) 573-1360
Contact: Personnel

Fireman's Fund Insurance Companies
200 W. Monroe St.
Chicago, IL 60606
(312) 580-6000
Personnel Director: Robert Holden

Arthur J. Gallagher & Co.
10 Gould Center, Golf Road
Rolling Meadows, IL 60008
(708) 640-8500
Personnel Director: William Hornig

Frank B. Hall & Co.
230 W. Monroe St., Suite 1000
Chicago, IL 60606
(312) 641-1900
Contact: Office Manager

Hay Group
205 N. Michigan
Boulevard Towers, Suite 4000
Chicago, IL 60601
(312) 819-2100
Contact: Personnel
Benefits consultants.

Hewitt Associates
100 Half Day Road
Lincolnshire, IL 60069

(708) 295-5000
Personnel Contact: John Zerba
Benefits consultants.

Holzman, Post, Ludwig & Schwartz
125 S. Wilke Road, Suite 300
Arlington Heights, IL 60005
(708) 392-2999
Personnel Director: Julie Bassett
Benefits consultants.

Inter Cargo Corp.
1501 Woodfield Road
Schaumburg, IL 60173
(708) 517-2990
Vice President: Brian D. Freund
Holding company, providing insurance for intenational trade.

Thomas L. Jacobs & Associates
230 W. Monroe St., Suite 545
Chicago, IL 60606
(312) 346-0155
Contact: Personnel
Benefits consultants.

Fred S. James Co.
230 W. Monroe St.
Chicago, IL 60606
(312) 346-3000
V. P., Human Resources: Cynthia Ferrara

Jardine
2122 York Road, Suite 220
Oak Brook, IL 60521-1923
(708) 990-2200
Personnel Director: Maureen Kolvow

Johnson & Higgins
500 W. Madison, Suite 2100
Chicago, IL 60606-2511
(312) 648-4200
Contact: Personnel

Kemper Group
Route 22
Long Grove, IL 60049
(708) 540-2000
Employment Supervisor: Gary Slettum

KFS James Insurance Agency
806 Arthur Ave.
Arlington Heights, IL 60006

(708) 392-8550
Contact: Personnel

KPMG Peat Marwick
303 E. Wacker Drive
Chicago, IL 60601
(312) 938-1000
Personnel Director: Patricia Gamble
Benefits consultants.

Kruger Insurance Agency
39 S. LaSalle St., Suite 300
Chicago, IL 60603
(312) 726-1002
Personnel Director: Carol Najdowski

Lamb, Little & Co.
5301 Keystone Court
Rolling Meadows, IL 60008
(708) 398-7060
Personnel Director: Bob Power

Lubin-Bergman Organization
7101 N. Cicero Ave.
Lincolnwood, IL 60646
(708) 673-4900
Personnel Director: Steve Dubrow

Mack & Parker
55 E. Jackson Blvd.
Chicago, IL 60604
(312) 922-5000
Contact: Personnel

Marsh & McLennan
222 S. Riverside Plaza
Chicago, IL 60606
(312) 648-6000
Employment Coordinator: Beth Ward

Massachusetts Mutual Life Insurance Co.
8755 W. Higgins Road, Suite 1090
Chicago, IL 60631
(312) 380-8700
Contact: Personnel

McManus & Pellouchoud
141 W. Jackson Blvd.
Chicago, IL 60604
(312) 427-1961
Personnel Director: Florence Stafanik

Meeker Magner
2360 E. Devon Ave., Suite 3010
Des Plaines, IL 60018
(708) 699-1400
President: T.G. Magner, Jr.

William M. Mercer, Meidiger, Hansen
10 S. Wacker Drive
Chicago, IL 60606
(312) 902-7500
Director, Employee Benefits: Robert Lindgren
Benefits consultants.

Mesirow Financial
350 N. Clark
Chicago, IL 60610
(312) 670-6000
Managing Director: James C. Tyree
Provides services for insurance, financial, and real estate investments.

Metropolitan Life Insurance Co.
200 E. Randolph St.
Chicago, IL 60601-6804
(312) 861-3000
Contact: Personnel

Miller, Mason & Dickenson
123 N. Wacker Drive
Chicago, IL 60606
(312) 701-4800
Contact: Personnel
Benefits consultants.

Milliman & Robertson
55 W. Monroe, Suite 3790
Chicago, IL 60603
(312) 726-0677
Personnel Director: Gwen Mitchell
Benefits consultants.

Julius Moll & Sons
6160 N. Cicero Ave.
Chicago, IL 60646
(312) 286-7737
Contact: Personnel

Near North Insurance
875 N. Michigan Ave., Suite 2300
Chicago, IL 60611
(312) 943-2500
Personnel Director: Mark Ernst

New York Life Insurance Company
8831 Gross Point Road
Skokie, IL 60077
(708) 673-9200
Office Manager: Jerry Villanueva

Noble Lowndes
525 W. Monroe St., Suite 2405
Chicago, IL 60606
(312) 648-1010
Attention: Human Resources Director
Benefits consultants.

Old Republic Life Insurance Company
307 N. Michigan Ave.
Chicago, IL 60601
(312) 346-8100
Personnel Director: Charles Strizak
Insurance holding company.

Prudential Insurance Co. of America
Prudential Plaza
130 E. Randolph
Chicago, IL 60601
(312) 861-4500
Contact: Personnel

Rollins Burdick Hunter of Illinois
123 N. Wacker Drive
Chicago, IL 60606
(312) 701-4000
Personnel Manager: Mary Paulus
Life insurance

Ryan Insurance Agency Group
123 N. Wacker Drive
Chicago, IL 60606
(312) 701-3000
Contact: Personnel

Schwartz Brothers Insurance Agency
135 S. LaSalle St.
Chicago, IL 60603
(312) 630-0800
Personnel Director: Betsy Karalif

Martin E. Segal Co.
101 N. Wacker Drive, Suite 500
Chicago, IL 60606
(312) 782-1416
Director of Employee Benefits: Lall Bachan
Benefits consultants.

Thilman & Filippini
1 E. Wacker Drive, Suite 1800
Chicago, IL 60601
(312) 527-9500
Personnel Director: Barbara Schultz

Towers Perrin Forster & Crosby
200 W. Madison St., Suite 3300
Chicago, IL 60606
(312) 781-0300
Personnel Director: Pat Seng
Benefits consultants.

The Travelers Insurance Co.
100 Park St.
Naperville, IL 60566-1029
(708) 986-8700
Personnel Manager: Robert Howard

Washington National Corporation
1630 Chicago Ave.
Evanston, IL 60201
(708) 570-5500
Vice President: Richard W. Miller

Wyatt Co.
303 W. Madison, Suite 2400
Chicago, IL 60606
(312) 704-0600
Director of Employee Benefits: Robert Barnes
Benefits consultants.

Zurich-American Insurance Companies
Zurich Towers
1400 American Lane
Schaumburg, IL 60196
(708) 605-6000
V.P. Human Resources: Dan Borbas

Investment Institutions/ Stock Brokers

For networking in **finance** and related fields, check out the following professional organizations listed in Chapter 5:

PROFESSIONAL ORGANIZATIONS:

Chicago Finance Exchange
Chicago Midwest Credit Managers Association
Financial Managers Society for Savings Institutions
Investment Analysts Society of Chicago
Municipal Bond Club of Chicago
Municipal Women of Chicago
National Futures Association

For additional information, you can write to:

Financial Analysts Federation
1633 Broadway
New York, NY 10019

Futures Industry Association
2001 Pennsylvania Ave., Suite 600
Washington, DC 20006

National Association of Securities Dealers
1735 K St., N.W.
Washington, DC 20007

PROFESSIONAL PUBLICATIONS:

Business Credit
Commodity Journal
Corporate Financing Week
Dun's Business Month
Finance and Development
Financial Analysts Journal
Financial Executive
Financial World
Futures
Institutional Investor
Investment Dealers Digest
Securities Week
Wall St. Transcript

DIRECTORIES:

Corporate Finance Sourcebook (National Register, Wilmette, IL)
CUSIP Master Directory (Standard & Poors, New York, NY)
Money Market Directory (Money Market Directories, Inc., Charlottesville, VA)
Nelson's Directory of Investment Research (W.R. Nelson, Port Chester, NY)

Security Dealers of North America (Standard and Poor's, New York, NY)
Who's Who in the Securities Industry (Economist Publishing, New York, NY)

EMPLOYERS:

American National Bank
33 N. LaSalle St.
Chicago, IL 60690
(312) 661-6001

Ameritech Pension Fund
30 S. Wacker Drive
Chicago, IL 60606
(312) 750-5000
Human Resources Director: Neil Kulick

Amoco Corporation Pension Fund
P.O. Box 87703
Chicago, IL 60680-0703
(312) 856-2945

Bacon, Whipple, Stifel, Nicolaus
135 S. LaSalle St., Suite 2323
Chicago, IL 60603
(312) 704-7000
Contact: Office Manager

Baker, Fentress & Co.
200 W. Madison St., Suite 3510
Chicago, IL 60606
(312) 236-9190
Personnel Director: Jim Koeneman

The Balcor Co.
4849 Golf Road
Skokie, IL 60077
(708) 677-2900

Bear Stearns & Co.
3 First National Plaza, Suite 2500
Chicago, IL 60602
(312) 580-4000

William Blair & Co.
135 S. LaSalle St., Suite 2900
Chicago, IL 60603
(312) 236-1600

Blunt, Ellis & Loewi
111 W. Monroe St., Suite 1700E

Chicago, IL 60603
(312) 346-9000

Blunt, Ellis & Loewi
333 W. Wacker Drive, Suite 300
Chicago, IL 60606
(312) 630-8635

Capital Supervisors
20 N. Clark St., Suite 700
Chicago, IL 60602
(312) 236-8271

Chicago Board Options Exchange
400 S. LaSalle St.
Chicago, IL 60605
(312) 786-5600
Contact: Personnel
Trading in stock options.

Chicago Board of Trade
141 W. Jackson Blvd.
Chicago, IL 60604
(312) 435-3500
Contact: Personnel
Trading in grain and financial futures.

Chicago Corporation
208 S. LaSalle St.
Chicago, IL 60604
(312) 855-7600

Chicago Mercantile Exchange
30 S. Wacker Drive
Chicago, IL 60606
(312) 930-8200
Contact: Personnel
Trading in commodities.

Clayton Brown & Associates
500 W. Madison
Chicago, IL 60606
(312) 559-3000

Dean Witter Reynolds
6000 Sears Tower
233 S. Wacker Drive
Chicago, IL 60606
(312) 984-4321

Dimensional Fund Advisors
1800 Sherman Ave.

Evanston, IL 60201
(708) 492-3050

Donaldson, Lufkin & Jenrette
3 First National Plaza
Chicago, IL 60602
(312) 419-4230

Duff and Phelps Investment Management
55 E. Monroe St., Suite 3600
Chicago, IL 60603
(312) 263-2610

A.G. Edwards and Sons
222 S. Riverside Plaza
Chicago, IL 60606
(312) 648-5200
Vice President: Morris Hofstetter

Ernst & Co.
209 W. Jackson St., Room 900
Chicago, IL 60606
(312) 554-2200

Ernst & Young
150 S. Wacker Drive
Chicago, IL 60606
(312) 368-1800

First Boston Corporation
135 S. LaSalle St., Suite 735
Chicago, IL 60603
(312) 750-3000

First Chicago Investment Advisors
3 First National Plaza, 9th Floor
Chicago, IL 60670
(312) 732-6400

Freehling & Co.
190 S. LaSalle St., 22nd Floor
Chicago, IL 60603
(312) 346-2680

Gofen & Glossberg
455 Cityfront Plaza, Suite 3000
Chicago, IL 60611
(312) 828-1100

Goldman, Sachs & Co.
4900 Sears Tower
233 S. Wacker Drive

Chicago, IL 60606
(312) 993-4600

Gruntal & Co.
135 S. LaSalle St.
Chicago, IL 60603
(312) 269-0380

Hamilton Investments
30 N. LaSalle St.
Chicago, IL 60602
(312) 444-2100

Harris Associates
2 N. LaSalle St., Suite 500
Chicago, IL 60602
(312) 621-0600

Heitman Financial
180 N. La Salle St., Suite 3600
Chicago, IL 60601
(312) 855-5700

Heller Financial
200 N. LaSalle
Chicago, IL 60601
(312) 621-7000

Howe Barnes Investments
135 S. LaSalle St., Suite 1500
Chicago, IL 60603
(312) 930-2900

Wayne Hummer & Co.
175 W. Jackson Blvd., Suite 1700
Chicago, IL 60604
(312) 431-1700

Illinois Municipal Retirement Fund
100 S. Wacker Drive
Chicago, IL 60606
(312) 346-6722

Institutional Capital Corporation
303 W. Madison, Suite 1800
Chicago, IL 60606
(312) 641-7200

Investment & Capital Management Corporation
10 S. LaSalle St.
Chicago, IL 60603
(312) 220-7550

JMB Institutional Investment
900 N. Michigan Ave.
Chicago, IL 60611
(312) 440-4800

Edward D. Jones & Co.
9 N. Vail St.
Arlington Heights, IL 60005
(708) 577-6377

Kemper Financial Services
120 S. LaSalle St.
Chicago, IL 60603
(312) 781-1121

Kidder, Peabody & Co.
125 S. Wacker Drive
Chicago, IL 60606
(312) 984-2300

Ladenburg, Thalmann & Co.
20 N. Clark St., Suite 525
Chicago, 60602
(312) 782-4200

LaSalle Partners
11 S. LaSalle St., Suite 400
Chicago, IL 60603
(312) 782-5800

Lehmann Brothers
190 S. LaSalle, 24th Floor
Chicago, IL 60603
(312) 609-7200

Lincoln Capital Management Co.
200 S. Wacker Drive
Chicago, IL 60606
(312) 559-2880

Loomis Sayles & Co.
3 First National Plaza, Suite 5450
Chicago, IL 60602
(312) 346-9750

Manufacturers Hanover Trust
10 S. La Salle St., 22nd Floor
Chicago, IL 60603
(312) 580-1011

Merrill Lynch Piercc Fenner & Smith
1 S. Wacker Drive

Chicago, IL 60606
(312) 347-6000

Mesirow Financial Co.
350 N. Clark St.
Chicago, IL 60610
(312) 670-6000

Mid-America Commodity Exchange
141 W. Jackson Blvd.
Chicago, IL 60604
(312) 341-3000
Contact: Personnel
Trading in commodity futures.

Midwest Stock Exchange
440 S. LaSalle St.
Chicago, IL 60605
(312) 663-2222
Contact: Personnel
Trading in securities.

Morgan Stanley & Co.
440 S. LaSalle St.
Chicago, IL 60605
(312) 765-6000

Northern Investment Services Group
50 S. LaSalle St.
Chicago, IL 60675
(312) 630-6000

Northern Trust Financial Futures
50 S. LaSalle St.
Chicago, IL 60675
(312) 630-6000

David A. Noyes & Co.
208 S. LaSalle St.
Chicago, IL 60604
(312) 782-0400

John Nuveen & Co.
333 W. Wacker Drive
Chicago, IL 60606
(312) 917-7700

Oppenheimer & Co.
1 S. Wacker Drive, Suite 2300
Chicago, IL 60606
(312) 621-6800

Paine Webber, Mitchell Hutchins
55 W. Monroe St.
Chicago, IL 60603
(312) 580-8000

Prescott, Ball & Turben
230 W. Monroe St., Suite 2800
Chicago, IL 60606
(312) 641-7800

Prudential-Bache Securities
1 S. Wacker Drive, Suite 2900
Chicago, IL 60606
(312) 630-7000

Prudential-Bache Securities
233 S. Wacker Drive
Chicago, IL 60606
(312) 630-7300

Public School Teachers' Pension and Retirement Fund of Chicago
205 W. Wacker Drive, Room 820
Chicago, IL 60606
(312) 641-4464

Rodman & Renshaw
120 S. LaSalle St., 10th Floor
Chicago, IL 60603
(312) 977-7800

Rothschild Securities Co.
33 W. Monroe
Chicago, IL 60603
(312) 781-8900

Salomon Bros.
8700 Sears Tower
233 S. Wacker Drive
Chicago, IL 60606
(312) 876-8700

Charles A. Schwab & Co.
70 W. Madison St., Suite 1300
Chicago, IL 60602
(312) 853-3030

Scudder, Stevens & Clark
111 E. Wacker Drive, Suite 2200
Chicago, IL 60601
(312) 861-2700

Sears, Roebuck and Co. Pension Fund
55 W. Monroe St.
Chicago, IL 60603
(312) 875-0450

Shearson Lehmann Hutton
141 W. Jackson Blvd., Suite 338
Chicago, IL 60604
(312) 435-3333

Shearson Lehmann Hutton
10 S. Wacker Drive
Chicago, IL 60606
(312) 648-3600

Smith Barney, Harris Upham & Co.
3 First National Plaza, Suite 5200
Chicago, IL 60603
(312) 491-3600

Bullish on LaSalle Street

Lisa Marini, a stock broker with Merrill Lynch Pierce Fenner & Smith, gave us this rundown on Chicago's trading scene.

"Chicago is the auction market capital of the world. On the trading floor, what you see is the most naked form of supply and demand in action. It's a public outcry market. Floor traders literally shout out their bids on stocks, options, commodities, metals, whatever.

"There are two classes of people in the auction—the traders and everybody else. You start out as a runner, running orders to the floor traders, who are the only ones who can actually bid. Next you become a phone clerk; they're the people who answer the phones and give the orders to the runners. From phone clerk you move up to crowd assistant or market-maker clerk. A crowd assistant helps the broker or trader execute the orders. A market-maker clerk monitors a trader's position and risk in the market.

"Some phone clerks earn upward of $50,000 a year. I know one market-maker clerk who made $140,000 last year. But you'll never be promoted to floor trader just by working hard. You have to take a national standardized test, which gives you a license to trade. It's called the R.O.P.—the Registered Options Principal test.

"Once you pass the test, you bid on a seat. In 1974, CBOE seats were around $10,000. In 1976 they went to $135,000. At the tail end of '77 they were down to $20,000. Now I think they go for $120,000.

"The major exchanges are the Midwest Stock Exchange, at 120 S. LaSalle, for stocks. Options are traded at the Chicago Board Options Exchange and the Midwest Options Exchange, both at 141 W. Jackson on the seventh floor. At the Chicago Board of Trade, 141 W. Jackson, the trading is in grains, beans, metals, and financial futures. The Mercantile Exchange, at Jackson and Canal, handles gold, currencies, and meats. The Mid-America Exchange, at 175 W. Jackson, is just like the Board of Trade but they deal in smaller amounts.

"About half the people on the floor work for big companies, and the others for small outfits, usually less than five people. The floor is treated as a completely separate hiring center. To be a Merrill Lynch floor clerk you go to the floor, not Merrill Lynch.

"The way to get a job on the floor is to know someone. There are a number of bars where brokers and traders congregate after hours. There's the Broker's Inn, 323 S. LaSalle; the bar in the lobby of the Board of Trade; and on the third Saturday of every month, Lou Mitchell's, 565 W. Jackson, is jammed with traders during breakfast, from about 7:30 to 10:30."■

Stein Roe & Farnham
1 S. Wacker Drive
Chicago, IL 60606
(312) 368-7700

Stifel Nicolaus & Co.
135 S. LaSalle St.
Chicago, Il 60603
(312) 704-7000

Teamsters Pension Fund
9377 W. Higgins Road
Rosemont, IL 60018
(708) 519-9800
Personnel Manager: Scott Robbins

Tucker Anthony
1 S. Wacker Drive
Chicago, IL 60606
(312) 853-6900

Van Kampen Merritt
1001 Warrenville Road
Lisle, IL 60532
(708) 719-6000

Warburg Paribas Becker
2 First National Plaza
Chicago, IL 60603
(312) 630-5555

The Yarmouth Group
2 Prudential Plaza, Suite 1300
180 N. Stetson
Chicago, IL 60601
(312) 861-1105

Ziegler Securities
1 S. Wacker Drive, Suite 3080
Chicago, IL 60606
(312) 263-0110

Law Firms

For networking in **law** and related fields, check out the following professional organizations listed in Chapter 5:

PROFESSIONAL ORGANIZATIONS:

American Bar Association
Association of Legal Administrators
Chicago Bar Association
Chicago Council of Lawyers
Chicago Women's Political Caucus
Independent Voters of Illinois
Lawyers for the Creative Arts
Women's Bar Association of Illinois

For more information, you can write to:

American Bar Association
750 N. Lake Shore Drive
Chicago, IL 60611

PROFESSIONAL PUBLICATIONS:

ABA Journal
Chicago Lawyer

DIRECTORIES:

ABA Directory (American Bar Association, Chicago, IL)
Martindale-Hubbell Law Directory (Martindale-Hubbell, Summit, NJ)

EMPLOYERS:

Adams, Fox, Adelstein, Rosen & Bell
208 S. LaSalle St., Suite 550
Chicago, IL 60604
(312) 368-1900

Altheimer & Gray
10 S. Wacker Drive
Chicago, IL 60606
(312) 715-4622
Administrator: Robert Wallwork

Arvey, Hodes, Costello & Burman
180 N. LaSalle St., Suite 3800
Chicago, IL 60601
(312) 855-5000
Administrator: Dean Niedospial

Baker & McKenzie
Prudential Plaza
130 E. Randolph Drive
Chicago, IL 60601
(312) 861-8000
Firm Administrator: Robert W. Cox

Bell, Boyd & Lloyd
3 First National Plaza
70 W. Madison St.
Chicago, IL 60602
(312) 372-1121
Administrator: William C. Allen, Jr.

Chapman & Cutler
111 W. Monroe St.
Chicago, IL 60603
(312) 845-3761
Administrator: Charles Stinnett

D'Ancona & Pflaum
30 N. LaSalle St., Suite 3100
Chicago, IL 60602
(312) 580-2081
Administrator: Al Silvian

Gardner Carton & Douglas
Quaker Tower
321 N. Clark St.
Chicago, IL 60610-4795
(312) 245-8850
Administrator: David D. Rose

Hinshaw, Culbertson, Moelmann, Hoban & Fuller
222 N. LaSalle, Suite 300
Chicago, IL 60601-1081
(312) 704-3000
Administrator: H. Joseph Plack

Hopkins & Sutter
3 First National Plaza
Chicago, IL 60602
(312) 558-6600
Administrator: Gregory P. Marren

Jenner & Block
One IBM Plaza
Chicago, IL 60611
(312) 222-9350
Administrator: Richard Wilkus

Katten, Muchin & Zavis
525 W. Monroe St., Suite 1600
Chicago, IL 60606-3693
(312) 902-5200
Administrator: Michael R. Marget

Keck, Mahin & Cate
3300 Sears Tower
233 S. Wacker Drive
Chicago, IL 60606
(312) 876-3400
Administrator: Donald L. Morris

Kirkland & Ellis
200 E. Randolph Drive
Chicago, IL 60601
(312) 861-2000
Adminstrator: Lois A. Strom

Lord, Bissell & Brook
115 S. LaSalle St.

Chicago, IL 60603
(312) 443-0410
Administrator: Harvey Lichterman

Mayer, Brown & Platt
190 S. LaSalle St.
Chicago, IL 60603
(312) 782-0600
Administrator: Robert A. Southern

McBride, Baker & Coles
Northwestern Atrium
500 W. Madison, 40th Floor
Chicago, IL 60603
(312) 715-5700
Administrator: Carol Lenkart

McDermott, Will & Emery
227 W. Monroe St.
Chicago, IL 60606
(312) 372-2000
Administrator: William Schaefer

Peterson, Ross, Schloerb & Seidel
200 E. Randolph Drive, Suite 7300
Chicago, IL 60601
(312) 861-1400
Administrator: Theodore Boundas

Pope, Ballard, Shepard & Fowle
69 W. Washington St., Suite 3200
Chicago, IL 60602
(312) 214-4200
Administrator: Steffani Francis

Rooks, Pitts, & Poust
55 W. Monroe St., Suite 1500
Chicago, IL 60603
(312) 372-5600
Administrator: Ruth Schumacher

Ross & Hardies
150 N. Michigan Ave.
Chicago, IL 60601
(312) 558-1000
Administrator: Duane A. Feurer

Rudnick & Wolfe
203 N. LaSalle St., Suite 1500
Chicago, IL 60601
(312) 368-4000
Administrator: Jack Gary

Schiff, Hardin & Waite
7200 Sears Tower
233 S. Wacker Drive
Chicago, IL 60606
(312) 876-1000
Administrator: Stephen B. Veitch

Seyfarth, Shaw, Fairweather & Geraldson
55 E. Monroe St., Suite 4200
Chicago, IL 60603
(312) 269-8844
Administrator: Helen E. Caroll

Sidley & Austin
1 First National Plaza
Chicago, IL 60603
(312) 329-5409
Administrator: D. James Lantonio

Wildman, Harrold, Allen & Dixon
225 W. Wacker Drive, Suite 2800
Chicago, IL 60606
(312) 201-2000
Administrator: Bruce Chisman

Winston & Strawn
35 W. Wacker Drive
Chicago, IL 60601
(312) 558-5882
Administrator: Douglas McLemore

Management Consultants

For networking in **management consulting** and related fields, you can write to:

PROFESSIONAL ORGANIZATIONS:

Association of Management Consultants
331 Madison Ave.
New York, NY 10017

Association of Management Consulting Firms
230 Park Ave.
New York, NY 10169

National Management Association
2210 Arbor Blvd.
Dayton, OH 45439

PROFESSIONAL PUBLICATIONS:

Academy of Management Review
Business Quarterly
Consultants News
Executive
Harvard Business Review

DIRECTORIES:

AMC Directory (Association of Management Consultants, New York, NY)
Consultants and Consulting Organizations Directory (Gale Research, Detroit, MI)
Directory of Management Consultants (Kennedy & Kennedy, Fitzwilliam, NH)
IMC Directory (Institute of Management Consultants, New York, NY)

EMPLOYERS:

American Management Systems
20 N. Clark St., Suite 3300
Chicago, IL 60602
(312) 269-0275
Vice President: Gary Curtis

Applied Information Developers
823 Commerce Drive
Oak Brook, IL 60521
(708) 574-3030

Arthur Andersen & Co.
33 W. Monroe St.
Chicago, IL 60603
(312) 580-0033
Director: John Oatman

Austin Co.
9801 W. Higgins Road
Rosemont, IL 60018
(708) 696-0500
Vice President: Milton Cooke

Theodore Barry & Associates
10275 W. Higgins Road, Suite 480
Rosemont, IL 60018
(708) 699-8010
V. P. of Personnel: Jim Hilvert

Benton Schneider & Associates
3030 Warrenville Road
Lisle, IL 60563
(708) 505-3030
President: William Benton

Booz, Allen & Hamilton
3 First National Plaza
Chicago, IL 60602
(312) 346-1900
Senior Vice President: Robert M. Howe

Boston Consulting Group
200 S. Wacker Drive
Chicago, IL 60606
(312) 993-3300
Senior V.P.: Carl Stern

Coopers & Lybrand
203 N. LaSalle
Chicago, IL 60601
(312) 701-5500
Managing Partner: L. Eugene Williams

Cresap
200 W. Madison St., Suite 3400
Chicago, IL 60606
(312) 263-7125
Vice President: Jeffrey A. Schmidt

Deloitte & Touche
2 Prudential Plaza
180 N. Stetson St.
Chicago, IL 60601
(312) 946-3000
Managing Partner: Thomas P. Flanagan

Ernst & Young
150 S. Wacker Drive
Chicago, IL 60606
(312) 368-1800
Managing Partner: James S. DiStasio

W. D. Farlow & Associates
1700 S. Westview Ave.
South Holland, IL 60473
(708) 331-5363
President: Dale Gowens

Grant-Thornton & Co.
700 Prudential Plaza
Chicago, IL 60601

(312) 856-0200
Director, Recruiting: Ed Spelde

A. T. Kearney, Inc.
222 S. Riverside Plaza
Chicago, IL 60606
(312) 648-0111
Personnel Director: Robert Sterling

Lester B. Knight & Associates
549 W. Randolph St.
Chicago, IL 60606
(312) 346-2100

KPMG Peat Marwick
303 E. Wacker Drive
Chicago, IL 60601
(312) 938-1000
Managing Partner: John L. Montogomery

Laventhol & Horwath
300 S. Riverside Plaza
Chicago, IL 60606
(312) 648-0555
Managing Partner: Kenneth I. Solomon

London House
1550 Northwest Highway
Park Ridge, IL 60068
(708) 298-7311

James H. Lowry & Associates
218 N. Jefferson, Suite 300
Chicago, IL 60606
(312) 930-0930

George S. May International Co.
303 S. Northwest Highway
Park Ridge, IL 60068
(708) 825-8806
President: D. Fletcher

McKinsey & Co.
20 S. Clark St.
Chicago, IL 60603
(312) 368-0600
Managing Director: Michael Murray

Planmetrics, Inc.
8700 W. Bryn Mawr Ave., Suite 300S
Chicago, IL 60631

(312) 693-0200
President: Larry Klock

Price Waterhouse
200 E. Randolph Drive
Chicago, IL 60601
(312) 565-1500
Managing Partner: Thomas Donahoe

Professional Computer Resources
2400 Cabot Drive
Lisle, IL 60532
(708) 954-3600
Chairman: Dave Eskra

Albert Ramond & Associates
5005 Newport Drive, Suite 600
Rolling Meadows, IL 60008
(708) 577-6868

ServiceMaster Limited Partnership
2300 Warrenville Road
Downers Grove, IL 60515
(708) 964-1300
Provides supportive management services to educational, health care, and industrial facilities.

Standards International
7511 Waukegan Road
Niles, IL 60648
(708) 647-1550

Technomic Consultants
330 S. Riverside Plaza, Suite 1940
Chicago, IL 60606
(312) 876-0004
President: Ron Paul

Tribrook Group
999 Oakmont Plaza Drive
Westmont Plaza
Westmont, IL 60559
(708) 990-8070
President: Richard L. Johnson

Manufacturers

PROFESSIONAL ORGANIZATIONS:

National Association of Manufacturers
1331 Pennsylvania Ave.
Washington, DC 20004

PROFESSIONAL PUBLICATIONS:

Assembly Engineering
Design News
Iron Age
Metalworking News

EMPLOYERS:

Aircraft Gear Corporation
6633 W. 65th St.
Bedford Park, IL 60638
(708) 594-2100
Personnel Director: Ken Zuncic
Aerospace manufacturing.

Application Engineering Corporation
801 AEC Drive
Wood Dale, IL 60191
(708) 593-5000
Personnel Director: Bob Zega
Involved in the design, engineering, manufacture, sale, installation, servicing and leasing of water cooling and treatment facilities; produces temperature control units used primarily in the production of plastics.

Axia, Inc.
122 W. 22nd St.
Oak Brook, IL 60521
(708) 571-3350
President: Dennis W. Sheehan
Manufacturer of construction-related products and tools; industrial mail media operations; metal products and cold steel bars.

Bally Manufacturing Co.
8700 W. Bryn Mawr Ave.

Chicago, IL 60631
(312) 399-1300
Director, Personnel Administration: Lois Balodis
Manufacturer of games and slot machines; owns and operates hotel-casino resorts.

Barber-Greene Corporation
3000 Barber Greene Road
Dekalb, IL 60115
(815) 756-5600
Recruiting Director: John Clementson
Principally engaged in the design, manufacture, and sale of specialized construction machinery.

Berkel, Inc.
1 Berkel Drive
LaPorte, IN 46350
(219) 326-7000
Personnel Manager: Carol Swan
Slicing machines, scales, tenderizers, bowl food cutters.

Bliss & Laughlin Industries
281 E.155th St.
Harvey, IL 60426
(708) 264-1800
Vice President: George W. Fleck
Produces cold, finished steel bars. Operates the Bliss & Laughlin Steel Co.

Bodine Electric Co.
500 W. Bradley Place
Chicago, IL 60618
(312) 478-3515
Chairman: Paul J. Bodine
Motor manufacturer.

Borg-Warner Corporation
200 S. Michigan Ave.
Chicago, IL 60604
(312) 322-8500
V.P. Human Resources: John D. O'Brian
Widely diversified company whose principal operations consist of the manufacture of environmental control equipment for homes, industry, and transportation; chemicals; power transmission components, pumps, and valves; transportation equipment; and a finance company, the Borg-Warner Acceptance Corp.

Calumet Industries
14000 Mackinaw Ave.
Burnham, IL 60633
(708) 862-9100

Vice President, Marketing: Philip A. Campbell
Refines and markets oils and asphalt products.

Caterpiller Tractor Co.
Channon Road, Box 504
Joliet, IL 60434
(815) 729-5511
Contact: Personnel
Manufacturer of earth-moving equipment and engines for that equipment.

Champion Parts Rebuilders
2525 W. 22nd St.
Oak Brook, IL
(708) 573-6600

Chicago Bridge & Iron Co.
800 Jorie Blvd.
Oak Brook, IL 60522
(708) 572-7000
Contact: Personnel
The Walker Process Division manufactures water treatment equipment; the Fibre Making Process Division manufactures paper mill equipment.

Combustion Engineering
650 Warrenville Road, Suite 100
Lisle, IL 60532
(708) 719-9800
District Sales Manager: Lyle Prince
Operates refractories.

Continental Can Co.
4711 W. Foster
Chicago, IL 60630
(312) 685-9000
Contact: Personnel
Diversified multi-industry company, including Continental Can Co., leading manufacturer of packaging; other divisions manufacture plastic containers and paper packaging products, explore for oil and gas, and provide financial and insurance services.

Danly Machine Corporation
2100 S. Laramie St.
Chicago, IL 60650
(312) 863-2800
Director, Employee Relations: G.K. Lorenz
Manufacturer of mechanical presses, die sets and die-makers' supplies, and milling and cutting machines.

Duraco Products
1109 E. Lake St.
Streamwood, IL 60107
(708) 837-6615
Personnel Director: Don Grimaldi
Manufactures industrial products.

Managing the factory

Bob Mikolashek is Vice President of Manufacturing for Champion Parts Rebuilders, Inc. We asked him to describe a typical career path in manufacturing supervision.

"A person coming out of school would probably apply for a job as a production line supervisor," says Bob. "That's an entry-level supervision job—you're overseeing employees who are paid by the hour. The next step, depending on the facility, would be a job as general foreman or superintendent, which means you're managing salaried, not hourly, employees. A general foreman or superintendent usually takes care of a whole department.

"From there you have two choices. You can continue to rise up through the ranks, gradually assuming production responsibility for several departments or the whole plant. But sometimes it's useful for a manager with basic production experience to branch off for a while and go into another area, such as quality control. It gives your career a broader base, makes you a more well-rounded manager."■

Elgin National Industries
120 S. Riverside Plaza
Chicago, IL 60606
(312) 454-1900
Vice President: Warren W. Browning
Consumer Products Group is engaged in importing, assembling, manufacturing, and distributing clocks and photographic equipment; company provides specialized engineering and construction for the coal and mineral industries.

Excelsior Manufacturing and Supply Corp.
1465 E. Industrial Drive
Itasca, IL 60143
(708) 773-5500
President: Robert Clement

Manufactures and distributes sheet metal to the heating and air conditioning industries.

Farley Industries
233 S. Wacker Drive, Suite 6300
Chicago, IL 60606
(312) 876-7000
President: William K. Hall
Metal-casting machinery.

Fiat-Allis Construction Machinery Co.
245 E. North Ave.
Carol Stream, IL 60188
(708) 260-4000
Contact: Personnel
Manufacturer of construction and earth-moving machines.

The Filtertek Companies
P.O. Box 135
11411 Price Road
Hebron, IL 60034
(815) 648-2416
Personnel Director: Jean Wilke
Manufactures specialty filtration elements.

FMC Corporation
200 E. Randolph St.
Chicago, IL 60601
(312) 861-6000
V.P., Human Resources: Lawrence Holleran
Diversified manufacturer of machinery and chemicals.

Gaylord Container Corp.
500 Lake Cook Road, Suite 400
Deerfield, IL 60015
(708) 405-5500
VP Human Resources: Lawrence G. Rogna
Produces paper packaging products.

Gerber Plumbing Fixtures
4656 W. Touhy Ave.
Lincolnwood, IL 60646
(708) 675-6570
VP Marketing: Lawrence Grabski
Manufactures brass and vitreous china plumbing fixtures.

Gold Bond Building Products
1400 E. Touhy Ave.
Des Plaines, IL 60018
(708) 296-9800
Contact: Personnel

Diversified manufacturer of gypsum and predecorated wallboard, vinyl siding, acoustical ceiling tile, glazed and unglazed flooring, wall coverings and fabrics, storm doors, and auto glass.

Goodman Equipment Co.
5430 W. 70th Place
Bedford Park, IL 60638
(708) 496-1188
President: Calvin A. Cambell
Injection-molding machinery.

W. W. Grainger, Inc.
5500 W. Howard St.
Skokie, IL 60077
(708) 982-9000
V.P., Human Resources: Neal Ormond III
National manufacturer and distributor of electric motors.

Hoffer Plastics Corp.
500 N. Collins St.
South Elgin, IL 60177
(708) 741-5740
Vice President: William A. Hoffer
Manufactures plastic products.

ICM Industries
122 S. Michigan Ave., Suite 1700
Chicago, IL 60603
(312) 939-5008
Holding company.

IDEX Corp.
630 Dundee Road, Suite 400
Northbrook, IL 60062
(708) 498-7070
Vice President: Kenneth Slawson
Manufactures a variety of industrial products.

Illinois Range Co.
708 W. Central Road
Mount Prospect, IL 60056
(708) 253-4950
President: Donald C. Browkaw
Manufactures food service equipment.

Illinois Tool Works
8501 W. Higgins Road
Chicago, IL 60631
(312) 693-3040
Vice President: Michael Gregg

Produces and markets engineered fasteners and components, packaging products, electronic keyboards, precision tools and gearing, and instruments.

IMC Fertilizer Group
2100 Sanders Road
Northbrook, IL 60062
(708) 272-9200
Senior Vice President: Richard J. Hedberg
Mines phosphate rock and potash for production of fertilizer. Also produces specialty chemicals and health products.

Interlake, Inc.
701 Harger Road
Oak Brook, IL 60521
(708) 572-6600
V.P. Human Resources: David R. Downs
A diversified manufacturer of metals and material-handling products.

ITEL Rail Corporation
200 S. Michigan Ave.
Chicago, IL 60604
(312) 322-7070
Personnel Director: Diane Kreja
Manufacturer of freight cars.

ITT/AC Pump
600 Enterprise Drive, Suite 105
Oak Brook, IL 60521
(708) 574-8145
Contact: Personnel
Manufactures high-technology products and systems for use in the processing of energy, food, water, and minerals.

Jepson Corporation
2 N. Riverside Plaza
Chicago, IL 60606
(312) 834-3710
Personnel Director: Jan Fensterman
A diversified manufacturing company.

Joslyn Manufacture and Supply Co.
30 S. Wacker Drive
Chicago, IL 60606
(312) 454-2900
Senior V.P.: Alwyn A. deSouza
Diversified company, operating in the fields of transportation, real estate, graphic arts, hobby and household products, mechanical contracting, heating and air conditioning.

Kewaunee Scientific Corporation
1144 Wilmette Ave.
Wilmette, IL 60091
(708) 251-7100
Manufactures scientific laboratory furniture and equipment.

Lawson Products
1666 E. Touhy Ave.
Des Plaines, IL 60018
(708) 827-9666
Personnel Administrator: Tracy Folano
Distributes repair and replacement supplies.

LiquidAir
Cardox Division
5230 S. East Ave.
Countryside, IL 60525
(708) 482-8400
Contact: Personnel
Manufacturer of dry ice and fire protection equipment.

Liquid Controls Group
Wacker Park
North Chicago, IL 60064
(708) 689-2400
VP, Marketing: Douglas W. Beattie
Manufactures and markets liquid measurement equipment.

MacLean-Fogg Co.
1000 Allanson Road
Mundelein, IL 60060
(708) 566-0010
President: Barry MacLean
Fasteners & fittings.

Magneco/Metrel
223 Interstate Road
Addison, IL 60101
(708) 543-6660
VP, Marketing: Madjid Soofi
Manufactures refractories.

Mark Controls
5202 Old Orchard Road
Skokie, IL 60077
(708) 470-8585
Senior V.P.: Eugene J. Tulley
Manufactures flow controls and energy-management equipment.

Microdot, Inc.
2 First National Plaza

Chicago, IL 60603
(312) 899-1925
President: Richard P. Strubel
Molds, fasteners, connecting devices.

The Middleby Corp.
8300 Austin Ave.
Morton Grove, IL 60053
(708) 966-8300
Vice President: John J. Hastings
Manufactures and markets food-service equipment.

Midwesco, Inc.
7720 Lehigh
Niles, IL 60648
(708) 966-2150
Contact: Personnel
Manufacturing and contracting services.

Miller Fluid Power
800 N. York Road
Bensenville, IL 60106
(708) 766-3400
Personnel Director: Tom Parker
Manufactures fluid power components.

Moline Corporation
P.O. Box 529
St. Charles, IL 60174
(708) 584-4600
Human Resources Director: Nancy Begalka

New York Blower Co.
171 Factory St.
LaPorte, IN 46350
(219) 362-1531
President: Peter Mathis
Unit heaters, propeller fans, blowers.

Outboard Marine Co.
100 Sea Horse Drive
Waukegan, IL 60085
(708) 689-6200
V.P. Employee Relations: F. James Short
Manufacturer of Evinrude and Johnson outboard motors and Lawn Boy mowers.

Patten Tractor and Equipment Company
635 W. Lake St.
Elmhurst, IL 60126
(708) 279-4400

Personnel Manager: T.C. O'Neil
Manufacturer of heavy machinery, including tractors.

Production Tool Co.
1229 E. 74th St.
Chicago, IL 60619
(312) 288-4400
President: A.E. Whisler, Jr.
Heavy machinery.

Protectaire Systems Co.
1353 N. McLean Blvd.
Elgin, IL 60123
(708) 697-3400
VP, Sales and Marketing: Michael F. Napadow
Produces, markets, and services spray paint finishing equipment and booths and overhead conveyor protection equipment.

Rockford Products Corporation
707 Harrison Ave.
Rockford, IL 61104-7197
(815) 397-6000
V.P. Human Relations: Dave Peterson
Manufactures fasteners.

Rockwell International
400 Maple Ave.
Carpentersville, IL 60110
(708) 426-4100
General Manager: Robert Carlson
Chicago operations consist of the Automotive Products Division, maker of leaf springs; Amforge, Inc., manufacturer of steel forgings; the Graphic System Group; and the Miehle Division, manufacturer of sheet-fed presses.

Scotsman Industries
775 Cororate Woods Parkway
Vernon Hills, IL 60061
(708) 215-4500
VP, Operations: Christopher D. Hughes
Manufactures commercial refrigeration products.

Schwinn Bicycle Co.
217 N. Jefferson
Chicago, IL 60606
(312) 454-7400
V.P. Human Resources: Brian Fiala
Leading manufacturer of bicycles.

Seeberg Phonograph Corporation
1105 Westwood Ave.

Addison, IL 60101
(708) 543-1274
Contact: Personnel
Manufacturer of video games and pinball machines.

Signode Corporation
3610 W. Lake Ave.
Glenview, IL 60025
(708) 724-6100
Manager of Employment: Marlene Haase
Manufacturer and distributor of strapping systems used in packaging; pneumatically operated stapling and nailing tools; and specialty wrapping papers.

Sommer & Maca Industries
5501 W. Ogden Ave.
Chicago, IL 60650
(312) 242-2871
VP, Sales: James P. Johnson
Manufactures glass-finishing machinery.

Sullair Coporation
3700 E. Michigan Blvd.
Michigan City, IN 46360-9990
(219) 879-5451
President: Robert Bloomberg
Portable and stationary air compressors, track-mounted rock drills, driven generator sets.

Tech/Ops Landauer
Two Science Road
Glenwood, IL 60425
(708) 755-7000
VP, Marketing: Brent R. Latta
Provides personal radiation dosimetry and radon detection equipment.

Whitman Corporation
111 E. Wacker Drive
Chicago, IL 60601
(312) 565-3000
Vice President: Ronald Wright
A diversified holding company, operating in three major business areas: consumer products, industrial products, and the Illinois Central Gulf Railroad.

Wilson Sporting Goods Co.
2233 West St.
River Grove, IL 60171
(708) 456-6100
Vice President: David Lumley

Manufactures and markets sports equipment and athletic apparel.

Woodward Governor Co.
5001 N. Second St.
Rockford, IL 61125-7001
(815) 877-7441
Personnel Director: Michael Schmit
Manufactures prime-mover controls.

Wozniak Industries
Two Mid America Plaza, Suite 706
Oakbrook Terrace 60181
(708) 954-3400
Contact: Personnel

Media: Newspapers and Magazines

For networking in the **magazine and newspaper publishing** business, check out the following professional organizations listed in Chapter 5:

PROFESSIONAL ORGANIZATIONS:

Agate Club of Chicago
American Medical Writers Association
American Society of Journalists and Authors
Chicago Headline Club
Chicago Newspaper Reporters
Chicago Press Photographers
Chicago Women in Publishing
Illinois Women's Press Association
Independent Writers of Chicago
Newspaper Representatives Association of Chicago
Professional Photographers of America
Social Service Communicators
Society of Professional Journalists
Suburban Press Club of Chicago
Women in Communications

For additional information, you can write to:

American Newspaper Publishers Association
11600 Sunrise Valley Drive
Reston, VA 22091

Audit Bureau of Circulations
900 Meacham Road
Schaumburg, IL 60195

Magazine Publishers Association
575 Lexington Ave.
New York, NY 10022

PROFESSIONAL PUBLICATIONS:

The Columbia Journalism Review
Editor and Publisher
Folio
The Writer
Writer's Digest

DIRECTORIES:

Editor and Publisher International Yearbook (Editor and Publisher, New York, NY)
Magazine Industry Market Place (R. R. Bowker, Inc., New York, NY)

FOR AN EXTENSIVE LIST OF CHICAGO'S NEWSPAPERS AND CONSUMER AND TRADE MAGAZINES, SEE CHAPTER 4.

Metals and Minerals (see also Steel Manufacturing)

Major trade publications in the field of **metals manufacturing** include:

PROFESSIONAL PUBLICATIONS:

Assembly Engineering
Design News
Iron Age
Metal Working Digest

EMPLOYERS:

Ace Fastener Corporation
1100 Hicks Road
Rolling Meadows, IL 60008
(708) 259-1620
Contact: Personnel
Division of Swingline, Inc., manufacturer of staples and staplers.

Advance Ross Corporation
111 W. Monroe St., Suite 2100E
Chicago, IL 60603
(312) 346-9126
Contact: Personnel
Provides products for the transportation and pollution control industries.

Advertising Metal Display Corporation
4620 W. 19th St.
Cicero, IL 60650
(708) 863-8900
Contact: Personnel
Produces and sells metal point-of-purchase advertising displays.

Allied Products Corporation
10 S. Riverside Plaza, Suite 1600
Chicago, IL 60606
(312) 454-1020
V.P. Human Resources: Leo Simmermeyer
Manufactures and markets farm implements, irrigation systems, and cotton-module equipment.

American Home Products
Ecko Products Division
5151 W. 73rd St.
Chicago, IL 60638
(312) 767-8460
Personnel Manager: James R. Luster
Manufacturer of quality cookwear.

American National Can Co.
8770 W. Bryn Mawr
Chicago, IL 60631
(312) 399-3000
Personnel Manager: Carol Jaggers
Manufacturer of packaging products in metal, glass, and plastic.

Anixter Brothers
4711 Golf Road
Skokie, IL 60076
(708) 677-2600
Contact: Personnel Director
Manufactures and distributes wire and cable used in the transmission of electric, telephone, and television signals.

Application Engineering Corporation
801 AEC Drive
Wood Dale IL 60191
(708) 595-1060
Personnel Director: Bob Zega

Primarily engaged in the design, engineering, manufacture, sale, installation, servicing, and leasing of products used in the processing of plastics.

Armstrong Containers
5200 W. Armstrong Ave.
Chicago, IL 60646
(312) 763-3333
Contact: Personnel
Manufacturer of metal and tin-plate containers.

Axia, Inc.
122 W. 22nd St.
Oak Brook, IL 60521
(708) 571-3350
Personnel Assistant: LaRue Carlson
Manufactures and markets commercial and industrial products.

Beatrice Foods
2 N. LaSalle St.
Chicago, IL 60602
(312) 782-3820
Senior V.P. Human Resources: William L. Chambers
Produces, processes, and distributes over 400 brands of food and dairy products; soft drinks, grocery and snack products; medical supplies through its Brunswick Labs Division; and fabricated metal products through its Chicago Specialty Manufacturing Co. division.

Bliss & Laughlin Industries
Bliss & Laughlin Steel Company
281 E. 155th St.
Harvey, IL 60426
(708) 264-1800
VP, Human Resources: Richard M. Bogdan

Borg-Warner Corporation
200 S. Michigan Ave.
Chicago, IL 60604
(312) 322-8500
V.P. Human Resources: John D. O'Brian
Widely diversified company whose principal operations consist of the manufacture of environmental control equipment for homes, industry, and transportation; chemicals; power transmission components, pumps, and valves; transportation equipment; and a finance company, the Borg-Warner Acceptance Corp.

Ceco Corporation
1 Tower Lane
Oakbrook Terrace, IL 60181
(708) 242-2000

V.P. Human Resources: Craig Grant
Manufacturer of fabricated structural materials.

Central Steel & Wire Co.
3000 W. 51st St.
Chicago, IL 60632
(312) 471-3800
Vice President: Richard Smith
Engaged in the warehousing and distribution of metals in forms produced by rolling mills.

Chicago Extruded Metals Co.
1601 S. 54th Ave.
Cicero, IL 60650
(708) 656-7900
Vice President: Eugene A. Riccio
Manufactures brass rods and steel.

Chicago Faucet Co.
2100 S. Nuclear Drive
Des Plaines, IL 60018
(708) 694-4400
Contact: Personnel
Manufacturer of quality plumbing hardware.

Chicago Mechanical
1400 E. 97th Place
Chicago, IL 60628
(312) 374-8505
Personnel Director: Stella Stokes
Mechanical contractor and metal fabricator.

Chicago Milwaukee Corporation
547 W. Jackson Blvd, Suite 1510
Chicago, IL 60606
(312) 822-0400
Contact: Personnel
Diversified company operates railroads and does business in areas of distribution, metal fabrication, and forest products.

Chicago Rivet & Machine Co.
901 Frontenac
Naperville, IL 60540
(708) 357-8500
Controller: Steve Voss
The country's largest manufacturer of semi-tubular rivets and rivet-setting machines.

J. L. Clark Manufacturing Co.
2300 6th St.
P.O. Box 7000
Rockford, IL 61125

(815) 962-8861
Personnel Director: Jack Kissinger
Major manufacturer of specialty packaging items for food, cosmetic, and drug industries; housewares; and automotive filters.

Dresser Industries
1601 W. 22nd St.
Broadview, IL 60153
(708) 450-6500
Plant Manager: Dan Hazelton
Manufacturer of energy-processing and conversion equipment, industrial specialty products, and consumer and mechanics' hand tools.

Duro Metal Products
2649 N. Kildare Ave.
Chicago, IL 60639
(312) 235-5000
Contact: Personnel
Manufacturer of mechanics' hand tools.

Elco Industries
1111 Samuelson Road
Rockford, IL 61125-7009
(815) 397-5151
Personnel Director: Gordy Anderson
One of the largest independent manufacturers of custom-designed fasteners, rivets, and metal components.

Excelsior Manufacturing and Supply Corp.
1465 E. Industrial Drive
Itasca, IL 60143
(708) 773-5500
President: Robert B. Clement
Manufactures and distributes sheet metal for use in the heating and air conditioning industries.

Fansteel, Inc.
One Tantalum Place
North Chicago, IL 60064
(708) 689-4900
Corporate Director, Human Relations: Robert E. Nelson
Manufacturer of refractory metals; fabricator of high-technology products for the automotive, appliance, metalworking, aerospace, recreational, electronic, and chemical industries.

Farley Industries
6300 Sears Tower
233 S. Wacker Drive
Chicago, IL 60606

(312) 876-7000
Contact: Personnel
A management and holding company that manufactures and markets industrial, chemical, and consumer products through its subsidiaries.

Illinois Tool Works
8501 W. Higgins Road
Chicago, IL 60631
(312) 693-3040
Vice President: Michael Gregg
Produces and markets engineered fasteners and components; packaging products; electronic keyboards; precision tools and gearing; and instruments.

Interlake, Inc.
701 Harger Road
Oak Brook, IL 60521
(708) 572-6600
V.P. Human Resources: David R. Downs
A diversified manufacturer of metals and material-handling products.

International Minerals & Chemical Corporation
2315 Sanders Road
Northbrook, IL 60062
(708) 564-8600
V.P. Personnel: John Stapleton
Produces phosphate and potash plant nutrients.

International Telephone & Telegraph Corporation
8200 N. Austin
Morton Grove, IL 60053
(708) 966-3700
Personnel Supervisor: Donald Flowers
Diversified producer of communications equipment and hydronic specialties through its Bell & Gossett Division.

Joslyn Manufacture and Supply Co.
30 S. Wacker Drive
Chicago, IL 60606
(312) 454-2900
Senior Vice President: Alwyn A. deSouza
Diversified company, operating in the fields of transportation, real estate, graphic arts, hobby and household products, mechanical contracting, heating and air conditioning.

MacLean-Fogg Co.
1000 Allanson Road
Mundelein, IL 60060
(708) 566-0010

Personnel Director: Linda Rica
Manufactures plastic components and engineered metal.

The Marmon Group
225 W. Washington St.
Chicago, IL 60606
(312) 372-9500
Personnel Director: George Frese
Manufactures pipe, tubing, metal products, wire and cable, automotive products, apparel accessories, and mining equipment.

McGill Manufacturing Co.
909 N. Lafayette St.
Valparaiso, IN 46383
(219) 465-2200
President: James C. McGill
Precision needle type, cam follower, and spherical roller bearings.

Oil-Dri Corporation of America
520 N. Michigan Ave., 3rd Floor
Chicago, IL 60611
(312) 321-1515
Personnel Director: Karen Jaffee
Develops and processes mineral products.

Phillips, Getschow Co.
1913 S. Briggs St.
Joliet, IL 60433
(312) 644-6116 (Chicago number)
Personnel Director: Joyce Wilson
Manufacturer of industrial and nuclear power piping.

Reflector Hardware Corporation
1400 N. 25th Ave.
Melrose Park, IL 60160
(708) 345-2500
Personnel Director: L. Lazzaro
Manufacturer of store fixtures, office and library furniture.

Regal-Beloit Corporation
5330 E. Rockton Road
South Beloit, IL 61080
(815) 389-1920
Corporate Personnel Director: Art Capitanoff
Manufacturer of cutting tools and power transmission systems.

Rego Corporation
4200 W. Diversey Ave.
Chicago, IL 60639
(312) 685-1121

Contact: Personnel
Manufacturer of copper and brass.

Rheem Manufacturing Co.
7600 S. Kedzie Ave.
Chicago, IL 60652
(312) 434-7500
V.P. Operations: Robert E. Jewell
Manufacturer of steel drum containers and shipping hardware.

Signode Corporation
3610 W. Lake Ave.
Glenview, IL 60025
(708) 724-6100
Manager of Employment: Marlene Haase
Manufacturer and distributor of strapping systems used in packaging; pneumatically operated stapling and nailing tools; and specialty wrapping papers.

Varlen Corporation
305 E. Shuman Blvd., P.O. Box 3089
Naperville, IL 60566-7089
(708) 420-0400
Contact: Personnel
Manufactures and sells variety of products in the metalworking industry.

Museums and Galleries

To help you learn more about running **museums** and other non-profit institutions, you can write to:

PROFESSIONAL ORGANIZATIONS:

American Association of Museums
1225 I St., N.W.
Washington, DC 20005

American Federation of Arts
41 E. 65th St.
New York, NY 10021

Arts and Business Council
130 E. 40th St.
New York, NY 10016

Illinois Arts Council
111 N. Wabash Ave.
Chicago, IL 60601

National Assembly of Local Arts Agencies
1420 K St., N.W., Suite 204
Washington, DC 20005

EMPLOYERS:

Adler Planetarium
1300 S. Lake Shore Drive
Chicago, IL 60605
(312) 322-0304
Director: Dr. Joseph Chamberlin
Museum of the stars, planets, galaxies, and beyond.

The Art Institute of Chicago
Michigan Ave. at Adams St.
Chicago, IL 60603
(312) 443-3600
Executive Director, Personnel: Marion Lang Alt
One of the foremost art museums; houses one of the world's richest collections of Impressionist, modern, oriental art and sculpture and decorative arts.

Balzekas Museum of Lithuanian Culture
6500 S. Pulaski Road
Chicago, IL 60629
(312) 582-6500
Contact: Personnel
Permanent exhibition of cultural artifacts; library; art gallery.

Brookfield Zoo
1st Ave. at 31st St.
Brookfield, IL 60513
(708) 242-2630
Contact: Personnel
200-acre zoological park.

Working in the non-profit world

Tom Sanberg is Director of Development for the Museum of Science and Industry. We asked him what it takes to make it in the non-profit world.

"Most of the people who enjoy non-profit work and are successful at it tend to be other-directed. They get satisfaction out of working for a so-called worthy cause. There are very few high- paying jobs in not-for-profit institutions. An executive-level job at the Museum, for example, probably pays about half what a job with similar responsibilities would pay in a profit-making company of the same size.

"One of the fastest-growing specialties within the non-profit world is fund-raising management, probably because non-profit institutions rely so heavily on grants and contributions," Tom adds. He notes that Northwestern University's extension division offers a course in fund-raising, and the local chapter of the National Society for Fund-Raising Executives (listed in Chapter 5) has had several seminars, workshops, and a certification program.■

Chicago Academy of Sciences
2001 N. Clark St.
Chicago, IL 60614
(312) 549-0343
Director: Dr. Paul Heltne
The earliest scientific institution in Chicago.

Chicago Historical Society
North Ave. at Clark St.
Chicago, IL 60614
(312) 642-4600
Director: Ellsworth Brown
The city's oldest cultural institution. Houses collections of Chicago costumes, memorabilia, and historical dioramas; mounts quarterly exhibitions.

Chicago Horticultural Society
P.O. Box 400
Lake Cook Road
Glencoe, IL 60022
(708) 835-5440
Contact: Personnel
300-acre botanical garden.

DuSable Museum of African-American History
740 E. 56th Place
Chicago, IL 60637
(312) 947-0600
Contact: Personnel
Museum houses a variety of permanent exhibitions dealing with black history and culture.

Field Museum of Natural History
Roosevelt Road at Lake Shore Drive
Chicago, IL 60605
(312) 922-9410
President: Willard Boyd

Natural history museum, specializing in the sciences of anthropology, botany, geology, and zoology and the composition and evolution of Earth and its near neighbors.

Garfield Park Conservatory
300 N. Central Park Blvd.
Chicago, IL 60624
(312) 533-1281
Contact: Personnel
Four and one-half acres of horticultural exhibitions.

Lincoln Park Conservatory
2400 N. Stockton Drive
Chicago, IL 60614
(312) 294-4770
Contact: Personnel
Indoor botanical garden.

Lincoln Park Zoo
2200 N. Cannon Drive
Chicago, IL 60614
(312) 294-4660
Director: Dr. Lester Fisher
The city's zoological park.

Morton Arboretum
Route 53
Lisle, IL 60532
(708) 968-0074
Contact: Personnel
Privately endowed 1,500-acre outdoor botanical garden, with emphasis on trees.

Museum of Contemporary Art
237 E. Ontario St.
Chicago, IL 60611
(312) 280-2660
Director: Kevin Consey
Dedicated to presenting the most provocative and significant developments in today's art.

Museum of Science & Industry
5700 S. Lake Shore Drive
Chicago, IL 60637
(312) 684-1414
Director: James S. Kahn
One of the world's most renowned science museums.

Oriental Institute
1155 E. 58th St.
Chicago, IL 60637
(312) 702-9520

Contact: Personnel
University of Chicago's museum of archaeology.

John G. Shedd Aquarium
1200 S. Lake Shore Drive
Chicago, IL 60605
(312) 939-2426
Director: William P. Braker
One of the world's most advanced indoor aquariums.

Spertus Museum of Judaica
618 S. Michigan Ave.
Chicago, IL 60605
(312) 922-9012
Director: Morris Fred
Maintains permanent collection of memorabilia related to Jewish life and history; mounts quarterly exhibitions.

Terra Museum of Art
664 N. Michigan Ave.
Chicago, IL 60611
(312) 644-3939
Director: Harold O'Connell
Specializes in 19th and 20th century American art.

Office Equipment and Supplies

For networking in the **office products** business, check out the following professional organizations listed in Chapter 5:

PROFESSIONAL ORGANIZATIONS:

Institute of Business Designers
Purchasing Management Association of Chicago

PROFESSIONAL PUBLICATIONS:

NOMDA Spokesman
Office Products Dealer

DIRECTORIES:

IWP Word Processing Directory (International Word Processing Association, Willow Grove, PA)
NOMDA Who's Who (National Office Machine Dealers Association, Elk Grove Village, IL)

NOPA Directory (National Office Products Association, Alexandria, VA)
Office Products Dealer Product Buying Guide (Hitchcock Publishing Co., Carol Stream, IL)

EMPLOYERS:

Acco International Corporation
770 S. Acco Plaza
Wheeling, IL 60090-6070
(708) 541-9500
Director of Personnel: Jackie Ray
Manufacturer of staplers and other office products.

Ace Fastener & Spotnails Co.
1100 Hicks Road
Rolling Meadows, IL 60008
(708) 259-1620
Director of Personnel: Karen Yoder
Manufacturer of staples and staplers.

Admiral Maintenance Service Co.
4343 W. Touhy Ave.
Lincolnwood, IL 60646
(708) 675-6000
Personnel Director: Roberta Blyton
Janitorial service.

AM International
333 W. Wacker Drive, Suite 900
Chicago, IL 60606
(312) 558-1966
Personnel Manager: Mary Ann Gruber

Arvey Paper & Supply Co.
3351 W. Addison
Chicago, IL 60018
(312) 463-6423
Contact: Personnel

Cook Electric Co.
6201 W. Oakton St.
Morton Grove, IL 60053
(708) 967-6600
Manager, Employee Relations: Cathy Brosmith
Manufacturer of data-handling systems.

Cummins-Allison Corporation
P.O. Box 339
Mount Prospect, IL 60056
(708) 299-9550
Personnel Director: Cherie McKane

A. B. Dick Co.
5700 W. Touhy Ave.
Niles, IL 60648
(708) 647-8800
Contact: Personnel
Major manufacturer of duplicating machines, offset printers, and word processors.

Duo-Fast Corporation
3702 N. River Road
Franklin Park, IL 60131-2176
(708) 678-0100
Contact: Personnel
Manufacturer of industrial nailers and staplers.

Duplex Products
1947 Bethany Road
Sycamore, IL 60178
(815) 895-2101
Personnel Director: Barbara Bauer

Fellowes Manufacturing Co.
1789 Norwood Ave.
Itasca, IL 60143
(708) 893-1600
Chairman: John Fellowes
Manufacturer of office products.

General Binding Corporation
One GBC Plaza
Northbrook, IL 60062
(708) 272-3700
Personnel Representative: Gary Smith
Manufactures and distributes business machines and related supplies that bind and laminate paperwork for the office, in-plant, education, government, and graphics markets.

Office Electronics
865 W. Irving Park Road
Itasca, IL 60143
(708) 773-1619
President: Michael Briggs
Makes stock and customized computer forms.

Pitney-Bowes, Inc.
225 W. Washington
Chicago, IL 60606
(312) 419-1550
Branch Manager: Robert Coyle
Manufacturer of postage meters and mailing equipment.

Publix Office Supplies
700 W. Chicago Ave.
Chicago, IL 60610
(312) 226-1000
President: David Kirshner
Contract office products distributor.

Quill Corporation
100 S. Schelter Road
Lincolnshire, IL 60069
(708) 634-4850
Human Resources Director: Robert Worobow
Catalog distributor of office products.

Reliable Corporation
1001 W. Van Buren St.
Chicago, IL 60607
(312) 666-1800
Chairman: Merrill Zehner
Catalog distributor of office products.

Rittenhouse, Inc.
250 S. Northwest Highway
Park Ridge, IL 60068
(708) 692-9130
Personnel Director: Diana Schultz
Printer of paper rolls, labels, and ribbons.

Sanford Corporation
2740 Washington Blvd.
Bellwood, IL 60104
(708) 547-6650
Human Resource Manager: Gerald Domke
Manufactures and markets office supplies.

Speed-O-Print Business Machine Corporation
3833 Swanson Court
Gurnee, IL 60031
(708) 249-8000
Personnel Director: Barbara Ault
Manufactures and sells business machines.

Uarco, Inc.
West County Line Road
Barrington, IL 60010
(708) 381-7000
Industrial Relations Mgr.: John O' Donnell
Manufacturer of business forms.

United Stationers
2200 E. Golf Road
Des Plaines, IL 60016

(708) 699-5000
V.P. Human Resources: Robert H. Cornell
Wholesalers of office products.

Xerox Corporation
3000 Des Plaines Ave.
Des Plaines, IL 60018
(708) 635-2335
Regional Personnel Manager: Ralph Volpe
Manufacturer of copy machines and xerography equipment used in offices, hospitals, and aerospace technology. Also owns magazine and book publishing interests.

Paper/Packaging

To help you learn more about the **paper industry** you can write to:

PROFESSIONAL ORGANIZATIONS:

American Paper Institute
260 Madison Ave.
New York, NY 10016

Paper Industry Management Association
2400 E. Oakton St.
Arlington Hts., IL 60005

Technical Association of the Pulp and Paper Industry
Technology Park, Box 105113
Atlanta, GA 30348

PROFESSIONAL PUBLICATIONS:

Packaging
Paper Trade Journal
Paperboard Packaging
Pulp and Paper

DIRECTORIES:

Lockwood-Post's Directory of the Pulp, Paper, and Allied Trades (Miller Freeman, New York, NY)
Paper Yearbook (Harcourt Brace Jovanovich, Cleveland, OH)

EMPLOYERS:

AES Technology Systems
140 Lively Blvd.
Elk Grove Village, IL 60007
(708) 437-3084
Produces customized documents.

AGI, Inc.
1950 N. Ruby St.
Melrose Park, IL 60163
(708) 344-9100
President: Richard Block
Manufactures folding cartons.

Album Graphics
1950 N. Ruby St.
Melrose Park, IL 60160
(708) 344-9100
Folding cartons, record jackets, paperback covers.

Arvey Corporation
3450 N. Kimball Ave.
Chicago, IL 60618
(312) 463-0030
V.P., Human Resources: Carol Larkin
Manufacturer of paper displays and printing.

Boise Cascade Corporation
800 W. Bryn Mawr Ave.
Itasca, IL 60143
(708) 773-5000
General Manager: Jack Stephenson
Engaged principally in the manufacture, distribution, and sale of paper products, wood products, and building materials.

Boise Cascade Corporation
Corrugated Container Div.
1201 East Lincolnway
LaPorte, IN 46350
(219) 326-5089
Contact: Personnel
Corrugated shipping containers, display sheets, solid fiber slip sheets, bulk shipping containers.

Bomarko, Inc.
1955 N. Oak Road
P.O. Box K
Plymouth, IN 46563
(219) 936-9901
Sells paper products used in food industry.

Bradner Central Co.
333 S. Des Plaines Ave.
Chicago, IL 60606
(312) 454-1852
Chairman: Richard S. Bull, Jr.
Paper distributor.

Champion International Corporation
8750 W. Bryn Mawr
Chicago, IL 60631
(312) 380-4000
Contact: Personnel
Maintains timberland; manufactures forest-based products, including newsprint, printing papers, packaging, and construction products.

Clarcor
2323 Sixth St.
P.O. Box 7007
Rockford, IL 61125
(815) 962-8861
Personnel Director: Dave Lindsay
Produces paper and plastic tubes and filters.

Consolidated Packaging Corporation
11 E. Adams St., 16th Floor
Chicago, IL 60603
(312) 984-1024
Personnel Director: Eugene Ryan
Producer of paperboard; marketer of corrugated shipping containers, folding cartons, and packaging materials.

DeSoto, Inc.
1700 S. Mount Prospect Road
Des Plaines, IL 60017
(708) 391-9000
V.P. Personnel: J. Barreiro
Manufacturer of furniture, chemical products, and paper products.

Field Container Corporation
1500 Nicholas Blvd.
Elk Grove Village, IL 60007
(708) 437-1700
Chairman: Eli Field
Manufactures paper and folding cartons.

Fort Howard
7575 S. Kostner Ave.
Chicago, IL 60652
(312) 767-3300

Employment Manager: Dorothy Stanis
Manufacturer of paper cups and products.

Gaylord Container Corp.
500 Lake Cook Road, Suite 400
Deerfield, IL 60015
(708) 405-5500
VP, Human Resources: Lawrence G. Rogna
Produces and markets paper packaging products.

A. J. Gerrard Co.
400 E. Touhy Ave.
Des Plaines, IL 60018
(708) 299-8000
President: Tony Tako
Steel and plastic strapping.

Inlander-Steindler Paper Co.
2100 Devon Ave.
Elk Grove Village, IL 60007
(708) 952-2000
Personnel Director: Pam Garza
Wholesale distributor for paper products.

Mead Container
7601 S. 78th Ave.
Bridgeview, IL 60455
(708) 458-8100
Contact: Personnel
Diversified manufacturer of paper and forest products marketed through its subsidiaries: Georgia Kraft Paper Co., Northwood Forest Industries, Brunswick Pulp & Paper Co., and Ft. Dearborn Paper Co.

Midland Paper Co.
5860 N. Pulaski
Chicago, IL 60646
(312) 583-0717
Personnel Director: Jim Sherry
Paper distributor.

Owens-Illinois, Inc.
2200 E. Devon Ave., 358
Des Plaines, IL 60018
(708) 695-0440
District Manager: Charles Rice III
Manufactures and sells packaging and paper products.

Packaging Corporation of America
1603 Orrington Ave.
Evanston, IL 60204
(708) 492-5713

Contact: Personnel
Manufacturer of paperboard, corrugated, and solid wood products used in food packaging, point-of-purchase displays, residential construction, and industrial uses.

Peck-Lynn Group
717 Forest Ave.
Lake Forest, IL 60045
(708) 295-6100
Chairman: Howard P. Hoeper
Holding company for paper manufacturers.

Schwarz-Exeter Paper Co.
8338 N. Austin Ave.
Morton Grove, IL 60053
(708) 966-2550
Personnel Director: Kathy Norris

Signode Industries
3610 W. Lake St.
Glenview, IL 60025
(708) 724-6100
Manager of Employment: Marlene Haase
Manufactures and distributes strapping systems.

Solo Cup Co.
1501 E. 96th St.
Chicago, IL 60628
(312) 721-3600
Plant Manager: Tony Graham
Manufacturer of paper cups and plates.

Stone Container Corporation
150 N. Michigan Ave.
Chicago, IL 60601
(312) 580-6660
V.P. Human Resources: Covington Shackleford
Manufacturer of corrugated and plastic containers.

Strombecker Corporation
600 N. Pulaski Road
Chicago, IL 60624
(312) 638-1000
President: Daniel Shure
Paper products.

Western Kraft Paper Group
1001 Knell St.
Montgomery, IL 60538
(708) 242-0922
Contact: Personnel
Manufacturer of corrugated packaging.

Petroleum/Rubber/Plastics

For networking in **oil, gas, rubber, plastics** and related fields, check out the following professional organization listed in Chapter 5:

PROFESSIONAL ORGANIZATIONS:

American Chemical Society

For more information you can write to:

American Gas Association
1515 Wilson Blvd.
Arlington, VA 22209

American Petroleum Institute
211 N. Ervay St.
Dallas, TX 75201

PROFESSIONAL PUBLICATIONS:

Drilling
Modern Plastics
National Petroleum News
Oil and Gas Digest
Oil and Gas Journal
Petroleum Independent
Pipeline & Gas Journal
Plastics Industry News
Plastics World
Rubber World

DIRECTORIES:

Energy Job Finder (Mainstream Access, New York, NY)
Modern Plastics, encyclopedia issue (McGraw Hill, NY)
Oil and Gas Directory (Geophysical Directory, Inc., Houston, TX)
Plastics Directory Issue (Cahners Publications, Newton, MA)
Rubber Directory and Buyers Guide (Crain Communications, Akron, OH)
Whole World Oil Directory (National Register Publishing Co., Wilmette, IL)
Worldwide Refining and Gas Processing Directory (PenWell Publishing, Tulsa, OK)

EMPLOYERS:

Amoco Oil Co.
200 E. Randolph Drive
Chicago, IL 60601
(312) 856-5111
V.P. Human Resources: Wayne Anderson
Petroleum refinery: gasoline, fuel oil, motor oils, paving materials, lubricating greases.

Ashland Oil
6428 Joliet St.
Countryside, IL 60525
(708) 579-2880
Contact: Personnel
Send resume to:
P.O. Box 5200
Paul G. Blazer Memorial Parkway
Dublin, OH 43017
ATTN: Gary Lyon
One of the nation's largest independent petroleum refiners and manufacturers of specialty chemicals.

CF Industries
Salem Walker Drive
Long Grove, IL 60047
(708) 438-9500
Contact: Personnel
Manufactures chemical fertilizers; operates petroleum refinery.

Clark Oil & Refining Co.
Box 297
131st and Kedzie Ave.
Blue Island, IL 60406
(708) 385-5000
Contact: Personnel
Refiner and retail marketer of gasoline.

Combustion Engineering
650 Warrenville Road, Suite 100
Lisle, IL 60532
(708) 719-9800
District Sales Manager: Lyle Prince
Operates refractories.

John Crane, Inc.
6400 Oakton St.
Morton Grove, IL 60053
(708) 967-2400
V.P. Human Resources: Jack Bucalo
Manufacturer of mechanical sealing units.

Goodyear Tire & Rubber Co.
1501 Nicholas Blvd.
Elk Grove Village, IL 60007
(708) 640-5000
Contact: Personnel
World's largest manufacturer of tires and rubber products.

Katy Industries
853 Dundee Ave.
Elgin, IL 60120
(708) 379-1121
Contact: Human Resources
Multi-industry corporation with interests in food processing, testing and measuring equipment, oil and gas exploration, industrial machinery, and consumer items such as jewelry, silver flatware, and clocks.

Martin Oil Service
P.O. Box 298
Blue Island, IL 60406
(708) 385-6500
Chairman: Carl Greer
Petroleum distributor.

Mobil Oil Corporation
I-55 and Arsenal Road
Joliet, IL 60434
(815) 423-5571
Refinery Manager: J.W. Eisenmann
Manufacturer of refined petroleum products.

Signode Corporation
3610 W. Lake Ave.
Glenview, IL 60025
(708) 724-6100
Manager of Employment: Marlene Haase
Manufacturer and distributor of strapping systems used in packaging; pneumatically operated stapling and nailing tools; and specialty wrapping papers.

Specialty Packaging
7400 W. Cermak Road
North Riverside, IL 60546
(708) 442-8800
Contact: Personnel
Manufacturer of aerosol valves and plastics.

Texaco, Inc.
3030 Warrenville Road, Suite 260
Lisle, IL 60532
(708) 505-9339

Contact: Human Resources Director
Major producer and marketer of petroleum products.

Torco Oil Co.
624 S. Michigan Ave.
Chicago, IL 60605-1975
(312) 341-1600
Chairman: Anthony M. Tortoriello
Markets and produces petroleum products.

Union Oil Co. of California
Union 76 Division Office
1650 E. Golf Road
Schaumburg, Il 60196
(708) 330-0076
Manager, Employment and Recruiting: Joyce Rodgers
Distributor of petroleum products and chemicals.

Printers

For more information, you can write to:

PROFESSIONAL ORGANIZATIONS:

National Association of Printers and Lithographers
780 Palisade Ave.
Teaneck, NJ 07666

Technical Association of the Graphic Arts
P.O. Box 9887
Rochester, NY 14614

PROFESSIONAL PUBLICATIONS:

American Printer
Graphic Arts Monthly
Printing Impressions
Printing News
Screen Printing

DIRECTORIES:

Directory of Typographic Services (National Composition Association, Arlington, VA)
Graphic Arts Green Book (A.F. Lewis & Co., Hinsdale, IL)
Graphic Arts Monthly buyer's guide/directory issue (Cahners Publishing, New York, NY)

Printing Trades Blue Book (A.F. Lewis & Co., New York, NY)

EMPLOYERS:

Alden Press
2000 Arthur Ave.
Elk Grove Village, IL 60007
(708) 640-6000
President: Jerome Spier
Direct-mail and catalog printing.

Berlin Industries
325 S. Lombard Road
Addison, IL 60601
(708) 543-0505
CEO: F.E. Schmitt
Printers of direct mailings and catalogs.

Bradley Printing Co.
2170 S. Mannheim Road
Des Plaines, IL 60018
(708) 635-8000
President: Richard D. Joutras
Prints catalogs, brochures, and annual reports.

Bowne of Chicago
325 W. Ohio St.
Chicago, IL 60610
(312) 527-3080
Contact: Personnel

Combined Communication Services
901 Warrenville Road, Suite 206
Lisle, IL 60532
(708) 810-1177
Human Resources Director: Dean McMillion
Trade magazine and catalog printing.

Continental Web Press
1430 Industrial Drive
Itasca, IL 60143
(708) 773-1903
CEO: Kenneth W. Field
Advertising, catalog, direct mailing, and magazine printing.

R. R. Donnelley & Sons Co.
2223 Martin Luther King Drive
Chicago, IL 60616
(312) 326-8000
V.P. Human Resources: J.E. Treadway

Fort Dearborn Lithograph
6035 W. Gross Point Road
Niles, IL 60648
(708) 774-4321
President: Thomas Adler
Label, calendar, and poster printing.

Merril Corporation
650 W. Washington St.
Chicago, IL 60606
(312) 332-4730
Contact: Personnel

Rand McNally & Co.
8255 Central Park Ave.
Skokie, IL 60680
(708) 267-6868
V.P. Industrial Relations: Don Helm

Ringler America
One Pierce Place, Suite 800
Itasca, IL 60143-1272
(708) 941-6000
President: Edward C. Nytko
Printers of books, magazines, and newspaper inserts.

Segerdahl Corporation
1351 S. Wheeling Road
Wheeling, IL 60090
(708) 541-1080
President: Earl Segerdahl

Sleepeck Printing Co.
815 25th Ave.
Bellwood, IL 60104
(708) 544-8900
President: Micheal W. Sleepeck
General commercial printers.

Tech Web
301 Alice St.
Wheeling, IL 50090
(708) 459-7000
President: Dan Weymouth

Wessel Co.
1201 Kirk St.
Elk Grove Village, IL 60007
(312) 595-7011
Personnel Director: Maryellen Des Remaux
Commercial printer.

Public Relations

For networking in **public relations** and related fields, check out the following professional organizations listed in Chapter 5:

PROFESSIONAL ORGANIZATIONS:

American Society of Journalists and Authors
Chicago Association of Direct Marketing
Independent Writers of Chicago
International Association of Business Communicators
Marketing Research Association
Public Relations Society of America
Publicity Club of Chicago
Social Service Communicators
Women in Communications

PROFESSIONAL PUBLICATIONS:

American Demographics
O'Dwyer's Newsletter
PR News
PR Reporter
Public Relations Journal
Public Relations Review

DIRECTORIES:

National Directory of Corporate Public Affairs (Columbia Books, Washington, DC)
O'Dwyer's Directory of Corporate Communications and *O'Dwyer's Directory of Public Relations Firms* (J.R. O'Dwyer Co., New York, NY)
Public Relations Journal—Directory Issue (Public Relations Society of America, New York, NY)

EMPLOYERS:

Bozell, Jacobs, Kenyon & Eckhardt
625 N. Michigan Ave.
Chicago, IL 60611
(312) 988-2000
Head, Chicago Office: Barbara Molotsky

Burson-Marsteller
1 E. Wacker Drive
Chicago, IL 60601
(312) 329-9292
Head, Chicago Office: John D. LeSage

Aaron D. Cushman & Associates
35 E. Wacker Drive, Suite 850
Chicago, IL 60601
(312) 263-2500
President: Aaron D. Cushman

Janet Diederichs & Associates
333 N. Michigan Ave.
Chicago, IL 60601
(312) 346-7886
President: Janet Diederichs

Dragonette, Inc.
303 E. Wacker Drive, Suite 218
Chicago, IL 60601
(312) 565-4300
President: Joe Dragonette

Daniel J. Edelman Co.
211 E. Ontario St.
Chicago, IL 60611
(312) 280-7000
Head, Chicago Office: Pamela Talbot

Financial Relations Board
150 E. Huron St., 8th Floor
Chicago, IL 60611
(312) 266-7800
Head, Chicago Office: Theodore Pincus

Drucilla Handy Co.
333 N. Michigan Ave., Suite 505
Chicago, IL 60601
(312) 704-0040
President: Drucilla Handy

Golin/Harris Communications
500 N. Michigan Ave.
Chicago, IL 60611
(312) 836-7100
President: Thomas Harris

Hanlen Organization
401 N. Michigan Ave., Suite 3120
Chicago, IL 60611

(312) 222-1060
President: Sy Handwerker

Hill & Knowlton
111 E. Wacker Drive
Chicago, IL 60601
(312) 565-1200
Head, Chicago Office: Arthur Wilbe

Martin E. Janis & Co.
919 N. Michigan Ave., Suite 3500
Chicago, IL 60611
(312) 943-1100
President: Martin Janis

Jasculca/Terman & Associates
730 N. Franklin St.
Chicago, IL 60610
(312) 337-7400
President: Rick Jasculca

Ketchum Communications
142 E. Ontario, 11th Floor
Chicago, IL 60611
(312) 828-9360
Head, Chicago Office: Judith Rich

Margie Korshak & Associates
211 E. Ontario, Suite 600
Chicago, IL 60611
(312) 751-2121
President: Margie Korshak

Manning, Selvage & Lee
303 E. Wacker Drive, Suite 440
Chicago, IL 60601
(312) 819-3535
Contact: Personnel

Porter Novelli
303 E. Wacker Drive, Suite 1214
Chicago, IL 60601
(312) 856-8888
Executive Vice President: Jerry Murray

Public Communications
35 E. Wacker Drive, Suite 1254
Chicago, IL 60601
(312) 558-1770
President: Richard Barry

Ruder, Finn & Rotman
444 N. Michigan Ave.
Chicago, IL 60611
(312) 644-8600
Head, Chicago Office: B. Richard Johnson

S & S Public Relations
40 Skokie Blvd., Suite 430
Northbrook, IL 60062
(708) 291-1616
President: Steven Simon

Selz, Seabolt & Associates
221 N. LaSalle St.
Chicago, IL 60601
(708) 372-7090
President: Paul Fullmer

Starmark, Inc.
240 E. Ontario St.
Chicago, IL 60611
(312) 944-6700
Personnel Director: Phyllis Martineau

Bernard Ury & Associates
307 N. Michigan Ave.
Chicago, IL 60601
(312) 726-3668
Contact: Personnel

Weiser Group
160 N. Wacker Drive
Chicago, IL 60601
(312) 368-1500
President: Michael Weiser

Real Estate Developers and Brokers

For networking in **real estate** and related fields, check out the following professional organizations listed in Chapter 5:

PROFESSIONAL ORGANIZATIONS:

American Institute of Real Estate Appraisers
American Planning Association
American Society of Real Estate Counselors
Building Managers Association of Chicago
Chicago Metropolitan Building Managers Club
Illinois Mortgage Bankers Association

National Association of Realtors
North Side Real Estate Board
Society of Real Estate Appraisers
Women's Council of Realtors

PROFESSIONAL PUBLICATIONS:

Real Estate News
Realty and Building

DIRECTORIES:

American Society of Real Estate Counselors Directory (ASREC, Chicago, IL)
Directory of Certified Residential Brokers (Retail National Marketing Institute, Chicago, IL)

EMPLOYERS:

American Invsco
505 N. Lake Shore Drive, Suite 100
Chicago, IL 60611
(312) 621-8660
Contact: Personnel

Baird & Warner
200 W. Madison St.
Chicago, IL 60606
(312) 368-1855
Personnel Director: Phoebe Heffner

Cambridge Realty Capital
200 W. Superior, Suite 303
Chicago, IL 60610
(312) 943-1911
President: Jeffrey Davis

Capital Realty Services
2 N. LaSalle St., Suite 1725
Chicago, IL 60602
(312) 853-3550
Managing Partner: Gordon Lee Pollock

Bernard Cohen & Co.
135 S. LaSalle St.
Chicago, IL 60603
(312) 236-0786
Managing Partner: Bernard Cohen

Cohen Financial Corporation
2 N. LaSalle St., Suite 1400
Chicago, IL 60602
(312) 346-5680
Vice President: Donald R. James

Coldwell Banker
200 E. Randolph St., Suite 6509
Chicago, IL 60601
(312) 861-7800
Personnel Director: Jenny Righeimer

Collins Tuttle & Co.
20 N. Clark St., Suite 1100
Chicago, IL 60602
(312) 427-6400
Personnel Director: Jeff Hoosin

Cushman & Wakefield of IL
150 S. Wacker Drive, Suite 3100
Chicago, IL 60606
(312) 853-0030
Personnel Director: Bonnie Richtman

Draper & Kramer
33 W. Monroe St.
Chicago, IL 60603
(312) 346-8600
Personnel Director: Marilyn Pry

Dwinn-Shaffer & Co.
55 W. Monroe, Suite 790
Chicago, IL 60603
(312) 346-9191
President: Leonard E. Wineburgh

Howard Ecker & Co.
400 N. State St., 4th Floor
Chicago, IL 60610
(312) 726-3330
President: Howard Ecker

First City Mortgage Corporation
115 S. LaSalle St., Suite 2806
Chicago, IL 60603
(312) 332-6200
Contact: Office Manager

First Interstate Mortgage Co.
100 S. Wacker Drive, Suite 400
Chicago, IL 60606

(312) 845-8500
President: A.G. Behnke

Focus Financial Group
200 W. Madison St., Suite 500
Chicago, IL 60606
(312) 726-9400
Attention: President

GMAC Mortgage Co.
20 S. Clark St., Suite 820
Chicago, IL 60603
(312) 346-7585
Vice President: Thomas Vivaldelli

Golub & Co.
625 N. Michigan Ave., Suite 2000
Chicago, IL 60611
(312) 440-8800
Director of Personnel: Rufina Lopez

Sheldon F. Good & Co.
333 W. Wacker Drive
Chicago, IL 60606
(312) 346-1500
Personnel Director: Michael Whiteman

Heitman Financial Services
180 N. LaSalle St.
Chicago, IL 60601
(312) 855-5700
Senior Vice President: Lester Rosenberg

Helmsley-Spear of Illinois
175 W. Jackson Blvd., A618
Chicago, IL 60604
(312) 781-2400
Contact: Personnel

Hoffman Group
300 Park Blvd., Suite 515
Itasca, IL 60143
(708) 250-7878
Personnel Director: Rose Cleary

Horwitz/Mathews
814 N. Franklin
Chicago, IL 60610
Personnel Director: Tem Horwitz
(312) 944-0589

Inland Real Estate Corporation
2091 Butterfield Road
Oak Brook, IL 60521
(708) 218-8000
Contact: Personnel

JMB Realty
900 Michigan Ave.
Chicago, IL 60611
(312) 440-4800
Contact: Personnel

Julian Toft & Downey
3 First National Plaza, Suite 5400
Chicago, IL 60602
(312) 704-0054
Managing Principal: Robert Julian

Jupiter Industries
400 E. Randolph St.
Chicago, IL 60601
(312) 520-4910
Contact: Personnel

Lane Industries
1 Lane Center
1200 Shermer Road
Northbrook, IL 60062
(708) 498-6789
Personnel Director: Linda Datz

LaThomas & Co.
15 E. Superior St.
Chicago, IL 60611
(312) 944-2611
Personnel Director: Sophia Worden

Levy Organization
980 N. Michigan, Suite 400
Chicago, IL 60611
Personnel Director: Margie Mintz
(312) 664-8200

Manufacturers Hanover
10 S. LaSalle St.
Chicago, IL 60603
(312) 726-7208

McKey & Pogue
112 S. Washington St.
Hinsdale, IL 60521

(708) 323-6710
Director of Personnel: Mary Berger

Metro Financial Group
220 S. State St., Suite 2014
Chicago, IL 60604
(312) 939-5155
Office Manager: Dawn Davidson

Mid-North Financial
205 W. Wacker Drive, Suite 202
Chicago, IL 60606
(312) 641-0660
President: Albert Hanna

Phillipsborn Group
222 S. Riverside Plaza, Suite 2820
Chicago, IL 60606
(312) 207-5500
Senior Vice President: Don Trossman

Prudential Preferred Properties
1571 Sherman Ave.
Evanston, IL 60201
(708) 864-2600
Director of Personnel: Kay Rasco

Rubloff & Co.
111 W. Washington St., Suite 2100
Chicago, IL 60602
(312) 368-5400
Director of Personnel: Carol Kearin

Salk Ward & Salk
116 S. Michigan Ave., Suite 800
Chicago, IL 60603
(312) 236-0825
President: Erwin A. Salk

Strobeck Reiss & Co.
223 W. Jackson Blvd.
Chicago, IL 60606
(312) 922-5820
Contact: Personnel

Sudler Marling
875 N. Michigan Ave., Suite 3250
Chicago, IL 60611
(312) 751-0900
Contact: Personnel

Synergy Realty Management Group
30 E. Adams, 12th Floor
Chicago, IL 60603
(312) 663-4800

Tishman Midwest Management Corporation
300 S. Riverside Plaza, Suite 1400N
Chicago, IL 60606
(312) 930-7300
Personnel Director: Irene Higgins

Universal Development Corporation
205 N. Michigan Ave., Suite 3909
Chicago, IL 60601
(312) 819-0200
Contact: Personnel

Urban Investment & Development Co.
333 W. Wacker Drive
Chicago, IL 60606
(312) 263-6000
V.P.Human Resources: William Holland

Wil-Freds, Inc.
P.O. Box 4050
Naperville, IL 60567
(708) 357-0222
Personnel Director: Carol Wittmann

Recreation/Sports

For networking in **recreation** and related fields, check out the following professional organizations listed in Chapter 5:

PROFESSIONAL ORGANIZATIONS:

American Fishing Tackle Manufacturers Association
National Employee Services and Recreation Association
National Sporting Goods Association
YMCA of Metropolitan Chicago

For additional information, you can write to:

National Recreation & Parks Association
3101 Park Center Drive
Alexandria, VA 22302

National Sporting Goods Association
1699 Wall St.
Mt. Prospect, IL 60096

World Leisure and Recreation Association
345 E. 46th St.
New York, NY 10017

PROFESSIONAL PUBLICATIONS:

Parks and Recreation
Sporting Goods Dealer
Sporting Goods Trade

DIRECTORIES:

Directory of Information Sources in Health, Physical Education and Recreation (ERIC Clearinghouse on Teacher Education, Washington, DC)
New American Guide to Athletics, Sports, and Recreation (New American Library, New York, NY)
Salesman's Guide to Sporting Goods Buyers (Salesman's Guides, Inc., New York, NY)
Sporting Goods Directory (Sporting Goods Dealer, St. Louis, MO)
Sports Administration Guide and Directory (National Sports Marketing Bureau, New York, NY)
Sports Marketplace (Sportsguide, Princeton, NJ)

EMPLOYERS:

Bally Manufacturing Co.
8700 W. Bryn Mawr
Chicago, IL 60631
(312) 399-1300
Manager of Employment: Lois Balodis
Manufacturer of games and slot machines; owns and operates hotels and casinos.

Balmoral Park
P.O. Box 158
Crete, IL 60417
(708) 568-5700
Horse racing track.

Better Boys Foundation
1512 S. Pulaski Road
Chicago, IL 60623
(312) 277-9582
Executive V.P.: Renee Ogletree

Conducts programs for all ages in educational and social development, theater, summer camping.

Boy Scouts of America
730 W. Lake St., 2nd Floor
Chicago, IL 60606
(312) 559-0990
Executive Director: Lin Carter
Provides direction for the operation of Cub packs, Scout troops and Explorer posts throughout the Chicago area.

Boys & Girls Clubs of Chicago
625 W. Jackson, Suite 300
Chicago, IL 60606
(312) 648-1666
Executive Director: W. Murray
Provides counseling and guidance through recreational, educational, cultural, and vocational activities.

Brunswick Corporation
One Brunswick Plaza
Skokie, IL 60077
(708) 470-4700
Contact: Personnel
A world wide leader in the leisure-time field, offering products and services through its Technical Group, Medical Group, Marine Power Group, Recreation Group, and Consumer Division.

Chicago Bears
250 N. Washington St.
Lake Forest, IL 60045
(708) 663-5408
Contact: Personnel
NFL professional football team.

Chicago Bulls
980 N. Michigan Ave., Suite 1600
Chicago, IL 60611
(312) 943-5800
Contact: Personnel
NBA professional basketball team.

Chicago Commons Association
915 N. Wolcott Ave.
Chicago, IL 60622
(312) 342-5330
Executive Director: Frank S. Seever
Maintains centers where people with the fewest alternatives meet for community, recreational, and educational activities.

Chicago Cubs
1060 W. Addison St.
Chicago, IL 60613
(312) 404-2827
Contact: Personnel
National League professional baseball team.

Chicago Park District
425 E. McFetridge Drive
Chicago, IL 60605
(312) 294-2200
Administrative Supervisor: Jessie Madison
An independent authority entrusted with the management and maintenance of Chicago's public parks and recreational facilities.

Chicago White Sox
324 W. 35th St.
Chicago, IL 60616
(312) 924-1000
Contact: Personnel
American League professional baseball team.

Chicago Youth Centers
231 S. Jefferson, 6th Floor
Chicago, IL 60606
(312) 648-1550
Executive Director: Delbert Arsenault
Provides recreational and educational opportunities to lower-income neighborhoods.

Ero Industries
8130 N. Lehigh Ave.
Morton Grove, IL 60053
(708) 965-3700
Director of Human Resources: Gene Dawson

Evanston Recreation Dept.
2100 Ridge Ave.
Evanston, IL 60204
(708) 328-2100
Superintendent: Richard Grodsky
Conducts comprehensive year-round recreation program.

Forest Preserve District of Cook County
536 N. Harlem Ave.
River Forest, IL 60305
(708) 366-9420
General Superintendent: Arthur Janura
Responsible for maintenance and preservation of Cook County forest preserves.

Forest Preserve District of DuPage County
P. O. Box 2339
Glen Ellyn, IL 60138
(708) 790-4900
Director: H.C. Johnson
Responsible for maintenance and preservation of DuPage county forest preserves.

Girl Scouts of America
55 E. Jackson Blvd., 14th Floor
Chicago, IL 60604
(312) 435-5500
Executive Director: Kathleen M. Bell
Maintains a contemporary Girl Scout and Brownie Scout program throughout metropolitan Chicago.

Homewood-Flossmoor Park District
18350 Harwood Ave.
Homewood, IL 60430
(708) 957-0300
Superintendent: Jill Bartholemew
Provides wide range of leisure, recreational, and educational activities to the community.

Hull House Association
118 N. Clinton St., Suite 200
Chicago, IL 60606
(312) 726-1526
Director: Patricia Sharpe
Provides recreational and social services through 24 neighborhood locations.

Hyde Park Neighborhood Club
5480 S. Kenwood Ave.
Chicago, IL 60615
(312) 643-4062
Executive Director: Irene M. Smith
Provides recreational and educational services to the community.

Jewish Community Centers of Chicago
1 S. Franklin St.
Chicago, IL 60606
(312) 346-6700
General Director: Jerry Witkovsky
Provides recreational, educational, and social services to all ages through numerous neighborhood centers.

Lake County Forest Preserve District
2000 N. Milwaukee Ave.
Libertyville, IL 60048
(708) 367-6640

Director: Jerrold Soesbe
Responsible for the maintenance and preservation of forest preserves in Lake County.

Wilmette Park District
1200 Wilmette Ave.
Wilmette, IL 60091
(708) 256-6100
Director: Terry Porter
Conducts athletic and sports events, recreational programs for the community.

Winnetka Community House
620 Lincoln Ave.
Winnetka, IL 60093
(708) 446-0537
Executive Director: Don Van Arsdale
Provides recreational programs for children of all ages.

YMCA of Metropolitan Chicago
755 W. North Ave.
Chicago, IL 60610
(312) 280-3400
Director of Personnel: Charlaine Robinson
Provides recreational, educational, and social services to men and women of all ages.

Young Men's Jewish Council
25 E. Washington St.
Chicago, IL 60602
(312) 726-8891
Executive Director: Nisson S. Pearl
Operates day camps and overnight camp; conducts after-school enrichment programs designed to enhance the social development of children.

YWCA of Metropolitan Chicago
180 N. Wabash
Chicago, IL 60601
(312) 372-6600
Executive Director: Audrey Peeples
Operates recreational, educational, and social programs primarily for women and girls.

Retailers/Wholesalers

For networking in **merchandising** and related fields, check out the following professional organizations listed in Chapter 5:

PROFESSIONAL ORGANIZATIONS:

American Warehousemen's Association
Greater North Michigan Avenue Association
Greater State Street Council
Illinois Food Retailers Association
Illinois Retail Merchants Association
Merchandising Executives Club
National Association of General Merchandise Representatives
National Association of Retail Dealers of America
National Association of Service Merchandising
National Network of Women in Sales
Retail Merchants Association

For more information, you can write to:

General Merchandise Distributors Council
5250 Far Hills Ave.
Dayton, OH 45429

Manufacturers' Agents National Association
23016 Mill Creek Road
Laguna Hills, CA 92654

National Association of Wholesale Distributors
1725 K St., N.W.
Washington, DC 20006

National Retail Merchants Association
100 W. 31st St.
New York, NY 10036

Warehouse Distributors Association
P.O. Box 1128
Waukegan, IL 60085

PROFESSIONAL PUBLICATIONS:

Chain Store Age
College Store Executive
Dealerscope Merchandising
Merchandising
Store Planning
Stores
Video Stores
Western Retailer News
Women's Wear Daily

DIRECTORIES:

Chicago Area Shopping Center Guide (The Sun-Times Co., Chicago, IL)
Fairchild's Financial Manual of Retail Stores (Fairchild Books, New York, NY)
Nationwide Directory—Mass Market Merchandisers (Salesman's Guide, Inc., New York, NY)
Shelton's Retail Directory (PS&H, Inc., New York, NY)

EMPLOYERS:

Ace Hardware Corporation
2200 Kensington Court
Oak Brook, IL 60521
(708) 990-6600
Personnel Director: Fred Neer
Dealer-owned hardware cooperative.

American Drugstores
Regional Headquarters
1818 Swift Drive
Oak Brook, IL 60521
(708) 572-5000
Contact: Personnel
Owns and operates large chain of retail drug stores in Chicago and suburbs.

American Stores—Jewel Cos.
1955 W. North Ave.
Melrose Park, IL 60160
(708) 531-6000

Ames
11535 S. Central Ave.
Worth, IL 60482
(708) 597-3500
Personnel Manager: Margot Zera
Owns and operates over 250 general merchandise stores offering a full line of hard and soft goods at discount prices.

Amlings Flowerland
540 W. Ogden Ave.
Hinsdale, IL 60521
(708) 654-8820
Personnel Director: Donna Handing
Floral, garden, and gift center.

Armanetti Corporation
508 W. Lake St.

Addison, IL 60601
(708) 543-9463
Personnel Director: Sylvia Stromberger
Liquor store chain.

B Dalton Bookseller
129 N. Wabash Ave.
Chicago, IL 60602
(312) 236-7615
Contact: Personnel
National chain of bookstores owned by Dayton Hudson Corporation.

Baker & Taylor Co.
501 S. Gladiolus St.
Momence, IL 60954
(815) 472-2444
General Manager: Richard Porter
Nation's largest wholesaler of hardcover books to retail stores and libraries.

Baskin, Inc.
Division of Hart, Schaffner & Marx
835 N. Michigan Ave.
Chicago, IL 60611
(312) 943-3000
Personnel Director: Beth Hahn
Retail clothing store chain with stores in Chicago and suburbs.

Bloomingdale's
900 N. Michigan Ave.
Chicago, IL 60611
(312) 787-5511
Contact: Personnel
Specialty department store.

Bosler Supply Co.
2332 W. Logan Blvd.
Chicago, IL 60647
(312) 772-7772
Personnel Director: Don Malpede
Wholesaler of industrial hardware.

Bradford Exchange
9333 N. Milwaukee Ave.
Niles, IL 60648
(708) 966-2770
President: Richard W. Tinberg
Retail and catalog sales of unusual products.

Butera's Finer Foods
1 Clocktower Plaza

Elgin, IL 60120
(708) 741-1010
President: Paul Butera
Retail grocery chain.

Carson Pirie Scott & Co.
1 S. State St.
Chicago, IL 60603
(312) 744-2000
Personnel Director: Mary Lou Pendergast
Retail department stores in city and suburbs; owns resorts, shopping centers, restaurants.

Century Shopping Center
2828 N. Clark St.
Chicago, IL 60657
(312) 929-8100
Retail shopping center serving the New Town area.

Chernin Shoes
1001 S. Clinton
Chicago, IL 60607
(312) 922-4545
Contact: Personnel
Discount retailer of mens, women's, and children's footwear.

Circle Fine Art Corporation
303 E. Wacker Drive
Chicago, IL 60601
(312) 943-0664
Distributes fine art; operates gallery chain.

Cotter & Co.
2740 N. Clybourn Ave.
Chicago, IL 60614
(312) 975-2700
Personnel Director: A. Fred Lobo
Cooperative owned by Tru-Value hardware stores.

Crate & Barrel
725 Landwehr Road
Northbrook, IL 60062
(708) 272-2888
Personnel Director: Lynn Saltzman

Crown Books
8811 S. 77th Ave.
Bridgeview, IL 60455
(708) 598-1590
Regional Manager: Tom Burke
Regional headquarters of national discount bookstore chain.

Dominick's Finer Foods
2132 W. Jefferson
Joliet, IL 60436
(815) 242-6160
Contact: Personnel
Retail grocery chain.

Dominick's Finer Foods
505 Railroad Ave.
Northlake, IL 60164-1696
(708) 562-1000
Contact: Personnel
Retail grocery chain

Evans, Inc.
36 S. State St.
Chicago, IL 60603
(312) 855-2000
Employment Manager: Dean O'Brecht
Retailer of women's apparel and furs; operates leased departments in 90 branches of 18 major department stores throughout the U.S. and its own stores in Chicago.

L. Fish Furniture Co.
4242 W. 42nd Place
Chicago, IL 60632
(312) 523-7700
President: Stephen Ehrlichman
Retail furniture stores.

Follett Corporation
1000 W. Washington Blvd.
Chicago, IL 60607
(312) 666-4300
Chairman: Robert Follett
Institutional services, distribution, college bookstores.

Fox Valley Center
195 Fox Valley Center
Aurora, IL 60506
(708) 851-7200
Retail shopping center serving the far western suburbs.

Frank Consolidated Enterprises
666 Garland Place
Des Plaines, IL 60016
(708) 699-7000
Personnel Director: P. Ruth Kurtz
Owns Z Frank, world's largest car dealership, and Wheels, Inc., car leasing organization.

Fretter Appliances
7440 S. Cicero Ave.
Bedford Park, IL 60638
(708) 594-6111

Gee Corporation
2600 W. 79th St.
Chicago, IL 60652
(312) 476-7400
Personnel Director: Nancy Gee
Retail lumber stores.

Gold Standard Enterprises
5100 W. Dempster St.
Skokie, IL 60077
(708) 674-4200
President: Harold Binstein
Liquor stores; wine & cheese shops.

GRI Corp
65 E. Wacker Drive
Chicago, IL 60601
(312) 977-3700
Personnel Director: Howard Horace
Markets mail-order products.

Hammond Organ Co.
4200 W. Diversey Blvd.
Chicago, IL 60639
(312) 283-2000
Manufacturer and marketer of musical organs.

I Magnin & Co.
830 N. Michigan Ave.
Chicago, IL 60611
(312) 751-0500
Personnel Director: Sue Lang
Specialty department store.

J.G. Industries
1615 W. Chicago Ave.
Chicago, IL 60622
(312) 421-5300
Personnel Director: Pam Egan
Retail merchandiser.

Karoll's Men's Fashions
32 N. State St.
Chicago, IL 60602
(312) 263-0600
President: Herb Karoll
Retail men's fashions.

K-Mart Corporation
Regional Headquarters
2300 B. West Higgins Road
Hoffman Estates, IL 60195
(708) 884-3850
Personnel Director: S.W. St. John
Variety and discount department stores in Chicago and suburbs.

Kroch's & Brentano's
29 S. Wabash Ave.
Chicago, IL 60603
(312) 332-7500
Personnel Director: Dolores Sledz
Nineteen-store chain of retail bookstores in Chicago and suburbs.

Land's End
1 Land's End Lane
Dodgeville, WI 53595-0001
(608) 935-9341
Personnel Contact: John Keenan
Apparel merchant, with outlets in Chicago area.

Lord & Taylor
835 N. Michigan Ave.
Chicago, IL 60611
(312) 787-7400
Personnel Manager: Diane Titche
Specialty department store, with branches in Chicago and suburbs.

Madigans
7440 W. Central Ave.
River Forest, IL 60690
(708) 771-7400
Personnel Director: Sharon A. Fitzpatrick
Chain of retail clothing stores.

Marshall Field & Co.
111 N. State St.
Chicago, IL 60690
(312) 781-1000
Personnel Director: Philip Johnson
Owns and operates retail department stores, offering a wide range of quality merchandise in the Midwest, South, and West; invests in shopping center development.

Montgomery Ward & Co.
Montgomery Ward Plaza
Chicago, IL 60671
(312) 467-2000

Contact: Personnel
Specialty retail stores.

Neiman-Marcus
737 N. Michigan Ave.
Chicago, IL 60611
(312) 642-5900
Personnel Director: Tracy Stewart
Specialty department store.

Nelson Bros. Furniture
2750 W. Grand Ave.
Chicago, IL 60612
(312) 489-3333
Retail home furnishings and appliances.

Northbrook Court Shopping Center
2171 Northbrook Court
Northbrook, IL 60062
(708) 498-5144

Oak Brook Center
UIDC Management
100 Oak Brook Center
Oak Brook, IL 60521
(708) 573-0700
Retail shopping center, serving the western suburbs.

Old Orchard Shopping Center
Skokie Blvd. at Old Orchard Road
Skokie, IL 60077
(708) 673-6800
Retail shopping center, serving the North Shore suburbs.

Getting the scoop on success

Our friend Trudy was 20 years old and desperate for a job when she saw an ad in the paper for a scooper at a newly opened ice cream parlor. Having spent a high school summer working in a soda shop, she applied for—and got—the job.

"When I started," Trudy recalls, "I was the only person working there full-time during the day—besides the manager. I made $4 an hour. Whether she did it deliberately or not, the manager sort of tutored me in a lot of the things she did—how to make deposits, how to order, that sort of thing. I guess she was sort of lazy because I did most of her chores.

"I had been there four months when the manager quit without notice. The owner, who had been out of town, returned the next day in a panic. He made me assistant manager—by default, I guess, because I was the only one who had any idea how to run the place. He placed an ad for a manager right away, and applications just poured in.

"Anyway, after a week went by, the owner told me to ignore the resumes that were coming in—even those from people with 20 years' experience. He made me the manager—at a salary of $22,000 a year."

Why Trudy?

"I worked really hard, right from the beginning, and I was there practically from the first day the place opened. I was always on time, and I never called in sick. All the other kids there were just trying to earn extra money for college. I was trying to make a living.

"The experienced people who applied for the job weren't willing to do the grunt work. They wouldn't scoop when things got busy, and they didn't want to deal with unloading 120 tubs of ice cream. All they wanted to do was paper work.

"I don't plan to be doing this the rest of my life. But as long as I'm doing it, I want to do it well. I think we have the best quality ice cream, and that's important to me. We're also one of the most successful places in the city, and I'm happy for the part I play in it."■

J.C. Penney Co.
Regional Headquarters
1750 E. Golf Road
Schaumburg, IL 60173
(708) 517-4600
Personnel Manager: Jim Fike
National retail merchandiser.

Pier 1 Imports
538 W. St. Charles Road
Elmhurst, IL 60126
(708) 834-9661
Regional Manager: Carl Stuecher

Polk Bros.
8311 W. North Ave.

Melrose Park, IL 60610
(708) 345-5555
Vice President: Michael Crane
Discount merchandiser of household goods, home furnishings, appliances, radios, and TVs.

Premark International
1717 Deerfield Road
Deerfield, IL 60015
(708) 405-6000
Vice President: John M. Costigan
Markets consumer products.

Radio Shack
Regional Headquarters
1350 S. Milwaukee Ave.
Libertyville, IL 60048
(708) 680-1800
District Manager: Bill Bartles
National retailer of electronic equipment and computers.

Saxon Paint and Home Care Centers
3840 W. Fullerton Ave.
Chicago, IL 60647
(312) 252-8100
Personnel Director: Kelly Berrington
Local chain of paint and wallpaper stores.

Sears, Roebuck & Co.
Sears Tower
Franklin and Adams Streets
Chicago, IL 60684
(312) 875-2500
Director, Professional Employment: Mary Misar
World's largest retailer; provides general merchandising, mail order, and financial services.

Seigle's Home & Building Centers
1331 Davis Road
Elgin, IL 60123
(708) 742-2000
Contact: Personnel
Retailer of building materials.

John M. Smyth Co.
1013 Butterfield Road
Downers Grove, IL 60515
(708) 960-4100
Personnel Manager: R. Slocum
Retail furniture stores located in Chicago and suburbs.

Spiegel, Inc.
1515 W. 22nd St.
Oak Brook, IL 60522
(708) 986-7500
V. P., Personnel: Harold Dahlstrand
National catalog merchandiser.

Sportmart, Inc.
7233 W. Dempster Ave.
Niles, IL 60648
(708) 966-1700
Contact: Personnel
Owns and operates discount sporting goods stores.

Spurgeon Mercantile Co.
822 W. Washington Blvd.
Chicago, IL 60607
(312) 738-5400
Personnel Director: Eric Anderson
Retail store chain.

Treasure Island Food Mart
3460 N. Broadway
Chicago, IL 60657
(312) 327-4265
President: Chris Kamberos
Retail grocery chain.

Waldenbooks, Inc.
Regional Office
251 Golfmill Shopping Center
Niles, IL 60648
(708) 824-2218
District Manager: Mark Gajewski
National chain of retail booksellers.

Walgreen Company
200 Wilmot Road
Deerfield, IL 60015
(708) 940-2500
V.P. Human Resources: John Rubino
National chain of drug and variety stores.

Lee Wards Co.
1200 St. Charles St.
Elgin, IL 60120
(708) 888-5800
Persident: John Popple
Manufacturer and marketer of hobby craft materials.

Warehouse Club
7235 N. Linder Ave.

Skokie, IL 60077
(708) 679-6800
Wholesale merchandiser.

Water Tower Place
845 N. Michigan Ave.
Chicago, IL 60611
(312) 440-3165
Retail shopping center and condominium development, serving the north Michigan Avenue area.

Wickes Furniture
351 W. Dundee Road
Wheeling, IL 60090
(708) 541-0100
V.P. Human Resources: Robert Ostrov
National chain of retail furniture outlets.

F. W. Woolworth Co.
Regional Headquarters
915 Lee St.
Des Plaines, IL 60016
(708) 827-7731
Personnel Director: Richard Enright
National chain of retail variety and discount department stores.

Yorktown Shopping Center
203 Yorktown Center
Lombard, IL 60148
(708) 932-7115
Retail shopping center, serving the western suburbs.

Steel Manufacturing (see also Metals and Minerals)

Major trade publications covering the **steel and metals industry** include:

PROFESSIONAL PUBLICATIONS:

Advance Materials and Processes
Industry Week
Metal Finishing
Metal Producing
Scrap Age

EMPLOYERS:

Acme Steel Co.
13500 S. Perry Ave.
Riverdale, IL 60627
(708) 849-2500
Personnel Director: Gerald Shope

American Colloid Co.
1500 W. Shure Drive
Arlington Heights, IL 60004
(708 392-4600
President: John Hughes
Mines and processes metals and ores.

Axia, Inc.
122 W. 22nd St.
Oak Brook, IL 60521
(708) 571-3350
Personnel Assistant: LaRue Carlson
Manufacturer of construction-related products and tools; metal products and cold steel bars.

Bethlehem Steel Corporation
737 N. Michigan Ave., Suite 1050
Chicago, IL 60611
(312) 951-5200
District Sales Manager: Hunter B. Harris

Bethlehem Steel Corporation
P. O. Box 248
Chesterton, IN 46304
(219) 787-2120
Plant Manager: Roger R. Penny
The nation's second-largest integrated steel production company.

A.M. Castle & Co.
3400 N. Wolf Road
Franklin Park, IL 60131
(708) 455-7111
Personnel Director: Thomas Prendergast

Chicago Heights Steel
P.O. Box 129
Chicago Heights, IL 60411
(708) 756-5619
President: Frank A. Corral
Rerolls rail and billet.

DeKalb Corporation
3100 Sycamore Road

DeKalb, IL 60115
(815) 758-3461
Personnel Director: Greg Olson

Dietrich Industries
1435 165th St.
Hammond, IN 46320
(219) 931-3741
Contact: Personnel
Steel processing.

Feralloy Corporation
12550 S. Stony Island Ave.
Chicago, IL 60633
(312) 646-4900
President: N. J. Murphy
Wholesaler of flat-roll steel.

A. Finkl & Sons
2011 N. Southport Ave.
Chicago, IL 60614
(312) 975-2500
Director of Labor Relations: R.J. Burgess
Steel producer.

Inland Steel Co.
30 W. Monroe St.
Chicago, IL 60603
(312) 346-0300
V.P. Human Resources: Judd R. Cool

Inland Steel Co.
3210 Watling St.
East Chicago, IN 46312
(219) 399-1200
President: Robert Darnall
The nation's seventh-largest steel company.

Interstate Steel Corporation
401 E. Touhy Ave.
Des Plaines, IL 60017
(708) 827-5151
Chairman: Howard Conant
Steel service center.

LaSalle Steel Co.
1412 E. 150th St.
Hammond, IN 46327
(219) 853-6000
Personnel Manager: Bob Kelley
Cold-finished steel bars.

L.T.V. Steel Co.
1701 Golf Road
2 Continental Towers, Suite 600
Rolling Meadows, IL 60008
(708) 364-0710
Contact: Personnel

National Steel Corporation
2850 E. Golf Road
Rolling Meadows, IL 60008
(708) 640-3300
District Sales Manager: Dennis Siewin

National Steel Corporation/Midwest Steel
U.S. Highway 12
Portage, IN 46368
(219) 762-3131
Director of Human Resources: Richard Shaughnessy
Manufacturer of fabricated metal warehouses and steel mill products.

Nelsen Steel & Wire Co.
9400 W. Belmont Ave.
Franklin Park, IL 60131
(708) 671-9700
Personnel Director: Joanne Fonseca
Manufactures cold heading wire and cold-finished steel bars.

Northwestern Steel & Wire Co.
121 Wallace St.
Sterling, IL 61081
(815) 625-2500
Personnel Director: K.J. Fritz
Produces steel.

N.P.S. Metal Service
1965 Pratt Blvd.
Elk Grove, IL 60007
(708) 806-4700
Contact: Personnel
Diversified producer of steel and metals.

Reynolds Metals, Corporation
47th St. & First Ave.
McCook, IL 60525
(708) 485-9000
Personnel Manager: Cornell Ward
Producer of sheet and plate metal.

J.H. Roberts Industries
3158 Des Plaines Road, Suite 231
Des Plaines, IL 60018

(708) 699-0080
Personnel Director: Larry Collins
Manufactures and distributes steel products.

Tuthill Corporation
908 N. Elm St., Suite 100
Hinsdale, IL 60521
(708) 655-2266
Corporate Controller: William Schilling

United States Steel Corporation
3426 E. 89th St.
Chicago, IL 60617
(312) 933-3102
Supervisor, Employment & Benefits: William R. Smith
Nation's largest integrated steel producer.

United States Steel Corporation
1 N. Broadway
Gary, IN 46402
(219) 888-3355
General Manager: John Goodwin
Nation's largest integrated steel producer.

UNR Industries
332 S. Michigan Ave.
Chicago, IL 60604
(312) 341-1234
Vice President: Henry Grey
Manufacturer of steel products for the industrial, commercial, consumer, communications, and transportation markets.

Travel/Transportation/Shipping

For networking in **travel and transportation,** check out the following professional organizations listed in Chapter 5:

PROFESSIONAL ORGANIZATIONS:

Chicago Transportation Club
Women in International Trade

For additional information, you can write to:

Airline Pilots Association
1625 Massachusetts Ave., N.W.
Washington, DC 20036

Airline Services Association and Regional Airline Association
1101 Connecticut Ave., N.W., Suite 700
Washington, DC 20036

American Society of Travel Agents
6 E. Monroe St.
Chicago, IL 60603
(312) 236-4035

Aviation Distributors & Manufacturers Association
1900 Arch St.
Philadelphia, PA 19103

Institute of Transportation Engineers
525 School St., S.W.
Washington, DC 20024

National Air Transportation Association
4226 King St.
Alexandria, VA 22302

PROFESSIONAL PUBLICATIONS:

AOPA Pilot
ASTA Travel News
Commercial Carrier Journal
Distribution
Fleet Owner
Heavy Duty Trucking
Traffic Management

DIRECTORIES:

Aviation Directory (E.A. Brennan Co., Garden Grove, CA)
Membership Directory (Aviation Distributors & Manufacturers Association, Philadelphia, PA)
Moody's Transportation Manual (Moody's Investor Services, New York, NY)
Travel Industry Personnel Directory (American Traveler, New York, NY)
World Aviation Directory (McGraw-Hill, New York, NY)

EMPLOYERS:

Air Canada
300 N. State St.
Chicago, IL 60610
(312) 836-6010

Air France
875 N. Michigan Ave.
Chicago, IL 60611
(800) 237-2747

Air Wisconsin
O'Hare International Airport
Chicago, IL 60666
(708) 569-3000

Alitalia Airlines
55 E. Monroe St.
Chicago, IL 60603
(312) 472-4720

Allied Van Lines
411 N. Halsted
Chicago, IL 60601
(312) 726-3588
Human Resources Director: Karen F. Klein
Moving service for families and high-value products.

American Airlines
1699 Wall St.
Mount Prospect, IL 60056
(708) 228-4290

American Express Travel
122 S. Michigan Ave.
Chicago, IL 60603
(312) 435-2595
Travel agency.

American Sightseeing Tours
530 S. Michigan Ave.
Chicago, IL 60605
(312) 427-3100
Chartered bus transportation.

American West Airlines
O'Hare International Airport
Chicago, IL 60666
(708) 372-2402

Arrington Travel Center
55 W. Monroe St., Suite 2450
Chicago, IL 60603
(312) 726-4900
President: Michael B. Arrington
Full service travel agency.

Ask Mr. Foster Travel Service
233 S. Wacker Drive, #9100
Chicago, IL 60606
(312) 993-0600
Travel agency.

Avis Rent-a-Car System
214 N. Clark St.
Chicago, IL 60601
(312) 782-6825
Car rental and leasing.

Brannif
O'Hare International Airport
Chicago, IL 60666
(800) 272-6433
Commercial airline.

Brink's, Inc.
234 E. 24th St.
Chicago, IL 60616
(312) 567-7100
Armored car service.

British Airways
67 E. Madison St.
Chicago, IL 60603
(312) 630-8700

Budget Rent-a-Car Corporation
500 N. Michigan Ave.
Chicago, IL 60601
(312) 580-5000
Car rental and leasing.

Burlington Northern R.R.
1230 E. Diehl Road
Naperville, IL 60566
(708) 505-5000
Commuter railroad.

Cast North America
2550 Golf Road, East Tower, Suite 102
Rolling Meadows, IL 60008
(708) 981-8700
Steamship line.

Chessie System
733 W. 136th St.
Riverdale, IL 60627
Chicago number: (312) 471-7181

Regional Sales Manager: L. E. Estill
Freight-handling railroad.

Chicago Motor Club
68 E. Wacker Drive
Chicago, IL 60601
(312) 372-1818
Travel and emergency road services to members.

Chicago & North Western Transportation Co.
One Northwestern Center
Chicago, IL 60606
(312) 559-7000
Commuter railroad.

Chicago Transit Authority
Merchandise Mart Plaza
P.O. Box 3555
Chicago, IL 60654
(312) 664-7200
Supplies public transportation to the city of Chicago.

Clipper Exxpress
15700 W. 103rd St.
Lemont, IL 60439
(708) 739-0700
Human Resources Director: Jean Weyer
Nationwide freight transportation.

Columbus Line
332 S. Michigan Ave., Suite 1505
Chicago, IL 60604
(312) 939-4857
Steamship line.

Continental Air Transport Co.
730 W. Lake St.
Chicago, IL 60606
(312) 454-7800
Provides bus service to and from Chicago's O'Hare airport; operates Gray Line Sightseeing and convention busses.

Continental Airlines
205 N. Michigan Ave., #800
Chicago, IL 60601
(312) 891-2879

Continental Charters
730 W. Lake St.
Chicago, IL 60606
(312) 454-0322
Chartered bus transportation.

Thomas Cook Travel
435 N. Michigan Ave.
Chicago, IL 60611
(312) 670-0664
Travel agency.

CP Rail
1200 Jorie Blvd., Suite 300
Oak Brook, IL 60521
(708) 990-3380
Freight-handling railroad.

Delta Airlines
999 Plaza Drive
Schaumburg, IL 60173
(708) 346-5344

Donlen Corporation
500 Lake Cook Road
Deerfield, IL 60015
(708) 831-0400
Personnel Director: Suzanne Gutowsky
Automotive fleet leasing.

Duchossois Industries
845 Larch Ave.
Elmhurst, IL 60126
(708) 279-3600
Chairman: C.A. Mapp
Designs, builds rail freight cars; railroad leasing.

Eastern Airlines
P.O. Box 66221
Chicago, IL 60666
(312) 601- 5200

Emery World Wide/Purolator
401 W. Touhy Ave.
Des Plaines, IL 60018
(708) 635-6210
Air freight.

Emkay, Inc.
805 W. Thorndale Ave.
Itasca, IL 60143
(708) 250-7400
Travel agency.

Federal Express Corporation
O'Hare Cargo Road, Bldg. 611
Chicago, IL 60666

(312) 601-2000
Air freight.

Federal Express Freight Service
O'Hare Cargo Road, Bldg. 611
Chicago, IL 60666
(800) 238-5355
Air freight.

Four Wheels Co.
666 Garland Place
Des Plaines, IL 60016
(708) 699-7000
Automobile leasing.

GATX Corporation
120 S. Riverside Plaza
Chicago, IL 60606
(312) 621-6200
Manufactures, leases, and sells railroad tank and freight cars.

Genway Corporation
500 N. Michigan Ave., Suite 920
Chicago, IL 60611
(312) 644-0200
Automobile and truck leasing.

Greyhound-Trailways Bus System
630 W. Harrison St.
Chicago, IL 60601
(312) 408-5971
Inter-city bus transportation.

Hanjin Container Lines
8750 W. Bryn Mawr, Suite 520
Chicago, IL 60631
(312) 693-7511
Steamship line.

Hertz Corporation
2400 E. Devon Ave.
Des Plaines, IL 60018
(708) 298-4810
Automobile and truck rental.

Illinois Central Gulf R.R.
233 N. Michigan Ave.
Chicago, IL 60601
(312) 819-7500
Commuter and freight-handling railroad.

Inter Ship, Inc.
P.O. Box 330
Palos Park, IL 60464
(708) 361-2525
Steamship line.

Itel Corporation
2 N. Riverside Plaza
Chicago, IL 60606
(312) 902-1515
Leases cargo containers.

ITOFCA, Inc.
1001 W. 31st St.
Downers Grove, IL 60515
(708) 963-3520
President: Leo McKenna
Provides transportation for shippers nationwide.

Japan Airlines
225 N. Michigan Ave., Suite 300
Chicago, IL 60601
(312) 565-7330

K & R Delivery
15 W 460 Frontage Road
Hinsdale, IL 60521
(708) 323-3230
Vice President: David Eggleston
Trucking service to the Midwest region and outlying states.

Keeshin Charter Service
615 W. 41st St.
Chicago, IL 60609
(312) 254-6400
Chartered bus transportation.

Lufthansa German Airlines
875 N. Michigan Ave.
Chicago, IL 60611
(312) 751-0111

Matson Navigation Co.
400 N. Michigan Ave., Suite 1616
Chicago, IL 60611
(312) 222-2470
Steamship line.

Mexicana Airlines
55 E. Monroe St.
Chicago, IL 60603
(312) 346-8414

Midway Airlines
5959 S. Cicero Ave.
Chicago, IL 60638
(312) 838-0001

MLS, USA
100 S. Wacker Drive, Suite 1820
Chicago, IL 60606
(312) 726-7250
Steamship line.

National Car Rental System
O'Hare Int'l. Airport
P.O. Box 66064
Chicago, IL 60666
(312) 694-4640
Automobile and truck rental.

Norfolk and Western R.R.
175 W. Jackson Blvd., Room 1121
Chicago, IL 60604
(312) 939-6702
Freight-handling railroad.

Northwest Airlines
203 N. LaSalle St., #2220
Chicago, IL 60601
(312) 984-0800

NYK Line
233 N.Michigan Ave., Suite 2500
Chicago, IL 60601
(312) 938-8600
Steamship Line

Pan American Air Lines
41 S. LaSalle St.
Chicago, IL 60603
(800) 221-1111

Santa Fe Railway System
224 S. Michigan Ave.
Chicago, IL 60604
(312) 786-8000
Freight-handling railroad.

Simmons Airlines
900 N. Franklin St.
Chicago, IL 60610
(312) 280-8222
Regional airline.

Soo Line
516 W. Jackson Blvd.
Chicago, IL 60606
(312) 860-4166
Freight-handling railroad.

Southern Pacific Transportation Co.
901 Warrenville Road
Lisle, IL 60532
(708) 719-5600
Freight-handling railroad.

Thillens, Inc.
4242 N. Elston Ave.
Chicago, IL 60618
(312) 539-4444
Armored car service.

Trailer Train Co.
101 N. Wacker Drive
Chicago, IL 60606
(312) 853-3223
President: Raymond C. Burton
Buys and maintains railroad freight cars.

Trans Union Corporation
111 W. Jackson St.
Chicago, IL 60604
(312) 431-0144
V.P. Human Resources: Sara Jo Light
Tank car leasing.

Trans World Airlines
225 N. Michigan Ave.
Chicago, IL 60601
(312) 558-7152

Union Pacific R.R.
436 W. 25th Place
Chicago, IL 60602
(312) 808-4450
Freight-handling railroad.

United Airlines
1200 E. Algonquin Road
Elk Grove Township, IL 60604
(708) 952-4000

United Parcel Service
1400 S. Jefferson St.
Chicago, IL 60607

(312) 920-2900
Shipping service for packages.

USAir
2800 River Road, Suite 173
Des Plaines, IL 60018
(708) 390-0095

U.S. Auto Leasing Co.
1800 N. Ashland Ave.
Chicago, IL 60622
(312) 278-7000
Automobile leasing.

Willett
3901 S. Ashland Ave.
Chicago, IL 60609
(312) 890-6700
Charter bus service.

Yellow Cab Co.
1730 S. Indiana Ave.
Chicago, IL 60616
(312) 225-7440
Manages Yellow and Checker taxi fleets.

Utilities

PROFESSIONAL PUBLICATIONS:

Electric Light and Power
Electrical World
Public Utilities

DIRECTORIES:

Brown's Directory of North American and International Gas Companies (Edgel Communications, Cleveland, OH)
Moody's Public Utility Manual (Moody's Investor Services, New York, NY)
Sourcebook (North American Telecommunications Association, Washington, DC)

EMPLOYERS:

Central Telephone Co. of Illinois
2004 Miner St.

Des Plaines, IL 60016
(708) 391-6023
Personnel Director: Brooke Rames
Supplier of telephone service.

Commonwealth Edison Co.
One First National Plaza
Chicago, IL 60609
(312) 294-4321
Vice President: George Rifakes
Electric utility.

Illinois Bell Telephone Co.
225 W. Randolph
Chicago, IL 60606
(312) 727-2445
Contact: Employment Director
Supplier of telephone and communications services.

Nicor, Inc.
P.O. Box 200
Naperville, IL 60566
(708) 242-4470
V.P., Human Resources: John Flowers
Develops and sells energy resources.

Northern Illinois Gas Co.
P.O. Box 190
Aurora, IL 60507
(708) 983-8888
Personnal Director: R.J. Lannon
Gas company.

Northern Indiana Public Service Co. (NIPSCO)
5265 Hohman Ave.
Hammond, IN 46320
(219) 853-5200
Contact: Personnel
Electric utility.

People's Energy Corporation
122 S. Michigan Ave.
Chicago, IL 60603
(312) 431-4000
Contact: Personnel
Parent firm of energy companies, including Peoples Gas Co.

Telesphere International
Two MidAmerica Plaza, Suite 500
Oakbrook Terrace, IL 60181
(708) 954-7700

Personnel Director: Patricia Wise
Provides long-distance telephone service.

Employers Index

A

B

C

D

E

F

G

I

J

K

L

M

N

O

P

Q

R

S

T

U

V

W

X,Y,Z

General Index